Disinformation Debunked

Disinformation Debunked: Building Resilience through Media and Information Literacy examines the way media and information literacy (MIL) can address disinformation in conjunction with fact-checkers and developers, to benefit from the expertise of these fields in fighting disinformation.

The book highlights the underlying stakes that are involved in the fight against disinformation, from producing smart tools to generalizing their use beyond the journalistic profession. It considers the MIL theories and methodologies at work in the digital era, especially from the perspective of digital visual literacy. Offering a comparative study of four European national experiences (France, Romania, Spain, and Sweden), the authors also make public policy recommendations to improve the fight against disinformation.

This book is of great importance to students, scholars, and educators working on media and information literacy, digital media, journalism, mass communication, misinformation and disinformation.

Divina Frau-Meigs is Professor of media and ICT sociology at Sorbonne Nouvelle University, France. She is a specialist of cultural diversity, internet governance and media and information literacy (MIL) as well as a researcher in the media uses and practices of young people and information disorders (radicalization, disinformation, hate speech etc.). She is the author and (co)editor of more than 40 books and 300 scholarly articles and book chapters. She holds the UNESCO Chair "Savoir Devenir in the era of digital development" (2015–), part of MILID and ORBICOM global networks. She founded the NGO Savoir*Devenir in 2017 to develop projects in MIL and digital citizenship. She is an expert with UNESCO, the Council of Europe and the European Union. As such, she was part of the EU high-level expert group on online disinformation (2018) and the high-level expert group on media literacy (2010–) as well as being a member of the Information for All Programme (IFAP) at UNESCO.

Nicoleta Corbu is Professor at the National University of Political Studies and Public Administration (SNSPA), Bucharest, Romania. She is the director of the Interdisciplinary PhD School (SNSPA) and executive director of the Center for Research in Communication. She is Vice Chair of ECREA Political Communication section. She is the recipient of a Fulbright grant in the United States (University of Georgia, 2008–2009), and was visiting professor at Florida Gulf Coast University (2012). She is currently part of BROD EDMO hub (European Media Digital Observatory) and member of the Network of European Political Communication Scholars (NEPOCS) since 2018. She has published books and papers on political communication and education policies.

Routledge Research in Media Literacy and Education
Series Editors: Pete Bennett and Julian McDougall

Media literacy is now established by UNESCO as a human right, and the field of media literacy education is both growing and diverse. The series speaks to two recurring concerns in this field: What difference does media make to literacy and how should education respond to this? Research and practice has aimed to protect against negative media messages and deconstruct ideology through critical thinking, developing media literacy through creative production and a social participatory approach which focuses on developing active citizens to play a constructive role in media democracy.

This series is dedicated to a more extensive exploration of the known territories of media literacy and education, while also seeking out 'other' cartographies. As such, it encompasses a diverse, international range of contexts that share a conceptual framework at the intersection of Cultural Studies/Critical Theories, (New) Social Literacies and Critical Pedagogy. The series is especially interested in how media literacy and education relates to feminism, critical race theory, social class, post-colonial, and intersectional approaches and how these perspectives, political objectives, and international contexts can 'decenter' the field of media literacy education.

The Routledge Handbook of Media Education Futures Post-Pandemic
Edited by Yonty Friesem, Usha Raman, Igor Kanižaj and Grace Y. Choi

Understanding Virtual Reality
Challenging Perspectives for Media Literacy and Education
Sarah Jones, Steve Dawkins and Julian McDougall

Media Literacy and Media Education Research Methods
Edited by Pierre Fastrez and Normand Landry

Disinformation Debunked
Building Resilience through Media and Information Literacy
Edited by Divina Frau-Meigs and Nicoleta Corbu

For more information about this series, please visit: https://www.routledge.com/Routledge-Research-in-Media-Literacy-and-Education/book-series/RRMLE

Disinformation Debunked

Building Resilience through Media and Information Literacy

Edited by Divina Frau-Meigs and Nicoleta Corbu

Routledge
Taylor & Francis Group
LONDON AND NEW YORK

First published 2024
by Routledge
4 Park Square, Milton Park, Abingdon, Oxon OX14 4RN

and by Routledge
605 Third Avenue, New York, NY 10158

Routledge is an imprint of the Taylor & Francis Group, an informa business

British Library Cataloguing-in-Publication Data
A catalogue record for this book is available from the British Library

ISBN: 978-1-032-48101-2 (hbk)
ISBN: 978-1-032-48102-9 (pbk)
ISBN: 978-1-003-38740-4 (ebk)

DOI: 10.4324/9781003387404

Typeset in Sabon
by SPi Technologies India Pvt Ltd (Straive)

Contents

Figures

Tables

Contributors

Alina Bârgăoanu, Professor, PhD, is the dean of the Faculty of Communication and Public Relations, National University of Political Studies and Public Administration (Bucharest); member of the Advisory Board of European Digital Media Observatory (EDMO) and of EDMO's task force on the war in Ukraine; Marcin Król Fellow at Visegrad Insight; member of the High-Level Expert Group on Fake News and Online Disinformation, EC (2018).

Joseph Beaudreau, a doctoral candidate at Université Sorbonne Nouvelle, serves as an assistant professor and researcher at the Pléiade laboratory, Université Paris Nord-Sorbonne. He is also acting as treasurer of Savoir*Devenir. Contributing to the critical discourse on contemporary information disorders, he is specialized in fact-checking, disinformation, and the political economy of communication. He was a lead researcher in European Erasmus+ project Fact-checking that mapped the state of disinformation studies in Europe and devised an online training course.

Adeline Bossu, a PhD in Information and Communication Sciences, is the director of operations for the PhDOOC association. She is a lecturer in information systems management and is a member of MICA Research Centre (University of Bordeaux-Montaigne). Her lines of research cover MOOCS, e-learning, and online information systems for which she has contributed a number of research chapters and articles.

Iuliana Călin is a PhD candidate in Communication Sciences at the National University of Political Studies and Public Administration (SNSPA) Bucharest. She is a teaching assistant and an assistant editor for digital archiving of scientific publications at the Faculty of Communication and Public Relations, SNSPA, as well as a member of the Centre for EU Communication Studies. She was part of the team involved in the European YouVerify! Project (2021–2022).

Flavia Durach, PhD, is Associate Professor at the National University for Political Studies and Public Administration, Bucharest, and Academic Coordinator of the MA in Digital Communication and Innovation. Her research interests include the study of media effects, with an emphasis on online disinformation. In recent years, she was involved in a number of international projects dedicated to media literacy and countering fake news.

Marina Enache is currently enrolled in the PhD programme at SNSPA București with a focus on Communication Sciences. Her main research interests are public communication and tackling disinformation in the public sphere. She has a bachelor's degree in Communication and Public Relations from the Faculty of Communication and Public Relations in SNSPA Bucuresti, where she is now involved in the development of the Project Management course for the Communication and Emerging Media bachelor programme. Marina has worked in several EU-funded projects, on both researcher and expert positions in the field of public awareness.

Roberto Feltrero holds degrees in Engineering and Philosophy, as well as a PhD in Cognitive Sciences with a doctoral award. He is currently a post-doctoral researcher at UNED, where he coordinates his group's research line on "Media education in the face of the development of digital technologies: Big Data and Artificial Intelligence". His research and publications cover topics related to technology, education, knowledge, and cognitive sciences, with special attention to developing educational technologies that address functional and cultural diversity through social innovation. He is responsible for functional and cultural diversity of the assistive software of www.proyectoheliox.org, a project in which some achievements of his national and international research works are being transferred to society.

Pascale Garreau, co-founder and editorial director of Savoir Devenir, provides training seminars, and participates to the creation of MIL resources, especially in data/AI-related projects. A graduate in sociolinguistics, she has been involved in MIL and digital citizenship for about 20 years. She was namely in charge of the Safer Internet Programme for France from 2008 to 2015. Her top priority is to make research results available in various formats to all citizens.

Javier Gil-Quintana, doctor in Education and Communication, is Professor at the Faculty of Education (UNED). He has a master's degree in Education and Online Communication and in Integrated Technologies and Society. He belongs to the CO-IP of the SMEMIU Research Group (UNED). He is the author of multiple publications on MOOCs, gamification, heritage education, and influencers.

Sophia Hamadi, a doctoral candidate at Université Sorbonne Nouvelle, works at Savoir*Devenir, contributing her expertise in communication and project implementation. She has thus been active in European projects YouCheck!, YouVerify!, Crossover, and ENID-TEACH. Her research interests deal with gender studies with a special focus on intersectionality as it is reflected on social media.

Michael Hameleers, PhD, University of Amsterdam, is an assistant professor of Political Communication at the Amsterdam School of Communication Research (ASCoR). His research interests include (right-wing) populism, disinformation, and selective exposure. He has published extensively on the content, causes, consequences, and counter-strategies of disinformation in a digital information setting.

Saeta Hernando (Alfredo C. Hernando) is co-founder and co-president of IDYL gUG (Berlin 2018) – Interdisciplinary, Dynamic, and Playful Learning (IDYL). He is a graphic communicator and designer, trainer in creativity and collaborative work and researcher in Educational Holistic Gamification. He has been a collaborator of the SMEMIU research group (UNED-Spain) since 2021.

José Javier Hueso Romero, a doctor in Education from National University of Distance Education (UNED) Cum Laude and extraordinary award, is a professor at the University of Nebrija (Madrid). He is a member of the SMEMIU research group (UNED). His research focuses on MOOCs, e-learning, educommunication, and gamification. He has participated as a speaker or organizer in various national and international scientific committees, and has published articles in impact journals and book chapters with publishers of recognized prestige in the scientific community.

Adina Ionescu, a PhD candidate, is an adjunct lecturer at Faculty of Communication and Public Relations, SNSPA. Her main research interests encompass disinformation, gamification, and MIL interventions. As a debate trainer for eight years, Adina is committed to non-formal educational methods, fostering critical thinking in high school students. She is part of national and international projects aimed to address disinformation, enhance the quality of fact-checking in Romanian journalists, and support the development of a strategy for governmental communicators in Romania.

Jade Azzoug Montané, has a PhD in History, is in charge of media literacy projects at Agence France-Presse (AFP), and is an associate professor at the University of Paris Saclay. She has worked for AFP on two European media literacy projects, YouCheck! (2019–2020) and YouVerify! (2020–2021). She has published *D'Havas à l'AFP, histoire d'une agence mondiale d'information* (2020) and *Le métier d'agencier à Havas et à l'AFP, deux siècles d'histoire* (2023).

Sara Osuna-Acedo is a professor of Communication and Education at the National University of Distance Education (UNED). She has held important educational management positions at UNED such as deputy vice rector for Lifelong Learning, and is coordinator of Institutional Courses and director of the Paulo Freire Chair of Educommunication by agreement between MESCYT and UNED. She is the principal researcher of the Consolidated Research Group on Social Media and Inclusive and

Ubiquitous Media Education (SMEMIU) at UNED. The most important research projects she has coordinated as principal investigator are the European Project "E-learning, Communication and Open-data: Massive Mobile, Ubiquitous and Open Learning" (ECO) and the Spanish project "Intelligent and Accessible Virtual Education. Integrated intelligent virtual spaces" (EVIA). She has been led the Spanish team in European projects "YouCheck!" and "YouVerify!".

Cristina Sánchez holds a degree in philosophy and educational sciences, a master's degree in educational technology, and a doctorate in Education from the UNED. She is an associate professor in the Department of Didactics, School Organization, and Special Didactics of the Faculty of Education (UNED). She has held management positions at the university as secretary of the master's degree, secretary of the faculty, and vice general secretary of the UNED exams, and she currently holds the position of academic coordinator of the master's degree in educational treatment of research diversity. She is a member of Research group SMEMIU. Her research lines are on inclusive media education, education for everyone and everyone, including vulnerable groups, in the process of social exclusion Research Line Coordinator.

Sonia Santoveña-Casal is a lecturer at the National University of Distance Education (Universidad Nacional de Educación a Distancia). She is currently the director of the Instituto Universitario de Educación a Distancia (IUED) and coordinator of the European network in D-flexible teaching project, Erasmus+ programme, European Commission.

Denis Teyssou is a senior journalist managing Agence France-Presse (AFP) Medialab R&D and a PhD candidate in Information and Communication Sciences at Paris Nanterre University. Denis has a long experience in participating for AFP into collaborative and innovation projects, mainly EU-funded and tackling disinformation. He is currently the innovation manager of the vera.ai (VERificiation Assisted by Articial Intelligence; https://veraai.eu/; 2022–2025) and is the founder of the InVID-WeVerify verification plugin (http://u.afp.com/plugin) named after two eponym previous EU innovation actions. Denis has co-edited the book *Video Verification in the Fake News Era* (2019, Springer) and co-authored the UNESCO report Balancing Act: Countering Digital Disinformation While Respecting Freedom of Expression (2020).

Loredana Vladu, PhD, MBA, is an associate professor and head of the Communication Department at the Faculty of Communication and Public Relations (National University of Political Studies and Public Administration, SNSPA). Since 2019, she has been a PhD supervisor in Communication Sciences position. In this role, she provides guidance and instruction in Media Literacy and Science Communication courses for PhD students.

Introduction

Divina Frau-Meigs and Nicoleta Corbu

0.1 Introduction

In 2018, the European Union took two landmark decisions about media literacy. It embedded media literacy in the Directive for Audiovisual Media Services and considered it as the second pillar for fighting disinformation in the report about the multidimensional approach to disinformation. In the former, media literacy becomes an obligation for all member states, who must report about its implementation every three years. In the latter, media literacy is a tool for building users' resilience in democratic societies (EU Audio-visual Media Services Directive, 2018).

Accordingly, an important budget was allocated for supporting projects in media literacy, within the "media literacy for all" five-year programme, coordinated by DG-Connect. The purpose was to foster good practices in the field and to spread them across Europe, as media literacy varies across regions and is dependent on the digital infrastructure of countries as well as their media ownership and political structures (linked to freedom of expression in particular). These measures and funding have had profound consequences on media literacy, as such expectations for democracy have put pressure on the media and information literacy (MIL) practitioners and researchers to provide golden standards to strengthen informational resilience for different age groups, as part of the effort to foster online prevention and promote responsible online participation.

To rise to these challenges, media literacy has undergone rapid changes, adjusting to the situation with relative alacrity, putting the EU in a pioneering position, as disinformation played as "a field-configuring process" (Frau-Meigs, 2022a), at macro level (organisations and programmes)—with external push—and micro level (individual or group actions and projects)—with internal pull. For those involved in the field for a long time, at the internal pull, it meant revisiting their vision of Media literacy and strengthening their theoretical stance. It also meant an opportunity, for the first time, to develop media literacy projects across several countries to test those theories against the responses from the practitioners. Finally, it also meant considering the implications for media literacy to keep its core principles, not being reduced to news literacy on the one hand and not being absorbed by

DOI: 10.4324/9781003387404-1

digital opportunism on the other hand. One key goal of the "Media literacy for all" framework was to ensure real field change and social transformation, as illustrated by projects YouCheck! and YouVerify! These two projects spanned a period of three years, including the Covid-19 crisis, with its series of confinements, that spurred an infodemic that put MIL to the test.

0.2 MIL theories in tension: Shifting paradigms between protection and participation

The definitions of MIL have increased over time, as the media perimeter evolved from the printed press and film to digital apps and immersive play systems. Accordingly, media theories have evolved, to encompass those changes, with two persistent trends: protection and participation leading to more regulation and more engagement, respectively (Frau-Meigs, 2013a).

Early definitions point to the development of media literacy education (MLE) as a highly critical and creative activity, in learning environments that include media (the printing press, film) as a tool for teaching and learning (Hobbs & Jensen, 2009). As early as the 1920s, MLE was used as a protection against propaganda and publicity in favour of quality news and consumer awareness, as they were present in commercial media that started to permeate youth cultures. In this protectionist approach, issues of violence and pornography (related to representations of gender and race) were case studies that led to effects theory and acculturation theory in order to explain how representations from media challenged representations from schools (Gerbner et al., 2002; Bryant & Oliver, 2013). Teachers started using the cheaper and cheaper media technologies (photography, video recorders) for educational purposes, with the aim of helping children to protect themselves by a hands-on approach, questioning the process via the practice. This innovative pedagogy has associated MLE with the Do It Yourself (DIY) movement and anchored the distinctiveness of the field in "learning by doing" (Moody, 1999), making media educators very responsive to media systems and technologies, with a strong visual component as different sorts of screens were invading the public spaces and, increasingly, the private homes.

The protectionist approach took some complexity with ideas that implied to avoid the "technicist trap" (Masterman, 1985, p. 26) by reducing MLE to the mechanics of media tools and formats when it was more important to learn about the power relations underpinning the media systems and the messages they emitted. This effects approach anchored MLE with citizenship values, with calls for regulation, be it protection of youth or public service obligations of media owners (clearly identifying advertising, parental warnings, equal airtime for parties, etc.). It brought about the multistakeholder nature of MLE as individuals, associations of civil society actors (parents, families, psychologists, etc.) and media businesses increased their relations and navigated the benefits as well as the risks of harms of full participation in mass and social media (Frau-Meigs & Torrent, 2009; Frau-Meigs et al., 2017a).

The protectionist approach lost some of its currency with media that became more participatory and less top-down (cable, radio, internet). From the 1980s on, uses and gratifications theory displaced the focus from power relations to the user and his/her agency, leading to increased empowerment (Hobbs & Jensen, 2009; Livingstone, 2004; Buckingham, 2003). The experiences of young people's everyday life were considered as key to understanding media and to the sense-making process (Hall, 1973). The stress was less on production systems and power relations and more on individual appropriation, user autonomy and self-expression. This in turn affected MLE's relation to citizenship, with participatory activities centred on community action and peer-to-peer movements (Mihailidis, 2018; Kotilainen and Rantala, 2009). The stress on the relevance to the lived cultural experience of young people aimed at turning them into critical thinkers aware of their rights as citizens.

This uses and gratifications theory leading to participation was supported by views coming from thinkers and researchers outside the Western Anglosphere—where, arguably, the media were born (Tunstall, 1977)—such as Paolo Freire (1968) or Vygotsky (1978). As MLE expanded through the world and localised, Western concepts and practices were further decolonised and adapted. Since the 1960s, in the Spanish-speaking sphere of Latin America, MIL evolved as edu-communication, a way to think of literacy at large as a sociocultural practice that reflects and reacts to power relations, inside and outside the classroom, into the streets and communities (de Soares, 2019; Kaplun, 1998). More recently, in the Asian sphere, Buddhist principles and reflective contemplative education were added to MLE so as to foster a mindful and introspective use of media among young people (Chompu & Sainampueng, 2018; Kajimoto et al., 2020).

0.3 The social turn and its disinformation disorders

This dual process of protection and participation has found new variations since the new millennium and its attendant digital media technologies. In the early 2000s, the opportunities for creativity and self-expression were extolled in MLE with more currency to uses and participation theory as social media platforms expanded. Issues of digital identity, self-expression and engagement found new validity as social media metrics provided users with options for their "quantified selves" (Lupton, 2016) and for their fan practices and influencer follow-ups (Jenkins et al., 2006). The uses and participation approach further complexified as "learning by doing" was increased with "learning by gaming" (game-based learning), as media intermixed with games. The evolution of games, as commercially more and more immersive, and pedagogically more serious, led to enhanced pedagogies with user intervention and agency.

Game-based learning engage participants to experience and explore some aspects of media while playing, with the machine and among themselves. The conversations across players are as important as their gameplay. Game-based learning is considered an effective tool for raising awareness and engagement, as it is appealing for young people and adults alike (Costa et al., 2018; Plass et al., 2015). It is even more powerful if it allows anyone playing to create their own examples or missions or modify their avatars. This is possible with browser games, with open content editors that allow personalisation (in classroom, workshops) as educators can use the game (and its platform) to create a custom educational game (Kerr et al., 2020; Charles et al., 2007). Games are applications that focus on experience, learning by doing, problem solving and can be used to build empathy and allow people to fail without penalty.

However, from the 2010s on, the social turn went from the fun of surfing online to the drudge of data mining, with various disinformation disorders and an increased push by digital media industries to consume ever updating new media without fostering critical engagement, and even less political resistance to their effects on social norms and values. The various crises (terrorist attacks, hacked elections and referenda, Covid-19 confinements, etc.) and disorders (radicalisation, polarisation, disinformation, etc.) have precipitated this trend and brought a new attention to MLE and its effects and risks of harm on large segments of the population. The protectionist approach re-emerged and led to collective regulatory policies and actions, with the rise of Internet governance to deal with complex global issues with a multistakeholder strategy.

In the face of information disorders, MIL has increased in currency, moving from a "shrinking violet" (McGonagle, 2011) to a composite expanding "multi-petaled daisy" (UNESCO, 2006, 2021). UNESCO extended MIL to encompass issues such as hate speech, radicalism, persuasive propaganda and cognitive biases. Consequently, more regulation has ensued with new definitions of MIL circulating. In 2011, Media and Information Literacy emerged, in the landmark Fez Declaration. UNESCO's emphasis since then has been on MIL as

> a set of competencies that empowers citizens to access, retrieve, evaluate and use, create as well as share information and media content in all formats, using various tools, in a critical, ethical and effective way, in order to participate and engage in personal, professional and societal activities.
>
> (UNESCO 2013)

In 2018, the European Union produced a landmark framework in its Audiovisual Media Services Directive (AMSD), which emphasises, inter alia, citizenship and the responsibility of digital platforms:

> Media literacy' refers to skills, knowledge and understanding that allow citizens to use media effectively and safely. In order to enable citizens to access information and to use, critically assess and create media content responsibly and safely, citizens need to possess advanced media literacy

> skills. Media literacy should not be limited to learning about tools and technologies, but should aim to equip citizens with the critical thinking skills required to exercise judgment, analyze complex realities and recognize the difference between opinion and fact. It is therefore necessary that both media service providers and video-sharing platforms providers, in cooperation with all relevant stakeholders, promote the development of media literacy in all sections of society, for citizens of all ages, and for all media and that progress in that regard is followed closely.
>
> (EU, 2018)

The competences that flow from these definitions extend MIL beyond schools and beyond personal or parental responsibility, to encompass governments and media organisations, with core values for democratic societies (freedom of expression, privacy, participation). MIL has been able to do so by developing its own set of competences, even though it is not part of the basic curricula in most countries. They are reflected, for instance, in the United States' "Core principles", as stated by the National Association for Media Literacy Education (NAMLE, 2007). In Europe, the core principles and competences appear in the "European charter for Media literacy" (Bachmair & Bazalette, 2007). Its three main tenets are around "the Cultural, the Critical and the Creative", so that citizens "broaden their experience of different kinds of media form and content; develop critical skills in analysing and assessing the media; develop creative skills in using media for expression and communication, and participation in public debate" (pp. 83–84). These varying core competences were construed as transversal to all subject matters in the schools, a subsidiary variable for any teacher or educator to adjust to his/her context and pedagogical repertoire.

0.4 Transliteracy and new challenges: Socialisation by design (and by law)

However, they are not enough to deal with times of uncertainty and rapid change as media become increasingly transborder and transnational and span both the IRL (the real life) and the URL (the virtual life), from printing press to metaverse. The unprecedented convergence produced by mediatisation, documentarisation and datafication makes it necessary to address contemporary crises related to the platformisation of media and learning as well as disinformation disorders while embracing the opportunities for transformative education. Such challenges call for MIL to become a scientific field of its own and not a poor relation of communication studies (effects and cultivation, uses and gratifications) or education sciences (competences). Defining the contours of MIL as a frontier field, supported by its own theoretical and methodological constructs, provides a framework for understanding how information via the digital media has become the crux of knowledge construction and identity formation.

The previous models predicated on the two-winged approach of protection vs participation are evolving to accommodate the platformisation of society (van Dijck et al., 2018). Platformisation refers to the fact that large Internet companies (such as Google, Amazon, Meta, Microsoft and Apple) organise public and private life and affect cultural norms and values. With processes that deal with dataveillance and engagement metrics, they can offer services such as search engines, data servers, game browsers and app stores. The platform ecosystem has incorporated both mass media outlets and social media networks, and used their combined capacities to manipulate political situations, as revealed by the recent scandals around "fake news" (Manokha, 2018). The core principles become those dealing with transparency, accuracy and privacy, as well as social responsibility and democratic sovereignty. As they are not embedded into the algorithmic processes operated by the platforms, such core principles need to be imparted to citizens so that they can enjoy their online and offline rights, thus totally within the MIL remit.

Effects theory has embraced datafication and its relation to digital tools, pointing to their design, their functionalities and their finalities (Drot-Delange & Bruillard, 2012). Effects theory developed in relation to disinformation effects show decreased trust in real information (van der Meer et al., 2023), engagement with questionable information (Corbu et al., 2020a; Glenski et al., 2020) and revisited early propaganda models, as well as the impact of the "third person effect" in fake news detection persuasive effects (Zerback et al., 2020), third person effects about disinformation (Corbu et al., 2020b, Corbu et al., 2022), to name just a few.

Effects theory has also extended to risks of harm and enlarged cultivation to go as far as referring to an "inoculation" technique (Basol et al., 2020; Cook et al., 2017). Inoculation refers to the creation of "mental antibodies" in people by exposing them to weakened versions of "fake news" and thus enabling them to resist future disinformation attacks. This is done by exposing the major mechanisms of disinformation (rogue actors' interference, plot theory rhetoric, etc.) using all sort of digital tools, in particular games such as the "Bad News" game.[1] It has addressed the old MIL conundrum about "the technicist trap" or the "tool competence" bias by recurring to techno-cognition, incorporating psychological principles with technological solutions to solve disinformation issues (Lewandowsky et al., 2017). This speedy re-education by games is presented as prebunking, the use of smart digital tools being supportive of verification processes (Wineburg & McGrew, 2019). Prebunking tries to foster audience resilience and prevent audience amplification by creating new heuristics in the minds of users. Often associated with "online civics" (Milhailidis, 2018; Wineburg & McGrew, 2019), prebunking lends itself more to educational preparedness than inoculation, as it is not a "one shot" intervention, but a strategy that can be embedded to MIL pedagogies (Nygren et al., 2022; Frau-Meigs, 2022a).

Uses and gratifications theory has extended to participatory cultures (Jenkins et al., 2006) and embraced mediatisation. It has nurtured the "edu-communication" paradigm, which has complexified "mediations" (Martin-Barbero, 1987), as youth and adult lives are mediated by all sorts of media, including self-made media (selfies, stories, streams, etc.). Mediations complexify with mediatisation as digital media cohabit with analogical ones, television feeding images that are reused on social media (Aparici, 2010). New mediated processes affect socialisation as they play on identity formation and agency, with actions on the real world (Erstad & Sefton-Green, 2012; Krotz, 2009). They also affect citizenship as they enable new participatory strategies in public life such as online petitions, crowdfunding etc. Understanding online participation has become key as it offers opportunities for activism and civic engagement (De Abreu et al., 2017; Mihailidis, 2018) but also risks for information disorders that are based on filter bubbles and echo chambers. New kinds of subjectivities have appeared, linked to emotions and cognitive biases that question the very notion of truth and may embrace "post truth" and "plot theories".

However, none of these approaches deals with the very convergence produced by mediatisation, and datafication in the platform society, aggregated to documentarisation. This is the tenet of transliteracy where mediatisation and datafication meet documentarisation and contributes to socialisation—not just protection or participation (Frau-Meigs, 2022b). Transliteracy purports to provide a compelling contribution to MIL theory, with core notions and innovative research intervention postures that have the potential of restructuring MIL into a frontier field. It transcends the traditional double-winged opposites of effects/protection and uses/participation by addressing socialisation and social learning via sedimented mass and social media (Frau-Meigs, 2013b).

Placing the theoretical cursor differently, at a meta-level, transliteracy blends effects and uses as well as protection and participation, as the new media environment blurs the frontiers between producer and consumer, private and public spaces. Transliteracy is one of the few theories that highlights how it is central for people to be able to navigate across media systems and platforms. It was first described as "the ability to read, write and interact across a range of platforms, tools and media", in a multimodal media world (Thomas et al., 2007, p. 101). It was later enlarged to embrace the double-meaning of digital convergence:

> 1) the multi-media dimensions of current literacy—being able to read, write, count and compute with print and digital tools and via all sorts of formats from book to blog; 2) the trans-domain requirements for digitally sustainable literacy—being able to code and to search, test, validate, modify information as understood in computation (code), in communication (news) and in library science (document and data).
>
> (Frau-Meigs, 2012, p. 15)

Transliteracy adds documentarisation to datafication and mediatisation, to explain how early information systems (e.g. cataloguing and indexing) have been augmented by digital treatments (Chartier, 1993; Goody, 1986). This has led to many formats (e.g. jpeg, ppt and excel), added new functionalities (e.g. traceability, interactivity, cloning and morphing, etc.) and affected organisational processes (e.g. search, recommendation, curation, etc.). These same opportunities and processes lend themselves to massive disinformation possibilities as each basic pixel can be programmed and modified independently, allowing infinite transformations of documents, including their falsification. As such, it has led to information disorders of a different kind, due to the ease with which documents can be modified, morphed, decontextualised. It has also increased participation and sociability as one of the main uses of social media is sharing and curating texts and images. More importantly, for MIL, it has displaced the circuits of recommendation, displacing the vertical gatekeeping of cultural elites and school systems with a more horizontal peer-to-peer sharing contract (Serres, 2012).

The meta-level of transliteracy is composed of three information cultures and their attendant competences: cultural and socialisation competences for media literacy (or infomedia), organisational and editorial competences for information literacy (or infodocs) and operational and problem-solving competences for data literacy (or infodata) (see Figure 0.1).

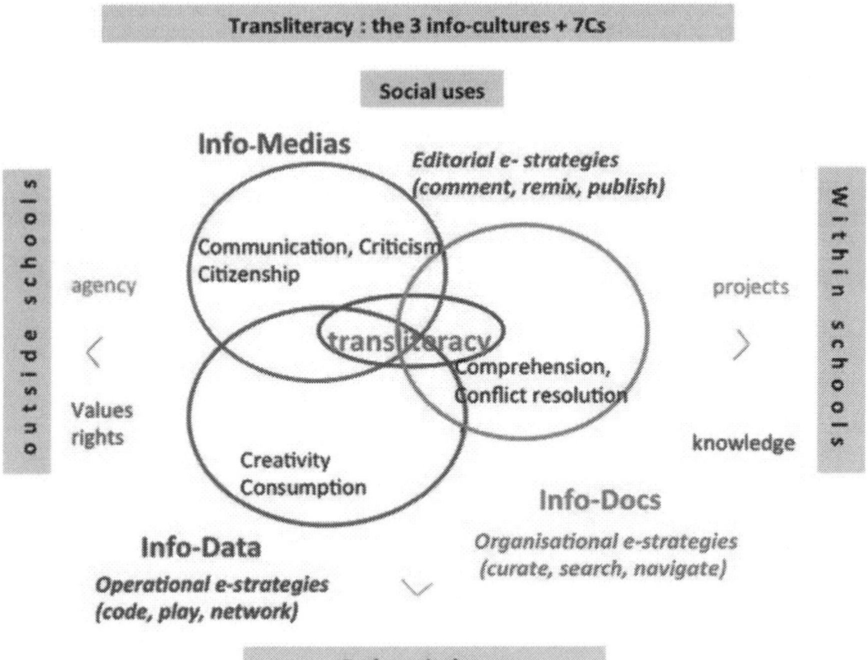

Figure 0.1 Transliteracy model: The three information cultures.

Source: Frau-Meigs, 2013b.

The transliteracy model was delineated by a large set of researchers united in a transdisciplinary project, ANR Translit (2013–2015), associated with European COST Action IS0906 "Transforming Audiences, Transforming Societies" (2010–2014) (Frau-Meigs et al., 2017a). This model was further tested and implemented in European Project ECO (open mobile and collaborative learning), through one of its Massive Open Online Courses (MOOC) created for the purpose, the MOOC DIY MIL (which received the Global MIL Award in 2016).

0.5 Innovative research developments and methodologies

Adopting a transliteracy stance paves the way for a series of theoretical and methodological developments, which revisit issues that have traversed the field of MLE/MIL since its beginning, especially the relation to technology, pedagogy and, ultimately, policy.

Transliteracy lends itself to interdisciplinary designs, across the social sciences (especially education, cognition and communication sciences) as well as transdisciplinary designs, across social sciences and data sciences (computing, game development). This combination can foster design experiments that combine critical and creative competences with evidence-based assessments, mixing theory and practice.

In terms of relation to the mind, cognition has shed new light on *socialisation* processes and *documentarisation.* Socio-cognition posits that the learners are capable of articulating knowledge (content level) and pertinent information search (access levels) in such a way as to construct their own understanding and to interact with others and their media environment (Perkins & Zimmerman, 1995; Salomon, 1994). Epistemic cognition enables critical thinking (Greene et al., 2018), multimodal text and image processing (Leu et al., 2015) and considers the learners' intellectual reasoning to build epistemic maturity (Frau-Meigs & Bossu, 2020). *Techno-cognition* uses smart AI-driven tools to gather and navigate information and to deal with cognitive biases that guide or misguide their uses (Lewandowsky et al., 2017).

In terms of the relation to technology, data sciences, in combination with *techno-cognition*, associate *socialisation* to the way algorithms shape media apps and services to bolster self-construction. Using *datafication* to conduct research on the platform society, and its information opportunities and information disorders, becomes possible with smart tools that can help identify the integrity of online images and texts and, by reverse engineering, debunk disinformation (Bontcheva & Posetti, 2020). The multidimensional analysis of behavioural scripts, navigation histories, social media patterns can provide predictive models of users' habits and biases and explain how they can be susceptible to the effects of disinformation (Corbu et al., 2020a; Vosoughi et al., 2018). Developing text and image forensics with algorithms and smart tools can respond to the growing need to train users to detect and debunk fake media content (Nygren et al., 2021).

In terms of relation to learning and pedagogies, *competences* frameworks provided by education co-mingle with cognitive approaches to *experiences* and how they deal with the users' emotions to foster learning (Kahan, 2013, 2017; Kahne et al., 2014). *Socialisation* uses *mediatisation* for harnessing the dynamics of learning events, exploring the articulation between the individual and the collective, in the digital space as much as in the physical space. Mediations as understood by *edu-communication* make it possible to describe the combined mechanisms of emotions and reasonings to engage learners and induce them to participate in self-empowering processes (Sanchez et al., 2017). Games, as they are increasingly shifting to engagement by design, lend themselves to new pedagogies that are gamified or use game-based learning for participatory activities and civic engagement (Osuna-Acedo, 2021).

In relation to citizenship, policy changes that are brought about to make MIL into a quick-fix solution to fight information disorders, often alongside with fact-checking, need to be evaluated with transliteracy lenses, with coherent indicators to assess their effectiveness. Particular attention should be paid to a balanced view of MIL, with opportunities in mind as much as risks of harm. The multistakeholder dimension of MIL and the governance of such heterogeneous actors is a challenge for researchers and practitioners in the field (Frau-Meigs et al., 2017b).

0.6 Implementing transliteracy to fight disinformation: Structure of this book

The first section of the book lays the theoretical background related to real-life solutions to combat mis- and disinformation: from prebunking and debunking approaches, fact-checking, to MIL. Additionally, the two projects are presented in a detailed manner, with a focus on objectives, outcomes, outputs and lessons learnt.

In Chapter 1, Hameleers presents an overview of the advances of the academic literature related to the solutions of prebunking and debunking to fight mis- and disinformation. In a first step, the author provides a synthesis of the main effects of mis- and disinformation [following Wardle & Derakhshan (2017) distinction], with the aim of setting the context for solutions to actively counter them through pre- and debunking. Next, the main sections of the first chapter focus on fact-checks as journalistic routines as a main debunking technique and on media literacy interventions and "inoculation" approaches as main prebunking techniques. Both paths of fighting mis- and disinformation are presented along with their own limitations, while the author further offers suggestions for more effective applications in the future.

In Chapter 2, Joseph Beaudreau focuses on fact-checking practices and their broader political and economic contexts, using a theoretical approach based on a critical political economy perspective. Starting with a well-documented historical overview on the fact-checking phenomenon, the chapter further presents up-to-date information about the main fact-checkers evaluation networks, International Fact-Checking Network (IFCN), and European Fact-Checking Standards Network (EFCSN). The European initiatives to support fact-checking, such as EDMO, AFP as a pan-European fact-checker, IFCN network, etc. are discussed in this chapter.

Most data presented in this book are the results of two international projects funded through *Media Literacy for all* EU initiative. In Chapter 3, Frau-Meigs et al. introduce the two projects (YouCheck! and YouVerify!) against a theoretical background related to the transliteracy paradigm of MIL (Brest, 2010; Taplin & Clark, 2012), with additional support from techno-cognition and edu-communication approaches. YouCheck! project (2019–2020) was an international project implemented in four countries (France, Romania, Spain and Sweden), aimed at empowering European citizens with the latest advances in image and video verification, through the InVID-WeVerify plugin developed in two different Horizon-funded European projects (https://www.invid-project.eu/ and https://weverify.eu). YouVerify! scaled-up the tools and instruments further developed and used in YouCheck!, embedding them in massive open online courses (MOOCs) implemented in three countries (France, Romania and Spain). Both projects are presented in detail, with a focus on outputs, outcomes and impact, and future regards about MIL real life interventions based on lessons learnt through these two projects.

The second section of the book looks as some resources and strategies used in the two MIL projects, and analyses their results as starting points for further evidence-based policy making.

In Chapter 4, Corbu et al. report data gathered in the YouCheck! project aimed at testing InVID-WeVerify plugin for image and video verification of information. The data relies on two quantitative and one qualitative studies, based on survey, experimental and focus groups-based methodologies. Results offer promising results related to the successful use in classrooms of new technological devices and tools to enhance media literacy among both teachers and students.

Chapters 5 and 6 both report on scaling up MIL interventions via MOOCs. Both chapters report on the implementation of the "Disinformation Step-by-Step" MOOC from two different perspectives. In Chapter 5, Frau-Meigs et al. focus on the effectiveness of the two seasons of the MOOC in terms of participants' satisfaction, while in Chapter 6, Bossu discusses MOOC facilitation as a means of getting participants involved and motivating them to make the best of this online learning experience. "Disinformation Step-by-Step", provided in three languages (French, English and Spanish) has been a successful media literacy large-scale programme, making use of both theoretical advances in MIL and practical facilities offered by ECO-Learning platform that hosted the courses, including embedding gamification strategies and InVID-WeVerify plugin. Both chapters discuss further developments of MOOCs of means of developing MIL in adult population throughout Europe and beyond.

In Chapter 7, Santoveña-Casal et al. offer a general overview of the results of MOOCs evaluation by Spanish participants and in-depth interviews with Spanish experts conducted in YouVerify! project. This chapter offers one-country insights and recommendations to actively fight mis- and disinformation through MIL and policy recommendation made by journalists, education experts and policymakers.

Feltrero et al. report on media literacy interventions through serious games, with the game BotBusters developed within the YouVerify! project as a case study. The game was developed around the InVID-WeVerify plugin, tested and largely used in the project, with the aim of becoming an open-access media literacy resource to further be used at a large scale. The chapter provides results of the use of the serious game, embedded in the MOOC Disinformation Step-by-Step. The gamification strategies used in BotBusters were developed based on the theoretical model of experiential learning, in which the learned is constantly involved and motived to learn through experience (Kolb, 2014). The high percentages of players who finished the serious game indicates that such games could become useful tools in media literacy interventions not only in classrooms but also in life-long learning settings.

The third section of the book is devoted to policies and policymaking with the intent to scale up and go further based on the evidence provided from the two projects. The two chapters included in this section provide evidence-based recommendation for policymaking based on focus groups with teachers and the educated ordinary people conducted in four countries in the YouCheck! project (Corbu et al., infra) and in-depth interviews with disinformation experts in three countries conducted in the YouVerify! project (Durach et al., infra). Both chapters adopt a cross-country comparison approach, building on differences specific for countries with different media policy approaches (Hallin & Mancini, 2004, revised 2011). Both chapters also point to several solutions that should become embedded in policies designed to purposefully fight mis- and disinformation: education, with an accent on life-long learning MIL interventions; tools and serious games developed with the aim of identifying questionable content and motivating people to fact-check the information they come across; fact-checking initiatives; media awareness campaigns; social media regulation to name just the most important ones.

Note

1 getbadnews.com

References

Aparici, R. (Ed.) (2010). *Educomunicación: más allá del 2.0*. Gedisa.

Bachmair, B., & Bazalette, C. (2007). The European charter for media literacy: Meaning and potential, *Research in Comparative and International Education*, 2(1), 80–87. http://doi.org/10.2304/rcie.2007.2.1.80

Basol, M., Roozenbeek, J., & van der Linden, S. (2020). Good news about bad news: Gamified inoculation boosts confidence and cognitive immunity against fake news. *Journal of Cognition*, *3*(2). https://doi.org/10.5334/joc.91

Bontcheva, K., & Posetti, J. (Eds.). (2020). (rep.). *Balancing act: Countering digital disinformation while respecting freedom of expression*. Broadband Commission for Sustainable Development. Retrieved from https://en.unesco.org/publications/balanceact

Brest, P. (2010). The Power of Theories of Change. *Stanford Social Innovation Review*, *8*(2), 47–51.

Bryant, J., & Oliver, M. B. (2013). *Media effects advances in theory and research*. Routledge.

Buckingham, D. (2003). *Media education: Literacy, learning and contemporary culture*. Polity Press.

Charles, D., Kücklich, J., & Kerr, A. (2007). Player-centered game design: Player modelling and adaptive digital games. In S. de Castell & J. Jenson (Eds.), *Worlds in play. International perspectives on digital games research*. Peter Lang.

Chartier, R. (1993). Du livre au lire. In R. Chartier (Ed.), *Pratiques de la Lecture* (pp. 81–117). Payot.

Chompu, U., & Sainampueng, R. (2018). The Buddhist Way of the New Media Literacy for the Youth in Bangkok. *Journal of MCU Peace Studies*, *6*(2), 460–473.

Clark, H., & Taplin, D. (2012). *Theory of change basics: A primer on theory of change*. Actknowledge.

Cook, J., Lewandowsky, S., & Ecker, U. K. H. (2017). Neutralizing misinformation through inoculation: Exposing misleading argumentation techniques reduces their influence. *PLoS One*, *12*(5), 1–21.

Corbu, N., Bârgăoanu, A., Buturoiu, R., & Ștefăniță, O. (2020a). Does fake news lead to more engaging effects on social media? Evidence from Romania. *Communications*, *45*(1), 694–717. https://doi.org/10.1515/commun-2019-0152

Corbu, N., Oprea, D., Negrea-Busuioc, E., & Radu, L. (2020b). They can't fool me, but they can fool the others! Third person effect and fake news detection. *European Journal of Communication*, *35*(1), 165–180. https://doi.org/10.1177/0267323120903686

Corbu, N., Oprea, D. A., & Frunzaru, V. (2022). Romanian adolescents, fake news, and the third-person effect: A cross-sectional study. *Journal of Children and Media*, *16*(3), 387–405. https://doi.org/10.1080/17482798.2021.1992460

Costa, C., Tyner, K., Henriques, S., & Sousa, C. (2018). Game creation in youth media and information literacy education. *International Journal of Game-Based Learning*, *8*(2), 1–13. https://doi.org/10.4018/IJGBL.2018040101

De Abreu, B. S., Mihailidis, P., Lee, A. Y., Melki, J., & McDougall, J. (2017). *International handbook of media literacy education*. Routledge.

de Soares, I. O. (2019). Educommunication landmarks in Latin America: What should be considered in the last 50 years. In J-C. Mateus, P. Andrada, & M. T. Quiroz (Eds.), *Media education in Latin America*. Routledge.

Drot-Delange, B., & Bruillard, É. (2012). Éducation aux TIC, cultures informatique et du numérique: quelques repères historiques. *Études de communication*, *38*, 69–80. https://doi.org/10.4000/edc.3393

Erstad, O., & Sefton-Green, J. (2012). *Identity, community, and learning lives in the digital age*. Cambridge University Press.

EU Audiovisual Media Services Directive. (2018). https://eur-lex.europa.eu/legal-content/EN/TXT/PDF/?uri=CELEX:32018L1808&from=EN

Frau-Meigs, D. (2012). Transliteracy as the new research horizon for media and information literacy. *Mediaeval Studies*, 2(Dec), 5–25.

Frau-Meigs, D. (2013a). *ANR TRANSLIT final report*. http://www.univ-paris3.fr/anr-translit-243520.kjsp

Frau-Meigs, D. (2013b). Child and adolescent well-being in Media and communication studies. In A. Ben-Arieh, I. Frones, F. Casas, & J. E. Korbin (Eds.), *Handbook of child well-being. theory, indicators, measures and policies*. Springer.

Frau-Meigs, D. (2022a). How disinformation reshaped the relationship between journalism and media and information literacy (MIL): Old and new perspectives revisited. *Digital Journalism*, *10*(5), 912–922.

Frau-Meigs, D. (2022b). Transliteracy and the digital media: Theorizing media and information literacy. In R. Tierney, F. Rizvi, & K. Ercikan (Eds.), *International encyclopedia of education* (4th ed.). Elsevier.

Frau-Meigs, D., & Bossu, A. (2020). L'agilité et l'interculturalité en question dans le dispositif global-local des MOOC: le cas du MOOC Pas à Pas. *Questions de communication 38*(2), 87–102.

Frau-Meigs, D., O'Neill, B., Soriani, A., & Tomé, V. (2017b). *Digital citizenship education: Overview and new perspectives*. Council of Europe Publishing.

Frau-Meigs, D., & Torrent, J. (Eds.). (2009). *Mapping media education policies worldwide: Visions, programmes and challenges*. UN AoC.

Frau-Meigs, D., Velez, I., & Flores-Michel, J. (Eds). (2017a). *Public policies in media and information literacy in Europe: Cross country comparisons*. Routledge.

Freire, P. (1968 Tr: 1970). *Pedagogy of the Oppressed*. Continuum.

Gerbner, G., Gross, L., Morgan, M., Signorielli, N., & Shanahan, J. (2002). Growing up with television: Cultivation processes. In J. Bryant, & D. Zillman (Eds.), *Media effects: Advances in theory and research* (2nd ed., pp. 43–67). Lawrence Erlbaum.

Glenski, M., Volkova, S., & Kumar, S. (2020). User engagement with digital deception. In K. Shu, S. Wang, D. Lee, & H. Liu (Eds.), *Disinformation, misinformation, and fake news in social media* (pp. 39–61). Springer.

Goody, J. (1986). *The logic of writing and the organization of society*. Cambridge University Press.

Greene, J. A., Copeland, D. Z., Deekens, V. M., & Yu, S. B. (2018). Beyond knowledge: Examining digital literacy's role in the acquisition of understanding in science. *Computers & Education*, *117*, 141–159. https://doi.org/10.1016/j.compedu.2017.10.003

Hall, S. (1973). *Encoding and decoding in the television discourse*. Birmingham Centre for Contemporary Cultural Studies.

Hallin, D. C., & Mancini, P. (2004). *Comparing media systems: Three models of media and politics*. Cambridge University Press.

Hobbs, R., & Jensen, A. (2009). The past, present, and future of media literacy education. *Journal of Media Literacy Education*, *1*(1), 1–11. https://doi.org/10.23860/jmle-1-1-1

Jenkins, H., Purushotma, R., Clinton, K., Weigel, M., & Robison, A. (2006). *Confronting the challenges of participatory culture: Media education for the 21st century*. The MacArthur Foundation.

Kahan, D. M. (2013). Ideology, motivated reasoning, and cognitive reflection. *Judgment and Decision making*, *8*(4), 407–424.

Kahan, D. M. (2017). Misconceptions, Misinformation, and the Logic of Identity-Protective Cognition. Cultural Cognition Project Working Paper Series No. 164, Yale Law School, Public Law Research Paper No. 605, Yale Law & Economics

Research Paper No. 575, Available at SSRN: https://ssrn.com/abstract=2973067 or https://doi.org/10.2139/ssrn.2973067

Kahne, J., Middaugh, E., & Allen, D. (2014). Youth, new media and the rise of participatory politics. *Youth and Participatory Politics Research Network*, *1*, 1–25.

Kajimoto, M., Ito, M., & Lim, M.-K. (Eds.). (2020). *Media and information literacy education in Asia: Exploration of policies and practices in Japan, Thailand, Indonesia, Malaysia and the Philippines*. UNESCO.

Kaplun, M. (1998). *Una pedagogia de la Comunicacion*. Ediciones de la Torre.

Kerr, A., Savage, J. D., & Twomey-Lee, V. (2020). Decoding and recoding game making events for diversity, inclusion and innovation. In *Report from the network in play and ReFiG research projects*. Maynooth University.

Kolb, D. A. (2014). *Experiential learning: Experience as the source of learning and development*. FT press.

Kotilainen, S., & Rantala, L. (2009). From seekers to activists: Characteristics of youth civic identities in relation to media. *Information, Communication & Society*, *12*(5), 658–677. https://doi.org/10.1080/13691180802345865

Krotz, F. (2009). Mediatization: A concept with which to grasp media and societal change. In K. Lundby (Ed.), *Mediatization: Concept, Changes, Consequences*. Peter Lang.

Leu, D. J., Zawilinski, L., Forzani, E., & Timbrell, N. (2015). Best practices in teaching the new literacies of online research and comprehension. In L. B. Gambrell & L. M. Morrow (Eds.), *Best practices in literacy instruction* (5th ed., pp. 343–364). Guilford.

Lewandowsky, S., Ecker, U. K., & Cook, J. (2017). Beyond misinformation: Understanding and coping with the "post-truth" era. *Journal of Applied Research in Memory and Cognition*, *6*(4), 353–369. https://doi.org/10.1016/j.jarmac.2017.07.008

Livingstone, S. (2004). Media literacy and the challenge of new information and Communication Technologies. *The Communication Review*, *7*(1), 3–14. https://doi.org/10.1080/10714420490280152

Lupton, D. (2016). *The quantified self*. Wiley.

Manokha, I. (2018). Surveillance, panopticism, and self-discipline in the digital age. *Surveillance and Society*, *16*, 219–237. https://doi.org/10.24908/ss.v16i2.8346

Martin-Barbero, J. (1987). *De los medios a las mediaciones: Comunicacion, cultura y hegemonia*. Gustavo Gili.

Masterman, L. (1985). *Teaching the media*. Comedia.

McGonagle, T. (2011). *Media literacy: No longer the shrinking violet of European audiovisual media regulation?* Iris-European Audiovisual Observatory.

Mihailidis, P. (2018). Civic media literacies: Re-Imagining engagement for civic intentionality. *Learning, Media and Technology*, *43*(2), 152–164. https://doi.org/10.1080/17439884.2018.1428623

Moody, K. (1999). *The children of Telstar. Early experiments in school television production*. Vantage Press.

National Association for Media Literacy Education (NAMLE). (2007). *Core principles of media literacy education in the United States*. http://www.amlainfo.org/uploads/r4/cE/r4cEZukacxNYaFFxlMONdQ/NAMLE-CPMLE-w-questions.pdf

Nygren, T., Frau-Meigs, D., Corbu, N., & Santovena-Casal, S. (2022). Teachers' views on disinformation and media literacy supported by a tool designed for professional fact-checkers: Perspectives from France, Romania, Spain and Sweden, *SN Social Sciences*, 2(40). https://doi.org/10.1007/s43545-022-00340-9

Nygren, T., Guath, M., Axelsson, C.-A., & Frau-Meigs, D. (2021). Combatting visual fake news with a professional fact-checking tool in education in France, Romania, Spain and Sweden. *Information*, *12*(5), 201. https://doi.org/10.3390/info12050201

Osuna-Acedo, S. (2021). Gamification and MOOCs. In D. Frau-Meigs, S. Osuna-Acedo, & Marta-Lazo, C. (Eds.), *MOOCs and the participatory challenge*. Springer. https://doi.org/10.1007/978-3-030-67314-7_6

Perkins, D., & Zimmerman, M. A. (1995).Empowerment theory, research, and application. *American Journal of Community Psychology*, *23*(5), 569–579. https://doi.org/10.1007/BF02506982

Plass, J. L., Homer, B. D., & Kinzer, C. K. (2015). Foundations of game-based learning, *Educational Psychologist*, *50*(4), 258–283. https://doi.org/10.1080/00461520.2015.1122533

Salomon, G. (1994). *Interaction of media, cognition, and learning*. Routledge.

Sanchez, E., Young, S., & Jouneau-Sion, C. (2017). Classcraft: From gamification to ludicization of classroom management. *Education and Information Technologies*, *22*, 497–513. https://doi.org/10.1007/s10639-016-9489-6

Serres, A. (2012). *Dans le labyrinthe: évaluer l'information sur internet*. C&F éditions.

Thomas, S., Joseph, C., Laccetti, J., Mason, B., Mills, S., Perril, S., & Pullinger, K. (2007). Transliteracy: Crossing divides. *First Monday*, *12*(12). https://doi.org/10.5210/fm.v12i12.2060

Tunstall, J. (1977). *The media were American*. Oxford University Press.

UNESCO (2006). *Media education. A kit for teachers, parents and professionals*. https://unesdoc.unesco.org/ark:/48223/pf0000149278

UNESCO. 2013. *Global Media and Information Literacy Assessment Framework: Country Readiness and Competencies*. Paris: UNESCO.

UNESCO. (2021). *Media and information literate citizens: Think critically, click wisely!* https://unesdoc.unesco.org/ark:/48223/pf0000377068

Van der Meer, T. G. L. A., Hameleers, M., & Ohme, J. (2023). Can fighting misinformation have a negative spillover effect? How warnings for the threat of misinformation can decrease general news credibility. *Journalism Studies*, *24*(6), 803–823. https://doi.org/10.1080/1461670X.2023.2187652

van Dijck, J. Poell, T., & De Waal, M. (2018). *The platform society*. Oxford Scholarship Online.

Vosoughi, S., Roy, D., & Aral, S. (2018). The spread of true and false news online, *Science*, *359*, 1146–1151.

Vygotsky, L. S. (1978). *Mind in society: Development of higher psychological processes*. Harvard UP.

Wardle, C., & Derakhshan, H. (2017). (rep.). *Information disorder: Toward an interdisciplinary framework for research and policy making*. Council of Europe. Retrieved from https://tverezo.info/wp-content/uploads/2017/11/PREMS-162317-GBR-2018-Report-desinformation-A4-BAT.pdf

Wineburg, S., & McGrew, S. (2019). Lateral reading and the nature of expertise: Reading less and learning more when evaluating digital information. *Teachers College Record: The Voice of Scholarship in Education*, *121*, 1–40. https://api.semanticscholar.org/CorpusID:227628758

Zerback, T., Töpfl, F., & Knöpfle, M. (2020). The disconcerting potential of online disinformation: Persuasive effects of astroturfing comments and three strategies for inoculation against them. *New Media & Society*, *23*(5), 1080–1098. https://doi.org/10.1177/1461444820908530

Section I

Fighting disinformation from a theoretical perspective

Designing projects YouCheck! and YouVerify!

1 The state-of-the-art in combating mis- and disinformation

Lessons from pre- and debunking approaches

Michael Hameleers

1.1 Introduction

Mis- and disinformation may have severe ramifications for society and democracy at large. Whereas misinformation refers to unintentional untruthfulness (e.g., Wardle & Derakhshan, 2017), disinformation can be understood as the goal-directed creation and spread of intentionally deceptive information (e.g., Bennett & Livingston, 2018). As false information – irrespective of its intentions – may have harmful consequences, such as the amplification of distrust and polarisation, it is important to understand how mis- and disinformation can be combatted or prevented. Against this backdrop, this chapter will review the state-of-the art in literature on corrective information, with a specific focus on how pre- and debunking approaches have been found to be effective under different conditions. Based on this review, the chapter will end with a forward-looking perspective on how these different tools can be used effectively to both prevent and fight the uncontrolled dissemination of mis- and disinformation across the globe.

Pre-bunking approaches that prevent misperceptions and instil resilience among audiences are found to be effective (e.g., Roozenbeek & van der Linden, 2019; Tully et al., 2020). Here, pre-bunking is understood as any intervention to prevent or combat mis- or disinformation *before* it is disseminated, with the aim to make audiences more resilient and better equipped to resist the persuasive impact of false information. In this regard, inoculation strategies that expose people to a small 'dose' of false information before an actual threat are found to be effective in empowering citizens to distinguish false from true information (e.g., Roozenbeek & van der Linden, 2019). Likewise, media literacy interventions that offer citizens specific suggestions on how they can rely on critical skills to recognise misleading and false information are found to have a negative impact on the credibility and acceptance of mis- and disinformation (e.g., Tully et al., 2020).

Research on debunking initiatives, mostly understood as fact-checks that respond to mis- and disinformation *after* its spread, point to similar optimistic conclusions: Although important sources of resistance may be identified (Hameleers & van der Meer, 2020), fact-checks that offer a short, argument-based

DOI: 10.4324/9781003387404-3

refutation of falsehoods are found to be successful in correcting false information (e.g., Nyhan et al., 2019). Despite the indications on the effectiveness of pre- and debunking initiatives in extant academic research, we know little about the real-world impact of these interventions, or their combined influence in combating false information in current digital and fragmented information environments. Perhaps even more important, most literature has failed to consider the longer-term and unintended side effects that interventions may have for the acceptance and trust in real, authentic information.

Against this backdrop, this chapter not only offers an overview of the evidence that pre- and debunking interventions may work but also considers how they can be implemented and integrated in complex information ecologies, and how they can overcome the resistance and impediments of the technological and societal context in which they operate. Finally, this chapter considers how pre- and debunking should also consider the consolidation or recovery of trust in factually correct information that may easily be dismissed as mis- or disinformation in a post-factual information era.

1.2 The effects of mis- and disinformation

Disinformation is created with the intention to deceive, and make a predefined impact on people's beliefs (e.g., Hameleers, 2023). Misinformation may, in addition, unintentionally result in misperceptions among recipients (Wardle & Derakhshan, 2017). Considering that exposure to false information has been found to result in misperceptions, it is important to explore how these negative consequences can be prevented or remedied. But why are mis- and disinformation potentially harmful and effective forms of communication?

Extant research has shown that exposure to mis- and disinformation may, among other things, influence political perceptions (e.g., Hameleers et al., 2020), or people's trust in established information and the news media (e.g., Zimmermann & Kohring, 2020). Here, it is also important to note that experimental research shows that disinformation can be perceived as highly credible (e.g., Schaewitz et al., 2020). One explanation for the credibility of mis- and disinformation comes from the truth-default-theory (TDT) of information processing (Levine, 2014). This theory holds that, on average, people are more likely to perceive new information as honest than dishonest. Therefore, unless suspicion is actively triggered by information sources, content or style, mis- and disinformation are likely to be regarded as trustworthy (Hameleers, 2022). This truth bias can be exploited by malicious actors, who imitate credible news formats and authentic visual information as closely as possible to avoid triggering suspicion. This is especially the case with visual disinformation formats that are often used in online settings and can add persuasive power to deceptive narratives by offering 'proof' and a direct index of reality to false statements (Weikmann & Lecheler, 2022). Moreover, considering that mis- and disinformation are often repeated, they may come across as familiar and truthful information sources that can sidestep suspicion.

The often-delegitimising narrative of disinformation may undermine trust in real information and established media by foregrounding accusations of 'fake news' and misinformation, contrasted to alternative sources of allegedly trustworthy information (Hameleers, 2022). At the same time, discussions about the threats of mis- and disinformation and delegitimising accusations of false information may undermine trust in real information by disproportionally triggering suspicion (Van der Meer et al., 2023). For these reasons, it is crucial that pre- and debunking approaches to mis- and disinformation somehow maintain a balance between critical perspectives towards suspicious statements, without motivating a cynical view to all information encountered.

1.3 State-of-the-art in debunking techniques

Mis- and disinformation have been associated with severe ramifications for democracy, such as the delegitimisation of established knowledge, mounting relativism toward facts, polarisation and mistrust (e.g., Van Aelst et al., 2017; Waisbord, 2018). In this setting, the question on what should be done to correct and prevent misinformation has become more prominent than ever. From a journalistic perspective, fact-checking has been coined as an important response to the uncontrolled dissemination of misinformation. Here, we refer to fact-checks as stand-alone or embedded journalistic products and routines that offer verdicts about the level of (un)truthfulness of (political) information by checking dubious or prominent claims (e.g., Amazeen et al., 2015; Uscinski & Butler, 2013). Fact-checks can, first of all, be delivered by independent organisations, such as fullfact.org in the UK, Agence France Press in France, and factcheck.org in the US. In addition, fact-checks may be part of established journalistic formats, for example, in the form of a dedicated editorial section (i.e., *The Washington Post*'s Fact Checker section).

Irrespective of the format, fact-checking platforms are regarded as politically unbiased and neutral (e.g., Amazeen et al., 2015). Although these platforms may show a selection bias in their inclusion criteria, for example, by selecting only the most visible dubious claims, they may refrain from attaching political judgements to their verdicts. That being said, in the bipartisan setting of the US, fact-checkers have been accused of demonstrating a liberal bias (e.g., Shin & Thorson, 2017). Research has further demonstrated that Republicans are more likely to reject and counter-argue fact-checks (Shin & Thorson, 2017), and that people are generally most likely to select fact-checks when they attack misinformation that is incongruent with prior beliefs (Hameleers & van der Meer, 2020). Thus, although they claim to be neutral and objective observers of the information ecology, fact-checks may be subject to mistrust and politically coloured interpretations. But why would fact-checkers be effective, and for whom are their effects (least) pronounced?

Basically, fact-checks should work as they present news users with a univocal verdict on the truthfulness of claims – using a factual and rational argumentation presented in easy-to-comprehend formats (Lewandowsky et al., 2012). The working of corrective information can also be understood through the perspective of the Truth-Default-Theory (TDT) coined by Levine (2014). The TDT states that humans are, as a default coping mechanism, wired to accept the honesty of the information they receive from others. As most information does not contain lies or misinformation (also see Acerbi et al., 2022), this default state of information acceptance should be valid most of the time, and helps news users to effortlessly navigate their information setting. Against this background, fact-checks should be effective in correcting misperceptions as they signal deception, and flag suspicious content to recipients. In other words, exposure to fact-checking information should prime suspicion, which should result in a deviation from the truth-default state.

There is ample evidence that exposure to fact-checking information lowers misperceptions, resulting in the successful debunking of misinformation. Meta-analyses, for example, show an overall positive and substantial effect of exposure to fact-checking information on the reduction of false beliefs (Chan et al., 2017; Walter et al., 2020). Even though some studies have pointed to negative or even 'backfire' effects of fact-checks (e.g., Nyhan & Reifler, 2010; Thorson, 2016), more recent experimental studies point out that exposure to fact-checking information lowers misperceptions (e.g., Hameleers & van der Meer, 2020; Nyhan et al., 2019).

Despite the potential of fact-checks, there are different limitations to their effectiveness. First of all, fact-checking information is most effective among recipients whose beliefs do not align with mis- or disinformation (e.g., Walter et al., 2020). In addition, fact-checking information is most likely to be selected by people who are already opposed to the claims of the debunked misinformation (Hameleers & van der Meer, 2020). Related to this, in an information era where facts are often disputed and mainstream media and journalism distrusted, fact-checkers may be regarded as biased, untrustworthy or even 'fake news' peddlers by growing parts of the population that have tuned out of established information sources (Primig, 2022). Here, it should also be noted that most research concluding that fact-checks are effective are based on artificial experimental study designs – which begs the question about fact-checks' effectiveness in real life media settings.

All in all, we can conclude that fact-checking information faces different challenges. Although people strongly inclined to believe mis- and disinformation may need fact-checking information most, they may be less likely to expose themselves to it and take the verdict into account. Even more so, their alternative media diets and distrust in established information sources may mean that they do not even come across debunking information. For this reason, it is important to present fact-checking information in a format that can overcome resistance and enhance the likelihood of selection among distrusting segments of the audience. But what kind of effective formats have been suggested and tested in extant literature?

First of all, the use of explicit rating scales and verdicts may enhance the clarity of fact-checks. Importantly, fact-checks should not emphasise and repeat the false statements that are debunked, as repetition of false information can enhance its credibility (Pennycook et al., 2018). A suggested format of fact-checking is therefore to present the verdict and arguments for the rejection of misinformation in a clear and accessible manner (e.g., Graves, 2017). It is also relevant to present the verdict early in the correction. Hence, in an overburdened information ecology, news users spend only very little time on reading news articles and background stories. Having only limited processing resources at their disposal, they may look for easy-to-process cues or heuristics. Responding to this bias, fact-checks may be most effective when they present recipients with a concrete and repeated verdict early on in the message, potentially supplemented with a visual rating scale that illustrates the level of untruthfulness (see also Amazeen et al., 2015, on the effectiveness of visual rating scales). A concrete example of such clear rating scales is the use of the truth-o-meter used by PolitFact.[1]

Second, as fact-checking information may be avoided by news users who need them most – such as citizens with stronger anti-establishment or disinformation perceptions – extant literature has experimented with different formats of fact-checking that should overcome resistance and selective avoidance. Hence, as literature shows that many citizens perceive the verdict of fact-checkers as biased or hostile against their views (e.g., Brandtzaeg & Følstad, 2017; Shin & Thorson, 2017), it is important that people do not perceive the correction as an attack on their beliefs. One way to overcome resistance and hostile perceptions towards fact-checks is to use humour or satire. As these formats are less likely to be associated with persuasive intent and political agendas, they may overcome the belief of political bias and hostility. In line with this, evidence shows that satirical refutations can be more effective than regular fact-checks among segments of the audience that are aligned with misinformation's false statements (Boukes & Hameleers, 2020). In a similar vein, Young et al.'s (2018) findings show that using humour in videos can enhance the effectiveness of corrective information.

Third, extant literature has offered indications that the source matters. More specifically, using regular source cues to present fact-checking information, such as established news sources and independent fact-checking platforms, may cause resistance among people who distrust such formats. As these citizens are most likely to encounter mis- and disinformation whilst avoiding regular established journalistic formats, it is important to find ways to reach them with corrections. One strategy proven to be successful is to use fictional cartoon characters or ordinary citizens to present and promote corrective information (Opgenhaffen, 2021). Fact-checks presented by cartoon figures did not cause resistance, and were overall perceived as credible and accurate sources of corrections. In a later application, the cartoon figures were replaced for a realistic fictional avatar called 'Anna'. Although more research is needed to explore the effectiveness of using alternative sources on social media in direct response to false information, it is plausible that presenting corrective information on the same channels as misinformation and via non-elitist sources that resemble regular news users may overcome an important source of resistance and avoidance.

Taken together, extant research has shown that fact-checks may offer an influential remedy to mis- and disinformation in the digital age. Although there are important pitfalls and barriers that may limit its scope and effectiveness, there is convincing evidence that fact-checks can enhance resistance to mis- and disinformation, albeit not all segments of the population may be reached. Considering that false information spreads at a way faster rate than corrections, which are also extremely costly and time intensive to make, it is important to look beyond debunking approaches. An important question is therefore how resistance to mis- and disinformation can be enhanced among news users *before* they are confronted with false information in their newsfeed.

1.4 State-of-the-art in pre-bunking techniques

The limited reach of fact-checks, at times, and the potential barriers to their selection may be partially remedied by relying on a more elaborate toolkit of fighting misinformation. One major alternative or supplement to fact-checking is pre-bunking. As an umbrella term for interventions that aim to instil resilience to the effects of misinformation, 'pre-bunking' involves all techniques and approaches to prevent the negative impact of misinformation before people are exposed to misleading content. The envisioned effectiveness of pre-bunking can, just like the effect of fact-checks, be understood as a consequence of priming suspicion and herewith motivating a deviation from the truth-default state (Levine, 2014). In other words, pre-bunking makes news users aware of deception in their information environment, which should motivate them to critically assess the veracity and biases of information.

Pre-bunking has mostly been studied in the form of media literacy interventions (e.g., Hameleers, 2020; Vraga et al., 2020) or 'inoculation' techniques (e.g., Roozenbeek & van der Linden, 2019). Media literacy interventions typically contain a stepwise description about how people can detect misinformation, offering concrete recommendations to news users navigating their information environment (e.g., Vraga et al., 2020). Inoculation also offers a warning about false information and exposes people to a small 'dose' of misinformation that should protect them from the actual harms of misinformation (Roozenbeek & van der Linden, 2019). Hence, encounters with smaller doses of the threat helps people to recognise misinformation and enables them to defend themselves when actual threats of deception arise.

Recent experimental research has shown that pre-bunking techniques can be effective in enhancing resilience towards misinformation. Roozenbeek and van der Linden (2019) show that inoculation with 'fake news games' – in which people are confronted with misinformation as producers and consumers – helps news users to accurately identify misinformation presented to them later. In a similar vein, experimental studies in which people are exposed to a media literacy intervention that tells them how to detect fake news lowers the credibility and believability of misinformation (e.g., Guess et al., 2020; Hameleers, 2020; Vraga et al., 2020). In a similar vein, using a pre-bunking intervention in education, Nygren et al. (2021) show that pupils were better equipped to detect false visual information after a two-hour intervention, whereas the credibility of real news was not affected. Although experimental research comes with clear drawbacks – such as the artificial and forced exposure setting and the short time frame between treatment and measurements – there is ample evidence that exposure to pre-bunking messages or games can help people to detect misinformation.

However, the priming of suspicion that is part of pre-bunking messages comes with an important drawback. Hence, by making people suspicious towards 'fake' news and deceptive content, a disproportionately cynical outlook on media content can be cultivated. Although misinformation is estimated to play a very small role in people's newsfeeds in terms of prominence (Acerbi et al., 2022), the focus on fake and deception in media literacy interventions may also lead news users to identify authentic and factually accurate information as misinformation. In support of this, Hameleers (2020) found that, although media literacy interventions lowered the credibility of misinformation, they also had a negative spillover effect on the credibility of authentic news. Modirrousta-Galian et al. (2022) also found that gamified inoculation treatments lowered the credibility of real information, and therefore did not improve the discernment between factually accurate information and misinformation.

These findings emphasise the importance of striking a balance between stimulating critical media literacy skills and maintaining trust in factually accurate information. Thus, although pre-bunking needs to help citizens to detect misinformation, such interventions should not overemphasise the threats of misinformation. Even more so, trust in factually accurate information needs to be consolidated, which means that the discernment between factually accurate information and misinformation is the targeted outcome instead of the detection of misinformation (Guess et al., 2020). This means that, looking beyond the effects on the recognition of just false information, interventions should also take into account the effects of interventions on trust in real news or factual information (also see e.g., Nygren et al., 2021). Against this backdrop, it is meaningful to approach the intended consequences of interventions as the extent to which news users are better equipped to make critical and well-informed decisions on the veracity and honesty of the information that surrounds them in today's overburdened information ecologies.

1.5 Suggestions for effective applications of remedies

At this stage, it can be concluded that both fact-checking information and pre-bunking techniques are proven to be effective remedies against misinformation. Yet, both routes towards more resilient societies come with important drawbacks. Does this mean that we need to abandon these interventions altogether? The answer is negative. The identified barriers to interventions' effectiveness should be regarded as challenges that future research and applications need to combat and overcome. It shows that we may need to revise existing interventions, carefully considering sources of resistance and negative side effects. This section more specifically forwards four concrete suggestions on how interventions may be improved in order to overcome the identified challenges. The main assumption here is that although no solution on its own is perfect or best able to combat misinformation, the combination of different tools and their strategic targeting to vulnerable audiences may make a crucial difference in society's resilience to false and deceptive information.

1.5.1 Use channels, sources and formats to overcome avoidance and resistance

Both pre- and debunking messages may be perceived as biased and unreliable by segments of society that have lost faith in the established political order and the media (Primig, 2022). Ironically, distrusting segments of society may be attracted most to alternative and hyper-partisan media that are most likely to disseminate counterfactual narratives or disinformation. In addition, experimental research shows that fact-checks are most likely to be avoided by people whose perspectives align with mis- or disinformation (Hameleers & van der Meer, 2020). The problem we face is therefore that interventions are most likely to be rejected or avoided by segments of society that are most susceptible to misinformation.

Responding to this challenge, the first major suggestion is to present corrective information or media literacy interventions on less established platforms and channels. More specifically, interventions may be most effective if they are presented on the same platform as misinformation, and part of the same networks as citizens with mis- and disinformation diets. A concrete example would be to present fact-checks directly as false flags on the social media platforms that are more likely to contain misinformation to and target media literacy warnings to community pages, platforms and environments that are likely to be visited by segments of society that tend to be exposed to misinformation. Thus, to increase the likelihood of selection among distrusting citizens, it is meaningful to not only present fact-checks or media literacy messages on independent stand-alone platforms of established media but also embed warnings and corrections on platforms that contain false information.

It also matters how the correction is presented, and which sources forward the verdict and correction. Importantly, people may feel attacked if an elitist institution – such as a fact-checking platform associated with the mainstream media – claims that they are wrong. For this reason, corrective information may be presented as subtle warning messages coming from ordinary people or sources people may identify with (see the example of cartoon figures or ordinary citizens on social media by Opgenhaffen, 2021). Importantly, these sources should avoid a direct attack on people's beliefs by stating that their perceptions on the world are wrong, false or even 'stupid'. A more subtle approach that points people to factually accurate information contrasted to false beliefs may be more constructive – overcoming the resistance caused by a direct attack or a label that states that people are wrong. Formats such as a truth sandwich – which focuses on factually accurate information instead of repeating false claims – may also be used to reach the same goal. Essentially, corrective information should be presented carefully and should avoid the impression that people feel that their identities are under attack by labelling recipients as misinformed, wrong or even ignorant.

Related to this, corrective information may acknowledge the drivers of believing misinformation or disinformation. Too often, corrections fail to respond to the reasons why misinformation may be believable. A concrete suggestion is to acknowledge contexts of insecurity, uncertainty or the emotions associated with certain developments or events. As an example, the COVID-19 pandemic was surrounded by a context of uncertainty, high stakes, fear and disagreeing expert voices. Corrective information, however, typically failed to acknowledge this context and the drivers of believing misinformation – herewith potentially neglecting disenchanted voices in society. Based on this, corrective information may be most effective when it acknowledges and relativises the underlying drivers of supporting and believing misinformed claims. Acknowledging that COVID-19 is surrounded by uncertainty and fears about the causes and treatment of the virus may help to engage people who typically avoid corrective information as they may attack their beliefs and identities whilst failing to resonate with their worldviews.

1.5.2 Consolidate trust and motivate critical (but not cynical) media skills

Considering that interventions may backfire by priming disproportionate levels of cynicism and distrust in factually accurate information (e.g., Hameleers, 2022), it is crucial to consolidate trust in factually accurate information. Therefore, instead of exclusively warning about the threats of deception, media literacy interventions and inoculation strategies need to relativise and contextualise the threats of mis- and disinformation embedded in an information ecology of mostly accurate information (Acerbi et al., 2022). In other words, current interventions that only offer tips on how to recognise fake news may cultivate disproportionate negative views on the information ecology and prime suspicion beyond a constructive level that helps them to discern between factually accurate information and misinformation.

Concretely, media literacy interventions and fact-checkers may offer suggestions on where recipients can find factually accurate and reliable information on different issues. A reading list of selected sources for different issues may help, such as the official sources of informing citizens about COVID-19. Moreover, interventions can relativise the threats of mis- and disinformation by emphasising that most information that people encounter in their newsfeed is reliable. However, some claims may be false or deceptive – which calls for a critical (but not cynical) approach to information. In any case, interventions can offer details on where misinformation is most and least likely to occur – which relativises the negatively biased worldview that misinformation is all around.

Another way to avoid cynicism is to focus less on the falsehoods and deception and more on the actual factual reality in the verdicts of a refutation. Fact-checkers may, for example, not simply repeat false information and stress the deceptive nature in their rating, but rather focus on the facts and the actual situation or evidence for reality. In addition, instead of warning about the deceptive nature of information, inoculation and media literacy approaches may stress the need to be critical, motivating users to verify information themselves by consulting multiple sources and reflecting on their own biases. Essentially, resilience towards misinformation may be achieved by stimulating critical skills and the confidence that people themselves are able to navigate their information environment. This entails the skills needed to find the majority of factually accurate information whilst being sensitised to the deception that may occur at times.

1.5.3 Experiment with modalities, formats and tailoring

Although many fact-checking platforms aim to present their verdicts in accessible and clear manners, it takes considerate amounts of attention and cognitive resources to process corrective information. Fact-checking platforms typically aim to be rigorous and precise, which may pose a challenge on the scarce resources and attention of recipients. The often-technical and textual elaborations of fact-checkers may exclude vulnerable segments of the audience that do not want to – or are unable to – invest reading time and processing resources in consuming corrective information. But what can we do to grab the scarce resource of attention in a competitive media environment where misinformation is often more engaging and easy to consume than corrections?

Fact-checkers may use visually attractive formats to present their verdict in an easy to comprehend manner that requires only limited reading time. A concrete example is to embed two-sentence verdicts on social media to flag suspicious content, which also responds to the first recommendation to circumvent avoidance and rejection from citizens most likely to be exposed to misinformation. The two-sentence verdict may clarify why statements are regarded as suspicious, combined with a brief statement of factually accurate information that can be contrasted to the flagged suspicious claims. Although fact-checking platforms may intend to offer a complete and well-founded verdict, not all citizens will be able or motivated to read the entire analysis and the reasons why certain claims are disputed. Therefore, it is suggested to include a 'read more' option or a link to the full research and refutation when outlining and embedding a short and easy-to-comprehend verdict on social media or other platforms where misinformation is likely to be encountered. This way, fact-checking may still be based on a complete and thorough analysis of reality, whilst also presenting recipients with an easy to digest recommendation.

Another suggestion is to present fact-checks in a more attractive and engaging format, for example by using short videos of a refutation or infographics that show recipients why claims are disputed after a quick look. Although such refutations require even more effort and financial resources, they may grab the audience's attention. Such videos or infographics should not be presented as stand-alone products on separate platforms or websites, but should ideally be embedded in the response sections of false, disputed or suspicious content online. Videos may also be suitable to explain to news users how they can be more critical news users. Hence, an audiovisual demonstration on how to recognise reliable information whilst being sensitive to deception may be comprehensible for citizens at different levels of cognitive skills and processing resources.

1.5.4 An integrated approach towards resilient societies

It is important to emphasise that although the different responses to misinformation may only have limited effects, they may have a meaningful impact on resilience when combined, repeated, targeted and adjusted to developments in the digital age. Although fact-checks may have a relatively limited reach, repeated exposure to debunking messages may also teach news users how to verify information themselves, and what types of narratives may be suspicious. The same applies to media literacy interventions and inoculation strategies. Not all messages may reach all citizens, but encountering warning flags and learning about the reasons why certain statements were retracted, dubious or unreliable may contribute to a more critical audience that is resilient to the threats of mis- and disinformation.

Moreover, when fact-checkers and media literacy initiatives offer clear guidance on where factually accurate information can be found, and how citizens can determine when information is trustworthy and reliable, we can avoid the negative side effects of strengthening distrust and cynicism related to trustworthy information. Overall, interventions need to offer the much-needed guidance for citizens to navigate complex digital information flows. Although most information is accurate and reliable, the digital setting affords manipulation and targeted attacks on people's beliefs. In addition, the many-to-many communication flows, the lack of gatekeeping and the low thresholds for access in the public domain also implies that people may be exposed to unintentional misinformation, or unverifiable claims that remain unchecked and unflagged.

This complexity of the information ecology needs to be central in education – not just in the educational message of pre-bunkers but also in educational programmes in schools and targeted digital literacy campaigns intended for vulnerable groups (i.e., the elderly who may be reached through libraries or other institutions). Hence, the complex information flows require an understanding of misinformation embedded in the current information ecology, and approaches that only focus on the statement level or isolated suspicious narratives fall short in emphasising how the context of (deceptive) content matters for its identification and resistance to its influence.

1.6 What's next? A forward-looking perspective on corrective information

Although fact-checking and pre-bunking have been prominent strategies for multiple decades, new developments in digital communication and artificial intelligence may pose new challenges on the way forward. As deep fakes and other synthetic deceptive media are getting more widespread, corrective information may need to do more than just checking the accuracy and honesty of statements. Hence, they may increasingly need to verify the authenticity of materials that are seemingly real – moving beyond the correction of political statements and positions. Open-Source intelligence (OSINT) may offer an important aid in the process of tracing back the origins of synthetic materials, but the detection and creation of highly realistic deceptive media may always be entranced in an arms race. In this setting, it may become more important to teach recipients on how to detect discrepancies between reality and the viewpoints of known actors vis-à-vis the mediatised images of these persons. Simply pointing out technological glitches may be insufficient when technologies are improving rapidly. Therefore, the audience needs to be trained to critically scrutinise whether the depictions they observe are realistic. In this setting, it is helpful that news users are offered a toolkit to fact-check themselves, for example, by checking whether visual information is authentic (i.e., OSINT, Tineye, or InVID-WeVerify).

As misinformation is a relatively rare phenomenon compared to factually accurate information, future interventions may also need to focus on enhancing the credibility and trust in factually accurate information. As indicated by Acerbi et al. (2022), it may be more effective to enhance the trustworthiness of factually accurate information by 1 percent than to decrease the acceptance of misinformation to zero. Thus, the combined strategy of combating misinformation needs to be supplemented by strategies that increase the accessibility and comprehensibility of high-quality information. A main challenge in that regard is to lower society's resistance to established information sources and to motivate audience segments that avoid the news and mainstream media altogether. To enhance the appeal of high-quality trustworthy information, it may be needed to experiment with formats that are selected and accepted by disenchanted audience segments.

As part of this future endeavour, mainstream media, as well as corrective information initiatives, need to acknowledge and relativise the feeding ground of misinformation instead of rejecting or sidestepping the feelings and concerns of people likely to select or believe misinformation. Too often, established media and other official sources of information ignore or even ridicule the concerns and feelings of disenchanted citizens – which may fuel polarisation and distrust to a more extreme level (Hameleers, 2022). Hence, considering the existing barriers for the selection of fact-checks and media literacy interventions among citizens that need them most, more resources have to be invested in building bridges and demonstrating higher levels of mutual understanding. Finding common ground between fragmented and opposed segments of society (i.e., everyone is concerned about the consequences of COVID-19/there is a lot of uncertainty and unclarity in official information) may contribute to enhancing trust in official information among citizens that are likely to avoid established information sources.

Related to this, more transparency on how knowledge is created and subject to high levels of uncertainty, change is needed to involve citizens in the process of knowledge created. For most citizens, the process underlying the formation of knowledge remains a black box, which also means that sudden changes in perspectives (i.e., masks were first deemed unnecessary and later obliged during the COVID-19 pandemic in many countries) are left unexplained. Only stating that decisions and guidelines suddenly changed without explaining why may fuel distrust in society and leave explanation room open for alternative narratives, conspiracies and misinformation. Explaining how decisions, policy and guidelines are changed and why factual interpretations may shift as expert knowledge is subject to change may leave less room for misinformation's alternative explanations of events.

In the way forward, transparency may also be more central to the platform's policies and guidelines. At this stage, there is only little knowledge about how algorithms curate and amplify misinformation and how financial interests of commercial platforms may promote the spread of falsehoods. In addition, there are currently no clear formal guidelines in place for the curation of false information. We are therefore in need of a stronger legal framework that explicates the guidelines for content producers and disseminators. Related, content policies and digital services acts need to work towards a more transparent digital society, where users know why they see certain content, and how their media diets are subject to mechanisms that are fueled by (commercial) interests.

1.7 Conclusion

Misinformation has been regarded as a severe problem that may undermine deliberative democracy. Extant research has demonstrated that both fact-checking and media literacy interventions can offer viable treatments, although they come with drawbacks. This chapter aimed to foreground the conditions under which interventions may (not) work and which strategies and adjustments may enhance their effectiveness. First of all, this chapter concluded that although fact-checks and other interventions are effective in artificial lab settings (e.g., Walter et al., 2020), they face challenges of selective avoidance and rejection in real life. Hence, as growing segments of society are losing trust in established information sources – including journalists and fact-checkers – corrective information may not reach the most vulnerable users that are likely to approach misinformation that reassures their distrust in established sources.

Different strategies may be employed to increase the likelihood of selection and acceptance of interventions. For example, fact-checks can use less elitist sources, and experiment with sources that are more relatable for recipients. For example, it may be useful to use ordinary citizen sources that warn fellow social media users about suspicious content (Opgenhaffen, 2021), which may overcome resistance to fact-checking information. In any case, it is important to circumvent the growing levels of cynicism related to established information sources when correcting misinformation. Humour, ordinary citizen cues and argumentation styles that do not attack people who are inclined to support misinformation are recommended formats to present corrective information. Importantly, as different segments of society may have different (media) preferences, ideological biases and identities, the affordances of digital infrastructures may be used to tailor and target fact-checking information to recipients' preferences.

Beyond these specific recommendations, we can conclude that there is no single perfect intervention or solution to combat misinformation. Different interventions, such as fact-checking, media literacy messages, inoculation games or legal interventions, may all come with their own strengths and weaknesses. Individually, their effects may be limited. However, the combination of a mixture of interventions that are repeated, tailored and amplified may offer the best response to misinformation (see Hameleers, 2020). The combined impact of a well-balanced strategy based on a set of interventions may be bigger than the sum of their parts. For example, media literacy interventions may teach people how to be critical, and how to rely on fact-checking information when in doubt. Fact-checks, in addition to the general warnings offered by media literacy interventions, can offer specific guidelines for how the trustworthiness of statements may be rated.

Related to this, we have to critically ask what the desired outcome of fact-checking and media literacy interventions are: When is an intervention deemed effective? More specifically, reducing misperceptions in the short term may not be the desired endpoint or impact of corrections. Rather, to truly enhance resilience towards misinformation, citizens themselves need to have the toolkit to judge the veracity of information, whilst maintaining trust in factually accurate information. In line with this, interventions used to respond to misinformation should instil critical literacy skills that help people to discern between the majority of factually accurate and trustworthy information, while being sensitive to dubious and suspicious claims that warrant further attention. Ideally, critical news users are able to become fact-checkers themselves, and the interventions used to combat misinformation should offer them the tools they need to recognise when information is in need of verification. Here, maintaining and enhancing trust in reliable information may be even more important than lowering the acceptance of misinformation (Acerbi et al., 2022).

Despite these recommendations, we are in need of more research on the effectiveness of corrections in the real world. Most evidence-based recommendations are currently founded on lab experiments or artificial survey settings in which people voluntarily contribute. These studies may miss the most vulnerable audience segments, and citizens that are most likely to select misinformation and avoid fact-checking information specifically. Therefore, we are in need of field experiments, as well as qualitative and interpretive methods that engage with citizens that resist fact-checking information, and studies that use real-life monitoring of different interventions. Moving forward, the conclusions of such studies can be used to further redesign and improve the effectiveness of current interventions proven to be worthwhile.

Taken together, we can conclude this chapter by emphasising the importance of ongoing initiatives to fight misinformation. Although no solution is perfect on its own, all means that are proven to be effective need to be used as part of a global toolkit that aims to enhance society's resilience to the threats posed by misinformation – which includes its undermining impact on the trustworthiness of factually accurate information.

Note

1 PolitFact.com

References

Acerbi, A., Altay, S., & Mercier, H. (2022). Research note: Fighting misinformation or fighting for information? *Harvard Kennedy School Misinformation Review*. https://doi.org/10.37016/mr-2020-87

Amazeen, M. A., Thorson, E., Muddiman, A., & Graves, L. (2015). *A comparison of correction formats: The effectiveness and effects of rating scale versus contextual corrections on misinformation*. American Press Institute. Retrieved April 27, 2022, from https://www.americanpressinstitute.org/wp-content/uploads/2015/04/The-Effectiveness-of-Rating-Scales.pdf

Bennett, L. W., & Livingston, S. (2018). The disinformation order: Disruptive communication and the decline of democratic institutions. *European Journal of Communication*, *33*(2), 122–139. https://doi.org/10.1177/0267323118760317

Boukes, M., & Hameleers, M. (2020). Shattering populists' rhetoric with satire at elections times: The effect of humorously holding populists accountable for their lack of solutions. *Journal of Communication*, *70*(4), 574–597. https://doi.org/10.1093/joc/jqaa020

Brandtzaeg, P. B., & Følstad, A. (2017). Trust and distrust in online fact-checking services. *Communications of the ACM*, *60*(9), 65–71. https://doi.org/10.1145/3122803

Chan, M. P. S., Jones, C. R., Hall Jamieson, K., & Albarracín, D. (2017). Debunking: A meta-analysis of the psychological efficacy of messages countering misinformation. *Psychological Science*, *28*(11), 1531–1546. https://doi.org/10.1177/0956797617714579

Graves, L. (2017). Anatomy of a fact check: Objective practice and the contested epistemology of fact checking. *Communication, Culture & Critique*, *10*(3), 518–537. https://doi.org/10.1111/cccr.12163

Guess, A. M., Lerner, M., Lyons, B., Montgomery, J. M., Nyhan, B., Reifler, J., & Sircar, N. (2020). A digital media literacy intervention increases discernment between mainstream and false news in the United States and India. *Proceedings of the National Academy of Sciences*, *117*(27), 15536–15545. https://doi.org/10.1073/pnas.1920498117

Hameleers, M. (2020). Separating truth from lies: Comparing the effects of news media literacy interventions and fact-checkers in response to political misinformation in the US and Netherlands. *Information, Communication & Society*, 1–17. https://doi.org/10.1080/1369118X.2020.1764603

Hameleers, M. (2022). *Populist disinformation in fragmented information settings: Understanding the nature and persuasiveness of populist and post-factual communication*. Routledge.

Hameleers, M. (2023). Disinformation as a context-bound phenomenon: Toward a conceptual clarification integrating actors, intentions and techniques of creation and dissemination. *Communication Theory*, *33*(1), 1–10. https://doi.org/10.1093/ct/qtac021

Hameleers, M., Powell, T. E., Van Der Meer, T. G., & Bos, L. (2020). A picture paints a thousand lies? The effects and mechanisms of multimodal disinformation and rebuttals disseminated via social media. *Political Communication*, *37*(2), 281–301. https://hdl.handle.net/11245.1/a27a4957-6fd9-4a8f-b6d2-e21185fddc43

Hameleers, M., & van der Meer, T. G. L. A. (2020). Misinformation and polarization in a high-choice media environment: How effective are political fact-checkers? *Communication Research*, *47*(2), 227–250. https://doi.org/10.1177/0093650218819671

Levine, T. R. (2014). Truth-default theory (TDT): A theory of human deception and deception detection. *Journal of Language and Social Psychology*, *33*(4), 378–392. https://doi.org/10.1177/0261927X14535916

Lewandowsky, S., Ecker, U. K., Seifert, C. M., Schwarz, N., & Cook, J. (2012). Misinformation and its correction: Continued influence and successful debiasing. *Psychological Science in the Public Interest*, *13*(3), 106–131. http://www.jstor.org/stable/23484653

Modirrousta-Galian, A., Higham, P. A., & Seabrooke, T. (2022). Effects of inductive learning and gamification on news veracity discernment. *PsyArXiv*. https://doi.org/10.31234/osf.io/4wfds

Nygren, T., Guath, M., Axelsson, C. A. W., & Frau-Meigs, D. (2021). Combatting visual fake news with a professional fact-checking tool in education in France, Romania, Spain and Sweden. *Information*, *12*(5), 201. https://doi.org/:10.3390/info12050201

Nyhan, B., Porter, E., Reifler, J., & Wood, T. J. (2019). Taking fact-checks literally but not seriously? The effects of journalistic fact-checking on factual beliefs and candidate favorability. *Political Behavior*. https://doi.org/10.1007/s11109-019-09528-x

Nyhan, B., & Reifler, J. (2010). When corrections fail: The persistence of political misperceptions. *Political Behavior*, *32*(2), 303–330. https://doi.org/10.1007/s11109-010-9112-2

Opgenhaffen, M. (2021). Fact-checking interventions on social media using cartoon figures: Lessons learned from "the Tooties". *Digital Journalism*, 1–24. https://doi.org/10.1080/21670811.2021.2011758

Pennycook, G., Cannon, T. D., & Rand, D. G. (2018). Prior exposure increases perceived accuracy of fake news. *Journal of Experimental Psychology: General*, *147*(12), 1865–1880. https://doi.org/10.1037/xge0000465

Primig, F. (2022). The influence of media trust and normative role expectations on the credibility of fact checkers. *Journalism Practice*, 1–21. https://doi.org/10.1080/17512786.2022.2080102

Roozenbeek, J., & Van der Linden, S. (2019). The fake news game: Actively inoculating against the risk of misinformation. *Journal of Risk Research*, *22*(5), 570–580. https://doi.org/10.1080/13669877.2018.1443491

Schaewitz, L., Kluck, J. P., Klösters, L., & Krämer, N. C. (2020). When is disinformation (in) credible? Experimental findings on message characteristics and individual differences. *Mass Communication and Society*, *23*(4), 484–509. https://doi.org/10.1080/15205436.2020.1716983

Shin, J., & Thorson, K. (2017). Partisan selective sharing: The biased diffusion of fact-checking messages on social media. *Journal of Communication*, *67*(2), 233–255. https://doi.org/10.1111/jcom.12284

Thorson, E. (2016). Belief echoes: The persistent effects of corrected misinformation. *Political Communication*, *33*(3), 460–480. https://doi.org/10.1080/10584609.2015.1102187

Tully, M., Vraga, E. K., & Bode, L. (2020). Designing and testing news literacy messages for social media. *Mass Communication & Society*, *22*(1), 22–46. https://doi.org/10.1080/15205436.2019.1604970

Uscinski, J. E., & Butler, R. W. (2013). The epistemology of fact checking. *Critical Review*, *25*(2), 162–180. https://doi.org/10.1080/08913811.2013.843872

Van Aelst, P., Strömbäck, J., Aalberg, T., Esser, F., de Vreese, C., Matthes, J., Hopmann, D., Salgado, S., Hubé, N., Stępińska, A., Papathanassopoulos, S., Berganza, R., Legnante, G., Reinemann, C., Sheafer, T., & Stanyer, J. (2017). Political communication in a high-choice media environment: A challenge for democracy? *Annals of the International Communication Association*, *41*(1), 3–27. https://doi.org/10.1080/23808985.2017.1288551

Van der Meer, T. G. L. A., Hameleers, M., & Ohme, J. (2023). Can fighting misinformation have a negative spillover effect? How warnings for the threat of misinformation can decrease general news credibility. *Journalism Studies*, *2023*, 1–21.

Vraga, E. K., Bode, L., & Tully, M. (2020). Creating news literacy messages to enhance expert corrections of misinformation on Twitter. *Communication Research*. https://doi.org/10.1177/0093650219898094

Waisbord, S. (2018). Truth is what happens to news: On journalism, fake news, and post-truth. *Journalism Studies*, *19*(13), 1866–1878. https://doi.org/10.1080/1461670X.2018.1492881

Walter, N., Cohen, J., Holbert, R. L., & Morag, Y. (2020). Fact-checking: A meta-analysis of what works and for whom. *Political Communication*, *37*(3), 350–375. https://doi.org/10.1080/10584609.2019.1668894

Wardle, C., & Derakhshan, H. (2017). Information disorder: Toward an interdisciplinary framework for research and policymaking, Council of Europe Report. http://tverezo.info/wp-content/uploads/2017/11/PREMS-162317-GBR-2018-Report-desinformation-A4-BAT.pdf

Weikmann, T., & Lecheler, S. (2022). Visual disinformation in a digital age: A literature synthesis and research agenda. *New Media & Society*, https://doi.org/10.1177/14614448221141648

Young, D. G., Jamieson, K. H., Poulsen, S., & Goldring, A. (2018). Fact-checking effectiveness as a function of format and tone: Evaluating FactCheck. org and FlackCheck. org. *Journalism & Mass Communication Quarterly*, *95*(1), 49–75. https://doi.org/10.1177/1077699017710453

Zimmermann, F., & Kohring, M. (2020). Mistrust, disinforming news, and vote choice: A panel survey on the origins and consequences of believing disinformation in the 2017 German parliamentary election. *Political Communication*, *37*(2), 215–237. https://doi.org/10.1080/10584609.2019.1686095

2 The political economy of fact-checking

From hope to reality check

Joseph Beaudreau

2.1 Introduction

In recent years, disinformation has become a significant focus for various actors, including journalists, policymakers, and platform managers. This has led to the "field-configuring process" of new research within multiple disciplines, such as science and technology, public policy, communications, philosophy, law, and education (Frau-Meigs, 2022). Despite some coherence on the topology of disinformation, debates persist on the definitions of what counts and what does not, as the topic can encompass everything from satire, urban legends, conspiracies, and propaganda (Frau-Meigs, 2019).

The debate on countering disinformation has given rise to three primary strategies: government regulation, media and information literacy (MIL), and fact-checking, each with its strengths and weaknesses.

Government regulation is challenging, especially in more democratic structures with competing interests. First, the tech corporations at the heart of information distribution are extremely powerful, and many ambitious calls for regulation would impact their business models. Second, there are legitimate concerns about governments being arbiters of truth. In addition, the potential for government action in Western democracies is substantially constrained by the political will of the United States, as its jurisdiction contains most of the world's largest social media platforms. The European Union (EU) has demonstrated its willingness to pressure technology companies by implementing data protection regulations that impact targeted advertising. In addition, the EU Commission took the initiative to establish the Code of Practice on Disinformation (CPD) in 2018, involving multiple stakeholders in the process. While the CPD has raised the standards of commitment, its enforcement mechanism is weak, and it grants digital platforms too much discretion, leading to significant gaps in implementation and coordination. (Shattock, 2021).

MIL is advocated to stimulate critical thinking, provide effective counter-narratives, and engage multiple stakeholders in private/public/civic partnerships. MIL is an education tool that can foster better civic engagement in complex information societies. With the advent of Internet 2.0 in the early

DOI: 10.4324/9781003387404-4

2000s, MIL has been adapting to the new complexities of the media ecosystem, such as radicalisation and hate speech, which have flourished with the rise of social media. Consequently, they have also been compelled to tackle the alarming increase in disinformation. The limitations of MIL are that it can be time consuming and expensive because it is a form of education. It frequently requires resources and training within schools provided by governments or civil society. As with most education programmes, it is also time-consuming to develop human capacity.

Fact-checking has emerged as a widely promoted solution for addressing disinformation, endorsed by various stakeholders seeking a rapid response. It is often more cost-effective than media literacy education, less confrontational than government regulation, and provides an opportunity for various actors to demonstrate their commitment to combating disinformation. Surrounded by the tensions between social media platforms and governments, fact-checking offers a means of assuaging public concerns and circumventing regulatory measures.

Contemporary fact-checking grew as a reform movement in the early 2000s in the specific political economy of US media. The trends of heightened media concentration, staff downsizing, and decline of public trust have continued, as has the monopolisation of the internet by a few dominant US-based corporations. By contextualising the roots of fact-checking within the media political economy, we can better evaluate its limitations and potential in combatting disinformation, upholding journalistic standards, and promoting a robust democracy.

This chapter builds upon Martin Hirst's call for a critical political economy approach to tackle "fake news" and considers disinformation within the broader context of political and economic structures (Hirst, 2017). By examining fact-checking practices within their historical and economic contexts, this approach offers a broad analysis of the power dynamics influencing the production, distribution, and consumption of information and seeks to contribute to the ongoing discourse on its role and effectiveness in the fight against misinformation.

The analysis begins by examining the theoretical framework that underpins this study, which is rooted in critical political economy. This framework provides a lens through which we can understand the complex interplay between media, democracy, and disinformation. With this theoretical foundation in place, the focus then shifts to the historical origins of fact-checking, which has its roots in the United States, tracing its development and growth that eventually led to its widespread adoption worldwide. The analysis further explores the European context, where fact-checking initiatives have become particularly prominent due to the EU's complex and proactive regulatory framework.

In exploring the EU's approach, contradictions within the state of media trust, fact-checkers, and the epistemological challenges faced by fact-checking are highlighted. Furthermore, the power dynamics between media organisations and social media platforms, which play a significant role in shaping the dissemination and consumption of information, are examined.

2.2 Critical political economy: A theoretical framework

In the aftermath of the 2016 elections, discussions on disinformation surged to the forefront, primarily focusing on the spread of false information's impact on democratic processes. However, these early debates often neglected to address the decades of underlying political and economic structures that facilitated the conditions for the disinformation crisis. As the digital landscape rapidly evolves and disinformation remains a pressing concern, critical theories have become increasingly relevant in shedding light on the deeper issues at play.

Within critical disinformation studies, scholars have recognised the necessity of historical and contextual analysis. This emerging approach emphasises the need to go beyond surface-level analyses of misinformation and consider the intricate relationships between power dynamics within media systems and society (Kuo & Marwick, 2021). One perspective that provides valuable insights is the critical political economy approach, which challenges the perception of a "natural" order in the current media ecosystem and examines the broader political and economic forces that shape the dissemination and consumption of information (McChesney, 2012).

Acknowledging that the disinformation crisis cannot be isolated from the larger political and economic landscape is essential. By examining the complex interplay between power, media, and society, the critical political economy contributes valuable insights into how information disorders undermine democratic processes (Wasko, 2018). In this context, the critical political economy approach offers a comprehensive framework for understanding the multifaceted challenges posed by disinformation.

In pursuit of this goal, this chapter draws upon the works of notable scholars in the critical political economy of communications, including Janet Wasko, Robert McChesney, Vincent Mosco, Dallas Smythe, and Christian Fuchs. This discipline serves as a pivotal organising principle for assessing the digital revolution as the workings of capitalism, including profit motives and commodification, which significantly determine the role of the internet in society (Fuchs, 2009).

2.2.1 Democracy and the free press

In the realm of political economy, scholars have long emphasised the significance of democracy and the pivotal role played by the media in shaping public discourse and political processes. Central to this understanding is the recognition of the free press as a critical element in fostering an informed and engaged citizenry (McChesney, 2007). This perspective has driven researchers to investigate the power relations and economic motivations of various actors within the media landscape, with a keen focus on public access and its impact on civic engagement.

Among the rise of disinformation and its potential ramifications on democratic societies, the examination of fact-checking gains further importance. In its earlier forms, fact-checking functioned as a form of alternative media, advocating for transparency and accuracy in journalism. With the intensified focus on combating disinformation, fact-checking initiatives were justified by invoking democratic ideals to safeguard the integrity of public information.

However, the underlying economic distribution of information remains a concern beyond the challenges posed by the digital era in propagating misleading information and threatening public discourse and trust in media institutions. Critical theorists have long assessed the commercialisation of information, revealing its potential to distort content visibility and manipulate public access to reliable information. As Benkler et al. aptly pointed out in their pioneering research, the success of disinformation during the 2016 US presidential election can be attributed to the deep-seated structural roots of the political and media systems. These enduring structural factors provided fertile ground for the proliferation and dissemination of misinformation, allowing it to gain traction and influence in a polarised society (Benkler et al., 2018). Despite the evolution of digital media, this aspect of the media ecosystem has often remained unchanged, prompting a critical examination of the role and impact of fact-checking within this context.

2.2.2 Commercialisation of information

Fact-checking operates at the nexus of intricate forces, where both traditional journalism and digital platforms play pivotal roles in shaping the information landscape and influencing public opinion. The commercialisation of information, driven by profit motives and market forces, further complicates the availability of accurate information to the public (Birkinbine et al., 2016). Large media conglomerates often prioritise profitability over journalistic integrity and diversity, resulting in a limited representation of societal issues and a lack of critical analysis. This concentration marginalises alternative and counter-hegemonic voices, posing a threat to democratic societies. Local and independent media outlets struggle to compete with conglomerates, leading to closures and compromised editorial independence, ultimately undermining the pluralism and diversity of opinions available to the public (Knoche, 2021; Radebe & Chiumbu, 2022).

This same market logic has led critical political economy researchers to examine the ways capitalism works and does not work in determining the role the internet might play in society. Profit motive, commercialism, public relations, marketing, and advertising are foundational to any assessment of how the internet has developed and is likely to develop without a shift (McChesney, 2013; see also Chapter 1 of this book). Technology companies have faced criticism for disseminating false information, creating echo chambers, and facilitating surveillance. Ethical concerns regarding privacy and polarisation have arisen, sparking debates about the impact of these technologies on the media ecosystem. Addressing the dissemination of false information requires greater transparency and accountability from corporations to ensure a fair and balanced media landscape. While efforts are being made to regulate these technologies and promote media literacy skills among the public, the power balance is not equal. Although new forms of organisation and communication present opportunities for social movements, it is vital to recognise the significant influence and control powerful corporations have on the attention economy. Striking a balance between the benefits of information and communication technologies and their potential negative impacts is crucial for fostering an informed and inclusive society in the digital age (Fuchs, 2020; see also Chapter 4 of this book).

In examining the evolution of the internet, it is important to acknowledge its transformation into a predominantly closed system. During the early 2000s, there was widespread optimism surrounding the potential of the internet to inaugurate a new democratic era characterised by public access to information and the dismantling of traditional power structures. However, by 2010, this utopian vision had begun to recede as a handful of significant corporations emerged to dominate the digital landscape (Anderson, 2010).

At present, Amazon holds a commanding position in the market, controlling 33% of the internet through its Amazon Web Services (AWS) platform. In comparison, its closest competitors, Microsoft and Google, account for 18% and 9% of the market share, respectively (Runkevicius, 2020). Consequently, much of the internet is now controlled by a select few technology giants, with nearly one-third of it running on the AWS infrastructure.

In recent years, the internet's infrastructure has become increasingly consolidated under the control of four major technology corporations: Microsoft, Alphabet (Google's parent company), Meta (formerly Facebook), and Amazon. According to data from the subsea cable analysis firm TeleGeography, these four companies have significantly increased their share of global undersea fibre-optic capacity, rising from less than 10% before 2012 to approximately 66% today. Analysts indicate that this trend is only set to intensify. By 2024, these tech giants are expected to emerge as the primary financiers and owners of undersea internet cables connecting bandwidth-intensive countries along the Atlantic and Pacific coasts (Mims, 2022).

The growing dominance of these four corporations in shaping the internet's infrastructure raises critical questions about market concentration, access to information, and the potential implications of such control on the global digital and information landscape (Tworek, 2020). As a result, the contemporary landscape of the internet stands in stark contrast to the early 2000s' idealistic vision of an open and accessible information commons. The consolidation of market power in the hands of a few dominant players has engendered a closed system that is increasingly subject to commercial imperatives and corporate interests.

With partnerships between fact-checkers and social platforms, algorithms are being changed to help promote fact-checking. However, as with other journalists and information creators, fact-checking is not immune to the power imbalance. These corporations hold significant control over the flow of information, which can be leveraged to promote their commercial interests and corporate agendas. This control over the infrastructure of the internet can make it difficult for fact-checking organisations to access and disseminate accurate information, particularly if it runs counter to the interests of these dominant players.[1] Additionally, the agenda-setting function of the media and its ideological underpinnings can influence the areas of focus for fact-checking efforts, determining which issues receive scrutiny and which remain overlooked. Ideology as a theme of political economy is not just an issue of the messages within content but also a reflection of the underlying power relations that shape the creation and distribution of information.

2.2.3 Digital commodification

Within the digital media landscape, the commodification of media, audiences, and labour has transformed the industry, adding more layers of complexity to the role of fact-checking. Content, audience attention and media professionals have become profitable commodities (Fuchs, 2016). This commodification has led to skewed and sensationalised content as well as a power shift within the industry (McChesney, 2015). Even in countries where strong public media exists, they are still required to compete for attention within market logic. This is significantly true with the dominance of the internet as a primary source of information dissemination. Public and other non-commercialised media are forced to compete for attention on commercialised social media and search platforms. Labour commodification has also created precarious working conditions for media professionals, including freelancers and gig workers, affecting their livelihoods and hindering their ability to produce quality journalism or creative content. The commodification of audiences has resulted in the prioritisation of entertainment over informative content, leading to clickbait headlines and sensationalised news stories. Consequently, the algorithms used by online platforms prioritise attention retention over authenticity, which can make it difficult for fact-checking services to reach and influence audiences, which compromises the public's access to unbiased and reliable information (Mosco, 2009; see also Chapter 7 of this book).

Online platforms prioritise sensational and shareable content to maximise circulation and advertising revenue. This creates a circular content economy in which popular content is rewarded with greater visibility, regardless of its factual accuracy. Fact-checking services on Facebook and Google are built into algorithmic selection processes that enable the circulation of certain types of content and the production of "network bias." Meanwhile, the burden of quality content is placed on individual content creators and users while hiding the responsibility of the algorithms (Marres, 2018).

Tech companies and misinformation purveyors benefit from each other due to commodification. Frau-Meigs explains that platforms such as

YouTube, Facebook, and Instagram use advertising-driven business models to keep users engaged, granting content creators control over production and allowing the spread of sensationalised and inaccurate content (Frau-Meigs, 2019, pp. 50–54). In addition, users are often responsible for flagging false information without compensation.

Attention-grabbing tactics, or clickbait, often form the core of certain websites' marketing strategies, and influencers have become central to these efforts as friend and influencer recommendations increasingly replace traditional advertising approaches. Facebook and Google employ engagement algorithms that prioritise content based on interaction and attention retention, rather than assessing the authenticity or veracity of the information. Psychometric advertising techniques target consumers through surveillance and analysis of browsing habits and website themes, leveraging behavioural science and data mining to refine advertisements, minimise dispersion, and enhance conversion rates. These practices use relational and experiential assets, contributing to the proliferation of disinformation and fostering online engagement and consumerism. Ultimately, this results in the polarisation of attention towards specific products and political parties (Frau-Meigs, 2019, pp. 50–54). Regardless of the accuracy of the content, outsourcing its creation to users remains advantageous to the platforms' financial interests.

2.3 Historical origins of fact-checking

Fact-checkers emerged from reform movements predating the disinformation crisis, with origins in the historical sociopolitical context of journalism in the United States. Early American fact-checking organisations and early adopters, such as those in Europe, primarily viewed fact-checking as a response to political debate. "General interest" fact-checkers and debunkers investigated online rumours that circulated before the advent of social media platforms. This movement's globalisation led to the creation of an international network and partnerships with tech giants. This historical trajectory situates fact-checking within digital journalism and the ongoing convergence of media and technological communications.

2.3.1 Rise and fall of objectivity

The concept of objectivity in journalism emerged in the early 20th century, with Walter Lippman arguing that it was crucial for maintaining US democracy (McChesney, 2007). American media organisations such as *Time* created internal fact-checking departments in the 1920s, staffed primarily by women (Smith, 2004). These fact-checkers reviewed articles and ensured their accuracy, although conflicts with journalists over what was defensible were common.

As the principle of objectivity became more widely taught in journalism schools, it also became conflated with the idea of neutrality, which led to criticism from both journalists and media critics. This conflation of the two concepts obscured the importance of examining evidence and verifying facts as fundamental principles in professional journalism. As a result, public trust in the media began to decline. According to surveys conducted by Pew Research starting in 1985, the perception of the press being inaccurate and biased steadily grew among the public (Kohut et al., 2011).

In addition, financial and business pressures within the media industry led to the closure of many internal fact-checking departments, including *Time Magazine*, in 1996 (Silverman, 2010). For many articles published, it was the responsibility of individual journalists to fact-check themselves at a time when the speed of publishing was increasing (Smith, 2004; see also Chapter 9).

According to Pew Research Center (1999), media professionals surveyed also tended to agree with public perception, with half of journalists and news media executives citing issues related to quality, such as sloppy reporting, an erosion of standards, and a trend towards sensationalism. The decline of trust in the media was not just a perception but a real issue, which contributed to the crisis of legitimacy in the media long before social networks.

The downsizing of editorial staff continued through the 2008 financial crisis and the 2020 pandemic, leading to less internal verification and faster publishing demands to compete for audience attention. This has contributed to the crisis of legitimacy in US journalism, with increased errors and inaccuracies, which can have severe consequences for individuals, communities, and society. While journalistic errors are not considered disinformation due to their lack of malevolent intent, this is often an academic distinction that most audiences will not perceive. They still have the potential to undermine public trust in the media and contribute in the spread of misinformation.

2.3.2 Early internet debunking

The debunking style of verification began as myth-busting of urban legends. In the early 1990s, online discussion forums were a growing subculture with a limited audience due to limited internet access. In the 1980s and 1990s, urban legends, startling stories founded on rumours, were a popular trend in American culture (Aspray & Cortada, 2019, p. 98). These urban legends were frequently shared and debated on online discussion forums, which contributed to their notoriety and aided in their propagation. The documentation of paranormal sightings, alligators in sewers, or extraterrestrial encounters resulted in forums debunking these beliefs by analysing their veracity and plausibility.

David and Barbara Mikkelson were active members of the popular forum Alt.folklore.urban. When the internet went public, they decided in 1995 to establish a reference page for all the urban legends discussed there: Snopes.com. The Mikkelsons had no background in journalism and were just curious hobbyists at first. In the early years of Snopes, they ran the website using David's income as a software developer. In their pursuit of answers to online mysteries, the California State University library and freedom of information requests were their primary resources. Other debunk-style sites were created in the late 1990s, such as Hoaxbusters.org and TruthorFiction.com, but none had Snopes' reach. Eventually, Snopes became the Mikkelsons' full-time occupation, and in 2010, with over 300,000 daily visits, they had to employ two staff members (Aspray & Cortada, 2019, p. 28).

These early "general interest" fact-checkers who focused on online rumours and chain mails were largely ignored by academics who studied the more prominent organisations that emerged from the blogging movement. However, since 2016, the focus on information spreading online and the methods of these original debunkers has become a dominant practice (Graves & Cherubini, 2016).

2.3.3 Political fact-checking as journalistic reform

The term "external fact-checking" was developed by Craig Silverman, a writer who began his successful career by publishing a blog for the Poynter Institute called Regret the Error. His blog chronicled the decline in proofreaders, copyeditors, and internal fact-checkers in newsrooms across the nation. This could result in self-inflicted errors that harm an organisation's reputation and the entire information ecosystem. During this period, Silverman (2010) also witnessed the emergence of a new style of journalism among bloggers, which he called "external fact-checkers." In the early 2000s, he characterised this phenomenon as a "culture of warring facts" in the United States.

With the advent of widespread Internet access in the late 1990s and early 2000s, the conflict between media narratives and facts entered a new phase. No longer merely personal diaries, blogs were operated by upstart media critics and citizen journalists. Possibly, when viewed through the lens of contemporary social media and microblogging platforms, where journalists endure a daily flood of good and bad faith attacks, the bloggers of the past appear antiquated. However, at the time, blogging created a very unpleasant friction between journalists and their audiences, who were suddenly free to publish independently critical feedback. These blogs may be considerably more precise and spiteful than letters to the editor.

The media and public officials became targets of weaponised facts. These bloggers identified media errors far more frequently than those in the correction section. As conservative blogger Ken Layne famously stated: "It's the year 2001, and we can Fact Check your a**" (Layne, 2001). Whether this was due to a more significant number of errors or a greater level of scrutiny is debatable, but there was a change in audience–press relations. During this period, numerous sites, such as Media Matters and Accuracy in Media, emerged as prominent media critics. Famous online media sites, such as Gawker and Gizmodo, began as blogs in the early 2000s; however, they have evolved from their original vision through acquisition.

Traditional journalists did not respect the new bloggers, even those who were less aggressive towards them. In a 2005 foundational essay, media professor Jay Rosen (2005) criticised the media industry as losing control over narrative and opinion gatekeeping. In the same essay, he documented a decline in popular confidence in the objectivity of mainstream media. Bloggers challenged the legitimacy of objectivity, the ethical cornerstone of American journalism. The establishment of the *Huffington Post* and Garret Graff's issuance of the first White House press pass to a blogger in 2005 indicated a shift in the credibility of blogging. Soon, newspapers began incorporating blogs into their websites, bloggers were employed by mainstream media institutions, and some journalists even left the mainstream media to become professional bloggers.

The emergence of blogging has been instrumental in establishing the historical context for modern political fact-checking practices. The rise of blogging also presents a striking parallel to contemporary debates over media and journalism. If one substitutes references to Twitter, YouTube, and other online media platforms for blogs, many of the same dynamics remain. For example, the proliferation of blogging platforms and designs has enabled journalists to leave established media organisations in favour of potentially monetised independent blogs and websites (Shafer, 2021).

This blogging movement gave rise to some of the most notable political fact-checkers, including Fact-check.org, PolitiFact, and the Washington Post Fact Checker. Even though they took on the appearance of blogs, the creators of all three ventures were industry experts who were successful in establishing long-term operations and organisations. These newly established fact-checking organisations presented themselves to the public as arbiters of political debate. These individuals operating on the periphery of the news industry would, over the course of time, develop a novel approach to digital journalism, which the traditional news organisations would eventually adopt. Despite this, the reform efforts of political fact-checking had not significantly impacted the agenda-setting of the new media before 2016 (Vargo et al., 2018).

2.3.4 Fact-checking goes global

Political fact-checking has seen a rapid expansion beyond its origins in the United States over the past two decades. Although the practice had a slow start, it gained momentum with the launch of permanent independent fact-checking projects in France in 2008, followed by projects in the United Kingdom, Argentina, Italy, and South Africa in subsequent years. It has also continued to be seen as a reform movement to revitalise journalism and act as a democracy-building tool (Amazeen, 2020).

Graves and Cherubini found that the responsibility for political fact-checking in Northern and Western Europe has been assumed by established news organisations with a few independent outlets joining in. In contrast, in the eastern and southern parts of Europe, fact-checking is not so much a complementary practice to traditional journalism as it is an alternative to it (Graves & Cherubini, 2016).

According to reports by Duke's Reporters' Lab, the number of active fact-checking operations worldwide grew from 11 in 2008 to 44 in 2014, with 21 located in Europe and 15 in the United States. It was in 2014 that fact-checking began to be organised internationally (Adair, 2014). However, it was not until the media panic surrounding disinformation in 2016 that the number of fact-checking projects exploded. By 2023, there were 417 active fact-checking operations across the globe, based in 100 countries and covering 69 languages (Stencel et al., 2023).

In 2014, the first international fact-checking event was held in London as an initiative by the Poynter Institute with the help of Duke University's Reporters' Lab director Bill Adair. Of the 44 active fact-checkers, 40 attended. This would lead to the creation of the International Fact-Checking Network (IFCN), which would be housed at Poynter and establish an annual international conference called Global Fact. These Global Fact events, as well as the creation of an organisation dedicated to developing fact-checking standards, have been a "field-configuring event" (Graves & Lauer, 2020). By September 2016, 35 fact-checking organisations from 27 countries would become signatories to the new IFCN Codes of Principles.

The development of the IFCN and its eventual Code of Principles is noteworthy in the fight against disinformation at an international and institutionalised level. There is an aspect of this process that is unique to journalism globally. It is a reformation of the principle of objectivity, which has played a pivotal role in the development of the movement. The principles call for each signatory to demonstrate commitment to nonpartisanship and transparency, which includes funding, sources used, organisational structure, methodology, and transparent correction processes. These signatories must then be open to re-evaluation every year by the IFCN to maintain their status.

This status became even more valuable for a growing number of fact-checking organisations around the world in December 2016, when Facebook first announced its Third Party Fact-Checking Program. This partnership has spread to include all Meta platforms (Facebook, Instagram, and WhatsApp). The institutionalisation of fact-checking with standards has helped propel fact-checking around the world. In 2023, 131 global fact-checking projects were verified or in the renewal process with IFCN, with 95 being official Meta Partners. This partnership elevated the practice of debunking online discourse, leading political fact-checkers to adopt this model and new organisations built around it.

2.4 Mapping complex power relations with European fact-checking

When exploring the landscape of fact-checking in Europe, several organisations play pivotal roles within the political economy. Before delving into the European context, this section examines the broader impact of fact-checking on a global level, considering the influential role of the IFCN and its collaboration with major platforms. Subsequently, the focus will shift to Europe, where we will examine the regional institutions of the European Fact-Checking Standards Network and the European Digital Media Observatory (EDMO). To illustrate the intersections of these institutions, we will then analyse the fact-checking projects undertaken by Agence France-Presse (AFP) in the European region. For this section, a comprehensive database was created by synthesising information from multiple sources, including Meta's partner list, IFCN signatories, Duke's Reporter's Lab mapping, and EFCSN reports.[2]

2.4.1 IFCN and platform partnerships

The IFCN has played a significant role on fact-checking organisations since its establishment in 2015. Of the 257 fact-checkers in the dataset, 140 are IFCN signatories, accounting for nearly 55%.[3] Among these signatories, 95 (37%) have a partnership with Facebook, and 26 operate in more than one country. Notably, 25 of these multi-country fact-checkers maintain Facebook relationships. The top five include AFP Fact Check Hub (83 countries), Fatabyyano (17), PesaCheck (10), Deutsche Presse Agentur (6), and Reuters Fact Check (6).

The United States has the highest number of fact-checking operations based there with 74 fact-checkers solely operating within the country.[4] When these US-based organisations are excluded, the dataset consists of 183 fact-checkers, of which 132 (72%) are IFCN members, indicating the importance of IFCN in shaping the global fact-checking landscape. Moreover, 88 (48%) of these fact-checkers have established partnerships with Facebook, illustrating the collaborative efforts between fact-checking initiatives and the social media platform. IFCN membership is key to many opportunities for funding from Facebook and other platforms.

2.4.1.1 International fact-checking network

IFCN is a business unit of the Poynter Institute for Media Studies, a registered non-profit specialising in journalism training based in Florida, USA. Notably, the Poynter Institute is also home to PolitiFact, one of the most significant fact-checking operations in the United States. The IFCN operates under the guidance of the Poynter Institute, and its director and staff members are employees of the institute.

The IFCN collaborates with fact-checkers worldwide, primarily through its consultative IFCN Advisory Board, which reflects global diversity with 11 members from different fact-checking organisations in 10 countries spanning 4 continents. The organisation maintains a dedicated section on the Poynter website featuring its work, trends, formats and news related to fact-checking, "fake news," and misinformation. To remain impartial, the IFCN avoids engaging in policy discussions beyond those concerning access to information and fact-checking. Staff members are also prohibited from being members of political parties or publicly supporting candidates for elected office, thus upholding the organisation's nonpartisan stance (*International Fact-Checking Network Transparency Statement*, n.d.).

From a political economy perspective, examining the IFCN's funding sources becomes crucial as they can influence its agenda and priorities. The fact that the IFCN receives funding from diverse entities, including philanthropic foundations, tech companies, and government agencies, raises questions about potential competing interests and conflicting goals. While philanthropic foundations may prioritise promoting media literacy and transparency, tech companies may be more interested in combating misinformation affecting their platforms and managing their public image. Similarly, government agencies may be motivated by geopolitical considerations or domestic political priorities.

Although the IFCN is not a signatory of its own code of principles, its recent decision to disclose its income and expenses marks a positive step towards increasing transparency and accountability. This move can foster trust and confidence among stakeholders, including fact-checking organisations, media outlets, and the public. However, it is crucial to acknowledge that financial transparency alone may not suffice to address concerns about biases or conflicts of interest. As with many non-profits, sources of funding can be complex and seemingly contradictory, but with the role of fact-checking as a form of digital journalism that determines which claims are valid, it is reasonable to question how these sources may influence its priorities, such as the allocation of grants to global fact-checking organisations. For example, much of its funding originates in the United States, including tech giants, and billionaire philanthropists, as well as funding aligned with US foreign policy such as the US Department of State and the National Endowment for Democracy.[5] Ongoing scrutiny and evaluation of the IFCN's funding sources and activities are essential to ensure that the organisation remains steadfast in its mission of promoting accuracy and integrity in journalism.

2.4.1.2 Platforms

With the increasing influence of social media platforms as primary sources of information, it is crucial to explore their role in fact-checking initiatives and their funding sources. In this section, we examine the complex interplay between social media platforms and fact-checking organisations, shedding light on the implications of these partnerships and funding arrangements in the pursuit of accurate and reliable information. Through partnerships with different companies, fact-checkers gain both access and funding, while in exchange, the social media platforms outsource the task of moderating content.

A recent annual survey conducted by the IFCN revealed that despite an increase in budgets for fact-checking organisations, there remains a heavy reliance on funding from tech companies (*State of the Fact-Checkers Report*

2022, International Fact-Checking Network 2023). This reliance is noted as a concern, as recent staff layoffs at Google and Meta highlight the need for organisations to diversify their funding sources. The survey indicates that Meta's Third Party Fact-Checking programme remains the leading funding source for these organisations, contributing 45.2% of their total income. Grants constituted 29% of primary funding, whereas donations or membership subscriptions accounted for 6.5%.

Compared with 2021, there were some changes in funding sources. Meta's programmes, including Instagram, experienced a slight increase (from 44.2%), while grants remained relatively stable (29.1% in 2021). Donations or membership subscriptions saw a notable rise (from 4.7% in 2021), suggesting growing individual support. However, partnerships with academic institutions witnessed a marginal decrease (from 3.5% in 2021). Advertising revenue and training as funding sources remained constant. In 2022, the fact-checking partnership with TikTok emerged as a new funding source for several organisations, highlighting the expanding landscape of social network funding opportunities in the fact-checking sphere.

Meta, formerly known as Facebook, holds a dominant position in the digital information ecosystem, serving as a primary source of information for billions of individuals worldwide. As a substantial player, Meta's influence on disseminating information and combatting disinformation raises questions about its investment in fact-checking initiatives.

In 2016, IFCN created its first and most important partnership with Facebook. This partnership was born out of reaction to disinformation being used on the social network leading up to the 2016 presidential election, in which Facebook faced significant public pressure due to its commercial and advertising support for Donald Trump's campaign, as revealed in Operation Alamo (Frau-Meigs, 2019, p. 68). In November of that year, IFCN (2016), as a collective organisation, wrote an open letter to Mark Zuckerberg encouraging him to hire fact-checkers and offering IFCN as a partner. Eventually, as the company rebranded to Meta, this partnership was extended to Instagram and WhatsApp.

In 2023, 95 IFCN signatories (37%) are partners with Meta, and this has significant implications for these fact-checking projects. According to a recent IFCN report of their members, Meta's Third Party Fact-Checking Program is still the most important source of financing for fact-checking groups, generating 45.2% of their total income.

Meta has officially made clear its commitment to bolstering the fact-checking industry. Since 2016, Meta has funded over $100 million in projects that assist its fact-checking efforts, and it claims to have built the largest worldwide fact-checking network of any platform (*Meta's Investments in Fact-Checking*, 2023).

One must examine the ramifications and underlying drivers of Meta's investment in the fact-checking sector from a political economy perspective. On the surface, the project seems charitable and socially responsible, but it is crucial to consider the structural pressures and power dynamics at work.

First, it is important to consider Meta's significance as a key player in the ecosystem of digital information. Meta can have a large impact on this area by supporting and influencing the fact-checking sector. This calls into question the objectivity and independence of fact-checking organisations that receive funding from the platform. Fact-checkers may be discouraged from condemning Meta's own participation in the dissemination of false information or holding the platform accountable for its policies, so it is important to consider the possibility of conflicts of interest and undue influence.

Furthermore, it is possible to see Meta's investment in the fact-checking sector as a calculated attempt to avoid criticism and regulatory scrutiny. Meta may be trying to avoid calls for stricter government controls or interventions that could limit its activities or hurt its revenue by appearing to combat misinformation aggressively. In this view, Meta's support for fact-checking projects could be seen as a way for the company to maintain its independence and guarantee the expansion of its market dominance. It is a very affordable programme at $100 million over the past eight years, considering that in 2022 the net profit of Meta was over $32 billion (META, 2023).

The emphasis on fact-checking as a countermeasure against disinformation may help distract from the structural causes of the issue. The algorithms used by Meta and other social media platforms have come under fire for emphasising engagement over the truthfulness of information, which can magnify contentious and sensationalist content. Meta may be downplaying the necessity of systemic reforms to its own platform and business model by highlighting fact-check partners' function in reducing the spread of false material.

Turning attention to other prominent players in the fact-checking landscape, Google and its subsidiary platform, YouTube, wield significant influence as major players in the digital information landscape. As primary sources of information for millions of users worldwide, their role in combating misinformation and supporting fact-checking initiatives should be considered.

Similar to the open letter with Facebook, in January 2022, IFCN published an open letter to YouTube's CEO, Susan Wojcicki, signed by nearly 100 fact-checking organisations, urging the platform to enhance its efforts to combat the spread of false information. In response, YouTube sent a representative to a town hall event at IFCN's GlobalFact 9 conference. The representative had to endure a steady stream of criticism from fact-checkers for failing to enforce quality standards and address misinformation on its platform (Smalley, 2022).

By November 2022, in response to this pressure, Google and YouTube announced a $13.2 million grant to IFCN with the goal of launching a new Global Fact Check Fund, which will be used to help fact-checking projects. In addition, they committed financial support to the IFCN to improve reporting, monitoring, and evaluation and expand its capacity. They also agreed to work with the IFCN to explore areas of cooperation, analytics, and the development of tools for combating disinformation and expanding resources to non-English-speaking countries (Dyakon, 2022). Similar to the case with Meta, these collaborative initiatives could have some positive results, but it remains to be seen whether the systemic role that Google and YouTube hold in information disorders will change.

In this subsection, we have delved into the complex interplay between social media platforms and fact-checking organisations, highlighting the implications of their partnerships and funding arrangements in the pursuit of accurate and reliable information. The findings reveal a significant reliance on funding from tech companies, with Meta (formerly Facebook) emerging as the primary funding source for many fact-checking groups. While IFCN as a collective body has proven able to push social media platforms to open themselves up to fact-checkers, it has also notably toned down the criticism of platforms that are sponsors and partners. This gains significance when viewed through the lens of the theoretical framework of political economy. The power dynamics and economic interests of social media platforms play a pivotal role in shaping the landscape of fact-checking initiatives. Meta's significant funding support for fact-checking organisations raises important questions about the objectivity and independence of fact-checkers, as they may face pressures that influence their stance on specific issues or their willingness to hold the platform accountable for its content moderation policies. Moreover, the emphasis on fact-checking as a countermeasure against disinformation might inadvertently distract from the structural causes of the issue, including the algorithms used by social media platforms that prioritise engagement over the truthfulness of information.

2.5 Europe's swift ascent: From latecomer to trailblazer

While the Meta partnership still plays an important role in Europe, fact-checkers enjoy support from a diverse range of funding sources. Notably, the backing comes from various public entities. Of particular significance is the funding received from the EU, which serves as a unique feature in the European fact-checking landscape. Some fact-checking organisations within Europe benefit from the commercial resources of their parent organisations. Grants from private international or national donors also play a significant role in sustaining these fact-checking endeavours. In addition, it is worth noting that foreign embassies and aid programmes from other nations contribute to the financial landscape.

All of this provides the fact-checkers in the EU, with a particular advantage that is not seen systematically elsewhere in the world. This contrasting dynamic between public and private funding sources opens new avenues for exploring and analysing power structures at play within EU fact-checking initiatives.

By examining the partnerships and collaborations between these organisations and fact-checkers, we can develop an understanding of the political economy of information within Europe at a macro level. Our analysis will provide valuable insights into how various funding sources influence fact-checking practices, their autonomy, and their potential to counter disinformation effectively in the region. By contextualising funding arrangements within the broader political economy of Europe, we can gain a comprehensive understanding of the implications on fact-checking practices and their potential to combat disinformation while preserving democratic values.

2.5.1 *The European Fact-Checking Standards Network*

A new phase of cooperation between fact-checkers has arrived in Europe and has been more thoroughly prepared. In early 2022, a new project started led by six European fact-checkers with the support of the European Commission.[6] The European Fact-Checking Standards Network (EFCSN) project aims to unite Europe's fact-checking and open-source intelligence (OSINT) communities to develop a Code of Professional Integrity that will serve as a framework to effectively combat misinformation. The goal is to determine which organisations can call themselves independent fact-checkers or reliable open-source investigators.

By the fall of 2022, after a period of consultation with over 40 fact-checking organisations in Europe, the EFCSN announced the European Code of Standards for Independent Fact-Checking Organisations, a set of guidelines developed to ensure that organisations engaged in fact-checking adhere to the standards of methodology, ethics, and transparency (EFCSN, 2022). Compliance with these standards is necessary for organisations to become members of the EFCSN, with the first round of membership decisions to be announced in late 2023.

The EFCSN is open to organisations that are dedicated to fact-checking with a substantial focus on a country that is a member of the Council of Europe, Kosovo or Belarus. This area comprises 102 fact-checkers operating in 42 countries.[7] Of these, 68 are signatories of the IFCN, while 45 fact-checkers in this region have established partnerships with Facebook.

Among these fact-checkers, 49 have been involved in the creation of the EFCSN. Of these, 42 are active IFCN signatories, with only 2 (Mimikama and Faktabaari) having never been signatories of the IFCN's code of principles. For countries outside the EU, this could be a new source of funding.

According to Finnish Faktabarri's press release, the EFCSN is more transparent, detailed, and flexible than the international IFCN policy code; however, it is complementary and allows European organisations a comprehensive governance framework (Toimitus, 2022). Another unique aspect that makes EFCSN an attractive evolution of the practice in Europe is that they can act as a group when engaging with EU regulations. This was demonstrated in January 2023 when they submitted a position paper recommending changes that hinder the dissemination of disinformation to the European Commission's proposal for the Media Freedom Act (EFCSN, 2023).

2.5.2 The European Union

At the EU level, there are 71 fact-checkers operating in 26 member states (see Table 2.1).[8] Among them, 42 are active IFCN signatories, indicating a commitment to the principles promoted by the IFCN. Of these, 29 fact-checkers engage in partnerships with Meta platforms, a pragmatic approach that allows them to access additional resources and extend their reach in combating misinformation. However, this partnership dynamic underscores the complex interplay between public and private actors within the political economy of fact-checking.

Interestingly, the European landscape also reveals a counterbalancing trend. Some fact-check projects and tools, like EFCSN or EDMO (including regional EDMO hubs), have received EU support. These EU-funded projects represent an alternative approach that diversifies funding sources and reduces dependence on private platforms. This phenomenon reflects the broader political and economic dynamics within the EU, where an observable effort exists to exert greater control over information ecosystems.

Table 2.1 Number of fact-checkers operating in each country

Country	*Total Fact-Checkers*	*Facebook Partners*	*IFCN*	*EFCSN*
Austria	5	2	4	3
Belgium	6	4	6	3
Bulgaria	2	1	2	1
Croatia	1	1	1	1
Cyprus	1	1	1	1
Czech Republic	2	2	2	1
Denmark	2	1	1	1
Estonia	3	2	3	2
Finland	2	1	1	2
France	11	4	6	4
Germany	7	3	4	3
Greece	2	2	2	2
Hungary	3	1	2	1
Ireland	3	2	2	1
Italy	5	2	3	3
Latvia	3	2	2	1
Lithuania	4	3	2	3
Luxembourg	1	1	1	1
Netherlands	4	2	2	2
Poland	6	2	4	3
Portugal	4	2	4	2
Romania	3	2	1	2
Slovakia	2	1	1	1
Slovenia	1	1	1	1
Spain	7	4	4	5
Sweden	2	1	1	1

Moreover, 31 EU fact-checkers have actively participated in creating the EFCSN, indicating their commitment to enhancing fact-checking cooperation within the EU context. This cooperative effort within the fact-checking community further underscores the multifaceted nature of the political economy of fact-checking in Europe, where actors navigate various funding sources and partnerships to fulfil their democratic role in an evolving information landscape.

Another dynamic is organisational structure which contextualises other influences that shape fact-checking operations and assesses their potential impact on the accuracy and integrity of information dissemination. Within the EU, 34 fact-checking projects are affiliated with large media organisations operating as part of established media outlets with substantial resources and audience reach. While being backed by such media organisations offers visibility and support, it may also subject fact-checkers to editorial priorities and potential conflicts depending on their funding sources and perceived trustworthiness among different national audiences. There are 18 fact-checking projects associated with smaller, independent media outlets. These organisations often face challenges regarding resources and audience reach, but their independence may grant them more editorial autonomy and flexibility in conducting fact-checking work. A total of 19 organisations in the EU are dedicated solely to fact-checking. These independent initiatives focus exclusively on debunking misinformation and may have unique approaches and methodologies that set them apart from fact-checking projects within larger media structures.

When analysing the ownership structure of fact-checking projects within the EU, we find a diverse landscape that encompasses different types of ownership arrangements (see Table 2.2).

Among the 71 fact-checking initiatives in the EU, 10 operate under public media ownership and are based in six countries: France, Germany, Belgium, Latvia, Lithuania, and Denmark. This indicates a level of local government involvement in fact-checking efforts, potentially reflecting the recognition of fact-checking as a tool for promoting transparency and accuracy in public information dissemination. On the other hand, 26 fact-checking projects are situated within commercial ownership structures. While this enables potential access to resources and financial stability, it also raises concerns about the influence of market forces on fact-checking practices and the possibility of prioritising revenue generation over editorial independence. Notably, media policies in the EU and individual European countries have not successfully dismantled oligopolistic media structures harmful to democracy (Trappel & Meier, 2022). In addition, 35 fact-checking projects have a mixed ownership or funding structure, encompassing a range of arrangements that include NGOs with diverse funding sources and large news agencies. This mixed model presents both opportunities and challenges, as it allows for various financial support but also demands careful attention when communicating these funding sources to their audiences.

Table 2.2 Ownership of fact-checkers by country

Country	*Total Fact-Checkers*	*Public Funding (%)*	*Commercial Status (%)*	*Mixed Fund Sources (%)*
Austria	5	0.0	20.0	80.0
Belgium	6	16.7	50.0	33.3
Bulgaria	2	0.0	0.0	100.0
Croatia	1	0.0	0.0	100.0
Cyprus	1	0.0	0.0	100.0
Czech Republic	2	0.0	0.0	100.0
Denmark	2	50.0	0.0	50.0
Estonia	3	0.0	66.7	33.3
Finland	2	0.0	0.0	100.0
France	11	27.3	36.4	36.4
Germany	7	42.9	14.3	42.9
Greece	2	0.0	0.0	100.0
Hungary	3	0.0	33.3	66.7
Ireland	3	0.0	66.7	33.3
Italy	5	0.0	40.0	60.0
Latvia	3	33.3	33.3	33.3
Lithuania	4	25.0	50.0	25.0
Luxembourg	1	0.0	100.0	0.0
Netherlands	4	0.0	50.0	50.0
Poland	6	0.0	16.7	83.3
Portugal	4	0.0	100.0	0.0
Romania	3	0.0	0.0	100.0
Slovakia	2	0.0	0.0	100.0
Slovenia	1	0.0	0.0	100.0
Spain	7	0.0	42.9	57.1
Sweden	2	0.0	50.0	50.0

The EU's fact-checking landscape showcases intricate relations between public and private entities, underscoring the complex political economy of fact-checking. As these fact-checkers traverse this dynamic digital information environment, they must deftly navigate their partnerships and affiliations. Their challenge lies in reconciling their commitment to delivering accurate information with the pressing needs for sustainability and maintaining their independence in their work.

2.5.3 The European Digital Media Observatory

The European Commission created the EDMO in 2020, following EU guidelines to combat disinformation. It has allocated funding to support regional hubs, and EDMO and its regional hubs operate independently of any national or EU public authority. EDMO is not an organisation that creates standards, it is more of a repository and a regional centre for cooperation in confronting disinformation. EDMO is a community of experts from various fields, including literacy education and fact-checking, who work together to detect, analyse, and expose disinformation campaigns across Europe.

To achieve this, EDMO has established hubs in different countries that provide specific knowledge of local information environments, helping to strengthen the detection and analysis of disinformation campaigns, improve public awareness, and design effective responses for national audiences. This allows EDMO-aligned fact-checkers in their regional hubs an interface to find patterns of disinformation specific to their region as well as best practices for their local audiences.

2.5.4 Agence France-Presse

The AFP has emerged as the world's leading fact-checking organisation owing to its dedicated division AFP Factuel launched in 2017. With an impressive presence across 24 languages, AFP published over 8,500 stories in 2021 alone. Its unique structure of mixed funding sets AFP apart, potentially ensuring its autonomy from external influences. The organisation derives its income from the sale of its production to clients and financial compensation from the French state for fulfilling general interest missions, preserving its independent status (IFCN Code of Principles, 2022).

The partnership between AFP and Meta has led to a significant expansion of AFP's fact-checking services across the globe. AFP is listed as a Meta fact-checker in 83 countries, including 15 EU countries, 3 non-EU European countries, 19 countries in the Americas, 20 African countries, 24 Asian countries, and 2 Oceania countries. In fact, AFP operates as the sole fact-checker with Meta platforms in 22 of these countries, a unique advantage over local fact-checkers for example, in Bolivia, Finland, Hungary, and Slovakia, whose local fact-checkers lack such access to this partnership. It is worth questioning the impact of this dominance as it raises concerns about the potential for an unequal distribution of limited fact-checking resources.

In addition to its Meta partnership, AFP has entered into agreements with Google, TikTok, and Twitter. TikTok compensates AFP for fact-checking services in several countries across Asia, Oceania, Europe, the Middle East, and Spanish-speaking Latin America, while Twitter pays AFP to assess the accuracy of contributions to Community Notes in the United States.

In its new efforts to combat misinformation, the AFP has also taken a proactive role in collaborative programmes worldwide since 2021. The European Commission and other European organisations co-fund these initiatives, with AFP receiving funding from the EU to participate in several EDMO hubs. AFP was also part of six organisations charged with creating the EFCSN, which the EU also funded.

The AFP has positioned itself as a key player in fighting disinformation, giving it access to funding from commercial and public sources. This funding has enabled AFP to scale its operations with a substantial impact on public discourse and trust in media, particularly in the countries where it operates as the sole fact-checker with Meta platforms.

2.6 Further limitations in polarised environments

In the context of democracy, trust in the media is a cornerstone, which is why it should be considered within the political economy. It enables the free flow of reliable information, which is essential for informed public discourse and decision-making (Hanitzsch et al., 2018). However, trust in the media can be compromised in polarised societies, leading to a fragmented public sphere in which different population segments have vastly different perceptions of reality. This polarisation can be exacerbated by the media landscape, shaped by society's broader political and economic structures (Benkler et al., 2018).

For fact-checkers, this presents a delicate challenge. It is not just about producing accurate information, but it must also consider the audience and the attitudes of the receiver. This is where critical theory can contribute because it emphasises that the production and reception of information are not isolated processes but are deeply intertwined with the broader sociopolitical context.

In the European context, these challenges can vary significantly from one country to another, reflecting the diverse political, economic, and media landscapes across the continent (Curran et al., 2014). This underscores the importance of a localised approach to fact-checking and media literacy, where EDMO hubs can coordinate a response to address these country-specific challenges, fostering trust in media and enhancing the effectiveness of fact-checking in diverse and polarised environments.

This section contextualises the potential limitations of fact-checking in polarised countries, considering public trust in media and the epistemological framing of fact-checking.

2.6.1 Media trust and relations

Fact-checking was created as a new form of digital media to reform journalism that was losing the public trust. Trust in news media has been a subject of interest in recent years, with surveys by the EU, Edelman, and Reuters' Digital News Report, among others, tracking its levels globally. After the 2016 focus on disinformation, low trust in the media became a significant point of discussion. Following the coronavirus pandemic, trust in governments and the media increased, which projected a hopeful note. However, in recent years, the gains of the upward trend in confidence have been largely erased. While these surveys can be debated on their methodology, there is a consensus among reports using various methodologies that there is a lack of trust in many European countries (Sapir, 2022).

Trust in media varies across countries depending on their specific media ecosystem. This disparity in confidence should be noted by journalists, researchers, and policymakers, particularly when examining the expectations of fact-checking, which are often too high (Vinhas & Bastos, 2022). Both sides of the extreme of global trust, according to Reuters, are in the EU. For instance, Finland has the highest trust in its media sources (69%), while Greece has the lowest trust among all countries surveyed (Newman et al., 2023). Both countries have one local fact-checker, and the AFP operates in both. While Greece has a local fact-checker Ellinkia Hoaxes partnered with Meta, Finland does not. Faktabaari, a non-profit organisation in Finland, is a celebrated fact-checking and MIL educator; however, it has never been associated with the IFCN and therefore cannot be a part of Meta's partnership.

Public TV and radio stations are the most trusted news source in the EU, according to the EU Barometer Media and News Survey, followed by the written press (39%) and commercial TV and radio stations (27%) (2022). This could signify that fact-checkers associated with public media have a greater potential impact than others, but again this depends on the context of each country. For example, in Poland, 43% of respondents trust private television and radio the most, whereas in Hungary the highest trust (at 25%) is in people they follow on social media.

Another factor that adds to the difficulty in trusting media is the socio-economic climate of each country. The Edelman Trust Barometer is an annual report first produced in 2020 with seven EU countries included in its sample: France, Germany, Ireland, the Netherlands, Spain, and Sweden. In the 2023 report (Edelman, 2023), they noted that there is a trust divide based on income inequality, with the top 25% having more trust in a country's institutions than the bottom 25%. The survey also asked respondents how divided they felt their country was, and if these divides could be overcome. With the exception of Ireland, the six other countries in the report are either severely polarised or in danger of becoming severely polarised. France, Germany, Italy, and Spain have at least five operating fact-checkers in delicate national climates. This is another challenge that fact-checkers must consider in their country's context, and this also raises questions about the expectations of fact-checking as a tool against disinformation. In a severely polarised community, it can be dangerous to assume normative boundaries, and reasoning when determining objective facts can intensify information disorder (Vinhas & Bastos, 2022).

2.6.2 Epistemological problems in polarised countries

Earlier criticism of US fact-checkers before they became integrated into social media platforms is still relevant. For example, the epistemological question revolves around how facts are selected for checking, a process similar to traditional editorial selection and gatekeeping. While disputes over the epistemic nature of fact-checking played out in academic journals between Uscinski and Amazeen, the debate has never been convincingly resolved (Amazeen, 2015; Uscinski, 2015; Uscinski & Butler, 2013). The process of fact-checking assumes that facts are observable and verifiable information that can be presented to the audience without political bias. However, this assumption is epistemologically simple and fails to account for the nuances of controversial issues. As Vinhas and Bastos noted, the problem of epistemology also applies to the literature that focuses on identifying false news, which assumes that facts are fundamentally different from misinformation (Vinhas & Bastos, 2022).

This is a trap that Marres called "the politics of demarcation," the act of creating a clear distinction between knowledge and its supposed opposite, anti-knowledge (Marres, 2018). She argues that it is no longer assumed that the public will automatically respect facts based on the authority of experts or statements that are validated outside the public domain. If factual knowledge derives its authority from a realm that is inaccessible to the public, it is likely to be targeted by anti-elite movements. In today's ever-changing and varied public spheres, epistemic authority must be earned through the difficult process of exchanging diverse viewpoints.

Furthermore, Marres distinguishes between stable facts and experimental facts in public discourse, with the latter having an unstable epistemic status that changes over time. Using the pro-Brexit claim of "350 million pounds per week for the NHS" as an example, she demonstrates how such experimental facts can evolve, reflecting public concerns and issue articulation, despite initially being deemed misleading or false. Often, many aspects of disinformation are symptoms of systemic problems within society, rather than the root causes. In other words, it is not just algorithms that are responsible for the spread of disinformation, but rather a complex set of social, political, and economic factors.

Kuo and Marwick stress in their article that social and political history plays a role in how certain facts are perceived as well as in the role that power plays in producing disinformation (Kuo & Marwick, 2021). For example, historically marginalised communities in a country can have a reason to distrust institutions, including the media, that have played a role in discriminating against them.

Farkas and Schou's work builds on this idea by emphasising the importance of the floating character of truth in contemporary politics (Farkas & Schou, 2018). They argue that discourse on what constitutes truth and falsehood is an essential aspect of political struggles for power and dominance. This means that instead of accepting the idea that facts no longer matter in politics, we should recognise that negotiations over what counts as truthful are an integral part of the political process. In this hyper-factual era, the concept of factuality is at the centre of discursive struggles, and labels such as "fake news" are entangled in multiple and opposing hegemonic projects. By foregrounding the floating character of truth, we can better understand the complexity of contemporary politics and the challenges posed by disinformation.

In many countries, the current sociopolitical climate is a feedback loop within information disorders, which requires fact-checkers to avoid depoliticising facts too much. With journalistic ideals of objectivity and non-political bias being codified in fact-checking organisations, the expectation can be insurmountable in some countries where issues such as racism, income inequality, and climate change are politicised within the normative political discourse of powerful forces.

2.7 Conclusion

Fact-checking, examined through a critical political economy lens, highlights the challenges and dynamics in the media ecosystem. The evolution of the digital media has brought about opportunities and challenges to the information ecosystem. As the internet initially promised a democratised space for information, the ensuing consolidation of power by a few tech giants has reshaped this landscape, raising essential questions about the accessibility and authenticity of information. Meanwhile, the rise of these platform companies has overshadowed the role of legacy media ownership concentration and its impact on information disorder (Trappel & Meier, 2022).

While fact-checking has been a beacon of hope in combating disinformation, the prevailing power dynamics of capitalist forces underscore the need to re-examine the expectations of fact-checkers. A notable concern is the influence of funding sources on fact-checking priorities, especially from tech giants like Meta, which introduce potential conflicts of interest, challenging the very essence of objectivity that fact-checking seeks to uphold. Another limitation under scrutiny is the politics of demarcation, where normative assumptions are upheld as facts as well as the process of which claims get checked. This can inadvertently exacerbate information disorder, especially in highly polarised countries.

The EU is beginning to forge a new model with several pivotal organisations emerging, and playing crucial roles within the political economy of fact-checking. The establishment of regional institutions like the EFSCN and the EDMO underscores Europe's commitment to combating misinformation and providing more diverse forms of funding. These organisations have the potential to create a new model for fact-checking with standards and methods that meet local audiences.

The EU as a bloc has demonstrated regulatory power against tech giants and open up alternative sources of funding for combatting disinformation, though commendable, the EU's efforts do not yet fully capture the solution to the systemic crisis in media. It has failed to show a similar effort in regulating media concentration as a bloc, which limits the concept of fact-checking as the leading champion to combat misinformation if regional information creation is also concentrated (Trappel & Meier, 2022). Fact-checking itself was a reform movement within journalism. And while a few of these organisations continue this role, many projects have been folded into powerful media companies and platforms, which can limit their ability to target these economic and political centres of power.

In conclusion, while Europe has made commendable strides in institutionalising fact-checking, the endeavour is full of challenges in the face of polarisation, epistemological debates, and socio-economic divides. For fact-checking to truly serve its purpose in Europe, there must be a continuous effort to understand and address these complexities, ensuring that truth remains a democratic, inclusive, and resilient ideal in the digital age. Addressing the root causes of disinformation demands a holistic, multidisciplinary approach, encompassing MIL, critical thinking, and accountability throughout the information ecosystem.

Notes

1 This was a reality experienced by TruthOrFiction: "[I]n fact, our managing editor has publicly criticised Facebook's handling of third-party fact-checkers. The platform has also falsely claimed that our site is "clickbait" and has refused to explain that decision despite repeated inquiries." https://www.truthorfiction.com/facebook-block-fact-checkers/?utm_content=expand_article
2 The following steps were taken in building the dataset in June 2023: (1) All 95 of Meta's Global Third Party Fact-Checking Partners operating in 123 countries to gain insights into the global reach of fact-checking initiatives and the role of the IFCN in securing Meta partnerships. (2) To validate the information gathered on Meta's global presence, every IFCN signatory, active or under renewal, was considered. (3) Projects listed by Duke's Reporters' Lab and those involved in developing the EFCSN were examined with the aim of incorporating European projects within the Council of Europe members (including former member Russia). (4) The final dataset comprises 257 fact-checking projects operating across 123 countries.
3 It is important to note that this figure includes fact-checkers whose status may have expired in 2023, as there can be a delay in IFCN processing renewals.
4 Notably, Lead Stories is based in the United States but operates in European countries (Belgium, Russia, Ukraine) and was therefore not included in the US-based category.
5 IFCN lists the following sources: Arthur M. Blank Family Foundation, the Duke Reporters' Lab, the Bill & Melinda Gates Foundation, Google, YouTube, TikTok, Meta (Facebook, WhatsApp, Instagram), the US Department of State, the National Endowment for Democracy, the Omidyar Network (Luminate), the Open Society Foundations, Fritt Ord Foundation, Craig Newmark Philanthropies and the Park Foundation.
6 AFP (France), Correctiv (Germany), Demagog (Poland), Pagella Politica/Facta (Italy) and EU DisinfoLab (Belgium) led by Fundación Maldita.es (Spain).
7 There are 46 countries in the Council of Europe, but 6 do not have a fact-checker operating in them according to the dataset: Andorra, Iceland, Liechtenstein, Malta, Monaco, San Marino.
8 Malta is not included; see note above.

References

Adair, B. (2014, October 11). *Duke study finds fact-checking growing around the world.* https://web.archive.org/web/20141011160449/http://www.reporterslab.org/duke-study-finds-fact-checking-growing-around-the-world/

Amazeen, M. A. (2015). Revisiting the epistemology of fact-checking. *Critical Review*, 27(1), 1–22. https://doi.org/10.1080/08913811.2014.993890

Amazeen, M. A. (2020). Journalistic interventions: The structural factors affecting the global emergence of fact-checking. *Journalism: Theory, Practice & Criticism*, *21*(1), 95–111. https://doi.org/10.1177/1464884917730217

Anderson, C. (2010, August 17). The web is dead. Long live the internet. *Wired*. https://www.wired.com/2010/08/ff-webrip/

Aspray, W., & Cortada, J. W. (2019). *From urban legends to political fact-checking: Online scrutiny in America, 1990–2015*. Springer Nature Switzerland AG.

Benkler, Y., Faris, R., & Roberts, H. (2018). *Network propaganda: Manipulation, disinformation, and radicalization in American politics*. Oxford University Press. https://doi.org/10.1093/oso/9780190923624.001.0001

Birkinbine, B., Gomez, R., & Wasko, J. (Eds.). (2016). *Global media giants*. Routledge. https://doi.org/10.4324/9781315682334

Curran, J., Coen, S., Soroka, S., Aalberg, T., Hayashi, K., Hichy, Z., Iyengar, S., Jones, P., Mazzoleni, G., Papathanassopoulos, S., Rhee, J. W., Rojas, H., Rowe, D., & Tiffen, R. (2014). Reconsidering "virtuous circle" and "media malaise" theories of the media: An 11-nation study. *Journalism: Theory, Practice & Criticism*, *15*(7), 815–833. https://doi.org/10.1177/1464884913520198

Dyakon, T. (2022, November 29). Google and YouTube partner with Poynter's international fact-checking network on $13.2 million grant for the global fact-checking community. *Poynter*. https://www.poynter.org/fact-checking/2022/google-and-youtube-partner-with-poynters-international-fact-checking-network-on-13-2-million-grant-for-the-global-fact-checking-community/

Edelman. (2023). *Edelman trust barometer global report*. https://www.edelman.com/trust/2023/trust-barometer

European Fact-Checking Standards Network. (2022). *European code of standards for independent fact-checking organisations*. https://eufactcheckingproject.com/app/uploads/2022/10/EU-CODE-EFCSN-.pdf

European Fact-Checking Standards Network. (2023, January 20). *Feedback from: European fact-checking standards network*. European Commission - Have Your Say. https://ec.europa.eu/info/law/better-regulation/have-your-say/initiatives/13206-Safeguarding-media-freedom-in-the-EU-new-rules/F3375867_en

Farkas, J., & Schou, J. (2018). Fake news as a floating signifier: Hegemony, antagonism and the politics of falsehood. *Javnost-the Public*, *25*(3), 298–314. https://doi.org/10.1080/13183222.2018.1463047

Frau-Meigs, D. (2019). *Faut-il avoir peur des fake news?* La Documentation Française.

Frau-Meigs, D. (2022). How disinformation reshaped the relationship between journalism and media and information literacy (MIL): Old and new perspectives revisited. *Digital Journalism*, *10* (5), 912–922. https://doi.org/10.1080/21670811.2022.2081863

Fuchs, C. (2009). Information and communication technologies and society: A contribution to the critique of the political economy of the Internet. *European Journal of Communication*, *24*(1), 69–87. https://doi.org/10.1177/0267323108098947

Fuchs, C. (2016). Dallas smythe today – The Audience commodity, the digital labour debate, Marxist political economy and critical theory. Prolegomena to a digital labour theory of value. In C. Fuchs & V. Mosco (Eds.), *Marx and the political economy of the media*. Brill.

Fuchs, C. (2020). *Communication and capitalism: A critical theory*. University of Westminster Press. https://doi.org/10.16997/book45

Graves, L., & Cherubini, F. (2016). *The rise of fact-checking sites in Europe*. Reuters Institute for the Study of Journalism.
Graves, L., & Lauer, L. (2020). From movement to institution: The "global fact" summit as a field-configuring event. *Sociologica*, *14*, 157–174. https://doi.org/10.6092/ISSN.1971-8853/11154
Hanitzsch, T., Van Dalen, A., & Steindl, N. (2018). Caught in the nexus: A comparative and longitudinal analysis of public trust in the press. *The International Journal of Press/Politics*, *23*(1), 3–23. https://doi.org/10.1177/1940161217740695
Hirst, M. (2017). Towards a political economy of fake news. *The Political Economy of Communication*, *5*(2), 82–94.
International Fact-Checking Network. (2016, November 17). An open letter to Mark Zuckerberg from the world's fact-checkers. *Poynter*. https://www.poynter.org/fact-checking/2016/an-open-letter-to-mark-zuckerberg-from-the-worlds-fact-checkers/
International Fact-Checking Network. (2022, July 11). Code of principles. AFP fact checking - IFCN application and assessment. *Poynter*. https://ifcncodeofprinciples.poynter.org/application/public/afp-fact-checking/BFC65C93-7D52-E06C-D7C9-71F30534104F
International Fact-Checking Network. (2023). State of the fact-checkers report 2022. *Poynter*. https://www.poynter.org/wp-content/uploads/2023/04/IFCN_2023_StateFactCheckers2022_v7a-1.pdf
International Fact-Checking Network Transparency Statement. (n.d.). *Poynter*. Retrieved June 30, 2023, from https://www.poynter.org/international-fact-checking-network-transparency-statement/
Knoche, M. (2021). Media concentration: A critical political economy perspective. *tripleC: Communication, Capitalism & Critique. Open Access Journal for a Global Sustainable Information Society*, *19*(2), 371–391. https://doi.org/10.31269/triplec.v19i2.1298
Kohut, A., Doherty, C., Dimock, M., & Keeter, S. (2011). *Press widely criticized, but trusted more than other information sources* (p. 37). Pew Research Center.
Kuo, R., & Marwick, A. E. (2021). Critical disinformation studies: History, power, and politics. *Harvard Kennedy School Misinformation Review*. https://doi.org/10.37016/mr-2020-76
Layne, K. (2001, December 9). Untitled. *KenLayne.Com*. https://web.archive.org/web/20011216191356/http://kenlayne.com/2000/2001_12_09_logarc.html#7775149
Marres, N. (2018). Why we can't have our facts back. *Engaging Science, Technology, and Society*, *4*, 423–443. https://doi.org/10.17351/ests2018.188
McChesney, R. W. (2007). *Communication revolution: Critical junctures and the future of media*. New Press.
McChesney, R. W. (2012). The political economy of communication: An idiosyncratic presentation of an emerging subfield. In A. N. Valdivia (Ed.), *The international encyclopedia of media studies* (p. wbiems031). Blackwell Publishing Ltd. https://doi.org/10.1002/9781444361506.wbiems031
McChesney, R. W. (2013). *Digital disconnect: How capitalism is turning the Internet against democracy*. The New Press.
McChesney, R. W. (2015). *Rich media, poor democracy: Communication politics in dubious times*. The New Press.
META. (2023, February 1). *Meta reports fourth quarter and full year 2022 results*. https://www.prnewswire.com/news-releases/meta-reports-fourth-quarter-and-full-year-2022-results-301736645.html

Mims, C. (2022, January 15). Google, Amazon, Meta and Microsoft weave a fiber-optic web of power. *Wall Street Journal*. https://www.wsj.com/articles/google-amazon-meta-and-microsoft-weave-a-fiber-optic-web-of-power-11642222824
Mosco, V. (2009). *The political economy of communication*. SAGE. https://doi.org/10.4135/9781446279946
Newman, N., Fletcher, R., Eddy, K., Robertson, C. T., & Nielsen, R. K. (2023). *Reuters institute digital news report 2023*. Reuters.
Pew Research Center. (1999). *Striking the balance, audience interests, business pressures and journalists' values*. https://www.pewresearch.org/politics/1999/03/30/striking-the-balance-audience-interests-business-pressures-and-journalists-values/
Radebe, M. J., & Chiumbu, S. H. (2022). Frames and marginalisation of counter-hegemonic voices: Media representation of the land debate in South Africa. *African Journalism Studies*, *43*(1), 89–106. https://doi.org/10.1080/23743670.2022.2033289
Rosen, J. (2005, January 5). Bloggers vs. journalists is over. *PressThink*. http://archive.pressthink.org/2005/01/21/berk_essy.html
Runkevicius, D. (2020, September 3). How amazon quietly powers the internet. *Forbes*. https://www.forbes.com/sites/danrunkevicius/2020/09/03/how-amazon-quietly-powers-the-internet/
Sapir, E. V. (2022). Can we trust measures of trust? Measurement invariance in trust in EU news media. *SN Social Sciences*, 2(10), 226. https://doi.org/10.1007/s43545-022-00534-1
Shafer, J. (2021, April 16). Opinion | How substack revealed the real value of writers' unfiltered thoughts. *POLITICO*. https://www.politico.com/news/magazine/2021/04/16/how-substack-revealed-the-real-value-of-writers-unfiltered-thoughts-482552
Shattock, E. (2021). Self-regulation 2:0? A critical reflection of the European fight against disinformation. *Harvard Kennedy School Misinformation Review*. https://doi.org/10.37016/mr-2020-73
Silverman, C. (2010). *Regret the error: How media mistakes pollute the press and imperil free speech* (ebook). Union Square Press.
Smalley, S. (2022, June 24). YouTube takes flak on the third day of GlobalFact. *Poynter*. https://www.poynter.org/ifcn/2022/fact-checkers-youtube-misinformation/
Smith, S. H. (2004). *The fact checker's bible: A guide to getting it right* (ebook). Anchor Books. http://site.ebrary.com/id/10064822
Stencel, M., Ryan, E., & Luther, J. (2023, June 21). *Misinformation spreads, but fact-checking has leveled off*. Duke Reporters' Lab. https://reporterslab.org/misinformation-spreads-but-fact-checking-has-leveled-off/
Toimitus. (2022, November 16). *Eurooppalaiset faktantarkistajat tiivistävät yhteistyötään EFCSN-laatukoodiston puitteissa*. Faktabaari. https://faktabaari.fi/avoinyhtk/eurooppalaiset-faktantarkistajat-tiivistavat-yhteistyotaan-efcsn-laatukoodiston-puitteissa/ (translated from the original Finnish work with Deepl)
Trappel, J., & Meier, W. A. (2022). *Chapter 7. Soaring media ownership concentration: Comparing the effects of digitalisation on media pluralism and diversity* (pp. 147–164). University of Gothenburg. https://urn.kb.se/resolve?urn=urn:nbn:se:norden:org:diva-12333
Tworek, H. (2020). Policy lessons from five historical patterns in information manipulation. In S. Livingston & W. L. Bennett (Eds.), *The disinformation age* (pp. 169–189). Cambridge University Press. https://doi.org/10.1017/9781108914628.007
Uscinski, J. E. (2015). The epistemology of fact checking (is still Naìve): Rejoinder to Amazeen. *Critical Review*, 27(2), 243–252. https://doi.org/10.1080/08913811.2015.1055892

Uscinski, J. E., & Butler, R. W. (2013). The epistemology of fact checking. *Critical Review*, *25*(2), 162–180. https://doi.org/10.1080/08913811.2013.843872

Vargo, C. J., Guo, L., & Amazeen, M. A. (2018). The agenda-setting power of fake news: A big data analysis of the online media landscape from 2014 to 2016. *New Media & Society*, *20*(5), 2028–2049. https://doi.org/10.1177/1461444817712086

Vinhas, O., & Bastos, M. (2022). Fact-checking misinformation: Eight notes on consensus reality. *Journalism Studies*, *23*(4), 448–468. https://doi.org/10.1080/1461670X.2022.2031259

Wasko, J. (2018). Studying political economies of communication in the twenty-first century. *Javnost - The Public*, *25*(1–2), 233–239. https://doi.org/10.1080/13183222.2018.1424031

3 MIL theories and the fight against disinformation in practice

Projects YouCheck! and YouVerify!

Divina Frau-Meigs, Nicoleta Corbu, and Sara Osuna-Acedo

3.1 Introduction

Fact-checking and media and information literacy (MIL) have been posited as the two main pillars to combat disinformation. The strengths and limitations of fact-checking have been evaluated by a number of researchers (for an overview, see Chapters 1 and 2 of this book). Prior research on evaluating the effectiveness of media literacy interventions has shown that the media-related interventions, aimed at increasing knowledge and critical thinking, are more effective than the behaviour-related ones, aimed at creative making and attitude change (Jeong et al., 2012). Research also suggests that the media literacy interventions tend to be more impactful if they are embedded in programmes reinforced through multiple sessions (Nygren et al., 2021; Scheibenzuber et al., 2023; Tully et al., 2020).

These elements suggest that an effective theory of change needs to be elaborated and shared within the transliteracy paradigm of MIL (Brest, 2010; Clark & Taplin, 2012). It should strive to

- clarify the assumptions and make the visions explicit as well as identify needs and necessary inputs and remediations for strategies and activities;
- identify the outputs (e.g. knowledge, technology and relationships) intended to result from the project;
- identify the outcomes (effects on actors, like changes in knowledge, attitudes, skills, relationships, or behaviour) that will result from the planned activities, engagement as well as the outputs produced (reports, tests and feedback at different stages of the process, i.e., intermediate/end-of-project outcomes, short-term/long-term outcomes);
- identify impacts, when possible (such as tangible social, economic and/or environmental benefits), that will be induced by the outcomes (with quantitative and qualitative evidence).

To encompass both knowledge acquisition and attitude transformation and to demonstrate impact, the transliteracy theory of change requires Analysis, Interpretation and then Reaction (AIR). The ultimate impact sought is to

DOI: 10.4324/9781003387404-5

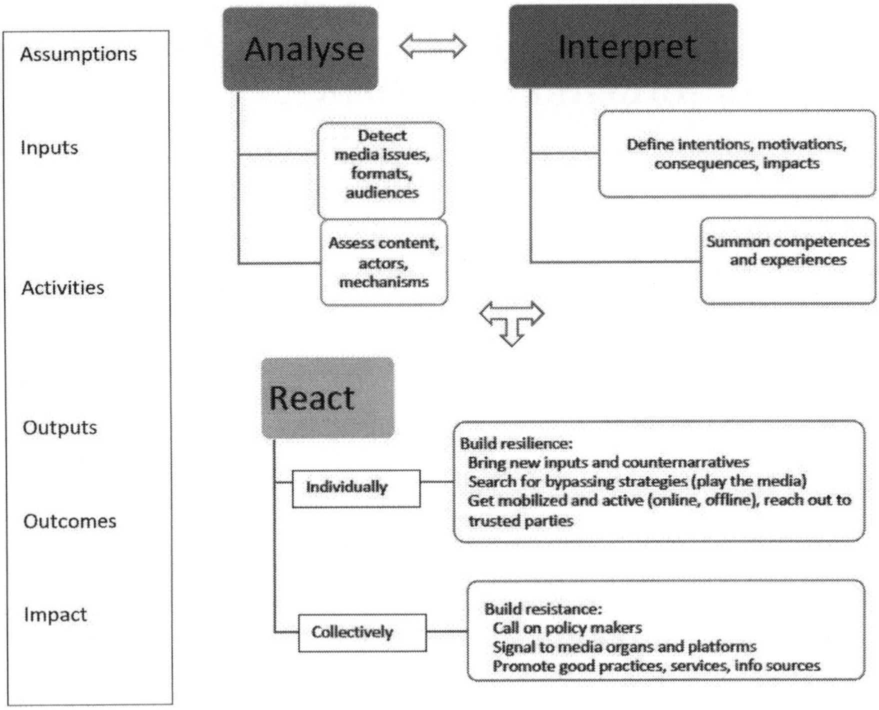

Figure 3.1 AIR Diagram and theory of change.
Source: Divina Frau-Meigs et al., Fresh AIR, 2018.

build resilience (at the individual level) and resistance (at the collective level), thereby mixing protection and participation, regulation and engagement (see Figure 3.1).

This points to pedagogical strategies and practices that are agile and iterative. The two projects YouCheck! and YouVerify! used transliteracy as the MIL theory of change, with additional support from techno-cognition and edu-communication:

Transliteracy and agility: the design experiments take into account the joint needs to deal with a complex process (disinformation in this case) and to facilitate the appropriation of a holistic pedagogical strategy by local teams. The triple process of agility (interactions, self-organisation and co-evolution) is key to outputs, outcomes and impact, and implies an iterative process that keeps improving the project until it reaches a stable and transferable stage, as one of the key values of agility is acceptance of change. This is facilitated by game-based learning, engagement by design inputs and modular pathways as used in MOOCs (Frau-Meigs & Bossu, 2020).

Transliteracy and techno-cognition: the design experiments include tools but these are never the entryway, neither are they used per se. For instance, the plug-in InVID-WeVerify is used to train journalists but also to show young people and educators how fact-checking works and how data and algorithms can create disinformation, but also help debunk it. This can imply a focus on the functionalities of the tool, in a reflexive manner, for the cognitive processes or biases that they reveal. What matters more is to create shared performance tools based on the negotiated needs of the various teams, and to provide feedback to the developers to keep improving their tool and the attendant services, in accordance with the agile methodology. This helps build trust across very heterogeneous MIL stakeholders.

Transliteracy and edu-communication: the design experiments take into account the new roles of educators as mediators and the enhanced attention to horizontal contributions by peers. The emphasis on creative teaching facilitates the trial-and-error methodologies where educators are moderators of situations of learning and animators of learning events, rather than mere transmissive agents. Such emphasis implies a focus on competences and experiences, an acceptance of various modes of learning, communicating and constructing identities and ideologies. It also suggests that transfer preoccupations need to be built in the early design of any project (Marta-Lazo & Gabelas-Barroso, 2023).

3.2 MIL in practice: YouCheck! as a pilot project (2019–2020)

The goal of project YouCheck! was to raise awareness of the public at large and the education and media literacy community about disinformation and "fake news" as a threat to democracy. YouCheck! also aimed at empowering European citizens with the latest advances in image and video verification so that they could be actors of their own resilience strategies when confronted with information disorders. Fostering citizens' agency with smart tools and adopting a solution-oriented approach to debunk "fake news" appeared as the most efficient way to change both their understanding of the "fake news" phenomenon and their daily behaviour with regard to information.

For such purposes, YouCheck! focused on the functionalities of the image verification plug-in InVID-WeVerify and provided pedagogical scenarios, gamification and self-paced tutorials for wider adoption. The project turned image and video checking technologies reserved to professionals into an accessible and usable tool for teachers, students and the public at large through a user-friendly environment created by the five project partners.

Adopting a multi-stakeholder MIL approach, the project united five partners: Savoir*Devenir (France), Agence France Press (France), Universidad Nacional de Educacion a Distancia – UNED (Spain), Uppsala University (Sweden) and National University of Political Studies and Public Administration – SNSPA (Romania). It capitalised on two existing independent EU-funded projects, the free verification plug-in designed by Agence France-Presse within the Horizon 2020 project InVID (2016–2018) and WeVerify (2018–2020) and free online training resources developed within the project ECO-LEARNING by partners Savoir*Devenir (France) and UNED (Spain). The effectiveness of this approach to increase students and citizens' media literacy and modify behaviours was evaluated by the Department of Education at Uppsala University (Sweden) in collaboration with SNSPA in Romania.

3.2.1 Rationale and assumptions

Disinformation, "fake news" and related information disorders have brought a lot of public attention to the dual need for fact-checking and for media literacy. Damages to the integrity of information and the integrity of the election process have evinced the societal costs of ignoring the necessary upskilling of the general population in the democratic process where quality information is key for decision-making in everyday life and for exerting one's digital citizenship rights and responsibilities, especially at crucial moments such as elections or referenda (Frau-Meigs et al., 2018).

Several fact-checking initiatives and tools have emerged as a response from the journalistic profession, sometimes with the support of the pure player platforms incriminated in the problem (Facebook and Google mostly). However, it seems crucial, in the European Single Digital Market context, to ensure that research in the field remains independent and publicly funded so as to produce really objective evidence-based results for policymakers.

Some of these initiatives have raised awareness on the need to reboot the public interest in seeking quality information and to rebuild trust in media, but most of them do not address the need to build the resilience of the general public, in particular young people. Research shows that building such resilience implies navigating online information in constructive ways. For this, people seem to need a mix of content knowledge and digital skills. Theories of media literacy like transliteracy and techno-cognition emphasise the importance of updated heuristics when navigating information as professional fact-checkers do (Wineburg & McGrew, 2019).

These theories stress the need for citizens to consider how images and videos may be manipulated and also be able to use digital tools, like reverse image search, to check their sources. But the use of such tools and how they might support people's transliteracy have not been studied in previous research. What prior research shows is that students struggle to separate credible from misleading digital multimodal information (Nygren et al., 2022).

Scholars also point to the fact that students are not more skilled at navigating online information in proportion to the time spent in front of screens (McGrew et al., 2018). To acquire effective and agile strategies when evaluating manipulated texts and images, the educational design should include a combination of challenging and stimulating tasks, together with cognitive scaffolding to support the use of online resources (Kirschner & De Bruyckere,

2017). It should also facilitate upscale and transfer across languages and cultures, in an edu-communicative manner.

Research revealed additional gaps: the thrust of journalistic fact-checking activities in most EU countries was mostly directed at journalists' interventions in the classrooms (ex: Factbar edu in Finland; Lie Detectors in Belgium and Germany; Entre les lignes in France), less at training and/or certifying teachers (Literacia dos medios e jornalismo in Portugal). Besides, the focus was mostly on text-based "fake news", much less on visual "fake news" though these are among the most prominent in social media used by young people and the public at large, especially on Facebook and YouTube (Frau-Meigs et al., 2019).

3.2.2 Inputs, objectives and activities

YouCheck! aimed at adapting a verification toolkit to MIL and at transferring the critical competences of fact-checkers to the classroom and to the public at large and to the classroom, with strategies and pedagogical procedures more largely applied to MIL via the open platform ECO DIGITAL LEARNING. This process was supposed to enable citizens, teachers and students to become familiar with fact-checking tools and to create an online community where such practices would be maintained.

The main specific objectives were organised around a set of activities:

1 The design of a simplified interface to handle InVID-WeVerify free verification plug-in
2 The facilitation and assistance to the exploration of the InVID-WeVerify plug-in by teachers in classrooms with pedagogical scenarios, to encourage them to create MIL projects
3 The co-design and co-creation of self-paced tutorials to help the public at large use YouCheck! toolbox, for exerting their critical thinking and digital citizenship
4 The evaluation of the efficiency of the materials in the YouCheck! toolbox to raise the level of media literacy
5 The systematic provision of MIL competences (skills, attitudes, knowledge and values)
6 The supply of a self-evaluation tool via gamification (quizz) to empower and provide agency to users in their everyday experiences

The research design and methodology adopted an agile approach, so as to ensure that the materials were tested twice, in two iterations, first by the developing partner and then by all partners in all languages. This entailed translation and localisation as well as feedback to all partners, including the team of InVID-WeVerify partners via AFP (see Figure 3.2).

The main beneficiaries were high school students (15–18 years old), teachers, librarians and journalists, as well as other actors from different

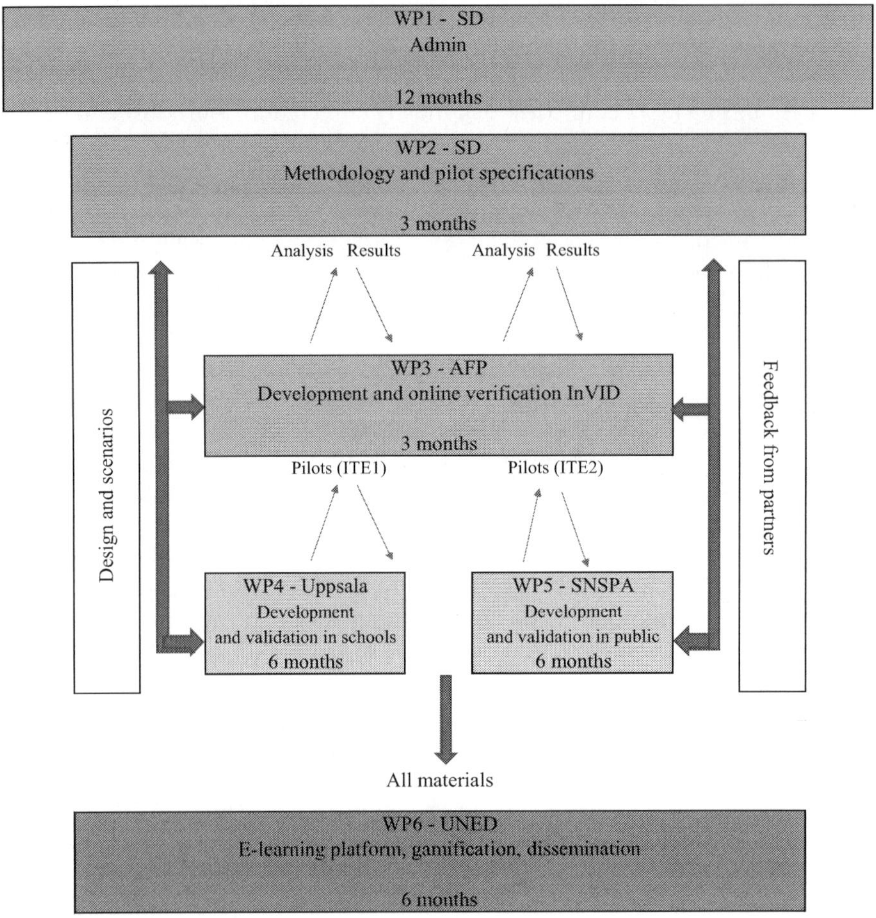

Figure 3.2 YouCheck! methodological design.

Source: Divina Frau-Meigs et al., S*D, 2018.

sectors likely to be confronted to visual fakes and deepfakes, such as political scientists, political communication specialists, media researchers and practitioners.

3.2.3 Outputs, outcomes and expected impact

There were various project outputs designed to help stakeholders in their work and/or daily activities. Teachers were provided with lesson plans (scenarios and pathways) to assist them in introducing media literacy topics and the InVID-WeVerify plug-in to their pupils. The serious game "YouCheck! Detectives" was created and made available to the public at large to introduce in a playful and pedagogical way the plug-in to large audiences. Online questionnaires were used to test the plug-in by beta testers, before presenting the tool to larger audiences. A toolbox with all materials, in five languages (English, French, Romanian, Swedish and Spanish), was made public on the project website. Research articles and conference presentations helped disseminate the results of the project to the academic environment and teaching communities.

The major expected outcomes were focused on facilitating the use of the enhanced InVID-WeVerify plug-in and YouCheck! toolbox for MIL as a significant breakthrough to enhance the traditional way of teaching about disinformation and propaganda. Additionally, we sought to embed the plug-in not just as an operational tool for users, but as an element in a full-fledged MIL transliteracy (project-based and competences-driven).

The impact evaluation involved two types of assessment. On the one hand, we focused on assessing students' media literacy as validated in previous research, using pre-and post-test questionnaires in interventions in classrooms, so as to identify how students' performances were affected by the interventions in the classrooms (two iterations). On the other hand, we assessed the plug-in uses with a larger group of the public via an online questionnaire designed for beta-testing individuals using InVID-WeVerify plug-in and focus groups with ordinary educated people and with teachers, so as to enrich the toolbox and make it available for all. In this perspective, the project also provided a self-assessment gamified quiz. This quiz aimed at helping each user to conduct his/her own evaluation of performance. It was based on the beta testers comments and optimised so as to improve the functionalities and resources of YouCheck! toolbox.

3.2.4 Main results and lessons learnt

3.2.4.1 Main results

The results show the effectiveness of the interventions planned in YouCheck! project. Particularly, they showed that using a visual media verification tool embedded in lesson plans can lead to attitude change in fact-checking among young people and improve media literacy skills.

The general results show that all participants believed that disinformation is a great challenge and they found the verification plug-in very useful but also complicated to use. Moreover, self-tutored adults agreed that the main measures to tackle disinformation should be development of critical thinking, media regulation, availability of technical tools and improvement of quality of news. Additionally, students performed better in visual fact-checking after being taught media verification skills and they improved their performance in detecting misleading images and videos after the class intervention. Generally speaking, students' attitudes changed significantly after using the plug-in embedded in the media literacy lesson plan. The most recurrent variables showing attitude change about fact-checking among students were the following: *relying less on "gut feeling" and on "journalist reputation" and relying more on "image design", "search of source" and "consulting fact-checking websites"*.

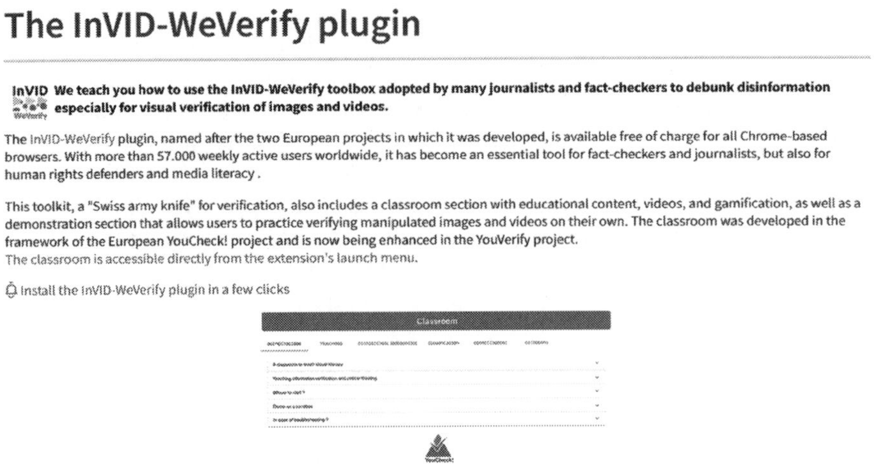

Figure 3.3 InVID-WeVerify open-access resource used in all activities of YouCheck! project.

Most outputs of the projects and its various outcomes are available as free resources at youverify.eu (see, as an example, Figures 3.3 and 3.4).

3.2.4.1.1 RESULTS OF SCHOOL INTERVENTIONS

In general, in all countries, the intervention with InVID-WeVerify was successful, with significant performance and increased interest in using digital tools and InVID-WeVerify in particular. The intervention does not show a "liar's dividend": the students clearly distinguished the true from the false, and this did not diminish their credibility in the news. Therefore, the idea that fact-checking efforts help to legitimise doubts about the veracity of information is not validated. This is especially true among students who used digital tools. Generally, the two countries showing the most progress are Romania and Spain. Those showing less progress are Sweden and France, although there is a notable improvement (see Figure 3.5). Other research has shown that too much self-confidence can affect performance (for detailed results of the interventions, see Nygren et al., 2021).

In general, the intervention in schools was very satisfactory. Students performed better in visual fact-checking after being taught media verification skills, and they improved their performance in detecting misleading images and videos after the class intervention. Students' attitudes changed significantly after using the plug-in embedded in the media literacy lesson plan. The most recurrent variables showing attitude change about fact-checking among students were relying less on "gut feeling" and relying more on "image design" and "search for a reliable source".

The positive results confirm that this experimental research should be moved to a broader stage of implementation, given its usefulness. They also

Figure 3.4 Screenshot of the main layout of YouCheck! Detectives serious game.

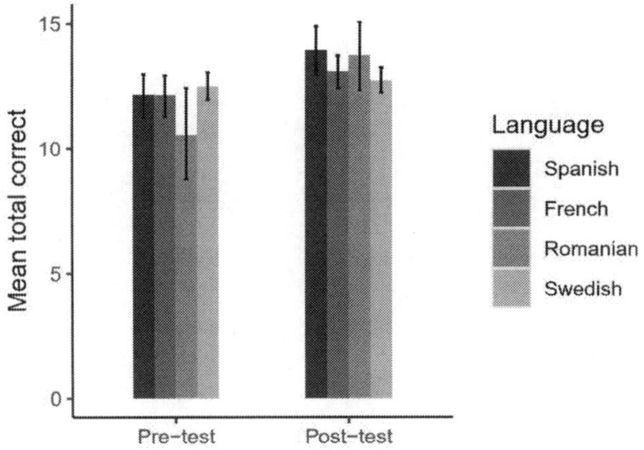

Figure 3.5 A notable increase in performance of detecting disinformation (Nygren et al., 2021).

confirm that MIL can be a rapid response strategy to societal problems of the magnitude of disinformation. It can increase the performance of students in detecting misinformation, and it can change behaviour and develop critical thinking. The differences across countries point to a necessary alignment of public policies in Europe.

3.2.4.1.2 RESULTS OF BETA TESTERS AND FOCUS GROUPS

The beta testers and focus groups showed an overall positive interest in InVID-WeVerify with some real interest in the tool, seen as useful and informative. People found the plug-in interesting, useful and easy to use. When evaluating the various dimensions of the toolkit, people appreciated its novelty, stimulation and efficiency. Perspicuity and attractiveness were slightly lower, but still highly evaluated (for a full presentation of the beta testers' evaluation of the tool, see Chapter 4 of this book).

The focus groups evaluated perceptions about and definition of "fake news", perceived prevalence and possible effects of fake news in online media, and measures to address the fake news phenomenon. The results showed that the definition is very fluid and not consensual across countries, with many formats (i.e. parody, satire) sometimes included under the broad umbrella of "fake news", and propaganda as the most mentioned concern. The prevalence of disinformation is perceived as very high, especially in school settings. The effects are perceived as very wide, mostly in health, democracy, with risks of alienation, anxiety and manipulation. The measures put forward related to media literacy measures, more tools and adequate regulation, as well as better quality of news overall. (Details about focus groups results are provided in Chapters 4 and 9 of this book.)

3.2.4.1.3 RESULTS OF GAMIFICATION AND TWO MEDIA CAMPAIGNS

The serious game was not tested per se, but the first media campaign provides indications as to its interest. The first campaign was conducted in June 2020 over 15 days. It had an overall positive impact and the indicators of performance were better than expected (considering briefness and low cost). The youth audience, between 13 and 24, was the most interested, and more men than women clicked on the link to the game (52% men, 48% women).

The toolkit was the object of the second media campaign and was aimed mostly at teachers and educators, over ten days in January 2021. The number of daily conversions (333 clicks) were above the expected (250 per day); the daily reach of the campaign was 27,494 people (expected 20,000 per day). The age distribution shows an overwhelming percentage of interest in ranges above 45 years (45–64), and women were roughly twice as many as men in impressions and clicks. (For more details, see Chapter 8 of this book.)

3.2.4.2 Lessons learnt

The impact of YouCheck! followed from the four main distinguishing features of the project design: image credibility evaluation, InVID-WeVerify user-friendliness and further development, critical thinking heuristics for visual digital literacy and cross-cultural insights. The main thrust of the project was to ensure that all main deliverables were tested (pilots in Semester 1) and deployed (interventions in Semester 2), in the four partner countries, in order to test whether a tool designed for professional fact checkers could stimulate adults and students' attention to visual literacy and better prepare them to determine the credibility of information.

In terms of MIL policy, the results of all activities in the project could help governments and educators better understand how to use media literacy tools and skills for rapid intervention. Following are the most meaningful lessons learnt and the takeaways for stakeholders:

- Online disinformation is still a somewhat confusing and understudied phenomenon, with important personal and social effects.
- Media literacy interventions using innovative tools are very positively received by educators, but there is still a general fear of using the new technologies in classrooms.
- Media literacy can be a rapid response strategy for combating online disinformation.
- Media literacy is efficient after interventions that sensitise to disinformation risks for democracy and develop self-awareness and critical thinking as to self-bias on credibility of news.
- Visual literacy tools developed in collaboration with media literacy educators can help raise critical thinking, improve fact-checking skills of the population and resilience against online disinformation.

3.3 MIL theories in practice: Scaling up YouVerify! (2021–2022)

The goal of project YouVerify! was to address the challenges brought by disinformation and its coming second wave, mostly AI-driven, by contrast with the first wave, mostly social media-driven. The project built on current tools and research and capitalised on the advances of previous YouCheck! project (2019–2020) by focusing on critical visual literacy training so as to scale up and disseminate competences in image and video verification across Europe.

YouVerify! used the much-enhanced InVID-WeVerify plug-in to foster information resilience among young people and youth educators (i.e. teachers, librarians, youth workers). Two main online deliverables were provided: a Massive Open Online Course (MOOC) on "Disinformation Step by Step" as well as a serious game named "Fake News Detectives". Additionally, the project looked into the feedback provided by the participants in the MOOC and the serious game to draw a series of recommendations for public policy with a set of indicators, as a diagnostic tool to evaluate the obstacles and opportunities in expanding media literacy in Europe (in terms of training, resources funding and evaluation mostly).

YouVerify! had a strong dissemination intent, and both deliverables were deposited as Open Educational Resources and hosted in the Eco Digital learning platform as well as in the site of the InVID-WeVerify plug-in. The partners were the same as for YouCheck!, without Sweden (as the focus was not on schools): Savoir*Devenir (France), Agence France Press (France), UNED (Spain), and SNSPA (Romania). the project also capitalised on the added functionalities of InVID-WeVerify plug-in: deepfake detection, Twitter analysis (metrics, charts, maps), chatbot assistant for dialogue with users, database of known fakes (debunks searchable by author, country, date), while keeping the previous ones (keyframes, reverse search, metadata, magnifier and forensics features). All partners were committed to promote replicating strategies in their respective countries and used the two "seasons" or "iterations" of the MOOC and the serious game to raise awareness about critical visual literacy and the verification and refutation strategies that can be put in place to combat disinfodemics. They solicited their dissemination networks (across journalists, local media, libraries, schools, etc.) at both national and European level, in order to broaden geographical coverage.

3.3.1 Rationale and assumptions

The digital environment provides new ways for producing and customising information, but also for manipulating and disrupting information flows. Terms such as "information disorders" or "fake news" have come to represent both the growing supply of disinformation across media and the receding trust in democratic institutions (science, journalism, politics, etc.). Disinformation was defined as "all forms of false, inaccurate, or misleading information designed, presented and promoted to intentionally cause public harm or for profit" (EU Commission, 2018, p. 13). It has disrupted elections and referenda, increased the spread of conspiracy theories and cast doubts on scientific research (as exemplified by the recent disinfodemic concerning Covid-19).

The public and private responses to this first phase of disinformation, mostly social media-driven, have been the promotion of fact-checking and of media education. Many initiatives and networks exist that provide verification tools and websites dealing with the first wave of disinformation, which has come to public concern in 2016. But, as with Covid-19, a second wave of disinformation arrived, AI-driven this time, with a continuous presence of viral fakes as GAN, algorithmic data mining and advanced image manipulation technologies became more sophisticated. This second wave points to the need to step up new types of MIL skills and tools and to train the general population so that quality information remains the main source for knowledge construction, critical thinking and decision-making for all. Of particular concern are "deepfakes" that can be fabricated using advanced neural-network approaches to manipulate video content (swapping faces and bodies in a quasi-undetectable manner).

Education remains key in debunking automated disinformation, especially visual fakes (Neekhara et al., 2020). So, increasing MIL levels is crucial to empower citizens to combat disinformation and its attendant evils for democracy (pandemics, climate change, migration crises, etc.). To address the challenges brought by disinformation and its coming second wave, it is important to build on current state-of-the-art tools and research and capitalise on previous advances by democratising access to them and spreading them as widely as possible, so as to build up "barrier gestures" as it were against the disinfodemic.

The research results of YouCheck! point to a certain number of lessons learnt upon which to draw the strategy of YouVerify! These lessons were used as feedback for adaptation of the InVID-WeVerify plug-in, one of the main objectives of YouCheck!. Just to give some examples, teachers and users would like a course in which to embed the tool, to avoid a strictly tool-oriented approach; they would prefer a database of known debunks to use when applying the tool, so as to make it more user-friendly in a teaching context; they would like a chat space to express their needs and queries; and they feel there is a gap between the official language and policies and what they are expected to do concretely in classrooms and with parents (Frau-Meigs et al., 2020; Osuna-Acedo et al., 2020).

These results are aligned with other studies in the field (Clark et al., 2020; Nygren et al., 2021). Further, research shows the lack of digital visual literacy and need for innovative approaches to create resilience among users (Breakstone et al., 2021; Lewandowsky et al., 2017).

Hence the necessity of expanding from these results and research and providing tools for massive training teachers and educators to media literacy with a strong component of visual literacy and a resource for making the access to InVID-WeVerify plug-in user-friendly and increasing motivation among young people to use it. Classroom interventions are one of the means of proceeding (and they were the main focus of YouCheck! project), but to amplify and disseminate further and across a more heterogeneous public, Massive Open Online Courses (MOOC) and Serious Games are a venue that can scale up the individual resilience and collective resistance against disinformation (see Figure 3.1: AIR diagram).

3.3.2 Inputs, objectives and activities

YouVerify! built on the lessons learnt from the previous pilot project YouCheck! in an agile way that facilitated scaling up. This made it possible to amplify the two main objectives:

1 Increasing the level of visual literacy in and out of schools via MOOCs and Games
2 Developing multiple dissemination strategies jointly with many stakeholders in the field, ranging from professionals in journalism and education to NGOs and public institutions

Through these two outputs (MOOC and Game), the project put special emphasis on visual competences and critical thinking competences. We defined competences as knowledge, skills, attitudes and values, along the Digital Citizenship Education framework developed by Council of Europe (Frau-Meigs et al., 2019). We described these main competences for MIL in the field of disinformation in a set of items measuring the following: (1) knowledge acquisition on disinformation/verification/refutation (recognising actors, motivations, consequences, responses), (2) skills (using tools, navigating websites, comparing search engines, discriminating across social media, devising counter-narratives), (3) attitudes (debunking "fakes", building resilience against disinformation, etc.) and (4) values (freedom of expression and opinion, dignity, respect for science and facts, participation).

We further developed digital visual literacy competences, unpacking them for the project, as the existing standards were drafted back in the 2010s (Avgerinou & Rutte, 2011; Spalter & Van Dam, 2008). We relied on input from researchers in digital visual literacy to upgrade its indicators and offer it to the participants in the MOOC (see Figure 3.6).

Additionally, YouVerify! relied on e-learning pedagogies, via MOOCs (Frau-Meigs et al., 2021; Osuna-Acedo et al., 2018a, 2018b). They present the advantage of structuring knowledge on the basis of active pedagogies, mostly learning by doing. They also are good replicating devices, especially if they encourage projects that involve many stakeholders. They can empower

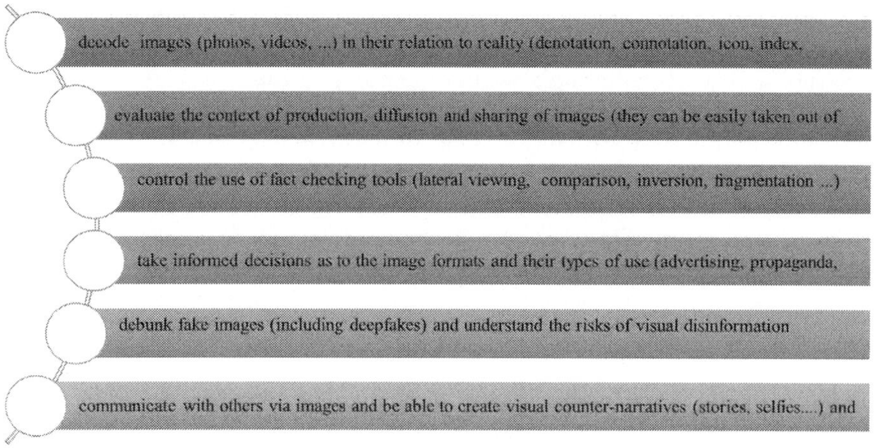

Figure 3.6 Visual literacy competences.

Source: Frau-Meigs, for Savoir*Devenir team, 2020.

participants by upskilling them for competences that they cannot acquire at university, such as critical digital literacy and verification and refutation strategies. The engaging pedagogical tools were developed in an agile way, with moderation during the two iterations, as well as gamification via a Serious Game, "Bot Busters". We applied the social MOOC model, or sMOOC, that fosters participation via social media and apps as well as transfer (Marta-Lazo et al., 2019).

The MOOC "Disinformation step by step", hosted in ECO platform, presented four main modules:

Module 1 on disinformation (definitions, actors, motivations)
Module 2 on verification strategies (tools, actors, resources)
Module 3 on refutation (cognitive biases, resilience, counter-narratives)
Module 4 on media education (competences, sense-making practices, project building)

Two additional modules were added, one on critical thinking and one on MIL projects, to embed the plug-in in MIL theory and practice. The MOOC offered several quizzes, including a final quiz to verify media education competences in disinformation and provide learning analytics. The MOOC also included a questionnaire to evaluate the perception of the users and probe into policy dimensions for future use. Open badges were offered to those who completed the course (for detailed results, see Chapters 5 and 6 of this book).

To emphasise game-based learning and the engagement by design trends in transliteracy, YouVerify! also used gamification strategies to improve learners' motivation and engagement. Building on the previous serious game developed for YouCheck!, the partners explored further the functionalities of InVID-WeVerify by offering a series of debunking missions to young people. The Serious Game "Bot Busters" provided game analytics that pointed to strengths and weaknesses and to areas of improvement that could be revised during the two iterations of the game in the MOOC.

Finally, YouVerify! pursued the "R" in the AIR theory of change, with more emphasis on collective solutions and public policies. It gathered data in order to propose policy recommendations for MIL and fighting disinformation, as the situation across European countries was highly heterogeneous (Frau-Meigs et al., 2017). Using questionnaires with MOOC participants and in-depth interviews with key actors and stakeholders involved in implementing media literacy actions within each country, the project elaborated a set of policy briefs and recommendations.

YouVerify! developed a set of specific objectives and activities:

1 Create the MOOC "Disinformation Step by Step" that focused on verification and refutation competences and developed best practices based on "learning by doing" with many embedded suggestions for project-building.
2 Develop the Serious Game "Bot Busters" with missions focused on digital visual competences.
3 Train people to Deep Fake detection tools and address emerging AI issues via the InVID-WeVerify plug-in and its new functionalities.
4 Establish an EU-wide dissemination network, involving medias, private and public sector actors as well as civil society NGOs to reach a larger audience.
5 Provide recommendations for country readiness in establishing policies for disinformation and MIL in the EU, with cross-country comparisons.

Following MIL transliteracy principles, and AIR theory of change, the research design and methodology adopted an agile approach, so as to ensure that the materials were tested twice, in two iterations, first by the developing partner and then by all partners in all languages. This entailed translation and localisation as well as feedback to all partners, including the team of InVID-WeVerify partners via Agence France-Presse (see Figure 3.7).

The main beneficiaries were teachers, librarians and journalists, as well as other actors from different sectors likely to be confronted with disinformation and to act on policy issues, such as political scientists, political communication specialists, media practitioners at large.

3.3.3 Outputs, outcomes and expected impact

The project outputs were the following: the "Disinformation Step by Step" MOOC (with workshops, scenarios and practices); the serious game "Bot

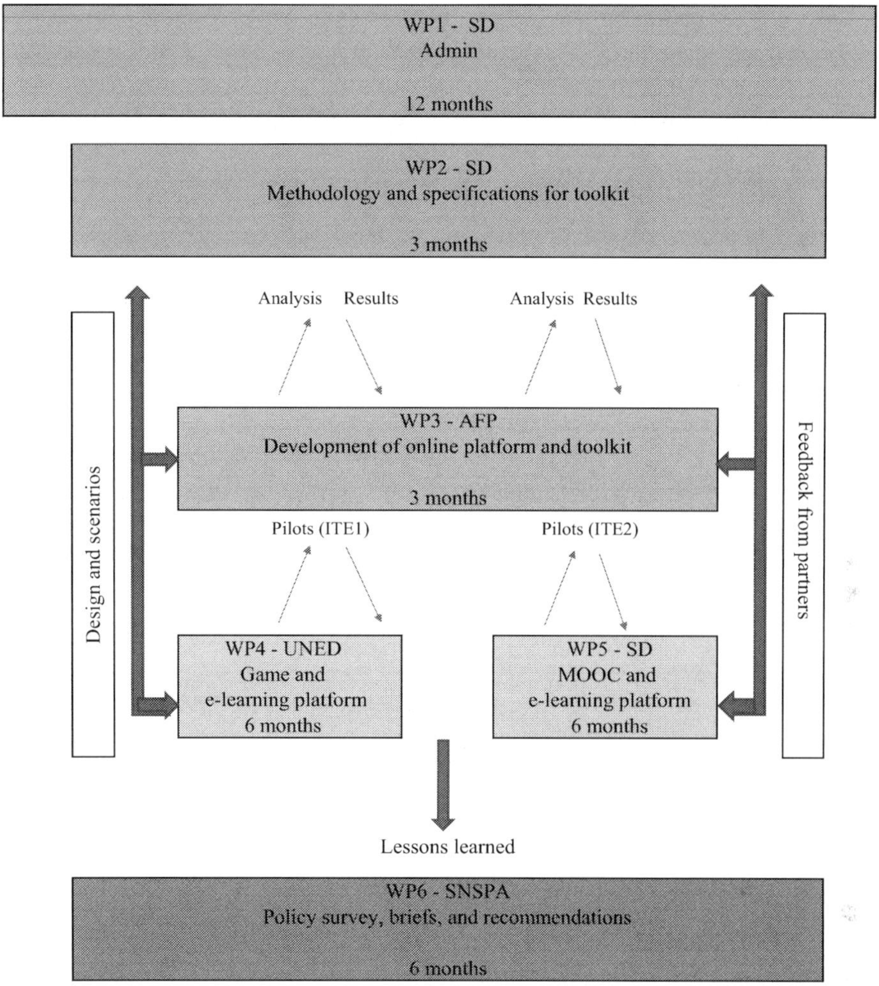

Figure 3.7 YouVerify! Methodological design.

Busters"; policy briefs for media and education policies; a toolbox with all materials (including those of previous project YouCheck!), available on the project's website and InVID-WeVerify website; and research articles to disseminate the results across the academic and teaching communities.

The major expected outcomes were threefold. First, promoting visual literacy of the enhanced version of InVID-WeVerify plug-in; second, transferring competences in MIL across partners and countries via game-based learning and social MOOCs; and third, contributing to policymaking by providing a set of recommendations for media and education national and European future policies.

The expected impact was related to increasing participants' performance in all aspects of media literacy and gathering key evidence (via expert interviews and satisfaction questionnaires of MOOC participants) to propose policy recommendations.

3.3.4 Main results and lessons learnt

3.3.4.1 Main results

The MOOCs gathered together 2,401 registered students, of which 1,373 were active. The results showed the effectiveness of the learning strategies planned in YouVerify! Particularly, they showed that critical thinking and visual literacy could be enhanced when the tools were embedded in MIL activities, workshops and practices.

As far as MOOC satisfaction was concerned, the participants were generally very satisfied with the content and information provided in the MOOC. All participants who took the satisfaction survey stated their satisfaction with the process and contributed their own local examples. Self-tutored participants kept their motivation at unexpected levels thanks to the facilitation techniques put in place during the iterations. Furthermore, policy actors supported the dual notions that MIL should be part of major school curriculum and that further coordination should exist across governmental agencies and ministries as well as across EU institutions.

Data about the project and educational resources are available on the project website, youverify.eu (see Figure 3.8) and on the MOOC platform, open access at present time (https://hub5.eco-learning.eu/course/disinformation-step-by-step/) (for examples of MOOC activities, see Figures 3.9 and 3.10).

Figure 3.8 The YouVerify website.

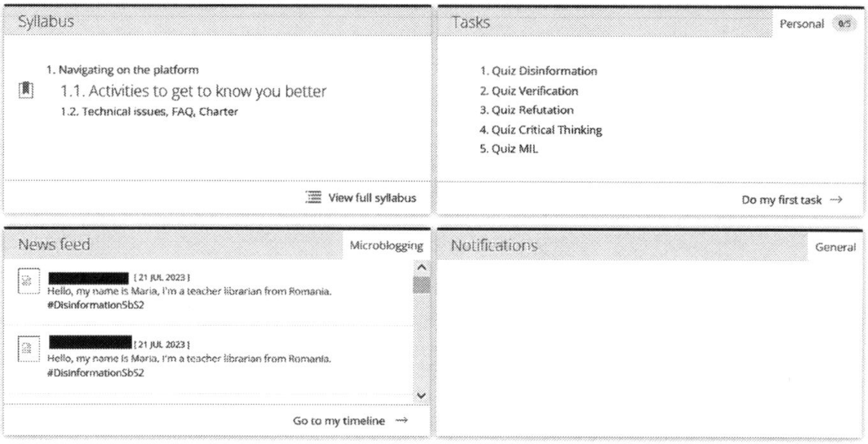

Figure 3.9 The dashboard of the MOOC on Ecolearning platform.

3.3.4.1.1 RESULTS OF MOOC ITERATIONS

The main quantitative results in figures are summarised below:

- Participants registered: 2,401
- Participants active in course: 1,373 = 57%
- Participants Quiz: 628 = 45.7%
- Open badges delivered: 383
- Participants Questionnaire: 333

The main quantitative results are well above average for what concerns e-learning and long-distance training. They can be attributed to a variety of factors: interest and timeliness of the topic; quality of contents and variety of resources; engagement of participants via a coordinated facilitation strategy (weekly meetings, challenges, forum and chats, webcast in three languages, etc.); incentive of micro-credits (open badges delivered). The second ITE had less participants but even more positive results, and points to a preference for the two paths format tried in ITE 2: path 1 "Disinformation", path 2 "MIL" (for detailed information about the MOOC implementation and results, see Chapters 5 and 6 of this book).

The main qualitative results show that the MOOC experience course design and engagement were up to expectations of participants and had a much lower rate of attrition than in most academic MOOCs. Participants' expectations were met in terms of their understanding of disinformation mechanisms as well as their use of fact-checking tools and techniques as well as refutation strategies. Overall, the potential of MIL dispensed massively via MOOCs to fight disinformation and create counter-narratives to disinformation was confirmed, and MIL effectiveness also, though projects are still baffling and maybe too ambitiously presented in MOOC design.

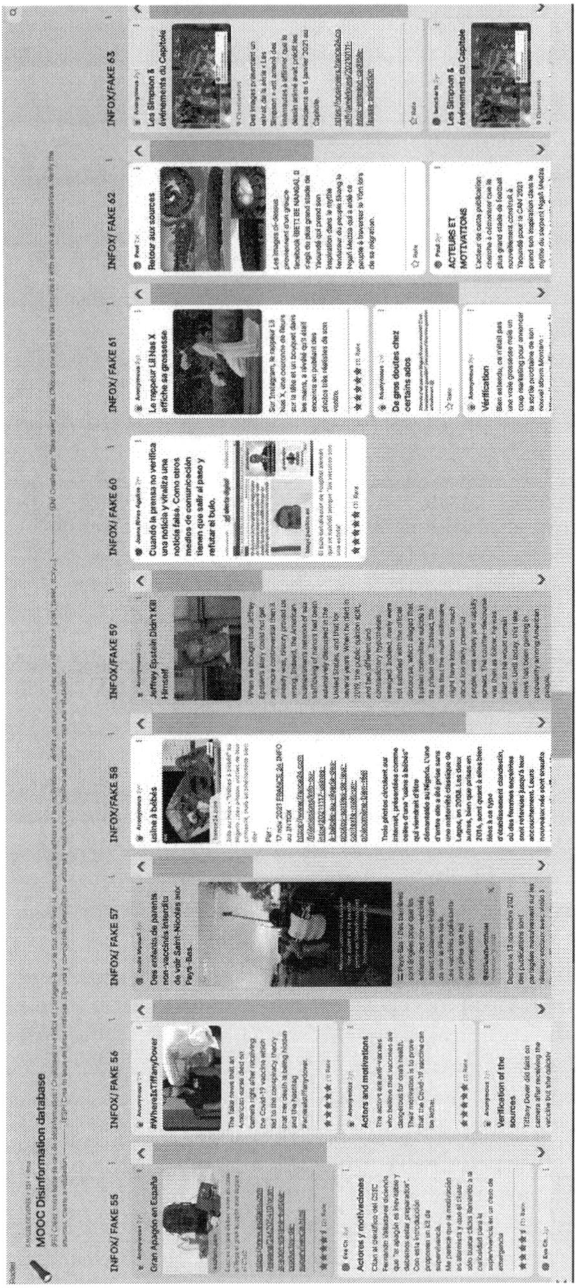

Figure 3.10 The disinformation database of examples, via Padlet.

3.3.4.1.2 RESULTS OF SERIOUS GAME

The highlights of game analytics showed the following:

- Number of visits received to the game: 15,281
- Number of players pressing the START button after watching the introduction animation, in percentage: French version: 82%; Spanish version: 98%; Romanian version: 85%; English version: 93%.
- Number of players who decide to start the game and complete all four missions: 83%. This percentage indicates that the game is understood and has been sufficiently attractive for players to complete all the missions – and get the Certificate (see Chapter 8 of this book for more details).

3.3.4.1.3 RESULTS FOR POLICY RECOMMENDATIONS

Policy recommendations were made based on the 30 expert interviews conducted in the three countries (10 experts, decision-makers, major stake-holders, journalists, per country), results of the MOOC, and prior YouCheck! outcomes. Two policy briefs, for education and for media, were elaborated and disseminated to specific stakeholders, including national ministries, and DG-Connect. The key recommendations were proposed based on key insights from the project:

Insight 1: There are significant differences in terms of an emerging framework for MIL interventions among the countries studies. Key recommendation 1: adapt measures to the stage (early/advanced/very advanced) each country is in and capitalise from an exchange of experiences and lessons learned.

Insight 2: In order to make a decisive contribution to countering disinformation, MIL needs to be formalised in the education system, and be provided with adequate resources. Key recommendation 2: increase the role of media education in the school curriculum and allocate financial and human resources needed.

Insight 3: MIL measures are effective, but they fail to reach important segments of society. Key recommendation 3: consider less obvious, but vulnerable target groups.

Insight 4: There is a persistent lack of coordination among stakeholders in the field of MIL, and between public and private initiatives. Key recommendation 4: establish clear intersectoral mechanisms and an MIL collaboration framework with permanent connections between public and private actors.

Insight 5: There are no comprehensive standards for evaluating the impact of MIL interventions, which can delay evidence-based policies in this area. Key recommendation 5: design a system of relevant Key Performance Indicators and implement a unified methodology for measuring the impact (see Chapter 10 for more details).

3.3.4.2 Lessons learnt

The various learning events of YouVerify! attested to the interest and motivation of adults that are amplifiers in MIL (many participants were part of libraries and youth workers associations).

The results from the participation questionnaire showed that the MOOC experience course design and engagement were up to expectations of participants and much lower rate of attrition than in most academic MOOCs. Moreover, participants' expectations were met in terms of their understanding of disinformation mechanisms as well as their use of fact-checking tools and techniques as well as refutation strategies. Additionally, the potential of MIL dispensed massively via MOOCs to fight disinformation and create counter-narratives to disinformation was confirmed, and MIL effectiveness also, though projects are still baffling and maybe too ambitiously presented in MOOC design (and absent in the structures where the participant work).

The interviews about policy showed that experts, be it policymakers, journalists, advocacy leaders or researchers, were aware of these challenges. Across all countries they tended to advocate for more public policies on MIL and on disinformation, for more multi-stakeholder partnerships and for a more legitimate presence of MIL in the core curricula of schools.

3.4 Conclusion

These results confirm the urgent need to carry out MIL strategies in order to recognise and disarm misleading information through social attitudes, which involve an active positioning of citizens' awareness of suspicion and vigilance. They show that regulation of disinformation and other fake news avatars is a challenging topic that demands balancing freedom of expression and protection from harm caused by untruthful information; such regulation calls for clear standards for assessing the quality of information on digital platforms.

People should be empowered and equipped with the tools to evaluate information quality as well as recognising manipulative tactics used to mislead information. MOOCs are ideal settings for critical MIL, although there are some hard challenges to be taken into account in some respects, such as achieving the necessary inter-creative attitude of participants and being aware of the responsibility of participants in the spread of misinformation by indiscriminate sharing, inside and outside the MOOC.

To ensure success, a multifaceted response is necessary, which engages a holistic approach involving governments, educators, digital platforms and civil society organizations so as to reach out to the entire citizenry. Critical MIL is therefore an essential component in the repertoire of strategies available to withstand disinformation and an evolving process for addressing new challenges.

NB: the precise descriptions of the two projects (rationales and results) are extracted from the initial deposit of the two projects and the final evaluation of the two projects as submitted to DG-connect by Savoir*Devenir. They have never been made public before. The full reports are available on request at contact@savoirdevenir.net.

References

Avgerinou & Rutte. (2011). Towards a cohesive theory of visual literacy, *Journal of Visual Literacy*, *30*(2), 1–19.

Breakstone, J., Smith, M., Wineburg, S., Rapaport, A., Carle, J., Garland, M., & Saavedra, A. (2021). Students' civic online reasoning: A national portrait. *Educational Researcher*, *50*. https://doi.org/10.3102/0013189X211017495

Brest, P. (2010). The power of theories of change. *Stanford Social Innovation Review*, *8*(2), 47–51. https://doi.org/10.48558/NPZS-C374

Clark, A. E., Nong, H., Zhu, H., & Zhu, R. (2020). *Compensating for academic loss: Online learning and student performance during the COVID-19 pandemic. HAL.* Available online at: https://halshs.archives-ouvertes.fr/halshs-02901505

Clark, H., & Taplin, D. (2012). *Theory of change basics: A primer on theory of change*. Actknowledge.

EU Commission (2018). A multi-dimensional approach to disinformation. Report of the independent High level Group on fake news and online disinformation. Available at: https://digital-strategy.ec.europa.eu/en/library/final-report-high-level-expert-group-fake-news-and-online-disinformation

Frau-Meigs, D., & Bossu, A. (2020). L'agilité et l'interculturalité en question dans le dispositif global-local des MOOC: le cas du MOOC Pas à Pas. *Questions de communication 38*(2), 87–102.

Frau-Meigs, D., Kotilainen, S., Pathak-Shelat, M., Hoechsmann, M., & Poyntz, S.R. (Eds.). (2020). *Handbook of media education research*. Wiley.

Frau-Meigs, D., O'Neill, B., Soriano, A., & Tomé, V. (2019). *Digital citizenship education: overview and new perspectives*. Council of Europe Publishing.

Frau-Meigs, D., Osuna-Acedo, S., & Marta-Lazo, C. (Eds.). (2021). *MOOCs and the participatory challenge. From revolution to reality*. Springer.

Frau-Meigs, D., Velez, I., and Flores Michel, J. (Eds.). (2017). *Public policies in media and information literacy in Europe. Cross-country comparisons*. Routledge.

Frau-Meigs, D., Velez, I., & Garreau, P. (2018). *Fresh AIR! MIL handbook*. https://savoirdevenir.net/wp-content/uploads/2023/10/INEDU-Manual-ENG.pdf

Jeong, S. H., Cho, H., & Hwang, Y. (2012). Media literacy interventions: A meta-analytic review. *Journal of communication*, *62*(3), 454–472.

Kirschner, P.A., & De Bruyckere, P. (2017). The myths of the digital native and the multitasker, *Teaching and Teacher Education*, *67*, 135–142. https://doi.org/10.1016/j.tate.2017.06.001

Lewandowsky, S., Ecker, U. K. H., & Cook, J. (2017). Beyond misinformation: Understanding and coping with the "post-truth" era. *Journal of Applied Research in Memory and Cognition*, *6*(4), 353–369. https://doi.org/10.1016/j.jarmac.2017.07.008

Marta-Lazo, C, Frau-Meigs, D, et Osuna-Acedo, S. (2019). Transfering a collaborative digital pedagogy: The transition from the sMOOC Model to the tMOOC in the "step by step", *Australasian Journal of Educational Technology*, *35*(5), 111–127.

Marta-Lazo, C., & Gabelas-Barroso, J. A. (2023). *Diálogos posdigitales: Las TRIC como medios para la transformación social*. Gedisa.

McGrew, S., Breakstone, J., Ortega, T., Smith, M., & Wineburg, S. (2018). Can students evaluate online sources? Learning from assessments of civic online reasoning. *Theory & Research in Social Education*, *46*, 165–193. https://doi.org/10.1080/00933104.2017.1416320

Neekhara, P., Hussain, S.S., Jere, M., Koushanfar, F., & McAuley, J. (2020). Adversarial Deepfakes: Evaluating Vulnerability of Deepfake Detectors to Adversarial Examples. *2021 IEEE Winter Conference on Applications of Computer Vision (WACV)*, 3347–3356.

Nygren, T., Frau-Meigs, D., Corbu, N., & Santovena-Casal, S. (2022). Teachers' views on disinformation and media literacy supported by a tool designed for professional fact-checkers: Perspectives from France, Romania, Spain and Sweden. *SN Social Sciences*, *2*(40), 1–22. https://doi.org/10.1007/s43545-022-00340-9

Nygren, T., Guath, M., Axelsson, C.-A., & Frau-Meigs, D. (2021). Combatting visual fake news with a professional fact-checking tool in education in France, Romania, Spain and Sweden. *Information*, *12* (5), 201; https://doi.org/10.3390/info12050201

Osuna-Acedo, S., Marta-Lazo, C, & Frau-Meigs, D. (2018a). From sMOOC to tMOOC, learning towards professional transference: ECO European project. *Comunicar, Media Education Research Journal*, *26*(55), 105–114. https://doi.org/10.3916/C55-2018-10

Osuna-Acedo. S, Frau-Meigs, D., & Marta-Lazo, C. (2018b). Educación Mediática y Formación del Profesorado. Educomunicación más allá de la Alfabetización Digital. *Revista Interuniversitaria de Formación del Profesorado (RIFOP)*, *32*(1), 29–42.

Osuna-Acedo, S., Frau-Meigs, D., Nygren, T., & Durach, F. (2020). Developing media literacy outside the classrooms for fighting visual disinformation: The Youcheck Project. In E. Lopez Meneses et al., (Eds.), *INNOVAGOGIA 2020, V Congresso Internacional sobre Innovación Pedagógica y Praxis Educativa* (pp. 533–543).

Scheibenzuber, C., Neagu, L. M., Ruseti, S., Artmann, B., Bartsch, C., Kubik, M., Dascalu, M., Trausan-Matu, S., & Nistor, N. (2023). Dialog in the echo chamber: Fake news framing predicts emotion, argumentation and dialogic social knowledge building in subsequent online discussions, *Computers in Human Behavior*, *140*. https://doi.org/10.1016/j.chb.2022.107587

Spalter, A. M., & Van Dam, A. (2008). Digital visual literacy. *Theory into Practice*, *47*(2), 93–101. https://doi.org/10.1080/00405840801992256

Tully, M., Bode, L., & Vraga, E. (2020). Mobilizing users: Does exposure to misinformation and its correction affect users' responses to a health misinformation post? *Social Media + Society*, *6*(4). https://doi.org/10.1177/2056305120978377

Wineburg, S., & McGrew, S. (2019). Lateral reading and the nature of expertise: Reading less and learning more when evaluating digital information. *Teachers College Record: The Voice of Scholarship in Education*, *121*, 1–40. https://api.semanticscholar.org/CorpusID:227628758

Section II

Fighting disinformation from a practical perspective

Results of projects YouCheck! and YouVerify!

4 Using tools to fight disinformation in and outside the classrooms

Evidence from four countries

Nicoleta Corbu, Divina Frau-Meigs, Adina Ionescu, and Jade Azzoug Montané

4.1 Introduction

Disinformation is one of the most important challenges facing democratic societies due to its amplification via social media and chatbots. The nature of false information is dynamic, as it rapidly changes its characteristics, techniques, and modalities of production and dissemination, making it more difficult to determine the accuracy of the information or the credibility of the source. Some users may be social bots, some texts may be half-truths suffused with false details, and some images may be edited to serve financial or ideological purposes (Frau-Meigs, 2019). Even people who are trusted by individuals, such as family and friends, can become victims of manipulated content and propagators, without their knowledge. Because disinformation is voluntarily generated, and shared intentionally or accidentally, it is vital to consider multiple elements and techniques to combat the phenomenon.

Disinformation is also multimodal, through both text and visuals or videos (Alam et al., 2022) and it is becoming more prevalent on the internet and social media platforms, exposing people to a range of risks, from believing urban legends to falling prey to plot theories and hybrid threats. Individuals tend to give credit to a claim when it has an image attached to it, even if the image is not relevant to the text (Newman & Zhang, 2020), underlining how easy it is to "hijack" the cognitive processes. Such situations are increasing the probability that false images emphasise the fake news overall effects. The advanced tools and methods to manipulate visual content are being addressed timidly in the research fields, as emergent studies indicate a gap in the literature about visual disinformation and how it can be tackled. Interventions such as fact-checking (done by human experts) and automated analysis of models and programmes using machine learning and deep learning networks indicate good results but many more new features are surfacing, from the online forgers. Along with the institutional and technological approaches, individuals need to have autonomy, knowledge, and tools to protect themselves from multimodal disinformation, a central purpose of the media and information literacy (MIL) initiatives, such as European project YouCheck! that was conducted in four countries: France, Romania, Spain, and Sweden.

DOI: 10.4324/9781003387404-7

YouCheck! was a European project funded by the European Commission within the "Media Literacy for All Programme", centred on stimulating critical thinking skills to fight disinformation and disseminate educational resources and digital tools that can help the teachers in classrooms (Savoir*Devenir, 2022). The project aimed to develop competences in visual disinformation identification and evaluation for teachers, students (16–18 years old), and the general public. The project consisted in producing educational resources for teachers such as lesson plans, a serious game (*YouCheck! Detectives*), and training for using the INVID-WeVerify plugin. These were used in MIL intervention with high school students, whereas beta-testers were asked to test the plugin on their own. The plugin offered six main functionalities: reverse image, keyframes, magnifier, forensic, similarity analysis, and metadata. It was supported by a browser extension, presenting multiple sections, including a "classroom" section for additional materials[1].

Implementing the educational framework of MIL as a modality to combat visual disinformation and emphasising the important role of digital tools in limiting the negative effects of fabricated content, our study was placed at the intersection of various fields: educational, MIL, disinformation (visual), methods of fighting disinformation and technological approaches to increase critical thinking skills and identification of visual manipulation.

Based on three studies using mixed methodology (survey and focus groups), we aimed to understand the perceptions and feedback of adults (Study 1), teachers (Study 2), and pupils (Study 3) that tested the INVID-WeVerify plugin. Following multiple phases with diversified participants using the plugin created a more nuanced comprehension of how a digital tool for combating disinformation can be effectively used in various contexts.

The purpose of the study was also to explore the contextual features, in which a digital tool for visual disinformation could be applied in culturally different learning spaces, to better understand the user experience in the educational realm (both teachers and students) and how individuals grasped the importance of anti-disinformation tools.

The results of our study were aimed at supporting teachers, designers, researchers, and MIL experts and helping them to learn about the effects and perceptions of introducing digital tools for disinformation in the classroom and outside of it, in different cultural contexts. Adapted instruments and knowledge, such as critical thinking and digital tools, were considered as crucial to healthy democratic societies because they are the most important weapons in the long term to win the war in favour of truth and credibility.

4.2 Mis- and disinformation: A technological and educational approach

Manipulated content circulating around the world is a problem that governments and societies can no longer ignore. With the large adoption of technological and digital innovations – from social media platforms to artificial intelligence – individuals are exposed to a large amount of new information and need to be able to discern whether the data and images they encounter are trustworthy or not. False information is not only a threat to individuals but also a real danger for digital communities and societies (e.g. anti-vaccination disinformation and increased levels of deaths from COVID-19).

In the academic field, the phenomenon has many names: "fake news", "false news", "misinformation", and "disinformation", indicating the importance of choosing an appropriate term that can encompass the relevant components and nuances of the process.

Fake news can be defined as "false information spread under the guise of being authentic news usually spread through news outlets or the internet with an intention to gain politically or financially, increased readership, biased public opinion" (Meel and Vishwakarma, 2020, p. 5). The concept gained mixed significance after it was weaponised (Tong et al., 2020) by some political actors in an attempt to attack journalistic materials that were portraying opposing views or shed light on questionable political activities. Due to its emotional charge and its assault on the credibility of media in general (Collier & Van Duyn, 2022; Egelhofer & Lecheler, 2019), the High-Level Expert Group on disinformation (2018) emphasised the urgency of adopting a distinct term for the description of the malignant phenomenon and its amplification.

Fake news cannot be accurately described as news as they only mimic the look and values of media articles – prominence, timeliness, and proximity, but lack the most important part of good quality journalism: objectivity (Tandoc et al., 2021). Furthermore, they are not entirely fake, as many articles labelled as fake news are based on truncated truths or real events reframed to serve other purposes (Gelfert, 2018). The term *fake news* therefore fails to describe the complexity and ever-changing nature of the process responsible for destabilising truth.

If *fake news* is not suitable, what term should be used? Academics pointed to *misinformation* and *disinformation*, both concepts adopted in many articles dealing with the subject of fabricated content shared online. Wardle and Derakhshan (2017) describe misinformation as false information created with no intention to deceive (often by honest mistakes) and disinformation as a voluntary and conscious process in which the creator disseminates the false information for particular purposes: political, financial, ideological, or reputational (Lecheler & Egelhofer, 2022). According to Tandoc and collaborators (2017), the difference lies in two elements: facticity and intentionality. Disinformation is produced with the intent to achieve specific goals (e.g. troll factories that share false data in the middle of presidential elections), while misinformation can include journalistic errors (hastily collected materials), unverified sources, or social media users sharing posts and news whether the information is authentic or not.

In project YouCheck!, we used the term *disinformation* predominantly, to refer to the process of generating and disseminating false information (textual, visual, or multimodal) designed to mislead the users, where the malicious intent of the creator is a fundamental component of the mechanism.

Disinformation is characterised by volume, veracity, and velocity (Zhang & Ghorbani, 2020) and needs to be addressed by many entities, through multiple tools that can respond to the volume continuously generated, the many subtypes of online disinformation, and explosive real-time proliferation. With the increasing levels of false content circulating on the internet and social media platforms, identification, assessment and verification efforts need to be enhanced. Besides the issue of regulation and self-regulation (Iosifidis & Nicoli, 2021; Mihajlov Prokopovic & Vujović, 2021; De Blasio & Selva, 2021), researchers tend to organise the fight against disinformation into three clusters: (1) institutional approach (through fact-checking organisations), (2) technological approach (through machine learning, deep learning, AI-automated detectors, and plugins), and (3) educational approach (by conducting courses and training on MIL, critical thinking, and analytical competences) (Nygren et al., 2022; Hangloo & Arora, 2022; Collins et al., 2020, Schuetz et al., 2021; HLEG, 2018). We focused on the last two approaches as we intended to help individuals bolster their resilience to disinformation.

Regarding *the technological approach*, Khan and collaborators (2021, p. 13) pointed out four paradigms in the academic field of disinformation identification: *hybrid approach* (including human and machine learning methods), *feature-based method* (a set of features used for training detection algorithms), *network propagation* (early detection of false news), and *fusing Artificial Intelligence models with human experts* for a better outcome in the decision-making process. Whether humans or machines are more accurate in identifying false news, one of the safest approaches should be the advancement of highly accurate identification tools, along with human assistance and expertise to mitigate the effects of disinformation generated by both humans and bots.

The methods and programmes employed for the detection of disinformation are constantly evolving, with many studies using Natural Language Processing (NLP), text mining, and machine and deep learning (Deep Neural Network, Convolutional Neural Network, classifiers, Generative Adversarial Networks, Propagation Networks, Advanced Graph Mining, etc.) (Nasir et al., 2021; Khan et al., 2021; Shu et al., 2020b; Collins et al., 2020). Figueira and colleagues (2017) attempted to classify the algorithms trained to combat disinformation into three categories: (1) based on content, (2) based on the message's diffusion dynamic, and (3) based on features meant to train the algorithm. The methods used to identify false content are diverse and tackle multiple issues: the message itself, how it is shared in the virtual communities, and what characteristics are important when users want to distinguish between real and doctored content. Additionally, multiple types of media used in manipulated content, such as images, should be considered, to increase the accuracy of fake detection (Reddy et al., 2019).

The challenges of detecting online disinformation fall into two categories, according to Shu and collaborators (2020a): content-based and user-based.

AI-powered models or machine learning approaches cannot accurately assess the truthfulness of false news because of specific vocabulary/context, inadequate databases, or lack of access in the early stages of fake information coagulation, making it difficult to stop disinformation proliferation. Conversely, using only human experts, even if they are able to discern nuances and general sentiment, can lead to errors and limitations in relation to the constantly large amount of fabricated information.

Regarding *the educational approach*, MIL (Frau-Meigs et al., 2017) provides spaces where individuals can learn to identify and evaluate text and visual media and prepares them for real-world situations, where fact-checkers or even algorithmic solutions are not already implemented.

In MIL interventions, the main emphasis is on creating learning spaces in which critical thinking, analytical abilities, and assessment of the creation and distribution of media products can be carried out step by step. This process encourages students' openness to use their critical thinking on what they encounter daily: social media feeds, news articles, videos and images, and websites.

4.3 Visual disinformation

Early research in the area of disinformation detection mostly focused heavily on text and context analysis, questioning which linguistic features, semantic structures, and writing patterns are involved in the "fake news formula" and its pattern of dissemination in virtual spaces and communities.

In addition to the text component however, images and videos were integrated into many disinformation-led articles because they create a sense of realism and authenticity (Hameleers et al., 2020), which can accelerate the cognitive processes leading to information acceptance and integration.

Weikmann and Lecheler (2022) classify visual disinformation along two axes: the level of modal richness (if the images are still or moving – GIFs) and the level of sophistication (the counterfeiter implements low-level or high-level techniques for falsifying the image). Qi et al. (2019) illustrate two categories of visual disinformation, based on the context in which the visuals appear: tampered images (digitally modified) and misleading images (visuals taken out of context or old images that reappear in other contexts).

Visual disinformation can be achieved by colour manipulation, elements repositioning, eliminating or adding components to the image, modifying the original photo by morphing it with other images/visual elements, retouching, cropping, and misattribution (Thomson et al., 2020). The type of visual disinformation does not matter, as long as the ill intent is present, as a central point of manipulation (Weikmann & Lecheler, 2022).

Individuals demonstrate lower abilities in recognising a manipulated image than they do for text (Kasra et al., 2016). Kanozia and collaborators (2021) observed that, in India, the most prominent categories of disinformation are videos and images added to a text, accentuating the need of using digital tools for identifying not only the text but also the multimedia content attached. Because pictures can evoke emotional responses, especially fear and anger (Cao et al., 2020), visual disinformation is subtler and even more insidious than only text and can have a long-lasting effect on users. The combination of text and images can act as a catalyst for the negative effects of disinformation (Alam et al., 2022) pointing out the necessity of new tools for detecting visual and multimodal disinformation (Meel & Vishwakarma, 2020).

Visual disinformation detection can follow the content of the post (the result of multiple media and their features) or external knowledge (where algorithms can skim through databases and compare different posts, images, and their features) (Cao et al., 2020). Because the manipulations become more and more ingenious, machine learning has developed multimodal systems and trained them to "catch" the manipulated images and videos, along with the text. Recent studies indicate that multimodal detection models (image, text, and additional features) perform better than single modality – either textual or image (Kirchknopf et al., 2021; Xue et al., 2021; Tuan & Quang Nhat Minh, 2021; Giachanou et al., 2020; Jindal et al., 2019).

Detection of images is still in its early stages, with many new models and techniques being implemented (as single or multimodal verification tools). One of the best-suited deep learning methods for identification and analysing doctored images are Deep Neural Networks (DNN) and Convolutional Neural Network (CNN), because they can be trained easily with examples of manipulated images with recognisable areas of forgery (Thomson et al., 2020). Machine learning approaches can identify two features that are different from real images: the physical level, with low quality of the image, and the semantic level, where pixels are modified (Qi et al., 2019).

As multimodal disinformation is perceived as slightly more credible than only textual disinformation (Hameleers et al., 2020), efforts in fighting manipulated content should be divided between fact-checkers, automated programmes, and media literacy experts. This approach can limit the negative effects by analysing the characteristics, diffusion patterns, and sources of false news, as well as imposing higher scrutiny in the journalistic field and increasing citizens' autonomy through knowledge. Researchers also need to pay more attention to visual disinformation, as concepts like *cheap fakes* and *deep fakes* (Paris & Donovan, 2019) start to enter the everyday vocabulary.

4.4 Tools to fight disinformation

Limiting the negative effects of disinformation is only possible if multiple tools are implemented because manipulated content is spreading much faster than real news (Vosoughi et al., 2018). Table 4.1 presents several tools for combatting visual disinformation, including plugins, deep learning methods, and search engines. The list is not comprehensive because numerous tools, models, and systems are being developed in the academic field and the private sector as well (e.g. Facebook).

Table 4.1 Tools for visual disinformation identification

Nr.	*Tool Name*	*Source*	*Type*	*Attributes*
1	Detection system	Jahankhani and Kapuku-Bwabw (2011)	Improved toolbar for fake news website detection	Three levels: URL identity, black list checking, and image-based screening
2	MVAE	Khattar et al. (2019)	Multimodal Variational Autoencoder	Encoder and Decoder of information from text and image + Fake News Detector
3	TikTec	Shang et al. (2021)	Multimodal Misinformation Detector	Detector for manipulated short videos on TikTok regarding COVID-19
4	PROVENANCE	Yosuf et al. (2021)	Web-based image and text verification tool	Video/Image Reverse Searcher, Video/Image Manipulation Detector (and many other settings)
5	Image Verification Assistant	Reveal (2016)	Web-based image verification tool	Has multiple settings: "image tampering detection", "metadata analysis", "reverse image search", "EXIF Thumbnail extraction", and "GPS geolocation"
6	RevEye	Steven van Vaerenbergh (2009)	Internet Browser Plugin	Reverse Image search on Google, Bing, Yandex, TinEye
7	TinEye	Tineye (2008)	Internet Browser Plugin Reverse Image Search Engine	Image source verification, Identification of modified images, Debunking images, Image Attribution
8	YouTube Data Viewer	Amnesty International (Koetl, 2014)	Web-based video verification tool	Extract Upload Time, Finding older versions of the video
9	Surfsafe	RoBhat (2018), Gutman-Wei (2018))	Internet Browser Plugin	Searching for the same image on different websites, alerting on photoshopped images, image source
10	InVID-WeVerify	InVID project[a]	Internet Browser Plugin	Audio and video content verification

[a] https://www.invid-project.eu/

In the end, combatting disinformation cannot be fully covered by algorithmic detection or by human flagging and fact-checking, given the immense volume of data generated every day, using multiple media types (video, image, text, and links). MIL interventions can support pupils (and individuals, in general) to develop the 21st-century competences needed to explore safely the internet and the present world, even if they do not follow fact-checkers' efforts or use an automated programme.

4.5 Evaluation of tools

In order to assess if the tools are relevant to the learning objectives and if they are appropriate for the user, researchers need to carry out a thorough evaluation of the instruments available.

User experience (or UX) can be defined as the result of the perceived usefulness and practicality of the product, mixed with the emotional and affective responses to the product/service, at any moment of the usage (Allam et al., 2013). Such an experience needs to be understood in order to design interfaces better and to develop digital features for facile use. How a user perceives the product or digital service is paramount for the tool's usability and efficiency.

In their article, Laugwitz, Held, and Schrepp (2008) proceed towards a standardised assessment tool for the subjective experiences of users regarding multiple types of digital programmes and systems. The authors created a User Experience Questionnaire and indicated three dimensions of the analysis implemented by the user: *perceived ergonomic quality* (task-based, pragmatic), *perceived hedonic quality* (non-task-based, aesthetic), and *perceived attractiveness of a product* (the relevance of the perceived quality of the product and its significance in a specific scenario). The perceived attractiveness of a product is operationalised in multiple factors: *perspicuity* (How easy to understand and navigate is the product?), *dependability* (How predictable and secure is the product?), *efficiency* (How organised and fast is the product?), *novelty* (How innovative is the product?), and *stimulation* (How captivating is the product?) (Laugwitz et al., 2008, p. 68). The level of importance of such a characteristics can be different for different types of users (short-usage, medium-usage, long-term/frequent, infrequent users) (Ilmberger et al., 2011), with the hedonic dimension (especially stimulation) having the biggest impact on the overall attractiveness of the interface. Researchers and UX designers need to balance the first two dimensions, pragmatic and hedonic (as defined by Ilmberger et al., 2011; Saleh et al., 2021 and based on Laugwitz et al., 2008), when they deal with how users explore a digital tool: new users are focused on goal-oriented behaviour, and the opposite is true for experienced users.

In this study, we used only five out of the six dimensions of the User Experience Questionnaire, as the users' experience was too short in the specific contexts to be able to correctly assess dependability. To better understand how a tool for fighting visual disinformation was perceived (specifically, the INVID-WeVerify plugin), we wanted to explore the experience of inexperienced users, leading us to our first research question:

RQ1. How do people generally perceive a new toolkit for fighting visual disinformation?

MIL has built, over time, a set of competences to enable citizens to improve their critical thinking and their evaluation of information, be it in the press or in digital spaces (e.g. social media platforms and video game websites). Positive outcomes of MIL interventions have shown an increase in the accuracy of disinformation identification among youth (Al Zou'bi, 2022; Kahne & Bowyer, 2016; Nygren et al., 2021), a surge in online political engagement and in targeted pressure on political institutions (Kahne & Bowyer, 2019), an improvement of critical thinking skills and in behavioural changes, and a rise in the intention to use reverse image search in the case of cheap fakes (Qian et al., 2022).

The role of technology in media literacy interventions becomes more important, with teenagers (13–18 years old) spending as much as eight hours on screens per day in 2021, a 17% increase from 2019 (Common Sense Media, 2022). Surfing constantly on social media platforms (YouTube, TikTok, Instagram), young people declare that it would be hard for them to give up on social media accounts, with many considering that they spend just the right amount of time on them (Vogels et al., 2022). As disinformation is spread deeper and faster on digital platforms (Vosoughi et al., 2018), the chances of encountering fabricated texts, images, and videos in scrolling on their timeline are higher than ever.

Because of their digitally filled life, teenagers are deemed capable, by default, of identifying false information that is circulating on the internet. However, studies showed that students tend to be confident in their cognitive skills to identify fabricated content but the confidence does not always lead to conclusive outcomes (Cruz & Morais, 2020), indicating that young people need to be trained and mentored to have a critical approach to disinformation and also to manage the necessary tools in order to tackle the manipulated content. Balakrishnan et al. (2022) in a study on disinformation dissemination during the COVID-19 pandemic demonstrated that the most probable false information spreader is a young male, with low education and a low ability to spot fabricated content.

With studies indicating that young people are not able to differentiate between false claims and authentic information (Veeriah, 2021) and that they can be swayed by disinformation that appears as news (Herrero-Diz et al., 2020), MIL interventions need to continue to address younger generations by reframing the use of a digital space that is not only for entertainment but also for their everyday life uses of information.

Students need to develop new abilities and metacognitive competences (Andersen, 2002) in order to be able to understand how to use digital technologies (in general and for disinformation evaluation purposes) and to grasp the impact new tools have on their lives as media consumers.

Phippen et al. (2021) emphasise an important idea: the expectation that students should be digitally literate as soon as they enter the classroom is unrealistic. Teachers should design the learning process to increase the pupils' confidence in themselves in order to acquire competences to mitigate disinformation.

Seen as "citizen-oriented direct interventions" (Yosuf et al., 2021, p. 3) and as having a positive impact on long-term media literacy, browser plugins can be a handy alert system for internet users, offering sophisticated tools (e.g. metadata analysis) at the tip of their fingers.

For a digital tool to be used, individuals need to perceive it as useful, interesting, and attractive. Our second research question focuses on the digital experience of the students when encountering an innovative toolkit for fighting visual disinformation:

RQ2. How do pupils in a classroom setting perceive a new toolkit for fighting visual disinformation (as part of an MIL intervention)?

Whether digital technologies are used in the classroom is influenced by the attitude of the teacher towards technology and innovative tools (Daniela, 2019). Fearing that introducing technology into students' learning processes may distract them from their educational purposes and learning goals and make organisation and relevant guidance more difficult (Loveless, 2011), many teachers are reluctant to create technology-enhanced learning spaces where digital tools are oriented towards educational goals.

Techno-cognition, or the ability "to design better information architectures that can build bridges between the socially-defined epistemic islands that define the post-truth era" (Lewandowsky et al., 2017, p. 30) needs to be developed based on critical thinking and new approaches in using digital spaces. Grounded in psychology and cognitive science, technocognition aims to use the knowledge of the human psyche to design better technologies, ideally disinformation-proof. Activities such as tagging the content on social media platforms or increasing verification through algorithms can facilitate the user journey on the internet and social media platforms, but they are not enough. Individuals, and especially teenagers, need to be guided and supported to develop digital competences in safe spaces where information can be shared step by step along with feedback.

MIL initiatives, supported by transliteracy and technocognition, can truly help students when tools for combatting disinformation and understanding the techniques used in false content are available to the pupils. They need to be mentored in the learning process of using the anti-disinformation tools but frequently, as in the adoption of ICTs at school, the competence level of teachers can make them technology-avoidant (Hassan & Mirza, 2021) and reluctant to integrate them in class lectures. According to MIL interventions design, the use of digital tools should not be "still" (top-down lectures full of information) but engaging, captivating, and flexible, to train pupils in the competences for mastering visual disinformation (Qian et al., 2022).

Interested in the teachers' perception of digital tools created to counter disinformation and their integration into classroom interventions, our third research question follows the teachers' perspective on technological interventions on media literacy:

RQ3. How do high school teachers perceive a new tool of fighting visual disinformation as a media literacy tool?

Regarding the adoption of ICTs in the classroom by teachers, Goh and Sigala (2020) observed three barriers: the extended period that the teacher and the student need to understand how to use the new technology, the lack of institutional support to integrate digital tools in the learning space (e.g. no training provided for the teacher, limited funds) and the subjective experience of the teacher (career length, attitude towards technology). Additionally, the perceived accessibility and availability of the tools (how easy they are to use) can influence the possibility of introducing them in the classroom.

Researchers need to assess the relevance of new tools such as smart plugins aimed to fight disinformation in the medium and the long term, in order to promote good results and practices. Many projects regarding browser extensions become inactive after a while (Yosuf et al., 2021), leaving a gap in the academic field and creating disadvantages for individuals that are navigating the internet and social media platforms.

The fourth research question aimed at exploring the methods in which a positive user experience could conduct to repeated usage of digital tools for fighting visual disinformation:

RQ4. What are the most efficient ways to introduce a plugin to fight disinformation, in order to maximise chances to be used in the future?

Being a "highly contextualised activity" (Hobbs & Jensen, 2009, p.2), MIL projects and classroom activities tend to be implemented differently in various countries, depending on the national curricula, the governmental support, the penetration of technologies in classrooms, and how well trained the educators are.

To understand better the role of media systems in a particular sociocultural space, Hallin and Mancini (2011, p.3) developed three media models – "Democratic Corporatist", "Polarized Pluralist", and "Liberal". They were based on four dimensions: "(1) the structure of the media market, (2) the degree of political parallelism, (3) the level of journalistic professionalism and (4) the role of the state". Following the economic, social, and political contexts in which media are involved and the standards that are implemented in their structure, Hallin and Mancini (2011) stated that every model has dominant characteristics in specific spaces: Liberal model in Anglophone countries and Atlantic region, the Democratic Corporatist model in North and Central Europe, and the Polarized Pluralist model in Southern Europe. A special case is represented by post-communist countries, where a mix of characteristics can be found because of their alternating authoritarian and democratic practices; they are integrated into a "Hybrid" media model.

The countries present in our study are part of different media models: Sweden relates to the "Democratic corporatist" model, France and Spain to "the Polarized Pluralist" model, and Romania to the "Hybrid" model. This spread offers different perspectives on MIL and disinformation effects and diverse approaches in initiatives focused to combat it. A previous study by Nygren et al. (2022) observed that teachers differ in the support given to develop the student's critical abilities, the level of professionalisation, and the importance given to digital tools for fighting disinformation.

The last research question explored the diverse perceptions of novel instruments to combat visual disinformation in the four countries involved in the project.

RQ5. Are there any important differences across countries in how a new tool to fight visual disinformation is perceived?

4.6 Methodology

In project YouCheck!, we conducted several pilot studies to test the InVID-WeVerify plugin and the attendant toolkit (with lesson plans, tips, and serious game). InVID-WeVerify was first developed in the INVID project[2] as a tool for professional journalists, to help them debunk visual disinformation. The challenge for YouCheck! was to transfer the uses of the plugin to a different group of professionals, the teachers, and to test it among the public at large.

In a first step (Study1), we used 56 beta-testers in the four countries, to play and evaluate the plugin, in February 2020. The beta-testers were not professional technology testers; they were a variety of mostly educated adults, 41% of which were men and 54% women (5% unspecified), with the mean age of 39 years ($M = 39.49$, $SD = 12.77$), and 94% having higher education. They had various professional backgrounds, with about half of them (49%) working in education (researchers, teachers, and students), 28% working in social media (influencers, consultants, etc.), and 17% in professions related to communication (journalism, social communication), while the rest occupied miscellaneous professions (business, computer and industrial engineering, etc.). Of the total sample, 43% lived in Spain, 27% in Romania, 21% in France, and 9% in Sweden. As a procedure, the testers were invited to download and install InVID-WeVerify, test its features for a minimum of 30 minutes, and then answer a series of questions in a feedback questionnaire.

In a second step (Study 2), we conducted a qualitative analysis, by means of four focus groups (one in each country of the project) with a total of N = 34 high school teachers, in February 2020. The interviews lasted between 66 and 90 minutes. We used a convenience sample, gathered using snowballing sampling: in France, the participants to the focus groups (N = 9) were based in Toulouse and were librarians working in upper secondary school documentation centres; in Romania, they were teachers in high schools across Bucharest (N = 9), teaching disciplines such as psychology, informatics, history, Romanian literature and language, etc.; in Spain, the participants (N = 7) were teacher trainers in Madrid, specialised in critical pedagogies, information technology in education, communication, digital culture, public relations, and information science; in Sweden, they were upper secondary school teachers from Uppsala (N = 9), specialised in civics, history, geography, religious studies, and informatics. Twelve of all respondents were men, and 22 women. As a procedure, teachers were introduced to the toolkit in meetings especially designed for this purpose, and later had the opportunity to use and play with the tool, before being asked about their impressions of the experience at a later time. We purposefully used the respondents of the focus groups as teachers for the schools media interventions, so as to make sure they had at least some prior experience with the tool and understood the importance of using such a technological product in a teaching-learning setting.

The third Study (Study 3) tested MIL interventions in high schools in the four countries, in the Autumn term of 2020, with two lessons: the first one dealt with the context and stakes of disinformation; the second one introduced the pupils to the InVID-WeVerify tool. They completed a questionnaire that included the evaluation of the plugin at the end of this second lesson. Each lesson lasted two hours, taught by the teachers we interviewed in focus groups.

The purpose of the high school intervention was larger than the testing of the toolkit in a teaching–learning setting. The strategy and structure of the intervention and its main outcome is presented in detail by Nygren et al. (2021). In this chapter, we only focus on the pupils who, at the end of the intervention, completed a questionnaire, which included questions about their impressions about the toolkit designed to debunk visual disinformation. Therefore, of the total sample of 373 pupils aged 16–18 involved in this study, we report on a sub-sample of N = 233 who completed the questions about the toolkit. The sample was composed of pupils from France (27%), Romania (9%), Spain (22%), and Sweden (42%): 54% were boys, 42% girls, and 4% either non-binary or non-specified.

Measures for Studies 1 and 3

To assess the InVID-WeVerify tool, we used an adapted version of the *Scale User Experience Questionnaire (short UEQ)* (Laugwitz et al., 2008), which assessed five (of the classic six) dimensions. The scale has been extensively used before in its six dimensions in various studies evaluating different technology-related tools, platforms, etc. (e.g. Al Gothami & Saeed, 2021;

Ilmberger et al., 2011; Rauschenberger et al., 2013; Silva & Borges, 2022). The six dimensions refer to pragmatic dimensions (*perspicuity*, *efficiency*, and *dependability*), hedonic dimensions (*stimulation* and *novelty*), and a global dimension (*attractiveness*). We left out the *dependability* dimension from the scale, as it usually covers aspects that need longer usage than the one we implemented in these studies. The five remaining dimensions were measured with semantic differentiator seven-point scales. *Attractiveness* was assessed with four items (annoying–enjoyable, unlikable–pleasing, unattractive–attractive, unfriendly–friendly), which formed a reliable scale in both Study 1 (α = .862, M = 4.95, SD = 1.13) and Study 3 (α = .786, M = 4.56, SD = 1.22). For *efficiency*, we used four items (slow–fast, inefficient–efficient, impractical–practical, cluttered–organised), which formed reliable scales (α = .831, M = 5.06, and SD = 1.11 for Study 1 and α = .830, M = 5.08, and SD = 1.27 for Study 3). *Perspicuity* was assessed with three items (not understandable–understandable, difficult to learn–easy to learn, confusing–clear), reliably grouped in scales (α = .865, M = 4.46, and SD = 1.31 for Study 1 and α = .822, M = 4.62, and SD = 1.42 for Study 3). For *stimulation*, we used three other groups of adjectives (boring–exciting, inferior–valuable, demotivating–motivating), with reliable scales for the two studies (α = .830, M = 5.09, and SD = 1.12 for Study 1 and α = .733, M = 4.49, and SD = 1.32 for Study 3). *Novelty* was assessed with other three groups of adjectives (dull–creative, conventional–leading edge, conservative–innovative), grouped in reliable scales (α = .843, M = 5.18, and SD = 1.25 for Study 1 and α = .793, M = 4.84, and SD = 1.33 for Study 3).

We added one item related to projected *future use of the tool*. In Study 1, we asked participants to what extent they expected to use the toolkit in the future, on a seven-point Likert scale, from 1 "never" to 7 "very often". In Study 2, we used a similar scale, but on a five-point Likert scale. We normalised the two scales, in order to have comparable values (from 0 to 1). The average evaluation about the future use was: M = .58 and SD = .28 for Study 1; M = .63 and SD = .28 for Study 3.

4.7 Findings

4.7.1 Results for Study 1 and Study 3

Generally speaking, both beta-testers and high school pupils perceived the InVID-WeVerify plugin in a positive manner on all dimensions (see Table 4.2).

The most valued dimensions were novelty and stimulation for the beta-testers, reflecting on the hedonic aspects of the tool, and efficiency and novelty for pupils, aspects related to both the hedonic and the pragmatic dimensions of the scale. It is noteworthy, though, that all participants in the two studies evaluated the plugin above the mean of the scales used for all dimensions. Overall, beta-testers appreciated the plugin slightly better, partly due to the good impression it made on them based on the novelty and excitement of a

Table 4.2 Evaluation of INVID-WeVerify toolkit by beta-testers and pupils

		Attractiveness	*Efficiency*	*Perspicuity*	*Stimulation*	*Novelty*	*OVERALL*
Study 1 (beta-tester)	Mean	4.95	5.06	4.46	5.09	5.18	4.93
	N	56	55	55	55	54	56
	SD	1.13	1.11	1.31	1.12	1.25	1.02
Study 3 (pupils)	Mean	4.56	5.08	4.62	4.49	4.84	4.71
	N	233	232	232	232	232	233
	SD	1.23	1.27	1.42	1.32	1.33	1.09

Table 4.3 Evaluation of InVID-WeVerify for each dimension, by gender

		Study 1 (beta-testers)			*Study 3 (pupils)*		
		N	*Mean*	*SD*	*N*	*Mean*	*SD*
Attractiveness	Men	23	4.91	1.15	125	4.44	1.20
	Women	30	5.00	1.16	97	4.75	1.28
Efficiency	Men	23	4.91	0.98	125	5.06	1.30
	Women	29	5.21	1.23	96	5.09	1.25
Perspicuity	Men	23	4.30	1.29	125	4.49	1.37
	Women	29	4.61	1.29	96	4.77	1.49
Stimulation	Men	22	5.12	1.04	125	4.41	1.34
	Women	30	4.94	1.17	96	4.62	1.32
Novelty	Men	22	5.08	1.34	125	4.64	1.31
	Women	29	5.21	1.25	96	5.07	1.36
Overall	Men	23	4.85	0.94	125	4.61	1.09
	Women	30	4.97	1.12	97	4.85	1.11

new technology tool. One possible explanation could be that young people are much more used to the novelty of ICTs, and are not that easily impressed by "yet another" tool.

One collateral finding worth reporting is the gender differences in evaluating tools. Even though we could identify only one significant difference between men and women, specifically on the novelty dimension in Study 3 ($t(219) = -2.38$, $p < .05$), there is an evident difference between the two genders: women usually evaluate all dimensions of the tool better than men, in both studies (see Table 4.3).

If we look at how people in individual countries assessed the InVID-WeVerify tool, there are some interesting differences that may reflect the differences between the way media literacy programmes and interventions are implemented in the different countries (see Table 4.4).

First of all, a general overview of the global evaluation shows that beta-testers evaluated slightly better the plugin in France ($M = 5.00$, $SD = 1.03$) and Spain ($M = 5.08$, $SD = 1.11$), while the pupils evaluated it better in Romania ($M = 5.61$, $SD = .94$) and Spain ($M = 5.08$, $SD = .87$). Romania shows the most striking difference between how beta-testers evaluated the

Table 4.4 Evaluation of InVID-WeVerify for each dimension, by country

		Study 1 (beta-testers)						*Study 2 (pupils)*					
		Attrac-tiveness	*Efficiency*	*Perspicuity*	*Stimulation*	*Novelty*	*Overall*	*Attrac-tiveness*	*Efficiency*	*Perspicuity*	*Stimulation*	*Novelty*	*Overall*
France	Mean	**4.85**	**4.94**	**4.89**	**5.17**	**5.14**	**5.00**	**4.36**	**4.97**	**4.47**	**4.37**	**4.69**	**4.57**
	N	12	12	12	12	12	12	62	62	62	62	62	62
	SD	1.07	1.13	1.22	1.23	1.23	1.00	1.03	1.04	1.29	1.28	1.16	0.94
Romania	Mean	**4.73**	**4.94**	**4.17**	**4.82**	**5.04**	**4.71**	**5.82**	**5.91**	**5.62**	**4.99**	**5.71**	**5.61**
	N	15	14	14	15	14	15	21	21	21	21	21	21
	SD	1.23	1.26	0.97	1.17	1.12	1.00	1.08	0.94	1.12	1.50	1.14	0.94
Spain	Mean	**5.18**	**5.19**	**4.64**	**5.18**	**5.21**	**5.08**	**4.78**	**5.35**	**4.77**	**4.80**	**5.69**	**5.08**
	N	24	24	24	24	24	24	51	51	51	51	51	51
	SD	1.17	1.10	1.38	1.09	1.40	1.11	1.07	1.05	1.34	1.21	0.94	0.87
Sweden	Mean	**4.70**	**5.10**	**3.40**	**5.33**	**5.67**	**4.72**	**4.30**	**4.84**	**4.42**	**4.31**	**4.31**	**4.43**
	N	5	5	5	4	4	5	99	98	98	98	98	99
	SD	0.86	0.98	1.67	1.05	1.12	0.80	1.27	1.47	1.50	1.34	1.34	1.16
Total	Mean	**4.95**	**5.06**	**4.46**	**5.09**	**5.18**	**4.93**	**4.56**	**5.08**	**4.62**	**4.49**	**4.84**	**4.72**
	N	56	55	55	55	54	56	233	232	232	232	232	233
	SD	1.13	1.11	1.31	1.12	1.25	1.02	1.23	1.27	1.42	1.32	1.33	1.09

plugin and how pupils assessed it, with almost one point difference on the seven-point scale. The Spaniards were the most consistent across the two studies (see Figure 4.1). The situation in Romania is most probably due to the different school curricula than all other countries. In Romania, at the time of the implementation of the school intervention, there were no mandatory classes of media literacy in the high school curricula. This might be the reason why such lessons raised much more enthusiasm among Romanian pupils.

In France and Sweden, pupils were less enthusiastic about the plugin than the beta-testers, probably due to their being much more familiar with classes of media literacy as they have long been inserted in the curricula, as a transversal field.

Overall, the presentation of the plugin in an MIL classroom setting is the best strategy to make the tool appealing to young people only in Romania, where the entire MIL topic in a classroom is a novelty. For France and Sweden, it seems that letting people discover the instrument on their own, at their own pace and in the limits of their curiosity works better than teaching about it in classrooms. For Spain, the setting did not make a difference at all.

When asked about the use of InVID-WeVerify in the future, both beta-testers and pupils estimated that they would likely use the tool in the future (M = .58 and SD = .28 for Study 1; M = .63 and SD = .28 for Study 3). However, none of the results is situated much higher than the middle point of the scale (normalised from 0 to 1). When looking at the country differences, they are quite large (see Table 4.5). Among the beta-testers, Romanians and Swedes scored lower than the middle point of the scale on future use projections, while the French and Spaniards scored consistently higher. The trend looks different for pupils. In Romania, there was a very enthusiastic

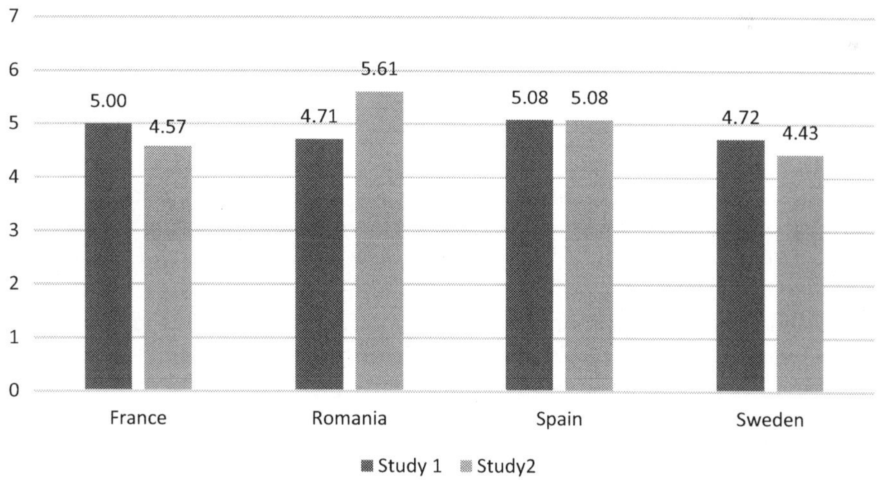

Figure 4.1 Evaluation of the InVID-WeVerify toolkit across countries (overall evaluation).

Table 4.5 Estimations about future use of InVID-WeVerify

		Study 1 (beta-testers)	*Study 3 (pupils)*
France	Mean	**0.72**	**0.51**
	N	12	61
	SD	0.22	0.28
Romania	Mean	**0.45**	**0.82**
	N	14	21
	SD	0.22	0.23
Spain	Mean	**0.62**	**0.71**
	N	23	51
	SD	0.29	0.29
Sweden	Mean	**0.42**	**0.62**
	N	4	99
	SD	0.44	0.26
Total	Mean	**0.58**	**0.63**
	N	53	232
	SD	0.28	0.28

projection for the future, pupils estimating that they would surely use the tool in the future. In Spain, there was also a high probability for the participants to use the tool in the future, whereas in Sweden and France there were mixed opinions about it (especially in France, where the mean was very close to the neutral point of the scale – $M = .51$ and $SD = .28$).

Due to the small number of cases in Study 1, even though One-Way ANOVA showed significant differences between the groups ($F(3,49) = 2.82$, $p < .05$), the post-hoc Tukey test did not yield any significant difference. In Study 3, the ANOVA test was again significant ($F(3,228) = 9.03$, $p < .01$), with significant post-hoc Tukey test differences between countries: results in France were significantly different from Romania and Spain, and results in Romania significantly differed from France and Sweden.

4.7.2 Results for Study 2

A more in-depth analysis of the way teachers received such a tool was performed using the data we collected via focus groups. In a first set of questions, teachers were asked about the various functionalities of the plugin, especially the three selected by the team as the most interesting, innovative, and robust: keyframes, forensics, and similarity analysis. We report on their views on the usefulness of the tool in various professions (including theirs) and intention to use it in the future in classrooms.

The tool was perceived in all countries as a useful artefact for professionals, but not necessarily for the general public or youth in schools. For example, in Romania the interviewees perceived the tool useful in politics ("Politics, this is clear to me" – Respondent 2, RO) or journalism, psychology, etc.

("I think media could use it, the journalists, provided they would be interested in good journalism... but also anthropologists, psychologists, teachers, statisticians" – Respondent 1, RO). In Spain, the respondents believed the plugin could be successfully used in business ("World in business strategy, where you have to consider ... contrasting a news story if it is viable or not (before making a decision)" – Respondent 7, ES). In France and Sweden, teachers discussed possible implementations of the tool in media literacy classes: "when students bring their facts from YouTube it could be helpful" (Respondent 6, SE); "not least when students themselves come from conflict areas like Syria with biassed information, then this could help us to challenge this which is part of our job" (Respondent 7, SE); "It would be necessary to have media education. Touch the fundamental values. Establish a real continuity along the curriculum" (Respondent 3, FR).

In France and Romania, participants also discussed the difficulty of using such a tool in classrooms: on the one hand, they felt the need to be trained ("We are not trained at that. I am very worried, there is no awareness among the teachers", Respondent 3, FR; "It is a matter of practice, as I told you, as any new sport" – Respondent 2, RO), and, on the other hand, the administration might reject the use of tools as part of the curriculum ("When I ask for tools, I am told that they are secondary, that there is no time", Respondent 4, FR).

When discussing intentions to use InVID-WeVerify in the future, the Spaniards and Swedes just stated they were willing to, with no further details. In France and Romania, participants were somewhat reluctant to future uses: while the French teachers thought of various ways to adapt the plugin to fit into the classrooms' setting ("There should be pedagogical scenarios with feedback on what is exploited and make them evolve accordingly" – Respondent 2, FR; "Ready-to-use sessions are simpler, in three hour long modules for instance" – Respondent 1, FR), the Romanians felt not competent enough to further teach others how to use the tool ("If I manage to learn how, I'd like to use it. To be honest, I thought of myself as being stupid for not being able to download it, at least" – Respondent 6, RO; "Of course this is the right way, the good way, it is a starting point, but to say that they will understand it and use it starting next week. [They will not use it] not necessarily as it is now, as it feels like a labyrinth to me... I don't know" – Respondent 7, RO).

Overall, teachers expressed mixed feelings about the new tool and its usefulness in media literacy classes. However, after getting used and trained about the tool, some of them adopted the idea of using the plugin in classrooms in the interventions described in Study 3.

As in the case of the quantitative studies, the qualitative one showed differences between countries: French, Spanish, and Swedish teachers were rather familiar with media literacy classes and tended to find ways to include the use of such tool in their (or their colleagues') classrooms, while the Romanian ones were rather reluctant and insecure.

4.8 Discussion

As regards the five research questions, the study yielded interesting responses to be used for further interventions aimed at fighting disinformation at large, not just visual disinformation.

Regarding RQ1, about the general perception of the new tool InVID-WeVerify, the User Experience Questionnaire proved to be a good measurement scale, as it reflects both pragmatic and hedonic dimensions structured by Laugwitz et al. (2008). The validity of the added dimension, future uses, could be added to advantage to their scale. The positive responses by young people and the larger public confirm the need to transfer such professional tools as the verification plugin to professions outside the field of journalism.

Regarding RQ2, about the pupils' perception of the new plugin, in MIL classes, the results confirm the need to embed the use of the plugin in scaffolded lesson plans. This tends to increase pupils' confidence and motivation in fighting visual disinformation. The plugin needs to be inserted in sense-making practices that are both realistic and engaging, with examples and functionalities likely to raise the pupils' curiosity. This confirms the move in project YouCheck! from providing the plugin to providing a full-fledged toolkit (with lesson plans, games, etc.). The fact that Romanian pupils were by far the most interested in the MIL intervention and performed better fits with prior research showing that in school settings that are rich in MIL interventions, pupils' exposure to new tools is less impactful than in school settings that are less rich. As novelty wanes and as alternative strategies are also available to them, pupils in MIL rich countries are reaching a kind of plateau that should alert MIL practitioners (Nygren et al., 2021).

Regarding RQ3, about the teachers' perception of the new plugin, the appreciation of its usefulness is mitigated by the reluctance to integrate it in the classroom, which confirms prior research (Hassan & Mirza, 2021). The mixed feelings about transferring a professional technical tool in the curriculum seem related to lack of training and institutional support rather than the teachers' prior experience and relation to technology at large.

Regarding RQ4, about the most efficient ways to introduce the plugin in the classrooms, the design of MIL interventions seems key, and confirms the active and agile approaches fostered by transliteracy and technocognition (Frau-Meigs, 2012; Lewandowsky et al., 2017). Setting the plugin within a series of missions and challenges can engage the pupils' interests and can stimulate their willingness to use the plugin in future cases, beyond the duration of the intervention. Also, encouraging developers to make the plugin as accessible as possible to end users (beyond journalists and fact-checkers) hints at a possibly fruitful dialogue with teachers, who often feel they are not consulted in the early stages of design and development of pedagogical tools. The results of the focus groups were shared with developers at the end of the project, and they added more tutorials and a database of fact-checked cases for ready-to-use examples as well as a chatbot, all asked for by teachers in their exchanges.

Regarding RQ5, about the cross-country comparison, the dimensions developed by Hallin and Mancini (2011) are confirmed, in their distribution across the four countries of the project. The results confirm the need to add MIL as an added dimension, as suggested by Matovic et al. (2017). This is particularly the case with the results in Romania, where external factors like the role of EU policies for MIL (including research programmes on MIL like YouCheck!) have played a role in the "hybrid" model. The increased involvement of fact-checking and journalism in MIL confirms that the more or less large presence of MIL in schools and in the training of journalists itself can enrich the media systems model. The state of MIL in each country can be used as a criterion for understanding the quality of its civic culture. The manner in which the state, through its public policies, provides a more or less favourable environment for MIL (integration in school curriculum, provision of resources and training, cooperation with other stakeholders, etc.) can be an important thermometer for measuring democratic engagement. This suggests, for further research, to take into account the mediatisation process that has become so important in education as MIL projects are incorporated in schools and out of schools (in libraries, museums, media, etc.).

4.9 Conclusion

Educating the new generation of young European citizens requires the involvement of many stakeholders: parents, teachers, journalists, key policymakers, researchers, developers, and designers. They have a responsibility to create an environment that has all the tools and knowledge students need to transform themselves into active citizens with critical and creative thinking as developed via MIL full set of competences. As MIL becomes "a social necessity" (Al Zou'bi, 2022, p. 60), MIL interventions in the classrooms, with trained teachers and technology-enhanced learning spaces, can be one of the most effective responses in the face of multimodal disinformation.

Notes

1 https://www.invid-project.eu/tools-and-services/invid-verification-plugin/; see also https://www.youverify.eu
2 https://www.invid-project.eu

References

Al Gothami, S. S., & Saeed, S. (2021). Digital transformation and usability: User acceptance of Tawakkalna application during Covid-19 in Saudi Arabia. In S. Saeed, M. P. Rodríguez Bolívar, & R. Thurasamy (Eds.), *Pandemic, lockdown, and digital transformation* (pp. 95–109). Springer.

Al Zou'bi, R. M. (2022). The impact of Media and Information Literacy on students' acquisition of the skills needed to detect fake news. *Journal of Media Literacy Education*, *14*(2), 58–71. https://doi.org/10.23860/jmle-2022-14-2-5

Alam, F., Cresci, S., Chakraborty, T., Silvestri, F., Dimitrov, D., Da San Martino, G., Shaar, S., Firooz, H., & Nakov, P. (2022). A survey on multimodal disinformation detection. In *Proceedings of the 29th International Conference on Computational Linguistics*. https://doi.org/10.48550/arXiv.2103.12541

Allam, A. H., Hussin, A. R., & Dahlan, H. M. (2013). User experience: Challenges and opportunities. *Journal of Information Systems Research and Innovation*, *4* (1), 28–36. https://seminar.utmspace.edu.my/jisri/download/F1_FinalPublished/Pub4_UserExperienceChallenges.pdf

Andersen, N. (2002). New media and new media literacy. *Thinking critically about media: Schools and families in partnership cable in the classroom*. CMC Report (pp. 30–35). https://www.medialit.org/sites/default/files/391_CIC_ML_Report.pdf

Balakrishnan, V., Ng, W. Z., Soo, M. C., Han, G. J., & Lee, C. J. (2022). Infodemic and fake news – A comprehensive overview of its global magnitude during the COVID-19 pandemic in 2021: A scoping review. *International Journal of Disaster Risk Reduction*, *78*, 103144. https://doi.org/10.1016/j.ijdrr.2022.103144

Cao, J., Qi, P., Sheng, Q., Yang, T., Guo, J., & Li, J. (2020). Disinformation, misinformation, and fake news in social media. *Lecture Notes in Social Networks*. https://doi.org/10.1007/978-3-030-42699-6

Collier, J. R., & Van Duyn, E. (2022). Fake news by any other name: Phrases for false content and effects on public perceptions of U.S. News Media. *Journal of Applied Communication Research*, *51*(4), 424–443. https://doi.org/10.1080/00909882.2022.2148487

Collins, B., Hoang, D. T., Nguyen, N. T., & Hwang, D. (2020). Trends in combating fake news on social media – A survey. *Journal of Information and Telecommunication*, *5*(2), 247–266. https://doi.org/10.1080/24751839.2020.1847379

Common Sense Media. (2022). (rep.). *The common sense census: Media use by tweens and teens, 2021*. Retrieved from https://www.commonsensemedia.org/sites/default/files/research/report/8-18-census-integrated-report-final-web_0.pdf

Cruz, M., & Morais, N. S. (2020). Fake news identification: Are future communication professionals prepared? *EDULEARN Proceedings*. https://doi.org/10.21125/edulearn.2020.1959

Daniela, L. (2019). Smart Pedagogy for technology-enhanced learning. *Didactics of Smart Pedagogy*, 3–21. https://doi.org/10.1007/978-3-030-01551-0_1

De Blasio, E., & Selva, D. (2021). Who is responsible for disinformation? European approaches to social platforms' accountability in the Post-Truth Era. *American Behavioral Scientist*, *65*(6), 825–846. https://doi.org/10.1177/0002764221989784

Egelhofer, J. L., & Lecheler, S. (2019). Fake news as a two-dimensional phenomenon: A framework and research agenda. *Annals of the International Communication Association*, *43*(2), 97–116. https://doi.org/10.1080/23808985.2019.1602782

Figueira, Á., & Oliveira, L. (2017). The current state of fake news: Challenges and opportunities. *Procedia Computer Science*, *121*, 817–825. https://doi.org/10.1016/j.procs.2017.11.106

Frau-Meigs, D. (2012). Translisteracy as the new research horizon for media and information literacy, *Medijske Studije/Media Studies*, *3*(6), 14–27.

Frau-Meigs, D. (2019). *Faut-il avoir peur des 'fake news'?* La Documentation Française.

Frau-Meigs, D., Velez, I., & Michel, J. F. (Eds.). (2017). *Public policy in media and information literacy in Europe. Cross-country comparisons*. Routledge.

Gelfert, A. (2018). Fake news: A definition. *Informal Logic*, *38*(1), 84–117. https://doi.org/10.22329/il.v38i1.5068

Giachanou, A., Zhang, G., & Rosso, P. (2020). Multimodal fake news detection with textual, visual and semantic information. In P. Sojka, I. Kopeček, K. Pala, & A.

Horák (Eds.), *Text, speech, and dialogue. TSD 2020. Lecture Notes in Computer Science, 12284*. Springer. https://doi.org/10.1007/978-3-030-58323-1_3

Goh, E., & Sigala, M. (2020). Integrating Information & Communication Technologies (ICT) into classroom instruction: Teaching tips for hospitality educators from a diffusion of innovation approach. *Journal of Teaching in Travel & Tourism*, *20*(2), 156–165. https://doi.org/10.1080/15313220.2020.1740636

Gutman-Wei, R. (2018, June 29). A web tool that lets people choose their own 'sources of truth'. *The Atlantic*. Retrieved from https://www.theatlantic.com/technology/archive/2018/06/robhat-labs-surfsafe-fake-news-images/564101/

Hallin, D. C., & Mancini, P. (2011). *Comparing media systems beyond the western world*. Cambridge University Press.

Hameleers, M., Powell, T. E., Van Der Meer, T. G. L. A., & Bos, L. (2020). A picture paints a thousand lies? The effects and mechanisms of multimodal disinformation and rebuttals disseminated via social media. *Political Communication*, *37*(2), 281–301. https://doi.org/10.1080/10584609.2019.1674979

Hangloo, S., & Arora, B. (2022). Combating multimodal fake news on social media: Methods, datasets, and future perspective. *Multimedia Systems*, *28*(6), 2391–2422. https://doi.org/10.1007/s00530-022-00966-y

Hassan, M. M., & Mirza, T. (2021). The digital literacy in teachers of the Schools of Rajouri (j&k)-India: Teachers perspective. *International Journal of Education and Management Engineering*, *11*(1), 28–40. https://doi.org/10.5815/ijeme.2021.01.04

Herrero-Diz, P., Conde-Jiménez, J., & Reyes de Cózar, S. (2020). Teens' motivations to spread fake news on WhatsApp. *Social Media + Society*, *6*(3), 205630512094287. https://doi.org/10.1177/2056305120942879

High Level Expert Group. (2018). (rep.). *Final report of the high level expert group on fake news and online disinformation*. European Commission. Retrieved from https://digital-strategy.ec.europa.eu/en/library/final-report-high-level-expert-group-fake-news-and-online-disinformation

Hobbs, R., & Jensen, A. (2009). The past, present, and future of Media Literacy Education. *Journal of Media Literacy Education*, *1*(1), 1–11. https://doi.org/10.23860/jmle-1-1-1

Ilmberger, W., Schrepp, M., & Held, T. (2011). Attractiveness of social platforms: An investigation on studiVZ. In *Proceedings IADIS International Conference Interfaces and Human Computers Interaction* (pp. 257–264).

Iosifidis, P., & Nicoli, N. (2021). *Digital democracy, social media and disinformation*. Routledge Taylor & Francis Group.

Jahankhani, H., & Kapuku-Bwabw, W. (2011). Improved awareness on fake websites and detecting techniques. In T. Jayaraveendran (Ed.), *Global security, safety and sustainability & e-democracy*. Springer.

Jindal, S., Sood, R., Singh, R., Vatsa, M., & Chakraborty, T. (2019). NewsBag: A multimodal benchmark dataset for fake news detection. *CEUR Workshop Proceedings* (vol. 2560, pp. 138–145).

Kahne, J., & Bowyer, B. (2016). Educating for democracy in a partisan age. *American Educational Research Journal*, *54*(1), 3–34. https://doi.org/10.3102/0002831216679817

Kahne, J., & Bowyer, B. (2019). Can media literacy education increase digital engagement in politics? *Learning, Media and Technology*, *44*(2), 211–224. https://doi.org/10.1080/17439884.2019.1601108

Kanozia, R., Arya, R., Singh, S., Ganghariya, G., & Narula, S. (2021). A study on fake news subject matter, presentation elements, tools of detection, and social media platforms in India. *Asian Journal for Public Opinion Research*, *9*(1), 48–82. https://doi.org/10.15206/ajpor.2021.9.1.48

Kasra, M., Shen, C., & O'Brien, J. (2016). Seeing Is Believing: How People Fail to Identify Fake Images on the Web. Available at SSRN: https://ssrn.com/abstract=3051561 or https://doi.org/10.2139/ssrn.3051561

Khan, T., Michalas, A., & Akhunzada, A. (2021). Fake news outbreak 2021: Can we stop the viral spread? *Journal of Network and Computer Applications*, *190*, 103112. https://doi.org/10.1016/j.jnca.2021.103112

Khattar, D., Goud, J. S., Gupta, M., & Varma, V. (2019). MVAE: Multimodal variational Autoencoder for fake news detection. *The World Wide Web Conference*. https://doi.org/10.1145/3308558.3313552

Kirchknopf, A., Slijepcevic, D., & Zeppelzauer, M. (2021). Multimodal detection of information disorder from social media. *2021 International Conference on Content-Based Multimedia Indexing (CBMI)*. https://doi.org/10.1109/cbmi50038.2021.9461898

Koetl, C. (2014, December 11). *YouTube data viewer*. Citizen Evidence Lab. Retrieved from https://citizenevidence.org/2014/07/01/youtube-dataviewer/

Laugwitz, B., Held, T., & Schrepp, M. (2008). Construction and evaluation of A user experience questionnaire. In Holzinger, A. (Ed.), *HCI and usability for education and work. USAB 2008. Lecture Notes in Computer Science, 5298* (pp. 63–76). Springer. https://doi.org/10.1007/978-3-540-89350-9_6

Lecheler, S., & Egelhofer, J. L. (2022). Disinformation, misinformation, and fake news. In *Knowledge resistance in high-choice information environments* (pp. 69–87). Routledge. https://doi.org/10.4324/9781003111474-4

Lewandowsky, S., Ecker, U. K., & Cook, J. (2017). Beyond misinformation: Understanding and coping with the "post-truth" era. *Journal of Applied Research in Memory and Cognition*, *6*(4), 353–369. https://doi.org/10.1016/j.jarmac.2017.07.008

Loveless, A. (2011). Technology, pedagogy and education: Reflections on the accomplishment of what teachers know, do and believe in a Digital age. *Technology, Pedagogy and Education*, *20*(3), 301–316. https://doi.org/10.1080/1475939x.2011.610931

Matovic, M., Juraitė, K., & Gutiérrez, A. (2017) The role of non-governmental actors in Media and Information Literacy: A comparative media systems perspective. In D. Frau-Meigs, I. Velez, & J. Flores Michel (Eds.), *Public policies in media and information literacy in Europe: cross-country comparisons* (pp. 159–193). Routledge.

Meel, P., & Vishwakarma, D. K. (2020). Fake news, rumor, information pollution in social media and web: A contemporary survey of state-of-the-arts, challenges and opportunities. *Expert Systems with Applications*, *153*, 112986. https://doi.org/10.1016/j.eswa.2019.112986

Mihajlov Prokopovic, A., & Vujović, M. (2021). The European approach to regulating disinformation. *Facta Universitatis, Series: Law and Politics*, *175*. https://doi.org/10.22190/fulp2003175m

Nasir, J. A., Khan, O. S., & Varlamis, I. (2021). Fake news detection: A hybrid CNN-RNN based deep learning approach. *International Journal of Information Management Data Insights*, *1*(1), 100007. https://doi.org/10.1016/j.jjimei.2020.100007

Newman, E. J., & Zhang, L. (2020). Truthiness: How non-probative photos shape belief. In *The psychology of fake news* (pp. 90–114). Routledge. https://doi.org/10.4324/9780429295379-8

Nygren, T., Frau-Meigs, D., Corbu, N., & Santoveña-Casal, S. (2022). Teachers' views on disinformation and media literacy supported by a tool designed for professional fact-checkers: Perspectives from France, Romania, Spain and Sweden. *SN Social Sciences*, 2(4). https://doi.org/10.1007/s43545-022-00340-9

Nygren, T., Guath, M., Axelsson, C.-A., & Frau-Meigs, D. (2021). Combatting visual fake news with a professional fact-checking tool in education in France, Romania, Spain and Sweden, *Information, 12* (5), 201. https://doi.org/10.3390/info12050201
Paris, B., & Donovan, J. (2019). *Deepfakes and cheapfakes. The manipulation of audio and visual evidence.* Data & Society. Retrieved from https://datasociety.net/wp-content/uploads/2019/09/DS_Deepfakes_Cheap_FakesFinal-1-1.pdf
Phippen, A., Bond, E., & Buck, E. (2021). Effective strategies for information literacy education: Combatting 'fake news' and empowering critical thinking. *Future Directions in Digital Information*, 39–53. https://doi.org/10.1016/b978-0-12-822144-0.00003-3
Qi, P., Cao, J., Yang, T., Guo, J., & Li, J. (2019). Exploiting multi-domain visual information for fake news detection. *2019 IEEE International Conference on Data Mining (ICDM)* (pp. 518–527). https://doi.org/10.48550/arXiv.1908.04472
Qian, S., Shen, C., & Zhang, J. (2022). Fighting cheapfakes: Using a digital media literacy intervention to motivate reverse search of out-of-context visual misinformation. *Journal of Computer-Mediated Communication, 28*(1). https://doi.org/10.1093/jcmc/zmac024
Rauschenberger, M., Schrepp, M., Pérez Cota, M., Olschner, S., & Thomaschewski, J. (2013). Efficient measurement of the user experience of interactive products. How to use the user experience questionnaire (UEQ). Example: Spanish language version. *International Journal of Interactive Multimedia and Artificial Intelligence, 2*(1), 39–45. https://doi.org/10.9781/ijimai.2013.215
Reddy, H., Raj, N., Gala, M., & Basava, A. (2019). Text-mining-based fake news detection using ensemble methods. *International Journal of Automation and Computing, 17*(2), 210–221. https://doi.org/10.1007/s11633-019-1216-5
Reveal. (2016). *Reveal image verification assistant.* RAND Corporation. Retrieved December 29, 2022, from https://www.rand.org/research/projects/truth-decay/fighting-disinformation/search/items/reveal-image-verification-assistant.html
RoBhat Labs. (2018). *SurfSafe.* Retrieved from https://www.getsurfsafe.com/
Saleh, A. M., Abuaddous, H. Y., Enaizan, O., & Ghabban, F. (2021). User experience assessment of a COVID-19 tracking mobile application (Aman) in Jordan. *Indonesian Journal of Electrical Engineering and Computer Science, 23*(2), 1120– 1127. https://doi.org/10.11591/ijeecs.v23.i2
Savoir*Devenir. (2022). *YouVerify! Final report.* Savoir*Devenir. Retrieved December 29, 2022, from http://savoirdevenir.net/you-verify/
Schuetz, S. W., Sykes, T. A., & Venkatesh, V. (2021). Combating covid-19 fake news on social media through fact checking: Antecedents and consequences. *European Journal of Information Systems, 30*(4), 376–388. https://doi.org/10.1080/0960085x.2021.1895682
Shang, L., Kou, Z., Zhang, Y., & Wang, D. (2021). A multimodal misinformation detector for covid-19 short videos on TikTok. *2021 IEEE International Conference on Big Data (Big Data).* https://doi.org/10.1109/bigdata52589.2021.9671928
Shu, K., Bhattacharjee, A., Alatawi, F., Nazer, T. H., Ding, K., Karami, M., & Liu, H. (2020a). Combating disinformation in a social media age. *WIREs Data Mining and Knowledge Discovery, 10*(6), 1–23. https://doi.org/10.1002/widm.1385
Shu, K., Wang, S., Lee, D., & Liu, H. (Eds.). (2020b). Mining disinformation and fake news: Concepts, methods, and recent advancements. In *Disinformation, misinformation, and fake news in social media. Lecture Notes in Social Networks* (pp. 1–19). Springer. https://doi.org/10.1007/978-3-030-42699-6_1
Silva, A., & Borges, L. C. (2022). Evaluating user experience of the Portuguese district archives websites. *Qualitative and Quantitative Methods in Libraries, 11*(3), 587–601.

Tandoc, E. C., Lim, Z. W., & Ling, R. (2017). Defining "fake news." *Digital Journalism*, *6*(2), 137–153. https://doi.org/10.1080/21670811.2017.1360143

Tandoc Jr., E. C., Thomas, R. J., & Bishop, L. (2021). What is (fake) news? Analyzing news values (and more) in fake stories. *Media and Communication*, *9*(1), 110–119. https://doi.org/10.17645/mac.v9i1.3331

Thomson, T. J., Angus, D., Dootson, P., Hurcombe, E., & Smith, A. (2020). Visual mis/disinformation in journalism and public communications: Current verification practices, challenges, and future opportunities. *Journalism Practice*, *16*(5), 938–962. https://doi.org/10.1080/17512786.2020.1832139

TinEye Reverse Image Search. (2008). *TinEye reverse image search*. Retrieved from https://tineye.com/

Tong, C., Gill, H., Li, J., Valenzuela, S., & Rojas, H. (2020). "Fake news is anything they say!" — Conceptualization and weaponization of fake news among the American public. *Mass Communication and Society*, *23*(5), 755–778. https://doi.org/10.1080/15205436.2020.1789661

Tuan, N. M., & Quang Nhat Minh, P. (2021). Multimodal fusion with Bert and attention mechanism for fake news detection. *2021 RIVF International Conference on Computing and Communication Technologies (RIVF)*. https://doi.org/10.1109/rivf51545.2021.9642125

van Vaerenbergh, S. (2009). *STEVEN2358/reveye: Reverse image search extension for Google chrome*. GitHub. Retrieved December 29, 2022, from https://github.com/steven2358/reveye

Veeriah, J. (2021). Young adults' ability to detect fake news and their new media literacy level in the wake of the covid-19 pandemic. *Journal of Content, Community & Communication*, *13*. https://doi.org/2456-9011

Vogels, E., Gelles-Watnick, R., & Massarat, N. (2022, December 15). *Teens, social media and technology 2022*. Pew Research Center: Internet, Science & Tech. Retrieved December 29, 2022, from https://www.pewresearch.org/internet/2022/08/10/teens-social-media-and-technology-2022/

Vosoughi, S., Roy, D., & Aral, S. (2018). The spread of true and false news online. *Science*, *359*(6380), 1146–1151. https://doi.org/10.1126/science.aap9559

Wardle, C., & Derakhshan, H. (2017). (rep.). *Information disorder: Toward an interdisciplinary framework for research and policy making*. Council of Europe. Retrieved from https://tverezo.info/wp-content/uploads/2017/11/PREMS-162317-GBR-2018-Report-desinformation-A4-BAT.pdf

Weikmann, T., & Lecheler, S. (2022). Visual disinformation in a digital age: A literature synthesis and research agenda. *New Media & Society*. https://doi.org/10.1177/14614448221141648

Xue, J., Wang, Y., Tian, Y., Li, Y., Shi, L., & Wei, L. (2021). Detecting fake news by exploring the consistency of multimodal data. *Information Processing & Management*, *58*(5), 102610. https://doi.org/10.1016/j.ipm.2021.102610

Yosuf, B., Qureshi, M. A., Spillane, B., Munnelly, G., Carroll, O., Runswick, M., Park, K., Culloty, E., Conlan, O., & Suiter, J. (2021). PROVENANCE: An Intermediary-Free Solution for Digital Content Verification. *Fourth Workshop on Knowledge-Driven Analytics and Systems Impacting Human Quality of Life (KDAH-CIKM-2021)*, arXiv:2111.08791. https://doi.org/10.48550/arXiv.2111.08791

Zhang, X., & Ghorbani, A. A. (2020). An overview of online fake news: Characterization, detection, and discussion. *Information Processing Management*, *57*(2), 102025. https://doi.org/10.1016/j.ipm.2019.03.004

5 Scaling up the fight against disinformation

The MOOC "Disinformation Step by Step" in project YouVerify!

Divina Frau-Meigs, Flavia Durach, Roberto Feltrero, Sophia Hamadi, and Pascale Garreau

5.1 Introduction

The digital environment provides new ways not only for producing and customising information but also for manipulating and disrupting information flows. Terms such as "information disorders" or "fake news" have come to represent both the growing supply of disinformation across media and the receding trust in democratic institutions (science, journalism, and politics). Disinformation, defined as "all forms of false, inaccurate, or misleading information designed, presented and promoted to intentionally cause public harm or for profit" (European Commission High Level Expert Group on Fake News and Online Disinformation, 2018, p. 13), has disrupted elections and referenda, increased the spread of conspiracy theories, and cast doubts on scientific research (as exemplified by the infodemic concerning Covid-19).

Several fact-checking initiatives and tools have emerged as a response from the journalistic profession. Such tools are mostly geared to journalists, not to teachers, students, or citizens at large. Research reveals additional gaps: the focus is mostly on text-based "fake news", much less on image-based "fake news", though these are among the most prominent in social media used by young people and the public at large. Besides, building resilience implies navigating online information in new ways, not unlike professional fact-checkers do (McGrew et al., 2018). For this, people need a mix of content knowledge and digital skills as underscored by theories of media and information literacy (MIL) such as transliteracy (Frau-Meigs, 2012; Nygren et al., 2021). Education remains key in debunking automated disinformation, especially visual fakes (Neekhara et al., 2020).

The research results of pilot project YouCheck! pointed to a certain number of lessons upon which the strategy for full-scale project YouVerify! capitalised. The feedback provided by teachers pointed at several felt needs: they wanted a course in which to embed the InVID-WeVerify plugin, to avoid a strictly tool-oriented approach; they needed a database of known debunks to use when applying the plugin, so as to make it more user-friendly in a

DOI: 10.4324/9781003387404-8

teaching context; they wished for a chat space to express their needs and queries directly to the plugin developers; and they felt there was a gap between the official language and policies and what they are expected to do concretely in the classrooms, in relation to the implementation of MIL projects (Nygren et al., 2022; Osuna-Acedo, 2020).

These results were aligned with other professionals' experiences in the field regarding the difficulties of designing efficient MIL interventions (McGrew et al., 2017; McGrew et al., 2018). Further, research shows the lack of digital visual literacy and need for innovative approaches to create resilience among users (Breakstone et al., 2021; Lewandowsky et al., 2017). Hence, the necessity of expanding from these results and providing MIL strategies and tools for the massive training of teachers and educators, with a strong component of visual literacy. To amplify MIL interventions and disseminate them further and across a more heterogeneous public, a Massive Open Online Course (MOOC), with its embedded modules featuring serious games, interactive workshops, and agile toolkits, was considered a means that can scale up the resilience against disinformation.

5.2 The scaling-up appeal of MOOCs for MIL

5.2.1 MOOCs as amplifiers and replicating devices

MOOCs are evolving and have been at the forefront of e-learning (Marta-Lazo et al., 2018; Osuna-Acedo et al., 2018). They present the advantage of structuring knowledge based on active pedagogies, mostly learning by doing. They also are good replicating devices, especially if they encourage projects that involve many stakeholders. They can empower participants by upskilling them for competences that they cannot acquire at university, such as critical digital literacy and verification and refutation strategies.

MOOCs present the possibility of acting as a means of training and dissemination because they offer the members of their virtual community a wide range of proposals for interaction and communication, valuing their applications in different ways according to the activities, resources, media, methodology, evaluation processes (Camarero Cano & Cantillo Valero, 2016), and interactivity. Those possibilities go beyond a traditional course structure to become a new model called social MOOC (sMOOC), where interactions, intercreativity, and communication are the main goals in the learning process (Gil-Quintana & Osuna-Acedo, 2020).

In the sMOOC model, teachers become mediators and facilitators to engage students to the collective learning experience (Marta-Lazo et al., 2018; Osuna-Acedo et al., 2018). A bidirectional, horizontal communication is very fruitful to empower participants towards the socio-constructivist learning methodology. The teaching methodology is also oriented towards collaborative learning, using interactive tools such as Padlet to allow participants to share knowledge and resources and to facilitate adaptive learning.

Like many online learning environments though, the risk of attrition is high: 90% of enrollees never finish the MOOC (Aldowah et al., 2020; Eriksson et al., 2017). This dropout rate produces the "funnel of participation" effect (Clow, 2013), characterised by a steep drop-off in activity from the beginning to the end of the MOOC session. Participants are likely to abandon the course if left to their own devices and if not provided with engaging pedagogical tools, unless they find what they were looking for while browsing the contents (Osuna-Acedo et al., 2017). Participants' engagement is another key feature of the sMOOC model (Martínez Pérez, 2016). Participants should play a central role in the learning process, assuming a co-responsible approach to their own learning. In the case of MIL, allowing participants to create collaboratively their own final projects on disinformation topics was one of the options chosen to foster adaptive learning and empowerment, allowing learners to become teachers on MIL.

To maintain the participants' engagement, activities of various kinds need to be provided. This calls for gamification, which can take the shape of serious games (such as "YouCheck! Detectives", from previous pilot project YouCheck!), interactive quizzes (to verify competences), online workshops with facilitators and mentors, etc. Serious Games are part of game-based learning that is raising increased interest in e-learning strategies (Costa et al., 2017; Frau-Meigs & Bossu, 2019; Sánchez & Olivares, 2011). Games develop recognised skills and competences to improve learners' motivation and engagement (Osuna-Acedo, 2020; Costa et al., 2016) (see Chapter 8 for results on serious games).

This leads to RQ1: *Can the MOOC experience deliver learning gains about MIL and disinformation and how?*

5.2.2 Fighting disinformation as a democratic emergency

Online disinformation has negative effects for democratic societies, such as growing distrust, polarisation, confusion regarding essential topics, disagreement over the shared meaning of basic notions, and election disruption (Colomina et al., 2021). Disinformation affects the organic formation of opinion and the decision-making process, thus damaging two key elements of good quality democracy.

Building resilience to online disinformation through education has been put at the forefront of all response strategies:

> Strengthening societal resilience is the only truly future-proof way to counter disinformation while maintaining fundamental rights, including through fact-checking, media- and information literacy for young and old, media pluralism and the contribution of academic institutes as independent agents well positioned to foster balanced multi-dimensional and sustainable approaches.
>
> (De Cock Buning et al., 2019, p. 11)

Low education is considered as one of the structural factors that makes societies less resilient to online disinformation (Humprecht et al., 2020). Educational interventions can help overcome challenges such as limitations of automated fact-checking or the difficulty for platform companies and fact-checkers struggling to act as fast as disinformation spreads (Dobrescu et al., 2022).

Initiatives to fight disinformation mostly tend to sensitise users and develop their knowledge about its mechanisms. Other initiatives focus on verification, with a heavy emphasis on verification, often led by fact-checkers. Much less is done on refutation, beyond published fact-checks by journalists, that do not necessarily meet the targeted audience of plot theorists, denialists, etc. (Frau-Meigs, 2019). A comprehensive and holistic MIL approach should hold the whole disinformation chain, from its mechanisms to its verification and refutation, as the last phase illustrates participants' empowerment and citizens' resilience.

This leads to RQ2: *Can MIL strategies support the fight against disinformation?*

5.2.3 Media and information literacy as a complex strategy to fight disinformation

Within the education needs revealed by research, MIL has a special place as it purports to develop critical thinking as regards mass and social media, while upholding freedom of expression values. MIL has moved from a traditional view of the press and the information factory to a more complex and holistic approach, due to information disorders especially among social media, pushed by data and algorithms. Consequently, MIL has been incorporating some smart tools in order to train students and adults to spot "fake news" and apply verification strategies. This is the case with such a tool as the InVID-WeVerify plugin, which has stimulated digital visual literacy and shown that there was a proven MIL efficacy in class interventions (Nygren et al., 2022).

But MIL cannot be improvised. The need to be trained is the recurring wish of teachers, who complain that the school curriculum leaves little space for project-based initiatives. Learning to scaffold MIL competences and values is key to the success of MIL interventions. So is the insertion of MIL projects in sense-making practices, like the fight against disinformation and for the value of quality information and sources. Consequently, empowering teachers in MIL strategies for fostering students' confidence in their critical analysis of content, fake or not, requires the sharing of a repertoire of strategies for facilitation, gamification, content production, etc.

This leads to RQ3: *Can MIL engage heterogeneous MOOC participants in the fight against disinformation effectively?*

5.3 Methodology

5.3.1 A qualitative-quantitative approach

Considering the complexity of the research questions and their multiple layers, we used a combination of qualitative and quantitative methods. The quantitative method took the shape of a satisfaction questionnaire, optional, for participants to fill in at the end of the MOOC. The qualitative method was embedded in the questionnaire, in the shape of two open-ended questions that made it possible to conduct a qualitative thematic analysis. According to Creswell (2018), "research methodology continues to evolve and develop, and mixed methods is another step forward, utilising the strengths of both qualitative and quantitative research" (pp. 41–42).

The research design strategy paid attention to timing, weighting, mixing, and theorising (Bryman, 1988; Creswell, 2018). The data set of the questionnaires were established with two iterations, each separated by three months, leading to two data sets. Having the open-ended questions created a counterbalance to the closed questions of the questionnaire and encouraged more inductive responses, suggesting patterns that were not oriented by prior expectations of the researchers. The mixing of verbatims and percentages provided an overall picture that could show the intrinsic value to all the segments of the research questions and their interpretation, as it identified measurable items and separate variables calibrated with the research questions, while remaining empirical and exploratory by nature. In terms of theorising, the approach was experimental and exploratory, as in qualitative research, partly because the purpose was to understand the MIL experience of participants (and indirectly, the funnel of participation phenomenon). In the choice of variables used for the questionnaires, the emphasis was on the sense-making that people construct of MIL and disinformation. In the open questions, the participants were encouraged to reflect on their own experiences, share their stories and practices, and define solutions for improvement and for action. This choice also had implications about the MOOC design per se.

5.3.2 MOOC design

"Disinformation Step by Step" was pedagogically designed within a sMOOC model. This model is intended to stimulate the culture of participation, triggering new forms of co-creation and collective co-authorship among students (Frau-Meigs et al., 2021; Gil-Quintana & Osuna-Acedo, 2020). The sMOOCs model encourages socio-constructivist learning by means of keeping strong social connections between participants. In this regard, the European MOOC platform Eco-Learning was used because it incorporated tools for that purpose: forums, microblogging, and links to be used on social networks. In fact, the platform integrated all the communication tools through the hashtag #Disinformation, making social interactions a must for the teaching methodology.

Three dimensions are key to sMOOC participatory design: resources; design and evaluation/monitoring. The facilitation and moderation of the MOOC were considered important (Frau-Meigs & Bossu, 2019), and a facilitation team was active during the first month of each MOOC iteration: 12 teachers distributed across the three languages of the MOOC where deployed, to keep group interactions and knowledge sharing processes. The target audience of participants was large and heterogeneous: any person interested in fighting disinformation was accepted, but teachers, facilitators, librarians, and journalists were the most targeted public.

The course design stated the following learning goals: understanding MIL, developing critical thinking in relation to MIL, mastering disinformation mechanisms, elaborating strategies for verification, fostering refutation, and setting up an MIL project. The course was organised around six modules, each adjusted to the six learning goals: critical thinking, MIL, disinformation mechanisms, verification strategies, refutation solutions, and MIL projects. This resulted in 8 published modules (introduction and assessment being added to core content modules); 77 published nuggets, 5 tasks to which were added 3 facilitation tasks for engaging participants in collaborative co-construction: a database of "fake news", a database of MIL projects and a FAQ "what if …?" to deal with thorny issues in MIL and disinformation.

The MOOC applied an MIL methodology, with special emphasis on digital visual competences and critical thinking competences. The project defined competences as knowledge, skills, attitudes, and values, along the Digital Citizenship Education framework developed by Council of Europe (Frau-Meigs et al., 2017). It described these main competences for MIL in the field of disinformation in a set of items measuring (1) knowledge acquisition on disinformation/verification/refutation (recognising actors, motivations, consequences, responses); (2) skills (using tools, navigating websites, comparing search engines, discriminating across social media, devising counter-narratives); (3) attitudes (debunking "fakes", building resilience against disinformation, etc.); (4) values (freedom of expression and opinion, dignity, respect for science and facts, participation).

At the end of each MOOC iteration, a satisfaction questionnaire was offered, organised under three main dimensions of relevance for our research questions. The first section evaluated whether the course could deliver its educational objectives, in terms of initial expectations versus learning goals achieved. The second section focused on learner experience: organisation, time management issues, such as the length of the training, strategy used for learning, personal time management strategies, and facilitation. The third section measured satisfaction with the topics of the course: critical thinking, MIL, disinformation, verification, refutation, and project creation. A final section was dedicated to the overall assessment of the course: positive elements, difficulties, suggestions for improvement, and overall evaluation of the training. Two open-ended questions to collect opinions were inserted as well: the first one dealt with the felt effects of disinformation and the second one with the solutions for countering disinformation. Participant information (gender, occupation, and age) was also collected. Full results of the satisfaction questionnaires for the two iterations of the MOOC can be retrieved on the YouVerify! Website.[1]

5.3.3 Corpus

The corpus was collected over two iterations over two months each (15 November–15 January 2022 and 15 February–15 April 2022) (see Figure 5.1). The first session (ITE1) provided all six modules without hierarchy. The second session (ITE2) organised the modules according to two paths: Path 1, "Disinformation"; Path 2, "MIL". In both cases, the participants were invited to fill in the participation questionnaire.

Most of the participants reflected the three countries of the main partners: France, Spain, and Romania (a great part of the English sample). But there were also some participants from French-Speaking countries and Latin America, showing the networking options opened by linguistic and cultural networks.

For the first iteration, a total number of 270 responses were collected across the three languages. The gender distribution shows more women in the Spanish (54%) and English (58%) samples than the French one (30%). The age range is 28–38 across the three countries. The occupation distribution

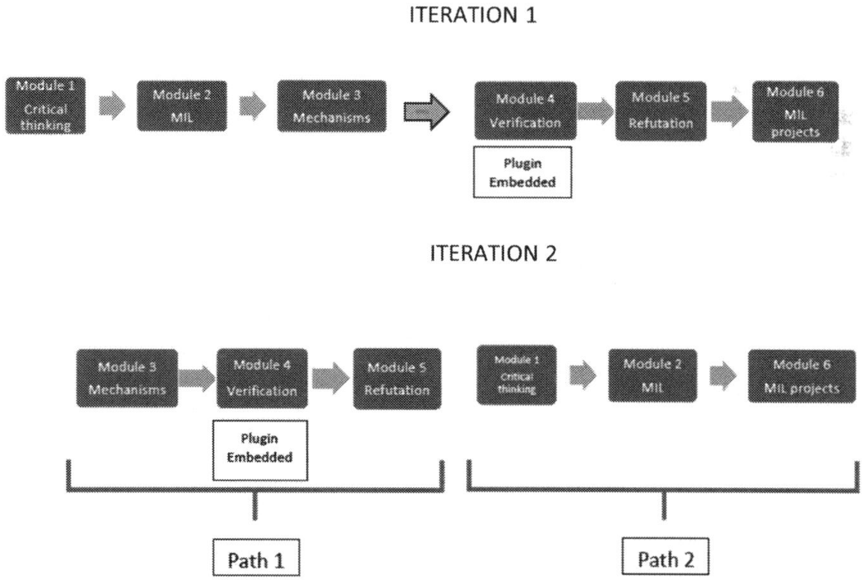

Figure 5.1 The structure of the MOOC (first and second iterations).

shows a majority of students in English and Spanish samples, followed by teachers in all samples and then other kinds of educators (librarians, social workers, etc.). Other occupations showed journalists and fact-checkers.

For the second iteration, a total number of 63 responses were collected. The gender distribution showed more women in the Spanish (81%) and English (70%) samples than the French one (40%). The age range is 29–42 across the three countries. The occupation distribution shows more students in all samples, especially the French, followed by teachers in all samples.

5.4 Results

5.4.1 General results

For the first iteration: 1,758 registered participants, with 1,049 actual participants active in the course, tantamount to 60% attendance rate, illustrating the funnel of participation effect, as numbers decreased from beginning to end, yet much less than for MOOC average (15% or less). Questionnaire responses totalled 270, which is about one-third (26%) of actual participation ratings. The general evaluation of the MOOC showed very high levels of satisfaction ("excellent" and "very good)", across the samples (89% for French, 75% for English, and 65% for Spanish).

For the second iteration: 637 registered participants, with 321 actual participants active in the course, tantamount to 50% attendance rate. Questionnaire responses totalled 63, which is about one-fifth (21%) of actual participation ratings. While they illustrate the funnel of participation effect, these numbers show a high level of engagement of participants, compared to the average in MOOCs (15% and less). The general evaluation of the MOOC showed even higher levels of satisfaction across the samples (93% for French, 71% for English, and 88% for Spanish).

Generally speaking, participants were very satisfied with all aspects of the MOOC in both ITE1 and ITE2. But ITE2 showed a higher satisfaction rate, pointing at the preference for the two clearly marked paths, one for training about disinformation and one for MIL projects.

5.4.2 On the MOOC experience (organisation; time management; facilitation, goal achievement, continuation)

The questionnaire included several items that were designed to test the MOOC experience, in terms of organisation of the modules, facilitation, and time management. Three questions addressed the perceived success for the participants, asking about goal achievement, temptation to quit course and desire to continue with more MOOC experience.

For the first iteration, most participants followed the proposed MOOC organisation because 62% were "following the units in order day by day", as was pedagogically designed. There is a big distance regarding the 16% that decided "doing everything at once", which is, usually, the more popular option when taking a MOOC course. This was a great methodological result since this day-by-day work was feeding social tools adequately. This result is also supported regarding time management. Of the total participants, 72% rated their own time management as "satisfied" or "very satisfied". Finally, the satisfaction with facilitation tasks was very high in the case of Spanish-speaking participants (almost 90% of satisfaction with facilitators), and it was good in the case of French-speaking and English-speaking students (more than 60% "satisfied" or "very satisfied"). Finally, the MOOC experience was also evaluated in terms of "dropping out intention". In this case, results are very good for Spanish-speaking and English-speaking students, just an average of 30% dropping intention, which is an excellent result for a non-formal open course. In the case of French-speaking students, dropping intention almost reached the 50%, as usual in this kind of course.

For the second iteration, MOOC organisation was successful too. In this case, 55% of participants were "following the units in order day by day", as was pedagogically designed, and 20% decided "doing everything at once", which is, usually, the more popular option when taking a MOOC course. Of the total participants, 67% rated their own time management as "satisfied" or "very satisfied", which goes in the same direction as iteration 1 for justifying methodological design. Finally, it is worth pointing out that participants' satisfaction with facilitation tasks was very high in the case of the second iteration. Across all samples, participants expressed over 90% of satisfaction with facilitation. Remarkably, in the case of English-speaking students, 76% were "very satisfied", which improved by far the 30% of the first iteration. About one-third of the English, almost half of the Spanish, and about half of the French-speaking people thought about dropping the course but finished it in the end. Results are even better for Spanish-speaking students since just 10% were thinking of dropping out, showing a very good satisfaction with the MOOC organisation and contents. In the case of French-speaking students, dropping intention almost reached the 50%, as usual in this kind of course.

5.4.3 On the learning experience about disinformation (mechanisms, verification, and refutation)

The questionnaire included several items that were designed to test the experience of the participants in their learning about the disinformation process: mechanisms, verification strategies, and refutation strategies. It also had an open-ended question about the felt effects of disinformation.

For the first iteration, concerning the first topic, disinformation mechanisms, the large majority of respondents had a positive opinion ("very interesting" and "interesting"), up to 97% across all samples. The French (63.6%) and English (62.8%) showed the most positive evaluations in this regard, while in the Spanish sample 43.9% believed that the topic was "very interesting". The respondents expressed positive evaluations of the second topic (verification strategies), but with greater differences between languages, up to 97% average all combined. As in the case of the previous topic, the French (59.1%) and the English (46.8%) scored higher than the Spanish (37.9%). The third topic about refutation strategies also received largely positive evaluations (95.8% for the English sample, 95.5% for the French sample, and 95.4% for the Spanish sample). The most positive evaluations were recorded in the case of the French sample (52.3% finding the topic "very interesting"), followed by the English (44.7%) and the Spanish (39.4%).

Overall, participants in all languages had a positive opinion of the topics about disinformation, with the French sample showing a greater inclination to find all the three topics to be of great interest. The results indicate a hierarchy of the most appreciated modules. For the French and English samples, the most interesting was "disinformation", followed by "verification", and "refutation". The preference of the Spanish sample goes to "disinformation", followed by "refutation", and, lastly, "verification".

For the second iteration, concerning the first topic, disinformation mechanisms, there were no negative evaluations: all answers ranged from "interesting" to "very interesting". The English sample showed the most positive evaluations in this regard, with 76.5% deeming the subject "very interesting", followed by the French sample (70%), and the Spanish sample (56.3%). The second topic, verification strategies, received highly positive evaluations as well. There were no negative evaluations; respondents found the topic to be "interesting" or "very interesting", and "moderately interesting" (in the French sample only 3.3%). In the English sample, 82.4% of respondents found the topic "very interesting". while 60% of the French sample and 56.3% of the Spanish sample shared the same view. The third topic, refutation strategies, received no negative evaluations from the respondents, although 3.3% of the French sample and 17.6% of the English sample found it only "moderately interesting". The most positive evaluations came from the French sample, with 56.7% or respondents finding the topic "very interesting", followed by the English one (52.9%), and the Spanish one (43.8%).

Overall, participants in all languages had a positive opinion of the topics about disinformation, with the English sample generally showing a greater inclination to find the topics to be of great interest. The results indicate a hierarchy of the most appreciated modules. For the French sample, the most interesting module was "Disinformation", followed by "Verification" and "Refutation". For the English sample, the most appreciated topic was "Verification", followed by "Disinformation" and "Refutation". In the case of the Spanish sample, "Disinformation" and "Verification" were equally interesting, followed by "Refutation".

5.4.4 On the felt effects of disinformation (open-ended responses)

In both iterations, the open-ended responses showed that participants were keenly aware of the negative effects of disinformation. They made comments about its impact at collective and individual levels. Disinformation was viewed as a multifaceted process that cannot be contained in a singular definition or a specific list of characteristics and effects. It can have a tremendous impact on how individuals make decisions, think, feel about themselves and the world around them, and consume information. Negative effects of fake news can affect the masses (manipulation, conflicts, violence, extremism, and social division), the emotional state of the citizens (panic, low self-esteem, depression, and apathy), cognitive processes (confusion, believing false information, and the impossibility of dialogue), democracy (general distrust in public actors and institutions), and the function of public key actors and mass media (censorship).

Some differences were found between our participants' responses, a part of them mentioning additional effects. The Spanish-speaking participants noticed that false information could create digital breaches and put the personal information of people at risk. They were also concerned with the vilification of experts as disinformation can lower the credibility of trustworthy sources: "increased b*llshit, discrediting professionals and amplifying controversial information" (R90, Spanish). The English-speaking respondents (most of them emanating from the Romanian partner) noted that technological and new digital tools such as the use of bots could accelerate the "virality of distribution" (R68, English) and amplify the fake news spiral. The French-speaking participants noted distrust in science and low self-esteem as two examples that affect how people view the credible academic process of research and how individuals that are reading, believing, and sharing fake news are feeling about themselves.

5.4.4.1 Iteration 1 (selection of verbatims)

5.4.4.1.1 AT COLLECTIVE LEVEL

Fake news produces a "systematic distrust of individuals with information and the manipulation of people for political purposes or the violence they may generate" (R12, French). False information "can lead to bad decisions, inappropriate behaviour, loss of control" (R20, French); "it can change people's behaviour, destroy the social trust in institutions and media" (R17, English/Romanian). False information incites informational disorientation:

> you do not know if it is the government, the citizens themselves, or the experts who are misinforming you because there is a severe problem with the ideologies that tend to misinform more and more on current issues and this happens with the government itself, with the citizens and even with the television. That is why there is less and less accountability, especially for journalists, and I think the most problematic is the fear that derives from it.
>
> (R27, Spanish)

Disinformation creates democratic erosion of public institutions:

> it raises questions related to where the liberty of expression stops and if it is necessary to impose censorship. These are facts that can lead to democratic erosion and the establishment of authoritarian regimes. Disinformation can aggravate the conflicts because. It diminishes trust in state institutions, leads to social conflicts, and becomes a risk to state security.
>
> (R41, English/Romanian)

The political sphere can be affected by "compromising the functioning of political elections and threatening democracy" (R30, Spanish), and by "the promotion of poorly developed discourses, which may benefit the political and economic interests of certain groups in favour of inequality" (R74, Spanish).

Social segregation can be the natural result if disinformation polarises the individuals by their values and opinions. Echo chambers are coming into reality from virtual space, with users that foster the same intention to keep closer to the people that are enforcing their beliefs and biases. "Us vs them" is a common trope in fake news that can create social problems, as our English-speaking participants stated. Segregation can provoke "denigration of an individual or a group, manipulation of a large part of the population so that it has a premeditated reaction by the perpetrators of misinformation, violence against an individual or a group, hate speech, stigma" (R5, French).

5.4.4.1.2 AT INDIVIDUAL LEVEL

Disinformation can inhibit how people perceive themselves, lowering their self-esteem. The disbelief fuelled by fake news affects not only the relation to public actors but also the self-awareness of individuals: "I see more and more disoriented and confused people…and they suffer" (R54, English/Romanian). Loopholes in the search for truth are real opportunities to keep people disconnected from reality: "Many people prefer to remain uninformed, don't want to corroborate the information they get, just to continue with their ideas" (R119, Spanish).

Emotions could lead to exaggerated responses and an impossibility of communication. Conflicts determined by negative feelings created by fake news can harm vulnerable groups: "disinformation is being used as a tool to harm specific communities by spreading lies, hate and fear within our societies" (R50, English/Romanian).

The ongoing spiral of disinformation has a lasting impact on the physical and mental health of citizens:

> fake news destabilizes the mental and physical health (if we are talking about disinformation that may lead a person to make a choice that will be bad for her health). When we are talking about the integrity of the human (spirit, body, mind), we have in our scope one of the most important things.
>
> (R91, English/Romanian)

"It can have an emotional impact on people" (R71, Spanish), with "alarm and risk, conditioning the way we think and act" (R12, Spanish). Powerful emotions, like panic, are prone to escalate in social tensions: "it can affect people on a larger scale and create panic or disorganization in society" (R32, English/Romanian).

The generalised intensification of violence and conflicts can lead to extremism, a state of mind where people are divided and unable to accept groups that are different from them, discriminating: "disinformation provokes extremist thinking in people. I notice that society is not informed, and their thoughts are not critical because they do not listen to the other party. It's hard for them to talk and listen" (R80, Spanish).

5.4.4.2 Iteration 2 (selection of verbatims)

5.4.4.2.1 AT COLLECTIVE LEVEL

With little analytical skills, people prone to believe fake news can become unable to tell the reality from the story or plot theory: "it can manipulate the opinions and create difficulties in knowing what is true from what is false" (R43, French). Manipulation can also create opinions in the individuals' minds that could later influence society: "it can confuse the public through false messages that can guide and transform the public opinion" (R49, Spanish).

Negative impact on society is illustrated through "loss of rights" (R10, English/Romanian), and, generally, a destabilisation of the social climate through instigation, violence, confusion, and inability to communicate with others. In addition, a series of unfortunate events is attached to the spiral of disinformation: "In case of disinformation, everyone receives false information; everyone is exposed to all risks including harassment, cybercrime, the presence of segregation in society" (R31, French). The fake news phenomenon not only manipulates citizens' opinions, but it can also deceive them, making them concerned about the credibility of the message, the reliability of the source, and, in the worst case, not even being able to realise that you are not encountering false information. Deception can lead to "quarrels between citizens, communicating false information that creates misunderstanding and mentally imprisons frightened people" (R21, French).

5.4.4.2.2 AT INDIVIDUAL LEVEL

Manipulation can "impact on both mental and physical health" (R14, English). Another negative influence of disinformation is violence, intolerance, hatred, and aggressive behaviour based on the worldviews promoted by fake news: "I think it's terrifying how disinformation can bring out the worst in people. It can lead to horrible things like murder and other types of crime" (R15, English/Romanian).

The respondents stressed the consequences of the lack of critical thinking because disinformation "directs our thoughts, without letting the critical spirit thrive" (R47, Spanish). Confusion was a subtle negative effect of disinformation because of its vague impact on our cognitive processes and decision-making systems. "The rise of digitalization and the amount of information we encounter daily, without thinking about how to filter it" (R6, English) can create an overabundance of data that individuals cannot comprehend and then integrate into coherent mental structures, being open to further manipulation and deception.

Social isolation leads to tension between individuals and, subsequently, in the society. Not only can the tension erupt in conflicts and violence, but it can also create real "psychosis of the populations" (R33, French) "due to mismanagement of the information" (R42, French). "Disinformation is a great danger to peace and social stability for a nation and also for humanity" (R41, French).

5.4.5 On MIL (critical thinking competence, MIL holistic approach, project building)

The questionnaire included several items that were designed to test the experience of the participants in their appreciation of MIL as a field and a competence, and the possibility of developing projects. It also incorporated an open-ended question on solutions to fight disinformation, to see if participants could put MIL in perspective.

For the first iteration, concerning critical thinking as a main MIL competence, the large majority of respondents had a high positive opinion ("interesting" and "very interesting"). The French respondents (95.4%) were the most satisfied, followed by the Spanish (88.7%) and the English (87.3%). Concerning MIL per se, the levels of satisfaction were also very high, with 95.4% for French sample, 87.9% for Spanish sample, and 84% for English sample. As for MIL projects, the results were more mitigated. The French respondents expressed 77.3% interest but 22.7% moderate interest ("moderately interesting" and "not interesting"). The Spanish sample showed 67.4% interest, but also 31.8% moderate interest. The English sample expressed 69.2% interest contrasted with 28.7% moderate to low interest.

For the second iteration, concerning critical thinking as a main MIL competence, all respondents expressed a very high positive opinion ("interesting" and "very interesting"). The Spanish and English respondents (100%) were the most satisfied, followed by the French (96.7%). Concerning MIL per se, the levels of satisfaction were also very high, with 80% of the French sample and 70% of the English sample expressing "very high interest", while the Spanish sample expressed 31.3% very high interest (and 68.8% interest). As for MIL projects, the results were more mitigated. The Spanish respondents expressed 100% interest, while the French sample showed 90% interest (and 10% moderate to low interest) and the English sample 70.5% interest contrasted with 29.4% moderate to low interest.

Overall, the respondents expressed a real interest in MIL as a field and a competence. The lesser interest in the "project" part of the respondents may be due to their being mostly students and teachers: students are not yet in a position to conduct full-fledged projects as encouraged in the project module; teachers suffer from the fact that MIL is not a compulsory matter in curricula.

5.4.6 On the solutions to combat disinformation (open-ended responses)

The majority of the respondents mentioned MIL as the most important measure to be taken in order to fight disinformation. The other solutions were awareness campaigns, fact-checking tools, and legislative measures. Some respondents mentioned more than one type of measure, while others did not provide any answer. A rather large number of respondents, especially among the English-speaking ones (primarily emanating from the Romanian partner sample) (16), did not make any suggestions or admitted they did not know the answer.

All the solutions proposed by the participants in the MOOC are based on media education and digital literacy, public awareness campaigns, proper legislative measures to sanction the actors of disinformation, as well as fact-checking initiatives to help people verify information's accuracy. This whole-society approach is meant to increase people's resilience against one of the biggest challenges of our times – disinformation.

5.4.6.1 Iteration 1 (selection of verbatims)

5.4.6.1.1 ON MIL

MIL was seen as a mandatory measure for the education in schools and universities, for journalists, as well as a solution that should be taken at the personal level, by following certain rules before believing certain information, such as conducting a thorough research on the topic, using a diversity of media, and trusting only reliable sources. An effective MIL education should build first one's critical thinking and develop a "truth-focused mindset" (R4, French). It should be based on "ethical principles when sharing information" (R20, English), as well as on "peer-to-peer learning and communication about disinformation" (R106, Spanish). More rarely mentioned measures dealt with "gamification for busting disinformation" (R78, Spanish), and "hacking courses" (R70, Spanish)

5.4.6.1.2 ON PUBLIC AWARENESS CAMPAIGNS

Some respondents focused on the connection between MIL and public awareness campaigns that should be done on "TV shows with people specialised in disinformation" (R29, English/Romanian), and implemented through "a communication strategy made by truly professionals" (R64, English/Romanian). The success of awareness campaigns was linked to the creation of a group of experts on new media or of "an official group at the Ministry of National Education" whose main goal would be "to analyse the disinformation phenomenon at any level and in any form, and to come up with a plan in order to reduce the impact and educate citizens to recognize and counteract disinformation" (R40, English/Romanian). They should be promoted during "open conferences organised in urban and rural areas" (R8, French).

5.4.6.1.3 ON FACT-CHECKING

A great responsibility also lies on journalists who should strengthen the information ecosystem by providing "high-quality journalism" and restoring public trust (R35, English/Romanian). Thus, journalists should verify their sources, be involved in fact-checking activities by debunking fake news on social media and generate "reputation scores for media agencies" (R131, Spanish).

Some respondents laid the emphasis on technology and "self-regulatory tools especially in social media" (R49, English/Romanian), allowing publication on different sites just for verified information (R39, English). These tools are meant to identify fake news, fact-check the results provided by search engines, and create a database with debunked content. The general agreement among all the respondents pointing to fact-checkers' role in preventing the spread of disinformation is to narrow human intervention, by implementing "automatic fake news detection software" (R19, French). Only one respondent referred to "better algorithms and human resources that verify social media posts in order to check disinformation" (R91, English/Romanian).

5.4.6.1.4 ON LEGISLATION

The policy solutions were related to the creation of an appropriate legislative framework to forbid anonymous posting on social media, to identify and ban posts or accounts spreading fake news, and to punish the ones involved in consciously spreading disinformation (R6, English/Romanian). Legislative measures also included media regulation, stating that journalists should share only trusted information, free from political influence.

5.4.6.2 Iteration 2 (selection of verbatims)

5.4.6.2.1 ON MIL

MIL was recommended by all respondents. It was considered necessary to increase people's awareness towards "the right usage of media" (R21,

French). It was presented as "the frontline of intellectual self-defence" (R18, English/Romanian). Some national differences appeared:

> The French-speaking participants considered it a volunteer activity conducted by the young generation, within awareness campaigns targeting all categories of people or as workshops/media projects for students organised in youth camps. The English-speaking respondents indicated MIL courses on social media, critical thinking, and digital literacy, as part of mandatory school curriculum, during all education stages. The Spanish-speaking respondents proposed that MIL courses should be taken by all citizens.

5.4.6.2.2 ON AWARENESS CAMPAIGNS

A significant number of respondents focused on the important role that should be assigned to public awareness campaigns, organised as conferences or meetings conducted by mass media representatives and social influencers (R14, French), during which "suitable tools for fighting against disinformation" should be presented to the public (R19, French). In particular, "more transparency" would be a good solution to combat disinformation (R7, Spanish). Awareness initiatives implemented at the personal level were also mentioned, in order to make people more responsible about disinformation.

5.4.6.2.3 ON FACT-CHECKING

Fact-checking or debunking activities were rarely mentioned measures. The French-speaking respondents called for "a fact-checking site for verifying information" (R12, 27, French), "groups of people fighting against disinformation" (R16, French) or "an anti-fake brigade to identify fake authors" (R18, French). One English-speaking respondent suggested to "use bots to write in red on the fake news sites and articles that they are fake" (R10, English/Romanian), while a Spanish-speaking respondent highlighted the importance of "an app where you can enter links to news, photos or videos and be able to know if they are true or not" (R3, Spanish)

5.5 On legislative measures

The legislative measures included laws adopted in order to sanction disinformation and cybercrime (R14, French), as well as the actors disseminating false content in social media (R29, French) or "non-neutral journalism" (R2, Spanish). Other respondents focused on the importance of "a department dealing with disinformation in every government" or "some policies to deal with this" (R15, English/Romanian).

5.6 Discussion

Overall, the participants' high expectations in the MOOC were met, be it in terms of prospective learning and teaching method (MIL relevance) and usefulness (disinformation relevance). Likewise, expectations regarding the MOOC experience per se were deemed relevant, in spite of the very heterogeneous sample of participants. Finally, the investment and effort applied by the participants were related to the level of interest throughout the MOOC (individual relevance), and to their shared experiences (collective relevance), especially visible in appreciation for facilitation and participation in forums and contributions to the three collaborative activities in the data bases (for "fake news", for MIL projects, and for FAQ).

The three research questions initially posed in the questionnaire were answered by the MOOC experience, over the two iterations. The main results showed the following:

1 MOOC experience, course design, and engagement were up to expectations of participants and resulted in much lower rates of attrition than in most academic MOOCs (RQ1).
2 Participants' expectations were met in terms of their understanding of disinformation mechanisms as well as their use of fact-checking tools and techniques as well as refutation strategies (RQ2).
3 Participants confirmed the effectiveness of MIL solutions dispensed massively via MOOCs to fight disinformation and create counter narratives to disinformation, though MIL project building was maybe too ambitiously presented in the MOOC design (RQ3).

5.6.1 Implications for MOOC experience and design

Generally speaking, participants were very satisfied with all aspects of the MOOC in both seasons: content, moderation, time management, interaction with others, and appreciated having achieved their goals to a large extent. More specifically, participants of all languages in the first and second iteration expressed very high levels of satisfaction with the content of the course that was related to disinformation.

Furthermore, the general evaluation of the MOOC indicated very high satisfaction rates, in particular for the French sample, who are probably more familiar with the MIL topics and with the MOOC format. The success rate of the course, measured as the percentage of participants who pass the final test, exceeds the average MOOC rates. This suggests that participants are engaged with the topic, and that the content of the course meets their learning goals and initial expectations.

An additional unintended dimension appeared: the change from one single path to two paths showed increased satisfaction. This adds to MOOC design discussions on size and length. It contributes to the analysis of the funnel of participation effect because it can explain the different levels of participation, beyond interest in the topic (see Chapter 6 for facilitation results). Presenting various paths might make MOOCs more engaging, because heterogeneous participants can choose their path according to their initial training and end objectives.

5.6.2 Implications for fight against disinformation

The three specialised modules – "Mechanisms of disinformation", "Verification strategies", and "Refutation strategies – received very positive evaluations, especially for the second iteration, where the path "disinformation" was clearly delineated and was offered first, followed in second time by path on "MIL".

The added insights provided by the open-ended question on effects of disinformation can shed some light on what motivated participants to take the online course and participate in its activities. They had personal and societal concerns. At the personal level, the quest for well-being online and offline seemed key as well as the need to regain self-esteem and a sense of control. At the societal level, the participants felt the need to overcome informational disorientation and to tool themselves to combat democratic erosion, social segregation, and media censorship.

The results are particularly promising in relation to the greater framework of measures for countering disinformation. Apart from systemic measures that target the technological, economic, and social drivers of disinformation, audience-centred solutions can empower citizens to fight against fake news in their personal and professional lives. Basic measures to guide the social media users through the overabundance of information – such as the use of credibility metrics and misinformation labels – are not enough in the absence of education on the broader mechanisms of disinformation. Fact-checking, as important as it is, has an impact only if the public actively follows fact-checks on topics of interest and becomes savvy at identifying fake news and refuting them.

5.6.3 Implications for MIL and its effectiveness

Given the results, MIL interventions can complement other measures and give the audience the ability to recognise and counter disinformation in a multitude of contexts. The participants clearly saw MIL as a field worthy of interest and appreciated the focus on critical thinking.

The added insights provided by the open-ended question on the solutions to combat disinformation confirmed the overall sense that MIL is the most effective education, far before awareness campaigns, fact-checking tools, and legislative measures to sanction the actors of disinformation. MIL is perceived as the best way to increase people's resilience against the challenges of disinformation.

The lesser results in conducting MIL projects should not detract from the interest in this potential. They probably reflect the fact that a substantive part of the general sample was composed of students and teachers. Such a population feels the lack of legitimacy of MIL in the curriculum (as expressed in the open-ended responses). This deficit makes it harder for them to embark on ambitious full-fledged projects.

The clear preference for the second iteration MOOC design, offering two paths, points to the full potential for the course to become a permanent resource for self-learning on how to identify and counter disinformation, with immediate and long-term implications on civic online engagement. This second version was turned into an Open Educational Resource (OER) at the end of the evaluation.

5.7 Conclusion

The sMOOC methodological design was aimed at ensuring the participants' motivation and engagement. On the one hand, due to the high degree of heterogeneity of the MOOC "Disinformation Step by Step" participants, both in previous knowledge and in motivation, and, on the other hand, due to the non-formal nature of the course, solutions were provided, in an agile way, over two iterations, in order to offer educational tools to adjust the learning experience to the ever-changing aims of each participant. The sMOOC model responded to their motivation and learning demands by means of communication and collaboration tools. The statistical results of this study, with a high degree of participant engagement, have proved that sMOOC can be a good methodological choice for scaling up the fight against disinformation.

This study thus contributes critical insights to digital visual literacy as well as guidance for students, educators, librarians, journalists, and youth workers. The implications for media literacy theory, teaching, and learning show that MIL can contribute effectively and massively to the current curricula debates about the importance of media literacy to support democratic engagement among young people and citizens at large.

Note

1 https://youverify.eu/en/resources (https://youverify.eu/en/node/36, https://youverify.eu/en/node/37)

References

Aldowah, H., Al-Samarraie, H., Alzahrani, A. I. (2020). Factors affecting student dropout in MOOCs: A cause and effect decision-making model. *Journal of Computing in Higher Education*, *32*, 429–454. https://doi.org/10.1007/s12528-019-09241-y

Breakstone, J., Smith, M., Wineburg, S., Rapaport, A., Carle, J., Garland, M., & Saavedra, A. (2021). Students' civic online reasoning: A national portrait. *Educational Researcher*, *50*(8), 505–515. https://doi.org/10.3102/0013189X211017495

Bryman, A. (1988). *Quantity and quality in social research*. Routledge.
Camarero Cano, L., & Cantillo Valero, C. (2016). La evaluación de los aprendizajes en los sMOOC. Estudio de caso en el Proyecto Europeo ECO. *Revista Mediterránea De Comunicación*, 7(2), 21–35. https://doi.org/10.14198/MEDCOM2016.7.2.2
Clow, D. (2013). MOOCs and the funnel of participation. *LAK'13: Proceedings of the Third International Conference on Learning Analytics and Knowledge* (pp. 185–189). https://doi.org/10.1145/2460296.2460332
Colomina, C., Margalef, H. S., & Youngs, R. (2021). The impact of disinformation on democratic processes and human rights in the world. In *Directorate-general for external policies, European parliament*. https://www.europarl.europa.eu/RegData/etudes/STUD/2021/653635/EXPO_STU(2021)653635_EN.pdf
Costa, C., Car, V., & Papadimitriou, S. (2017). Good Practices and emerging trends in media and information literacy. In D. Frau-Meigs, I. Velez, & J. Flores-Michel (Eds.), *Public policies in MIL in Europe: Cross country comparisons*. Routledge.
Costa, C., Tyner, K., Henriques, S., & Sousa, C. (2016). A review of research questions, topics and methodologies for media literacy in game-based learning research (2010–2016). *Journal of Content, Community & Communication Amity School of Communication*, 4(2), 2–16.
Creswell, J. W. (2018). *Research design: Qualitative, quantitative, and mixed methods approaches* (5th ed.). Sage.
De Cock Buning, M., Ginsborg, L., & Luca, S. A. (2019). *Online disinformation ahead of the European Parliament elections: towards societal resilience*. STG Policy Briefs, 3. https://hdl.handle.net/1814/62426
Dobrescu, P., Durach, F., & Vladu, L. (2022). Building resilience to disinformation through media and information literacy. In L. Gómez Chova, A. López Martínez, & I. Candel Torres (Eds.), *Proceedings of INTED2022 Conference* (pp. 3059–3068).
Eriksson, T., Adawi, T., & Stöhr, C. (2017). "Time is the bottleneck": A qualitative study exploring why learners drop out of MOOCs. *Journal of Computing in Higher Education*, *29*(1), 133–146.
European Commission High Level Expert Group on Fake News and Online Disinformation. (2018). *A Multidimensional approach to disinformation. Report of the independent High level Group on fake news and online disinformation*. https://digital-strategy.ec.europa.eu/en/library/final-report-high-level-expert-group-fake-news-and-online-disinformation
Frau-Meigs, D. (2019). *Faut-il avoir peur des fake news ?* La Documentation Française.
Frau-Meigs, D. (2012). Transliteracy as the new research horizon for media and information literacy. *Medijske Studije/Media Studies*, *3*(6), 14–27.
Frau-Meigs, D., Osuna-Acedo, S., & Marta-Lazo, C. (Eds.). (2021). *The challenge of MOOCs. From revolution to reality*. Springer.
Frau-Meigs, D., & Bossu, A. (2019). Participatory MOOCs at the crossroads of the logic guiding public and private actors in the open training of teachers: The European project ECO questions de communication. In L. Massou, B. Juanals, P. Bonfils, & P. Dumas (Eds.), *Questions de Communication, Sources ouvertes numériques. Usages éducatifs, enjeux communicationnels*. Série Actes 39. https://www.ticemed.eu/publication-sources-ouvertes-numeriques
Frau-Meigs, D., Velez, I., & Flores-Michel, J. (2017). *Public policies in MIL in Europe: Cross country comparisons*. Routledge.

Gil-Quintana, J., & Osuna-Acedo, S. (2020). Citizenship training through sMOOCs: A participative and intercreative learning. *Sustainability*, *12*(20), 8301. https://doi.org/10.3390/su12208301

Humprecht, E., Esser, F., & Van Aelst, P. (2020). Resilience to online disinformation: A framework for cross-national comparative research. *The International Journal of Press/Politics*, *25*(3), 493–516. https://doi.org/10.1177/1940161219900126

Lewandowsky, S., Ecker, U. K., & Cook, J. (2017). Beyond misinformation: understanding and coping with the "post-truth" era. *Journal of Applied Research in Memory and Cognition*, *6*(4), 353–369. https://doi.org/10.1016/j.jarmac.2017.07.008

Marta-Lazo, C., Frau-Meigs, D., & Osuna-Acedo, S. (2018). Collaborative lifelong learning and professional transfer. Case study: ECO European project. *Interactive Learning Environments*, *26*, 1–14. https://doi.org/10.1080/10494820.2018.1451346

Martínez Pérez, J. (2016). El empoderamiento del alumnado desde el modelo sMOOC. *Revista Mediterránea de Comunicación*, *7*(2), 69. https://doi.org/10.14198/MEDCOM2016.7.2.6

McGrew, S., Ortega, T., Breakstone, J., & Wineburg, S. (2017). The challenge that's bigger than fake news: Civic reasoning in a social media environment. *American Educator*, *41*(3), 1–9.

McGrew, S., Breakstone, J., Ortega, T., Smith, M., & Wineburg, S. (2018). Can students evaluate online sources? Learning from assessments of civic online reasoning. *Theory & Research in Social Education*, *46*, 165–193. https://doi.org/10.1080/00933104.2017.1416320

Neekhara, P., Hussain, S. S., Jere, M., Koushanfar, F., & McAuley, J. (2020). Adversarial deepfakes: Evaluating vulnerability of deepfake detectors to adversarial examples. *2021 IEEE Winter Conference on Applications of Computer Vision (WACV)* (pp. 3347–3356).

Nygren, T., Frau-Meigs, D., Corbu, N., & Santovena-Casal, S. (2022). Teachers' views on disinformation and media literacy supported by a tool designed for professional fact-checkers: Perspectives from France, Romania, Spain and Sweden. *SN Social Sciences*, *2*(4). https://doi.org/10.1007/s43545-022-00340-9

Nygren, T., Guath, M., Axelsson, A., & Frau-Meigs, D. (2021). Combatting visual fake news with a professional fact-checking tool in Education in France, Romania, Spain and Sweden. *Information*, *12*(5), 201.

Osuna-Acedo, S. (2020). Gamification and MOOCs. In D. Frau-Meigs, S. Osuna-Acedo, & C. Marta-Lazo (Eds.), *MOOCs and the participatory challenge*. Springer.

Osuna-Acedo, S., Marta-Lazo, C., & Frau-Meigs, D. (2018). From sMOOC to tMOOC, learning towards professional transference: ECO European project. *Comunicar: Media Education Research Journal*, *26*(55), 105–114. https://doi.org/10.3916/C55-2018-10

Sánchez, J., & Olivares, R. (2011). Problem solving and collaboration using mobile serious games. *Computers & Education*, *57*(3), 1943–1952. https://doi.org/10.1016/j.compedu.2011.04.012

Osuna-Acedo, S., Frau-Meigs, D., Camarero-Cano, L., Bossu, A., Pedrosa, R., & Jansen, D. (2017). Intercreativity and interculturality in the virtual learning environments of the ECO MOOC project. In M. J. Kinshuk & M. K. Hribi (Eds.), *Open education: From OERs to MOOCs* (pp. 161–187). Springer.

6 The role of facilitation to foster participation and ensure knowledge transfer in media and information literacy

The case of the MOOC "Disinformation Step by Step"

Adeline Bossu

6.1 Introduction

The rise of the internet and associated functionalities encourage individuals to share and participate within more or less extensive collectives. Connectivity is pushing back spatio-temporal barriers and digital networks are impacting social activities, both professionally and personally. The Covid-19 health crisis has also highlighted and reinforced the development of these emerging practices. The management of information and its distribution have become crucial issues in promoting communication and collaboration between individuals and groups of individuals. Digital systems are multiplying to allow the meeting of distributed competences and knowledge around the world in order to co-create and co-produce. In education and training, techno-pedagogical solutions for managing learning are developing very rapidly. The Massive Open Online Courses (MOOCs) are such solutions: they have largely participated in the hybridisation of education, that is, the mix of online and real-life learning experiences, since 2008, when the first MOOCs appeared (Frau-Meigs et al., 2021).

More than learning management, MOOCs allow community building and collaboration. The role of facilitation for such massive communities becomes a real issue for successful learning and social experiences, and, even more so, for intercultural participation. This role can be studied in different learning domains, such as maths or economics that use media as support for their discipline. But in the case of media and information literacy (MIL), the emphasis is not on the learning *with* media but on learning *about* media with media. The MOOC "Disinformation Step by Step" goes one step further, within the YouVerify! project, as it looks at how the media can amplify disinformation. Considering how the facilitation process works when dealing with media and disinformation can foster participation in the fight against the proliferation of "fake news" and promote MIL while ensuring knowledge transfer.

DOI: 10.4324/9781003387404-9

6.2 State of the art

The first MOOC designers, Siemens and Downes, proposed MOOCs in 2008, to take advantage of the internet and large-scale connectivism, applying them to learning environments (Downes, 2012; Siemens, 2005). At that early stage, MOOCs were developed to meet the needs of accessibility and dissemination of knowledge to as many people as possible and to deal with the absence of content that was not available locally. But they were rapidly used for other purposes, in particular to disseminate training by universities or other organisations (Davis et al., 2014; Ospina-Delgado et al., 2016). Some teachers and learners then used them as teaching resources for their own courses or as additional materials (Delgado-Kloos et al., 2015; Israel, 2015). The health crisis created by Covid-19 has largely contributed to this development (King & Lee, 2023). The need to provide distance training stimulated the use of MOOCs as a learning device, defined by the combination of hardware (tablet, mobile, etc.), software applications, and access to learning management systems and contents. They have been used sometimes as a teaching aid in its own right, sometimes as an adjunct learning method (flipped classroom, blended learning, etc.) (Bossu, 2020). Some of them have been left open and accessible as an Open Educational Resource (OER) (Hylén, 2005).

Institutions, albeit reluctantly at first, recognised their certification and have gone so far as to integrate them into their competences validation process, sometimes by mixing them with face-to-face courses. Participants can now validate, remotely and via MOOCs, a fully recognised learning path, as in the case of FUN, the French public platform for universities, or Openclassrooms, a start-up that collected agreements with universities in France to deliver such services.[1] ECOlearning, initially a European-funded experimental portal for MOOCs, became a public–private platform for National University of Distance Education (UNED) and for other institutions in Europe and beyond, including Savoir*Devenir, the NGO in charge of YouVerify! project (Savoir*Devenir, 2021, 2022).

However, the content of MOOCs as the only learning material appeared limited and insufficient for efficient learning and the validation of complete courses, with high levels of attrition (Cisel, 2016). The quest to improve engagement and completion has led teaching teams to personalise courses (Peltier & Séguin, 2021), to propose solutions to increase learner engagement and motivation. They then developed facilitation practices, added additional elements to the content (such as mentoring activities, peer-to-peer exercises, gamification, etc.).

Facilitation in a MOOC can be defined as the active process of creating such traces of interactions and building on them to ensure the transfer of knowledge and experiences (Bossu, 2020). The process must simultaneously guide, inform, encourage, and motivate participants to complete their pathway. Through specific online actions, open to all, the facilitator and his/her team must act with agility to reach and engage a large number but also a diversity of participants (Walji et al., 2016). However, meeting the needs of a "massive" community and individual needs at the same time is a complex and difficult task (Andersen & Ponti, 2014; Haavind & Sistek-Chandler, 2015; Hew & Cheung, 2014; Mackness et al., 2013).

Among the complexities, the level of acculturation to learning devices is specific to each person, and the absence or lack of such acculturation can be an obstacle to learning in a MOOC (Colas et al., 2016). In addition, participants do not always have the skills to complete courses independently (Beaven et al., 2014), especially since MOOCs are presented on platforms with various formats and offer a multitude of options, resources and activities (Hew et al., 2018; Mackness et al., 2013). Thus, some participants tend to ask for traditional support in learning (Knox, 2014; Karlsson & Godhe, 2016), while others prefer a certain freedom and autonomy. Besides, MOOCs are dependent on the different levels of initial knowledge of their participants as well as their levels of acquisition. MOOCs are also dependent on the cultural perspective of their authors, which compels participants to align themselves with it (Colas et al., 2016). The cultural perspective covers both the country values and the professional ecosystem, which influences the authors choice of communication channels, spaces of interaction, as well as tools and practices (Bossu & Frau-Meigs, 2018).

Facilitation in a MOOC must interconnect the participants' multiple needs with the pedagogical teams' practices and cultures. To meet the varied needs of a large intercultural community, several facilitation practices have been observed. The role of the facilitator, sometimes likened to that of a tutor (Rodet, 2016), is assigned to one or several members of the pedagogical team. But this role, in a context of online learning and particularly a MOOC, can undergo various changes. Facilitation functions are often provided by multiple actors: teachers, pedagogical engineers, community leaders, etc. Any pedagogical team develops, makes available, and activates a number of resources and interaction spaces, with various formats to enable learners to achieve their own goals (Littlejohn & Hood, 2018).

In the case of multilingual MOOCs, participation requires the creation of small groups of learners grouped by language (De Waard et al., 2014, Godwin-Jones, 2014). These learning groups promote interpersonal interactions and thus networking and mutual aid, which can go as far as the development of real peer tutoring. Small learning communities lighten the work of facilitators and the entire pedagogical team by relieving them of certain activities (Ross et al., 2014). The learners then take on a real role in the facilitation process. Thus, MOOC designers must promote various means of communication between participants, for example with activities promoting reflections and testimonials around content, experiences, and collaborations or peer reviews (Walji et al., 2016). These activities are conducive to individual interactions and reciprocal knowledge (Ferguson & Sharples, 2014; Walji et al., 2016; Watson et al., 2016), and the participants seem to be sensitive to feedback from their peers (Ferguson & Sharples, 2014).

The pedagogical team therefore has a vested interest in developing facilitation to encourage online conversations (Walji et al., 2016; Zhu et al., 2018). To engage participants to interact in the community and learning, facilitators use practices similar to those of community management on social networks (Kop et al., 2011; Medina-Salguero & Aguaded Gómez, 2013). But they also balance their actions and interventions to leave some space for interactions between peers and independent learning (Ross et al., 2014). However, the question arises of the legitimacy and competences of certain participants to facilitate and help. The question of MOOC adaptability to intercultural contexts also emerges (Colas et al., 2016) and facilitators must know both the context of the MOOC and the one of the learners to ensure that both massive and individual learning takes place (Bossu, 2021).

The study of knowledge management collectives such as work teams (McDermott, 1999), communities of practice (Gherardi & Nicolini, 2000), and learning communities (Tremblay, 2004) provides further analysis of structuring (Tremblay et al., 2003) around the creation, circulation, and transfer of knowledge (Gherardi & Nicolini, 2000). Thus, authors interested in the concept highlight the social theory of learning. Communities of practice are based on shared repertoires of know-how-oriented resources resulting from collective action (Brown & Duguid, 1991).

The facilitation process is supposed to foster appropriation by the participants. This requires cognitive and technical mastery of the MOOC as a learning device, social integration of use into daily life, and the emergence of innovation and creativity (Breton & Proulx, 2002). The MOOC is a technical innovation in the field of digital education that benefits from social appropriation (Collin & Saffari, 2015). Social appropriation takes place in three stages: a phase of emulation and overestimation, a phase of field testing and experimentation, and a phase of incorporation of the technical innovation into a sustainable social dynamic (Musso et al., 2007). Those stages can be supported by social media and online networks, which implies a certain mastery of MIL per se.

Transfer can take place when the conditions for facilitation and appropriation are in place (Cambien, 2008). The phenomenon of transfer, in management and educational sciences, is defined in relation to knowledge by the ability to use acquired competences in a new context (Devos & Dumay, 2006; Perrenoud, 2002; Tardif & Meirieu, 1996). Users must be able to reproduce practices in their own context. The effectiveness of transfer can be assessed by observing users' commitment, development, and sustainability of their own devices, as, for instance, with the creation of new MOOCs (Cohen & Levinthal, 1990).

Learning devices and their embedded artefacts can play a role in transfer as "boundary objects", linked to management supports and tools, models and prototypes (Brown & Duguid, 1991; Wenger, 1998). As they are circulated from one practice to another, they ensure the transfer of knowledge that users can mobilise in other practices. Devices and artefacts must be comprehensible to all actors in the collective, and they attest to the presence of a shared culture (Creplet et al., 2005).

6.3 Research questions

This research attempts to shed light on the levers that enable the facilitation process to meet the needs both of massive engagement and of individual participation in an intercultural context, as the three partners of YouVerify! (France, Romania, and Spain) delivered the MOOC in their respective languages (the Romanians preferring to work on the English version common to all, before translation into French and Spanish). The ECOlearning platform made this intercultural experience available to all members at the same time as it allowed all three languages and communities to be visible and accessible within a single space.[2]

In this study, we focus on a particular type of MOOC, in order to gain new insights about the role facilitation plays in improving the learning experience: an intercultural MOOC focused on MIL.

RQ1. Are facilitation practices and processes, used to facilitate intercultural communities, effective in a MOOC dedicated to MIL?

Interactions are crucial in a MOOC because they ensure both the participation of participants in the learning process and the sharing and transfer of knowledge. The study of interactions and collectives around and with digital systems offers the possibility of observing, via digital traces, relational and organisational dynamics.

RQ2. What are the key success factors to facilitate practices in an intercultural MOOC about MIL?

In addition, interactions allow the observation of the phenomena of appropriation, inter-culturation (Demorgon, 2005), and transfer of relational and organisational practices and strategies with new spatio-temporal relationships in an intercultural context.

RQ3. To what extent can facilitation practices help build a sense of community and ensure transfer of knowledge in an intercultural MOOC about MIL?

6.4 Methodology

The general research framework studies MOOCs as techno-pedagogical systems or devices (Boumazguida et al., 2022) composed of pedagogical, didactic, technical, and social artefacts (Bossu, 2020; Chevry-Pebayle & Rossini, 2017). The interactions of the participants take place via authentic artefacts, defined as developed by humans, coherently "architected" to meet a need, and associated with a "pattern of use" (Simon, 1979; Zacklad, 2013). These artefacts and digital systems are both supports and results of learning and make it possible to observe the traces of interactions and presence of the teaching teams and participants (Bossu, 2021; Peraya, 2019).

6.4.1 A systemic approach

Studying the MOOC device as a complex system offers the possibility of taking into account learning, leadership strategies, organisational groups, and interpersonal relationships. The expression "socio-digital ecosystem" related to information systems (Reix, 2011) comes close to it and confirms Trestini's proposal (Trestini, 2016) to study the MOOC as a device with its own ecosystem. As Morin (1992) suggested, the complexity of the system can be grasped by analysing how individuals and groups relate with each other and with the learning device itself, as well as share feedback. Ultimately, the systemic approach of Palo Alto (Picard & Marc, 2013), as reinterpreted by Mucchielli (2004), is used to understand the transfer phenomenon.

The research method used consists in collecting qualitative data (Paillé & Mucchielli, 2012), with an in-depth case study on a specific field (Hlady-Rispal, 2015). It does not study the effectiveness of the device per se, but all the interactions within the collectives, and particularly those in connection with the facilitation process. The study of several MOOC iterations and different cultural contexts thus provides an understanding of systemic influences and feedback loops within the learning device (Morin & Le Moigne, 1999).

6.4.2 Action research

The systemic approach when applied to learning devices such as MOOCs lends itself to action research, balancing problem-solving actions (how to fight disinformation) with a collaborative context (co-creation of knowledge and content materials) (Allard-Poesi & Perret, 2003; Morrissette & Desgagné, 2009). Action research requires the involvement of researchers in the actions of management, production, and facilitation of the MOOC "Disinformation Step by Step". The data collected are produced by traces of interaction and collaboration, i.e., communications mediated, synchronous and asynchronous. Observations are made on the MOOC platform and forum threads, but also on collaborative working documents, electronic messages, social networks, and artefacts created specifically for this particular project. The observation of these interactions offers the possibility of revealing the practices implemented as well as the cognitive and social strategies.

The approach is mainly deductive because it consists of confirming the results of previous research on the facilitation of intercultural online courses. But it can also propose new postulates that can enrich knowledge and theory in order to understand the phenomenon of transferability (Ihadjadene &

Chaudiron, 2008) and analyse the way in which interactions are mobilised in learning situations of co-construction, appropriation, and transfer, in a digital context.

6.4.3 "Disinformation Step by Step" MOOC case study and corpus

This research focuses on the two iterations of the MOOC "Disinformation Step by Step" produced in the context of the YouVerify! project, which aimed at combating disinformation on a large scale (see Figure 6.1).

The MOOC "Disinformation Step by Step" emerged a few years after the European project "ECO Digital Learning", which took place between 2013 and 2016. Its objective was to design MOOCs and train participants to create their own digital educational resources. On this same model, with the same platform, Eco-learning, and some of its actors, the Savoir*Devenir team elaborated the MOOC "Disinformation Step by Step", and relied on the support of its partners: Agence France-Presse (AFP) for disinformation tools, UNED for gamification, and National University of Political Studies and Public Administration (SNSPA) for additional facilitation support and policy observations (see Figure 6.2).

The instructional design derives from the sMOOC, or social MOOC (Osuna-Acedo et al., 2017), based on a pedagogical approach that is both socio-constructivist and connectivist (Siemens, 2005; Downes, 2012). It relies on situated action (Engeström, 1999; Vygotskij et al., 2003), and particularly on peer-to-peer learning. The MOOC was proposed and facilitated twice between November 15, 2021, and April 15, 2022, with no learning path on iteration 1 and two possible learning paths on iteration 2. Between the two

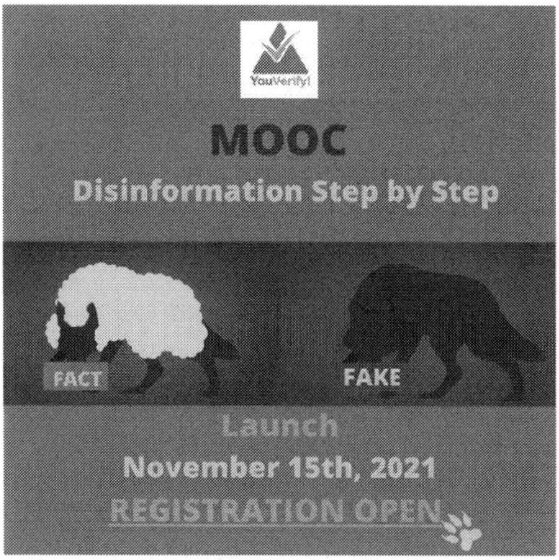

Figure 6.1 The visual for launching the MOOC (save the date).

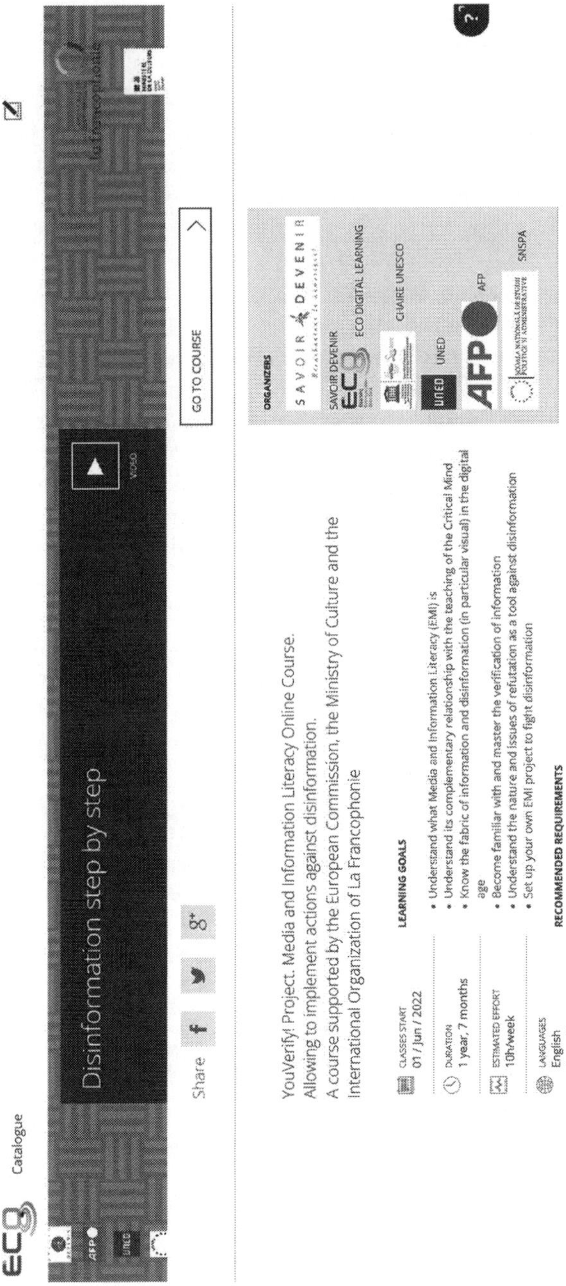

Figure 6.2 The landing page of the MOOC on ECO platform.

iterations, the course was adapted, improved, and enriched, based on the first iteration's feedback and outcomes; hence, the two paths proposed: path 1 on disinformation and path 2 on MIL. After the end of its second iteration, it was offered as an OER, without facilitation[3] (see Chapter 5 for MOOC results).

The MOOC "Disinformation Step by Step" consisted of six main modules with defined educational objectives: (1) understanding MIL, (2) developing critical thinking in relation to MIL, (3) mastering disinformation mechanisms, (4) elaborating strategies for verification, (5) Fostering refutation, and (6) setting up an MIL project.

Completion and validation of activities allowed participants to obtain an Open Badge on request. It was interdisciplinary, intercultural, and available in French, Spanish, and English (the language chosen by the Romanian partners). It was contextualised in each language, with additional resources. A special effort was made for European participants, including Romanians who benefited from resources adapted and contextualised by a dedicated Romanian facilitation team.

The design team was mainly made up of members of the Savoir*Devenir association. They are experts in the fields of MIL and have skills in pedagogical engineering and distance education. They organised the educational framework in which they centralised the resources and wrote the content. To ensure the facilitation, they joined forces with the European project teams and facilitators generally involved in other existing learning communities.

6.4.4 Observing interactions

The observations of the interactions were made via the traces of digital presence on the MOOC and are listed according to the supports and spaces of exchanges (see Table 6.1).

The interactions observed took place between many heterogeneous actors across many media, as collaborative online pads (Padlet, framapad, Google doc), to ensure the implementation and the proper functioning of the MOOC.

6.5 Results

Observations confirmed the need to organise and diversify facilitation practices with a configuration and strategic artefacts that were both triggers and results of interactions, to support massive teaching, individualise learning, and promote peer support.

6.5.1 Techno-pedagogical facilitation choices

The content and activities of the MOOC were mainly hosted by the *Learning Management System* (LMS; or Training Platform). To engage the

Table 6.1 Traces of presence associated with interactions on the exchange spaces of the MOOC "Disinformation Step by Step" (Bossu, 2020)

Supports	Exchange space	Identifiers or traces of presence
The MOOC	Forum	Image, profile name, message
	microblogging	Image, profile name, description, message
	Social networks	Image, profile name, description, message
	Web conference	Picture, profile name, description, video, voice, image
Electronic messaging	The messages	Signature
Google Collaborative Folder	Document d'organisation Google Doc et Tab	Image, profile name, comments, edit, suggestion, write
	Work documents	Image, profile name, comments, edit, suggestion, write
Social apps	Social networks	Image, profile name, description, message
	Private and public video conferencing	Voice, Image, Video
Mediating artefacts dedicated to the teaching and facilitation team	Organisation tables	Identifying teams with names
	The MOOC	Identifying teams with images, videos
	The FAQ and the charter	The identifiers and values of the project through the content
Mediating artefacts dedicated to MOOC participants and supplemented by their interactions	Activity sheets/templates	Project identifiers and values through content and images
	Co-creation spaces and collaborative wall (Padlet and Google doc)	Image, profile name, description of individuals and workgroups, message

participants, the facilitation team used the functionalities offered by the LMS, all accessible via the platform dashboard (see Figure 6.3).

On this dashboard, all the features offered by the platform appeared. As in most MOOCs, the facilitation team used the main features of the LMS to offer spaces for discussion such as the forum, group features, announcements, etc.

The ECO project community developed communication features specific to the pedagogical model based on connectivism and socio-constructivism: a microblogging tool and a forum were available to participants, while an announcement window allowed interaction with the facilitation team. This

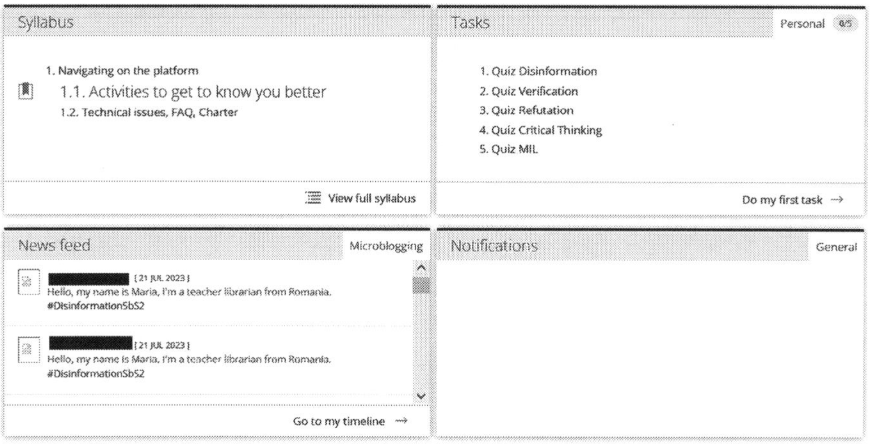

Figure 6.3 The dashboard of the MOOC on ECO (with units, activities, microblog, and announcements).

made it possible to facilitate the MOOC live on the platform, with the internal exchanges among the participants visible by all.

To propose the activities and also to encourage exchanges and interactions between the participants, the team used the platform's forum. On this forum, engaging activities were created: for example, having participants introduce themselves, answering questions elicited by the team for reflection, and inviting people to search for resources or react to content.

The discussion threads were separated by activity and by language (one thread per activity and one per language) but they remained visible and accessible to everyone regardless of the language used by the participant.

The team also used the groups feature and its internal micro-blog to encourage discussion. These spaces and functionalities were used by the animation teams not only to offer the activities but also to encourage exchanges and interactions between the participants.

The content and activities were mostly hosted by the LMS but, to complete the content initially produced by the team, external additions were made: videos offered on YouTube to refer to existing testimonials; resources to consult; "interactive" materials produced by the YouVerify! team (games, quizzes, etc.). To expand on this material, resources were also expected from MOOC participants. In addition to the platform's functionalities, "external" artefacts related to the activities were created and made available to participants. These were mostly collaborative writing documents with teaching instructions: Padlet collaborative walls and Google Doc writing documents. Two padlets were created to develop activities suggested in modules, one for disinformation strategies (mechanisms, verification, refutation) to create a database of ready-to-use examples of fakes news, one for MIL projects (see Figure 6.4). One participative Google Docs "Frequently Asked Questions" (FAQ) was produced and enriched over the two iterations.

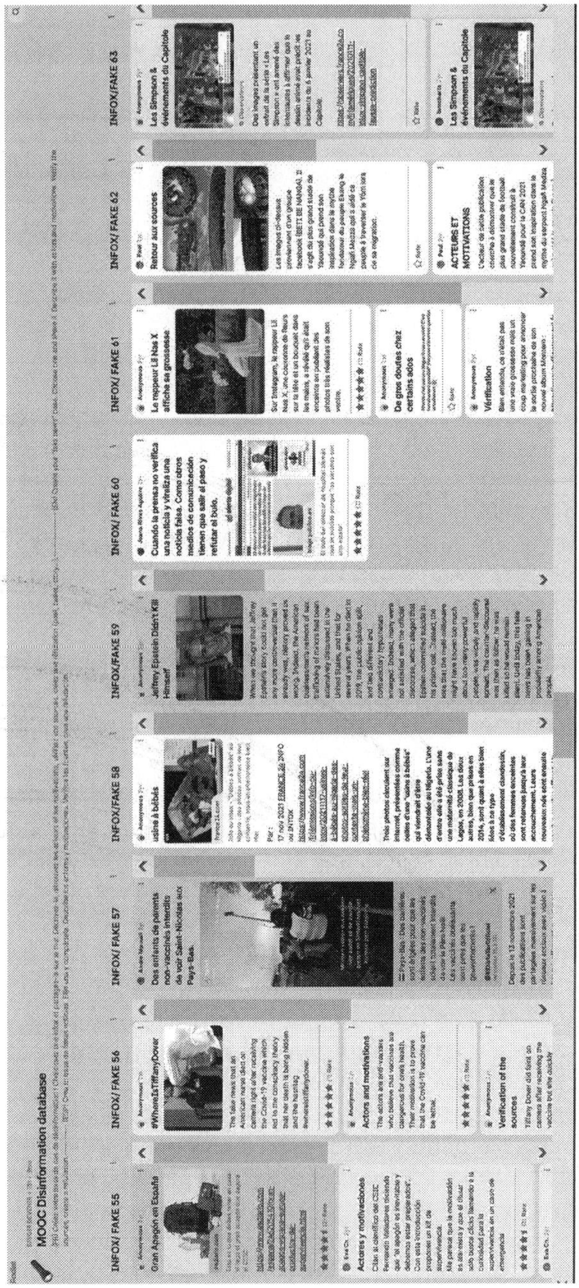

Figure 6.4 Screenshot of the Padlet MOOC Disinformation Database.

In the Padlet on disinformation, participants were invited to share a "fake news" of their choice and analyse it according to the method suggested in the course: find the actors and motivations, use a tool for verification, and publish a counter-narrative. In the padlet on MIL, participants were invited to create their own project, following MIL specificities and using a "roadmap". The facilitation team appended these additional apps to meet the sharing, interaction, and co-construction needs of the participants, taking advantage of their functionalities (ergonomic, responsive, and scalable). These spaces outside the platform were highly used sharing spaces by the participants. More than 200 cases were shared, in three languages, to create the common database of "fake news".

The pedagogical teams also added additional spaces and tools such as electronic messaging and mass mailing tools (Mailchimp type). Thus, ten newsletters were produced and sent by Savoir*Devenir to the participants of the MOOC to keep them abreast of new activities, new resources. Additionally, a weekly newsletter (in three languages) was sent by Savoir*Devenir to update participants about tasks, activities, and forum questions/responses. The pedagogical team advertised the MOOC via posts on social networks and microblogging tools, internal to the platform and external with Twitter, LinkedIn, Facebook, and Instagram on both professional (Savoir*Devenir, official pages of partners) and personal accounts (members of the pedagogical team's and facilitators' social networks pages) (see Figure 6.5).

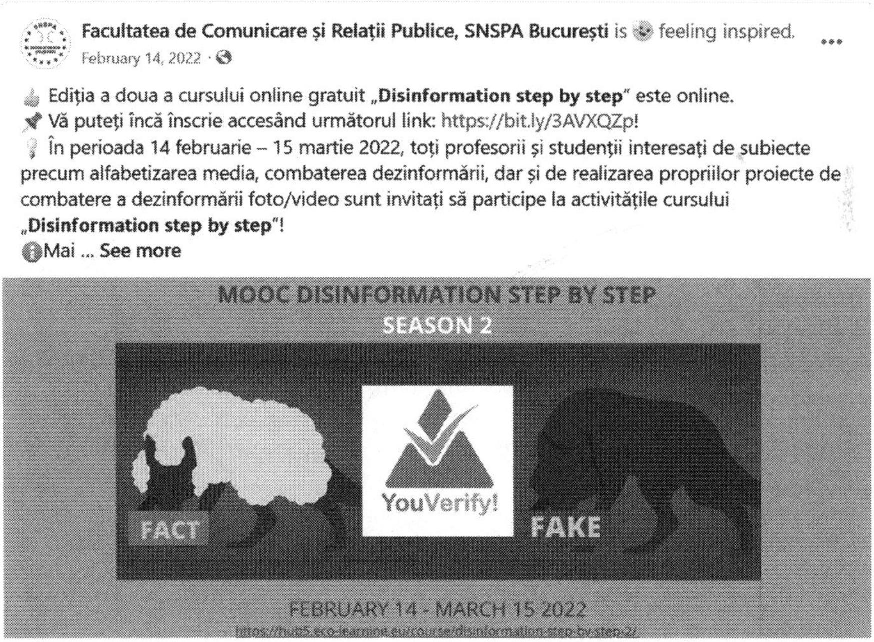

Figure 6.5 Screenshots of posts on social networks.

Moreover, video conferencing and streaming media were produced for live web conferences via Zoom and YouTube. These live events were carried out to bring in experts and get participants to react. Three web conferences were held live during both iterations of the MOOC in English, French, and Spanish, to answer the questions of participants.

The MOOC integrated various techno-pedagogical choices, not all of which were initially pedagogical tools, but were used for pedagogical purposes or at least for co-construction of knowledge, facilitation, and motivational support. The MOOC device extended beyond the platform that hosted its content and became the result of a juxtaposition of various heterogeneous artefacts.

6.5.2 *Organised facilitation with coordinated actors and supporting artefacts*

6.5.2.1 *Actors and their roles*

To engage a multicultural learning community, the facilitation teams were organised by language and country, in three teams: French, English, and Spanish. A team, composed mainly of three members of the SNSPA from Romania and two members of Savoir*Devenir, facilitated the English version with actions and contributions to additional and adapted resources. A recontextualisation effort was particularly developed for the Romanian participants on the English version. The Spanish team had a majority of members from the UNED to propose an adaptation to the Spanish version with resources, educational activities, and complementary spaces. The French team, mainly made up of members of Savoir*Devenir, also incorporated facilitators from French-speaking countries (Cameroon, Haiti, and Ivory Coast), to adapt the French version of the MOOC. Some of these actors belonged to the three teams; the teams were both independent and coordinated by the facilitation manager.

The teams were made up of teachers, PhDs, local facilitators, and civil society association leaders. These facilitators came from heterogeneous disciplines and geographical areas. Their mission was to engage communities and collectives of various natures, and, when possible, on site as well. In addition, the MOOC integrated other already-existing collectives. In short, the teams sought to engage local/national communities. To gather participants, each partner contacted their national networks. Savoir*Devenir as the project coordinator also reached out to European partners, especially in connection to the European Digital Media Observatory (EDMO) and some of its hubs: DE FACTO for France, IBERIFIER for Spain and Portugal, BELUX for Belgium, and EDUK-MEDIA as well as Benevoles EMI for French-speaking African countries. This strategy made it possible to be closer to users and their needs for MIL training in the field of fact-checking and disinformation. For example, face-to-face facilitators were able to help participants connect, access activities, and master the digital environment and pedagogical constraints.

The MOOC facilitation also relied on the participants themselves. They came from various professions, studies, and countries. To facilitate this process and peer-to-peer interactions, groups were self-formed by language with the features of the platform.

6.5.2.2 Organisation and artefacts

In order to meet the coordination and interaction needs of the teams, as well as the transfer of skills and practices, supervision was provided by the facilitation manager who set up the timing for the activities and shared collaborative artefacts. For example, pre-MOOC meetings and weekly meetings during the facilitation period were organised. These meetings were carried out by the facilitators team, and as some members belonged to different countries and backgrounds, they made the link between the collectives. Organisational tools were shared between the teams, and common summary emails were also sent to share feedback, experiences, and future actions.

Online organisation tools were created and shared like a general retro-planning of the MOOC. Collaborative documents helped complete the plan for the facilitation, week per week as for the distribution of moderation schedule (see Figures 6.6 and 6.7).

The tables and supports were mainly hosted on Google Doc and Tab and were open to writing to all users, so that everyone could register, for example, to ensure the moderation during a specific week. Facilitators could also report their doubts, problems, needs, or comments throughout the duration of the MOOC and as the weeks went by on a collaborative document: "the liaison document", shared with all the teaching teams.

To lead and manage these teams, other technologies were used, namely web conferencing service providers such as ZOOM and electronic messaging (WhatsApp) as well as weekly summary electronic messages. Artefacts were also created to guide and accompany the facilitators. Thus, the missions of the facilitator position were clearly identified, documented, and shared by all the actors of the educational teams.

The missions were broken down, and the document was open to collaborative writing to add, modify, and make suggestions on the facilitator's tasks. This strategy made it possible to clarify the areas of action of a facilitator and to modify the animation tasks as needed.

Other documents were initiated by the manager and then created collaboratively to facilitate the management and handling of the system. For example, the image of the facilitators was shaped by adding each of the actors' photo and their description on a Google Slide. This allowed the team players to spot their colleagues and become aware of their own position in the team. Tutorials, such as the registration guide (see Figure 6.8) or the use of a Padlet (see Figure 6.4), are also very good examples.

The registration tutorial allowed the various team members to connect correctly. This step was not always easy. This tutorial evolved over the two

FR	15 NOV - 21 NOV			22 - 28 NOV	29 - 5 DEC	6 DEC - 16 DEC	
UNITÉS	Bienvenue	**Unité 1** Esprit Critique	**Unité 2** Education aux Médias et à l'Information	**Unité 3** Décryptages Désinformation	**Unité 4** Stratégies Vérification	**Unité 5** Solutions Réfutation	**Unité 6** Projets EMI
BADGES	No quiz	**Quiz 1** **Badge 1**	Quiz (no badge)	**Quiz 3** **Badge 2**	**Quiz 4** **Badge 3**	**Quiz 5** **Badge 4**	No quiz
ACTIVITÉS	**Se présenter**	**Tester son esprit critique**	**Créer sa base d'infox**	**Décrypter sa base d'infox**	**Vérifier sa base d'infox**	**Réfuter sa base d'infox**	**Faire un projet EMI + FAQ Désinfox**
ATELIERS "Clés en main"		Test: quel citoyen numérique êtes vous?	Base d'infox	Vidéo Médiatropismes	**INVID-WeVerify** Utiliser plug-in	**INVID-WeVerify** Jouer BOT BUSTERS	Préparer émission radio/video ou story **Faire feuille de route EMI + FAQ Désinfox**
ATELIERS "Se lancer"		Vidéo « Les secrets des cycles cosmiques » E xercez votre esprit critique	Feuille de route (objectifs et cibles)	Vidéo au choix	**INVID-Werify** Construire une session/atelier autour du jeu Youcheck detectives (FR) Bot Busters (en /sp)	**INVID-WeVerify** Défi Detox de l'infox!	Préparer émission radio/video ou story **Faire feuille de route EMI + FAQ Désinfox**
ANIMATION		Briser la glace	Projet	Débat	Mise en situation	Jeu	Production
LIVES experts + animateurs			1 zoom activités	Jeudi 25 Nov 19h + 1 zoom activités	1 zoom activités	Jeudi 9 dec 19 h + 1 zoom activités	1 zoom activités (optionnel, sauf pour OIF)

Figure 6.6 Screenshots of the facilitation and activities schedules.

EN	15 NOV - 21 NOV			22 - 28 NOV	29 - 5 DEC	6 DEC - 16 DEC	
UNITS	Welcome	**Unit 1** critical thinking	**Unit 2** MIL	**Unit 3** Mechanisms of Disinformation	**Unit 4** Strategies of Verification	**Unit 5** Solutions of Refutation	**Unit 6** MIL Projects
BADGES	No quiz	**Quiz 1** **Badge 1**	Quiz (no badge)	**quiz 3** **Badge 2**	**Quiz 4** **Badge 3**	**Quiz 5** **Badge 4**	No quiz
ACTIVITIES	**Presenting oneself**	**Testing your critical thinking**	**Creating your fakenews database**	**Analyzing fakenews in your database**	**Verifying fakenews in your database**	**Refuting fakenews in your database**	**Building your MIL project + FAQ Disinfox**
WORKSHOP **Ready to use**		Testing what kind of digital citizen you are	**Fake news database**	Video Médiatropismes	**INVID-WeVerify** Using the plug-in	**INVID-WeVerify** Playing serious game BOT BUSTERS	Preparing radio/video programme or story/tweet/post **Make MIL roadmap + FAQ Disinfox**
WORKSHOP **Get Started**		Video « Les secrets des cycles cosmiques » Test ing your critical thinking	MIL Roadmap (objectives and public)	Video of your choice	**INVID-Werify** Building a session/workshop on serious game Bot Busters	**INVID-WeVerify** Challenge Disinfox (using plug-in preferably)	Preparing radio/video programme or story/tweet/post **Make MIL roadmap + FAQ Disinfox**
FACILITATION		Ice-breaker	Project	Debate	Role play	Serious game	Production
LIVES experts + facilitators			1 zoom activities	Thursday 25 Nov 19h (FR) + 1 zoom activities	1 zoom activities	Thursday 9 dec 19 h (FR) + 1 zoom activities	1 zoom activities (optional)

Figure 6.6 (Continued)

ES	15 NOV - 21 NOV			22 - 28 NOV	29 - 5 DEC	6 DEC - 16 DEC	
UNIDADES	Bienvenidos	**Unidad 1** Pensamiento critico	**Unidad 2** AMI	**Unidad 3** mecanismos de Desinformacion	**Unidad 4** Estrategias de Verificacion	**Unidad 5** Solutiones de Refutacion	**Unidad 6** Proyectos AMI
MEDALLAS	No quiz	**Quiz 1** **Medalla 1**	Quiz (no medalla)	**quiz 3** **Medalla 2**	**Quiz 4** **Medalla 3**	**Quiz 5** **Medalla 4**	No quiz
ACTIVIDADES	**Presentarse**	**Comprobar su pensamiento critico**	**Crear su base de "fakenews"**	**Descodificar las fakenews de su base**	**Averiguar las fakenews de su base**	**Refutar las fakenews de su base**	**Montar su proyecto AMI+ FAQ Desinformacion/Desint ox**
Taller **Listo para uso**		Test: que tipo de ciudadano digital eres? (o similar en español)	Base de Fakenews	Video Médiatropismes	**INVID-WeVerify** Utilisar el plug-in	**INVID-WeVerify** Jugar con BOT BUSTERS	Preparar un programa (radio, video) o un post, story… **Hacer su "hoja de ruta"** **+ FAQ Desinformacion**
Taller **DIY**		Vidéo « Les secrets des cycles cosmiques » Ejercer su pensamiento critico	Hoja de ruta AMI (objetivos y públicos)	Video elejida por participantes	**INVID-Werify** Construir una session/workshop para usar el juego Bot Busters	**INVID-WeVerify** Desafio "Detoxicacion"	Preparar un programa (radio, video) o un post, story… émission radio/ **Hacer su "hoja de ruta"** **+ FAQ Desinformacion**
FACILITACION		Romper hielo	Proyecto	Debate	Ponerse en el rol de un fact checker	Jugar	Produccion
LIVES expertos + facilidadores			1 zoom actividades	Jueves 25 Nov 19h (FR) + 1 zoom actividades	1 zoom actividades	Jueves 9 dec 19 h + 1 zoom actividades	1 zoom actividades (opcional)

Figure 6.6 (Continued)

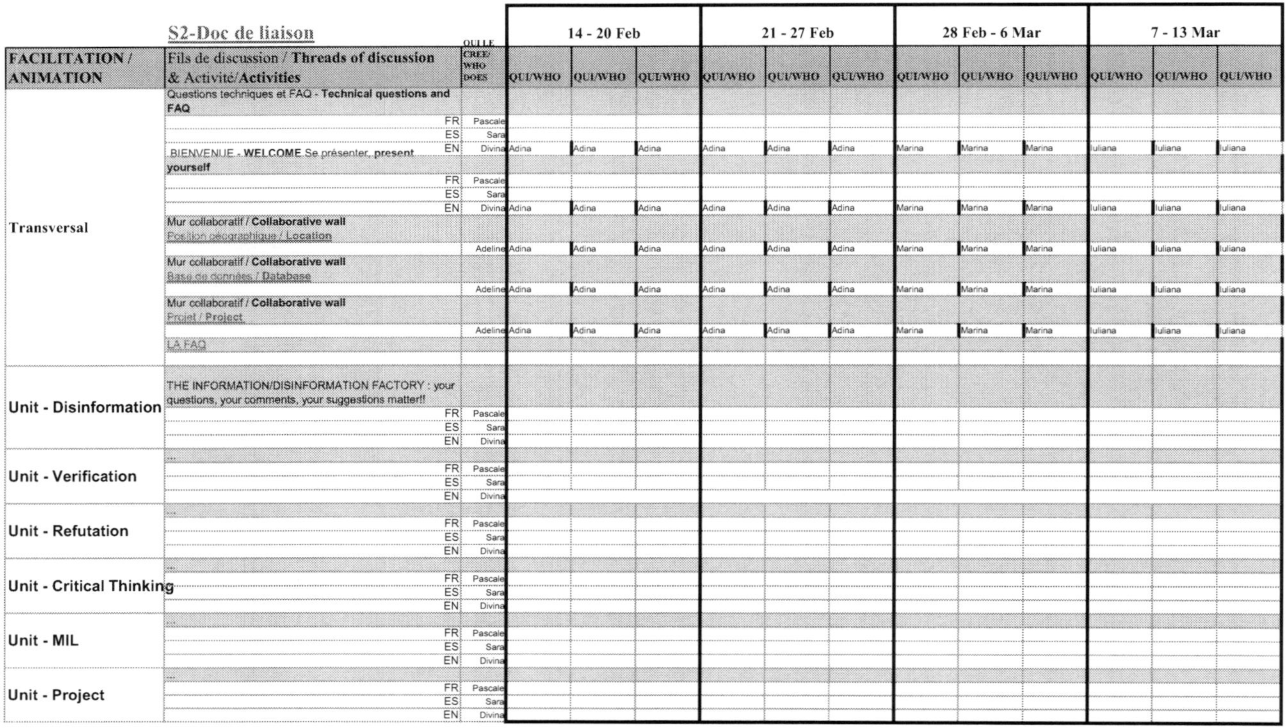

S2-Doc de liaison				14 - 20 Feb			21 - 27 Feb			28 Feb - 6 Mar			7 - 13 Mar		
FACILITATION / ANIMATION	Fils de discussion / **Threads of discussion** & Activité/**Activities**		QUI LE CREE/ WHO DOES	QUI/WHO	QUI/WHO	QUI/WHO	QUI/WHO	QUI/WHO	QUI/WHO	QUI/WHO	QUI/WHO	QUI/WHO	QUI/WHO	QUI/WHO	QUI/WHO
Transversal	Questions techniques et FAQ - **Technical questions and FAQ**														
		FR	Pascale												
		ES	Sara												
		EN	Divina	Adina	Adina	Adina	Adina	Adina	Adina	Marina	Marina	Marina	Iuliana	Iuliana	Iuliana
	BIENVENUE - **WELCOME** Se présenter, **present yourself**														
		FR	Pascale												
		ES	Sara												
		EN	Divina	Adina	Adina	Adina	Adina	Adina	Adina	Marina	Marina	Marina	Iuliana	Iuliana	Iuliana
	Mur collaboratif / **Collaborative wall** Position géographique / Location														
			Adeline	Adina	Adina	Adina	Adina	Adina	Adina	Marina	Marina	Marina	Iuliana	Iuliana	Iuliana
	Mur collaboratif / **Collaborative wall** Base de données / Database														
			Adeline	Adina	Adina	Adina	Adina	Adina	Adina	Marina	Marina	Marina	Iuliana	Iuliana	Iuliana
	Mur collaboratif / **Collaborative wall** Projet / Project														
			Adeline	Adina	Adina	Adina	Adina	Adina	Adina	Marina	Marina	Marina	Iuliana	Iuliana	Iuliana
	LA FAQ														
Unit - Disinformation	THE INFORMATION/DISINFORMATION FACTORY : your questions, your comments, your suggestions matter!!														
		FR	Pascale												
		ES	Sara												
		EN	Divina												
Unit - Verification	...														
		FR	Pascale												
		ES	Sara												
		EN	Divina												
Unit - Refutation	...														
		FR	Pascale												
		ES	Sara												
		EN	Divina												
Unit - Critical Thinking	...														
		FR	Pascale												
		ES	Sara												
		EN	Divina												
Unit - MIL	...														
		FR	Pascale												
		ES	Sara												
		EN	Divina												
Unit - Project	...														
		FR	Pascale												
		ES	Sara												
		EN	Divina												

Figure 6.7 Screenshot of the facilitation schedule per unit and facilitator.

				Animation du 22 - 28 Nov							Animation du 15 - 21 Nov					
FACILITATION / ANIMATION	Fils de discussion / **Threads of discussion** & Activité/**Activities**		QUI LE CREE/ WHO DOES	QUI/WHO > 22 NOV	QUI/WHO > 23 NOV	QUI/WHO > 24 NOV	QUI/WHO > 25 NOV	QUI/WHO > 26 NOV	QUI/WHO > 27 NOV	QUI/WHO > 28 NOV	QUI/WHO > 15 NOV	QUI/WHO > 16 NOV	QUI/WHO > 17 NOV	QUI/WHO > 18 NOV	QUI/WHO > 19 NOV	QUI/WHO > Name & date
Transversal	Questions techniques et FAQ - **Technical questions and FAQ**															
		FR	Pascale	Adeline	Adeline	Adeline	Adeline	Adeline	Adeline	Adeline	Adeline	Adeline	Adeline	Adeline	Adeline	Adeline
		ES	Sara													
		EN	Pascale								Adeline	Adeline	Adeline			
	BIENVENUE - **WELCOME** Se présenter, **present yourself**															
		FR	Pascale								Pascale, Sophia, Cyrille, Adeline, Jhony	Divina, Adeline	Adeline	Adeline	Adeline	Adeline
		ES	Sara													
		EN	Pascale								Adina	Adina	Adina	Adina	Adina	Adina
	Mur collaboratif / **Collaborative wall** Partagez une infox / **Share your fake**															
		FR	ADeline, Blaise	Adeline, Blaise	Adeline, Blaise	Adeline, Blaise	Adeline, Blaise	Adeline	Adeline, Blaise	Adeline, Blaise	Adeline, Blaise	Divina, blaise	Adeline, Blaise	Adeline, Blaise	Adeline, Blaise	Adeline, Blaise
		ES	ADeline													
		EN	ADeline				Joseph									
Unit 1 - 15 novCritical Thinking	Avez-vous été confronté à une infox? Have you been confronted with a fake?															
		FR	Pascale, Cyrille									Divina			Cyrille	
		ES	Sara													
		EN	Pascale				Joseph				Adina & Iuliana	Adina & Iuliana	Adina & Iuliana	Adina & Iuliana	Adina & Iuliana	Adina & Iuliana
Unit 2 - 15 novEMI/MIL	Avez-trouvé des infox pour faire votre base locale ? Have you found fake for your local infox base?															
		FR	Pascale													
		ES	Sara													
		EN	Pascale								Adina & Iuliana	Adina & Iuliana	Adina & Iuliana	Adina & Iuliana	Adina & Iuliana	Adina & Iuliana
Unit 3 - 22 NovDisinformation	Avez-vous décrypté des infox de votre base ? Have you analysed any infox of your base?															
		FR	Pascale												Cyrille	
		ES	Sara													
		EN	Pascale								Adina & Marina	Adina & Marina	Adina & Marina	Adina & Marina	Adina & Marina	Adina & Marina
Unit 4 - 29 NovVerification	Avez-vous vérifié des infox de votre base? Have you verified any fake of your base?															
		FR	Pascale													
		ES	Sara													
		EN	Pascale													
Unit 5 - 6 Dec Refutation	Avez vous réfuté des "infox" de votre base? Have you refuted any fake of your base?															
		FR	Pascale													
		ES	Sara													
		EN	Pascale													
Unit 6 - 6 Dec Project	Avez-vous créé une FAQ désinfo? Have you created a disinformation fake?															
		FR	Pascale													
		ES	Sara													
		EN	Pascale													

Figure 6.7 (Continued)

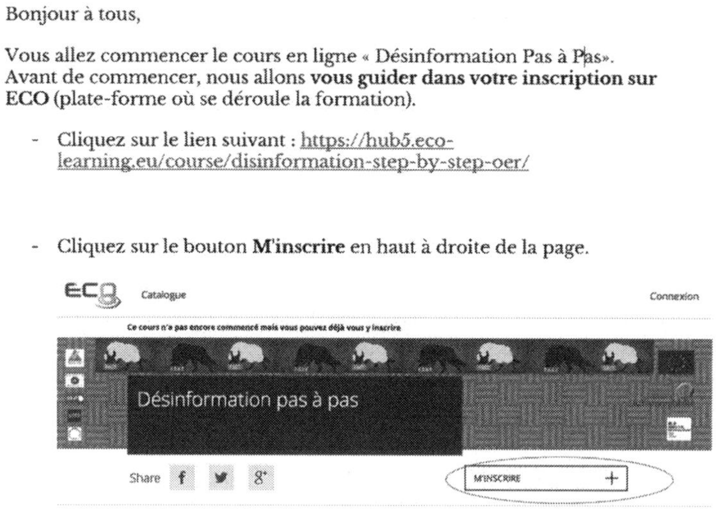

Bonjour à tous,

Vous allez commencer le cours en ligne « Désinformation Pas à Pas».
Avant de commencer, nous allons **vous guider dans votre inscription sur ECO** (plate-forme où se déroule la formation).

- Cliquez sur le lien suivant : https://hub5.eco-learning.eu/course/disinformation-step-by-step-oer/

- Cliquez sur le bouton **M'inscrire** en haut à droite de la page.

Figure 6.8 The registration tutorial.

iterations. Later, this tutorial was released to learners. The writing of a tutorial on how to use a Padlet was also carried out. This tutorial was produced collaboratively as evidenced by the comments. It was created to guide facilitators and participants in carrying out the activities hosted on the collaborative wall. It too evolved with the iterations.

6.5.2.3 Collectives and cultures

Several types of collectives and roles were in place to animate and organise the community (see Table 6.2).

As with previous ECO projects, YouVerify! brought together the logics of various kinds of actors (Bossu & Frau-Meigs, 2018). Each actor had a predetermined role: the teachers focused on the content and the activities; the facilitators on the follow-up that they could provide; the participants on their learning progress. But the borders were porous, and the actors oscillated from one role to another: from facilitator, to teacher, to peer. At the same time, various intercultural interactions took place, such as the exchanges between French and Romanian facilitators, or the co-creation of documents

Table 6.2 Summary of the natures of collectivities, roles, and interculturality

Roles	Participants, experts, facilitators, designers, partners, facilitation supervisor, peers
Collectives	Pedagogical team, facilitation team, community of practice, learning community, support groups
Cultures	Field, discipline, geographical origin

Table 6.3 Organisational choices and artefacts

Tools and artefacts	Virtual synchronous, asynchronous
Tools at the service of Management of tasks and animation teams	Videoconferencing service, collaborative organisation tool, instant messaging, electronic messaging
Artefacts	Tutorials, team image, facilitator missions, calendar, collaborative writing walls, collaborative liaison document

with teachers and community managers. This porosity was reinforced by the participation of some of the facilitators in several teams, which created a bridge between the cultural collectives. For instance, the Spanish were very active with peers in South America (Cuba in particular), the French with peers in French-speaking Africa.

Several organisational choices and artefacts were put in place to organise the community (see Table 6.3).

The artefacts and the organisation offered the possibility of bringing together various actors for the facilitation of the MOOC by promoting synchronous and asynchronous exchanges and common spaces accessible to all. In addition, the teams, in search of continuous and constant improvement, were co-developing the materials, the artefacts, and the organisation throughout the two iterations.

Thus, the artefacts and the organisation offered the possibility of having various actors collaborate for the facilitation of the MOOC in order to make individuals from various cultures and fields learn from the materials and from each other and to make them collaborate through the co-construction of the artefacts and activities offered.

6.5.3 The various methodologies used to develop the MOOC

All actions and facilitation materials were carried out with the aim of supporting and engaging participants into action. To automate and offer "constant" content, the MOOC was based on an instructivist pedagogical model with introductory resources, written content, a calendar, paths to follow, and lists of activities to carry out. To complete this approach and promote interactions between peers, learning was also based on exchanges and co-construction. The team emphasised approaches specific to socio-constructivism and connectivism. It developed participatory practices and moderation to strengthen the contribution of the entire collectivity. To these two active pedagogical approaches, the possibility of learning with a transmissive and self-training approach was added, with the validation of the course by simply reading the content in a linear manner and taking the various quizzes offered. The MOOC also became an OER at the end of the project.

The facilitation team sought to meet the heterogeneous needs of as many people as possible. The team also developed several modules, which were offered but not imposed (workshops 1 and workshops 2, Project construction unit, etc.). Participants could choose among these extra options but could also create their own journey, in a non-linear way. All participants were free to choose their resources and activities. To help and guide the participants in their self-training and empowerment, the team offered some benchmarks to "frame" the learning process with cross-cutting resources to help the participants find their way around the MOOC (tutorials, procedures, FAQs, participant charters, etc.). The teaching team in conjunction with the facilitation team provided redundant contents in the course modules, to accommodate various levels of participant knowledge (entry level, advanced level). Weekly mass mailings were made by electronic messages and notifications on the MOOC with reminders were sent. Web conferences were recorded and accessible at any time. Models and templates for carrying out activities and building projects were available for easy download (see Figure 6.9).

Using this template, the participants could carry out their activity by responding as they wished to the structured elements of the project. In this way, they had better chances of validating their project and their learning path.

Thus, even if based on socio-constructivism, the MOOC could be followed with an instructivist and transmissive pedagogical approach, with the consultation of resources and the validation of knowledge acquisition

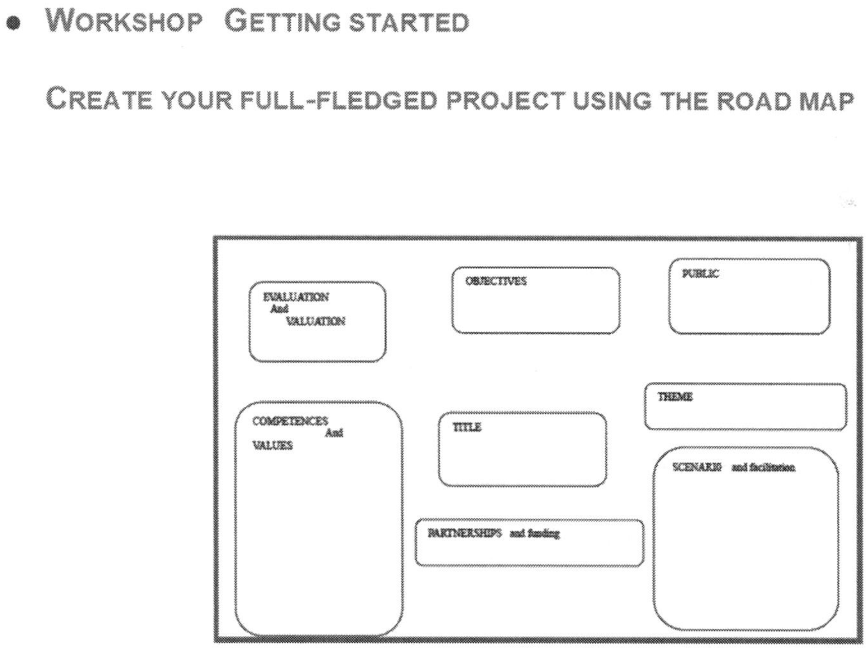

Figure 6.9 Screenshots of the "roadmap" to carry out MIL projects.

through quizzes. The proposed activities responded to the possibility of choosing one's path. They illustrated the integration of different educational approaches: activities to be carried out alone, such as the search for resources, viewing, reading and quizzes; collaborative activities such as the co-construction of the "fake news" database; peer-reviewed activities; resource creation activities – the team produced some elements to show the example, and some participants played the game of creation, they became content producers. The shared creations and co-productions were incorporated as learning material for the following iteration.

Participants could therefore, should they wish to, validate their course by accessing only the resources and content, by taking the quizzes, without any exchange or direct support. This last solution, without moderation, led to the final version of the MOOC, in OER, with no access to all the interaction spaces (forum, collaborative documents). This makes the MOOC accessible to everyone, while avoiding a re-mobilisation of the teaching team whose continuous availability is not sustainable. However, with the benefit of two iterations and facilitation, the materials provided in the final version show not only the knowledge base but also the learning process upon which new learners can build their competences. The learning device leaves participants free to choose, according to their aspirations and possibilities, how to use and carry out the MOOC.

Several teaching and learning processes were associated with the MOOC "Disinformation Step by Step" (see Table 6.4).

The objective of the facilitation process and its attendant artefacts and activities were to meet the needs of the participants, i.e., to consolidate while individualising and contextualising the learning experience and adapting to changes, user practices, and cultures, and emerging features of technology solutions. The multiplicity of supports, pedagogical models, and activities seem to favour the achievement of these objectives, or at least was chosen to try to respond to the greatest number while promoting interactions and co-construction.

But this multiplicity does not mean going in all directions because the facilitation process, like that of creation of the MOOC, cannot be improvised and requires organisation. This organisation seems to have positive consequences on the effectiveness of the facilitation and the level of satisfaction with the MOOC and its experience.

The general results about facilitation were captured in a satisfaction questionnaire that had two questions about the process (satisfaction with facilitation and satisfaction with interactions with others), in the two iterations.

Table 6.4 Summary of the teaching and learning processes of the MOOC "Disinformation Step by Step"

Connectivist and socio-constructivist pedagogical approaches	Activities of exchanges, sharing, co-construction, monitoring,...
Transmissive and instructivist approaches	Self-training, tests, OER,...

Those two questions yielded excellent results, with high levels of satisfaction, especially from the English language Romanian participants, much less exposed to this learning device than the other partners (see Chapter 5).

Among the other measures of success, the low level of attrition was a remarkable achievement, especially for a non-academic course, as usually 90% of enrollees never finish and drop out (Aldowah et al., 2020). There were 2,401 participants registered overall, of which 1,373 active, which brings the completion rate to an average of nearly 60%. Among them, 628 took quizzes, 383 obtained badges, and 333 completed the feedback questionnaire, all far above average results. In terms of appropriation and transfer of competences, the padlet on disinformation yielded 135 cases for the "fake news" database and the padlet on MIL projects 23 roadmaps. They testify to the success of such learning devices as the sMOOC for transfer and localisation.

6.6 Discussion

The objectives of the research questions were met as regards facilitation. Results showed that facilitation practices and processes identified by previous research to facilitate intercultural communities in a MOOC were effective in a MOOC dedicated to MIL, teaching with media about media. The observations helped to identify some key success factors to facilitate practices in an intercultural MOOC about MIL. And finally, results showed that facilitation practices helped build a sense of community and ensure transfer of knowledge in an intercultural MOOC about MIL.

Facilitation goals were completed on several levels: to transmit information, to support participants, and to engage learners. They were relatively successful in overcoming the difficulty in MOOCs to respond to each and everyone, with the risk that massification might reduce the consideration of individual specificities (Andersen & Ponti, 2014; Haavind & Sistek-Chandler, 2015; Hew & Cheung, 2014; Mackness et al., 2013). This challenge was even more difficult to achieve as the international dimension made it necessary not only to engage a large number of participants but also to respect their heterogeneous diversity (Walji et al., 2016). The facilitation team of the MOOC "Disinformation Step by Step" was able to meet these requirements by applying the practices identified to meet this challenge while going further with the idea of replicability and the transfer of the learning device and its attendant practices.

6.6.1 To meet individual requirements and multiple intercultural specificities, the facilitation team developed responses adapted to each culture (RQ1)

Having the facilitation teams organised by language and country around the learning device made it easier to engage the multicultural learning community. The content and teaching materials were recontextualised and, therefore, adapted for learning and engagement by country. Animation by intercultural groups was ensured by the constitution of groups by language, and the creation of spaces for exchanges or collaborative materials dedicated to each language, as recommended by De Waard et al. (2014) and Godwin-Jones (2014). This reinforced the commitment of learners from local communities, since the MOOC seemed adapted to their needs. Similarly, communications were made on social networks by each cultural team and contributed to appropriate, challenging, and engaging communication. This made it possible to overcome the cultural barriers of the MOOC creators (Colas et al., 2016). Participants did not have to adapt to the MOOC creators' culture because mediation was appropriate within their own culture.

Facilitators identified by language and community were also good points of reference for supporting learners who felt attended by people who were "close", because of their origin. Peers "identified" as a "cultural peer" when they were geographically close, which in turn fostered engagement and motivation. The MOOC as sMOOC offered activities between peers and by teams that were built around common interests or geographical locations, promoting trusted interactions (Ross et al., 2014). In addition, some learners followed face-to-face online training and met physically. Conversely, the peer-to-peer learning communities facilitated the work of facilitators (Ross et al., 2014).

The diversity of the actors, whether participants or members of the teaching and facilitation teams, grouped by geographical or disciplinary cultures around the resources, activities, methodologies, and artefacts adapted to the contexts and facilitated by an adjusted communication, made it possible to meet the intercultural requirements. This also promoted adaptation to the requirements of the skill and knowledge levels of the participants. Everyone could find the answer to their needs with the teachers present to meet more theoretical needs, the facilitators for more organisational questions, and the peers for the needs of interaction, sharing of practice, and feedback. The "pedagogical" presence (Frau-Meigs & Bossu, 2017) was ensured by contextualised content, appropriate media and apps, co-produced artefacts, facilitators, and "close" peers. It reduced attrition and disengagement by ensuring a social presence that was visible and accessible to all.

6.6.2 Developing specific artefacts and organisational tools made it possible to develop specific facilitation practices which were key success factors of engagement (RQ2)

The visibility and accessibility of artefacts made the participants' questions and answers visible to everyone, on forums, social networks, and other spaces. The artefacts then had a real role of mediation and support in the learning path of the MOOC. They provided solutions to counter the obstacles identified for the dual needs of a "massive" community and individual participants (Andersen & Ponti, 2014; Haavind & Sistek-Chandler, 2015; Hew & Cheung, 2014; Mackness et al., 2013). Visible artefacts and interactions were proof of presence and contained the answers to the questions asked or the examples and testimonials sought. They even encouraged participants to give access to their profiles, for peer networking, reinforcing the idea that peers promoted the engagement of participants.

Paradoxically, the more the MOOC was massive and fostered interactions, the more likely it was to meet everyone's needs. The socio-constructivist approach of the MOOC favoured this phenomenon as well as interculturality. The facilitation teams had chosen to leave the content and interactions visible to everyone without splitting by language or domain. Thus, exchanges and content in other languages, as well as all activities were accessible to all. The purpose of this openness was to capitalise on interculturality (Bossu, 2021).

6.6.3 *Transfer was ensured by specific, massive, and intercultural facilitation artefacts and mediation practices (RQ3)*

Artefacts created and practices used throughout the facilitation process of the sMOOC had several functions, at several stages. At the beginning of the MOOC production, some were created to manage, coordinate, inform, and train the facilitators and the teaching staff. The interactions they elicited were visible to all other teams. Then, during the iteration, the artefacts and interactions helped the facilitators foster collaboration, codesign, and feedback loops. Finally, during and after the iteration, they benefited the participants who were able to proceed with their own interactions and their own productions and projects.

The teams, in search of continuous and constant improvement, reflected together on the evolution of the system throughout the two iterations. They capitalised on interculturality by sharing the experiences, needs, practices, and solutions of all. The interactions between the pedagogical team and the facilitation team contributed to building the motivation of all actors involved. The fact of sharing common artefacts, of co-constructing them, and of following their evolution not only engaged the designer and facilitator levels but also snowballed into engaging the participants. Finally, after having appropriated these artefacts and collaboration practices, participants applied them in their own context, in relation to disinformation and to other MIL themes (hate speech, cyber-harassment, etc.). The facilitators in particular continued to maintain their communities active with these resources and these practices.

This intercultural facilitation was aligned with the socio-constructivist methodologies used in the MOOC as social MOOC. Users contributed their experiences to the making of the learning device, and they were able to reuse the artefacts and practices. Across the two iterations, the constant reflexivity as to the evolution of practices testified to a search for continuous intercultural improvement and appropriation to the chosen context.

The difficulties of designing the facilitation of the MOOC resided in the profusion of interactions, resources, actors, and practices which, while paradoxically being the driving force, hindered their identification. The use of people who were experts in agility and had reached a certain epistemological maturity (Frau-Meigs & Bossu, 2018) was a real advantage, as was the case with the YouVerify! Partners who had accumulated experience on dealing with disinformation and media amplification. Intercultural and digital competences were also essential to the success of a project of this magnitude.

6.7 Conclusion

The MOOC "Disinformation Step by Step" achieved its purpose, to scale up training on how to fight disinformation, particularly in a situation where constraints on spatial movement and time management were heavy due to the Covid-19 crisis and confinement. The choice of a MOOC learning device proved to be well suited to MIL. This project-based field already relied on communities of practice, which is one of the recommendations of research into MOOC facilitation. The facilitation challenges resided in getting such communities to interact in a meaningful way, so as to maximise engagement and transfer. The use of multiple actors, activities, artefacts, and tools contributed to the success of the MIL intervention, in terms of learning, interaction, and transfer of practices across communities. The hybridisation of forms of presence and pedagogical strategies was also a success factor, both triggering interactions and resulting from them.

The MOOC as a learning device became a digital common, empowering its participants and fostering collective intelligence in the fight against disinformation, as evinced by the responses in the satisfaction questionnaires. This device may be conducive to the development of the field of MIL, which also has the dual challenge of training people and developing innovative practices. Capitalising on engaging practices and intercultural training, with a particular attention to facilitation processes, can foster an international community of practice, to address a transborder phenomenon such as disinformation.

Notes

1 https://openclassrooms.com
2 https://hub5.eco-learning.eu/course/disinformation-step-by-step-oer/
3 https://hub5.eco-learning.eu/course/disinformation-step-by-step/oer

References

Aldowah, H., Al-Samarraie, H., & Alzahrani, A. I. (2020). Factors affecting student dropout in MOOCs: A cause and effect decision-making model. *Journal of Computers in Higher Education*, *32*, 429–454. https://doi.org/10.1007/s12528-019-09241-y

Allard-Poesi, F., & Perret, V. (2003). La Recherche-Action. In Y. Giordano (Ed.), *Conduire un projet de recherche, une perspective qualitative* (pp. 85–132). EMS. https://hal-upec-upem.archives-ouvertes.fr/hal-01490609

Andersen, R., & Ponti, M. (2014). Participatory pedagogy in an open educational course: Challenges and opportunities. *Distance Education*, *35*(2), 234–249. https://doi.org/10.1080/01587919.2014.917703

Beaven, T., Hauck, M., Comas-Quinn, A., Lewis, T., & de los Arcos, B. (2014). MOOCs: Striking the right balance between facilitation and self-determination. *MERLOT Journal of Online Learning and Teaching*, *10*(1), 31–43.

Bossu, A. (2020). *Système d'action agile et dispositif interculturel numérique: le cas du MOOC Pas à Pas du projet ECO*. PhD Thesis, Université Michel de Montaigne - Bordeaux III. https://tel.archives-ouvertes.fr/tel-03132056

Bossu, A. (2021). Interculturality and agility in MOOC design: The MOOC step by step project. In D. Frau-Meigs, S. Osuna-Acedo, & C. Marta Lazo (Eds.), *MOOCs and the participatory challenge: From revolution to reality* (pp. 71–88). Springer.

Bossu, A., & Frau-Meigs, D. (2018, March 28). L'agilité et l'interculturalité en question dans le dispositif global-local des MOOC: le cas du MOOC Pas à Pas. *Pré-Actes. TICEMED 11, Pédagogie et numérique: L'enseignement supérieur au défi de la mondialisation?*, University Cadi Ayyad Marrakech, Morocco. http://www.ticemed.eu/app/download/23659149/Pr%C3%A9-actes+Ticemed11+v180403.pdf

Boumazguida, K., Temperman, G., & Lièvre, B. D. (2022). Quels outils d'aide à la réussite pour quels profils d'apprenants dans un MOOC hybride? *Recherches En Éducation*, *46*. https://doi.org/10.4000/ree.10130

Breton, P., & Proulx, S. (2002). *L'explosion de la communication à l'aube du XXIe siècle*. La Découverte & Syros.

Brown, J. S., & Duguid, P. (1991). Organizational learning and communities-of-practice: Toward a unified view of working, learning, and innovation. *Organization Science*, *2*(1), 40–57. https://doi.org/10.1287/orsc.2.1.40

Cambien, A. (2008). *Une introduction à l'approche systémique: appréhender la complexité* (p. 87) [Research report]. Centre d'études sur les réseaux, les transports, l'urbanisme et les constructions publiques (CERTU).

Chevry-Pebayle, E., & Rossini, I. (2017). Besoins et dispositifs d'aide dans le contexte d'apprentissage des MOOC. *Distances et Médiations Des Savoirs*, *19*(19). https://doi.org/10.4000/dms.1940

Cisel, M. (2016). *Utilisations des MOOC: éléments de typologie*. Thèse, Université Paris-Saclay. https://tel.archives-ouvertes.fr/tel-01444125

Cohen, W. M., & Levinthal, D. A. (1990). Absorptive capacity: A new perspective on learning and innovation. *Administrative Science Quarterly*, *35*(1), 128–152. https://doi.org/10.2307/2393553

Colas, J.-F., Sloep, P. B., & Garreta-Domingo, M. (2016). The effect of multilingual facilitation on active participation in MOOCs. *The International Review of Research in Open and Distributed Learning*, *17*(4). https://doi.org/10.19173/irrodl.v17i4.2470

Collin, S., & Saffari, H. (2015). Le MOOC et le "hype": analyse critique des discours médiatiques sur les MOOC. *Revue internationale des technologies en pédagogie universitaire*, *12*(1–2), 124–137. https://doi.org/10.18162/ritpu-2015-v12n12-11

Creplet, F., Doupouet, O., Kern, F., & Munier, F. (2005). Organizational and cognitive duality based on interactions between communities. *European Journal of Economic and Social Systems*, *18*(1), 111–123. https://ideas.repec.org/a/ris/ejessy/0125.html

Davis, H. C., Dickens, K., Leon Urrutia, M., del Sanchéz Vera, M. M., & White, S. (2014, April). MOOCs for Universities and Learners An analysis of motivating factors. *6th International Conference on Computer Supported Education (03/04/14)*, Southampton. https://eprints.soton.ac.uk/363714/

de Waard, I., Gallagher, M. S., Zelezny-Green, R., Czerniewicz, L., Downes, S., Kukulska-Hulme, A., & Willems, J. (2014). Challenges for conceptualising EU MOOC for vulnerable learner groups. *Proceedings of the European MOOC Stakeholder Summit 2014* (pp. 33–42). http://www.emoocs2014.eu/sites/default/files/Proceedings-Moocs-Summit-2014.pdf

Delgado-Kloos, C., Munoz-Merino, P. J., Alario-Hoyos, C., Estevez Ayres, I., & Fernandez-Panadero, C. (2015). Mixing and blending MOOC Technologies with face-to-face pedagogies. *2015 IEEE Global Engineering Education Conference (EDUCON)* (pp. 967–971). https://doi.org/10.1109/EDUCON.2015.7096090

Demorgon, J. (2005). Langues et cultures comme objets et comme aventures. *Ela. Etudes de linguistique appliquée*, *140*(4), 395–407. https://www.cairn.info/revue-ela-2005-4-page-395.htm

Devos, C., & Dumay, X. (2006). Les facteurs qui influencent le transfert: une revue de la littérature. *Savoirs*, *12*(3), 9–46. https://www.cairn.info/revue-savoirs-2006-3-page-9.htm

Downes, S. (2012). *Connectivism and connective knowledge: Essays on meaning and learning networks.* http://www.downes.ca/files/books/Connective_Knowledge-19May2012.pdf

Engeström, Y. (1999). Activity theory and individual and social transformation. In *Perspectives on activity theory* (pp. 19–38). Cambridge University Press. https://doi.org/10.1017/CBO9780511812774.003

Ferguson, R., & Sharples, M. (2014). Innovative pedagogy at massive scale: Teaching and learning in MOOCs. In C. Rensing, S. De Freitas, T. Ley, & P. J. Muñoz-Merino (Eds.), *Open learning and teaching in educational communities* (vol. 8719, pp. 98–111). Springer. https://doi.org/10.1007/978-3-319-11200-8_8

Frau-Meigs, D., & Bossu, A. (2017). Towards e-presence at distance as a way to reach and share e-quality: The case of the ECO sMOOCs. In *Digital Education: Out to the World and Back to the Campus: 5th European MOOCs Stakeholders Summit, EMOOCs 2017, Proceedings* (pp. 38–47). Springer International Publishing.

Frau-Meigs, D., & Bossu, A. (2018). La maturité épistémique dans les MOOC: le cas du MOOC "Pas à Pas" du projet européen ECO. *Revue française des sciences de l'information et de la communication, 12.*

Frau-Meigs, D., Osuna-Acedo, S., & Marta-Lazo, C. (Eds.). (2021). *MOOCs and the participatory challenge. From revolution to reality.* Springer.

Gherardi, S., & Nicolini, D. (2000). The organizational learning of safety in communities of practice. *Journal of Management Inquiry*, *9*(1), 7–18. https://doi.org/10.1177/105649260091002

Godwin-Jones, R. (2014). Games in language learning: Opportunities and challenges. *Language Learning & Technology*, *18*(2), 9–19. http://dx.doi.org/10125/44363

Haavind, S., & Sistek-Chandler, C. (2015). The emergent role of the MOOC instructor: A qualitative study of trends toward improving future practice. *International Journal on E-Learning*, *14*, 331–350. https://www.learntechlib.org/primary/p/150663/

Hew, K. F., & Cheung, W. S. (2014). Students' and instructors' use of massive open online courses (MOOCs): Motivations and challenges. *Educational Research Review*, *12*, 45–58. https://doi.org/10.1016/j.edurev.2014.05.001

Hew, K. F., Qiao, C., & Tang, Y. (2018). Understanding student engagement in large-scale open online courses: A machine learning facilitated analysis of student's reflections in 18 highly rated MOOCs. *The International Review of Research in Open and Distributed Learning*, *19*(3). https://doi.org/10.19173/irrodl.v19i3.3596

Hlady-Rispal, M. (2015). Une stratégie de recherche en gestion: L'étude de cas. *Revue Française de Gestion*, *41*(253), 251–266. https://doi.org/10.3166/RFG.253.251-266

Hylén, J. (2005). Open educational resources: Opportunities and challenges. *OECD's Centre for Educational Research and Innovation, 10*. http://www.oecd.org/education/ceri/37351085.pdf

Ihadjadene, M., & Chaudiron, S. (2008). Quelles analyses de l'usage des moteurs de recherche. *Questions de communication*, *14*, 17–32. https://doi.org/10.4000/questionsdecommunication.604

Israel, M. J. (2015). Effectiveness of integrating MOOCs in traditional classrooms for undergraduate students. *The International Review of Research in Open and Distributed Learning*, *16*(5). https://doi.org/10.19173/irrodl.v16i5.2222

Karlsson, N., & Godhe, A.-L. (2016). Creating a community rather than a course—Possibilities and dilemmas in an MOOC. *Education Sciences*, *6*(4), 18. https://doi.org/10.3390/educsci6020018

King, I., & Lee, W.-I. (2023). Roles of MOOCs in times of crises. In I. King & W.-I. Lee, *A decade of MOOCs and beyond* (pp. 135–151). Springer. https://doi.org/10.1007/978-3-031-15241-2_8

Knox, J. (2014). Digital culture clash: "massive" education in the *E-learning and Digital Cultures* MOOC. *Distance Education*, *35*(2), 164–177. https://doi.org/10.1080/01587919.2014.917704

Kop, R., Fournier, H., & Mak, J. S. F. (2011). A pedagogy of abundance or a pedagogy to support human beings? Participant support on massive open online courses. *The International Review of Research in Open and Distributed Learning*, *12*(7), 74. https://doi.org/10.19173/irrodl.v12i7.1041

Littlejohn, A., & Hood, N. (2018). *Reconceptualising learning in the digital age*. Springer Singapore. https://doi.org/10.1007/978-981-10-8893-3

Mackness, J., Waite, M., Roberts, G., & Lovegrove, E. (2013). Learning in a small, task–oriented, connectivist MOOC: Pedagogical issues and implications for higher education. *The International Review of Research in Open and Distributed Learning*, *14*(4). https://doi.org/10.19173/irrodl.v14i4.1548

McDermott, R. (1999). Learning across teams: How to build communities of practice in team organizations. *Knowledge Management Review*, *8*, 32–38.

Medina-Salguero, R., & Aguaded Gómez, J. I. (2013). La ayuda pedagógica en los MOOC's: un nuevo enfoque en la acción tutorial. *@tic. revista d'innovació educativa*, *11*, 30–39. https://dialnet.unirioja.es/servlet/articulo?codigo=4550733

Morin, E. (1992). *Introduction à la pensée complexe*. ESF.

Morin, E., & Le Moigne, J.-L. (1999). *L'intelligence de la complexité*. L'Harmattan.

Morrissette, J., & Desgagné, S. (2009). Le jeu des positions de savoir en recherche collaborative: une analyse des points de vue négociés d'un groupe d'enseignantes du primaire. *Recherches qualitatives*, *28*(2), 118–144. https://papyrus.bib.umontreal.ca/xmlui/handle/1866/21551

Mucchielli, A. (2004). *Approche par la modélisation des relations*. Armand Colin.

Musso, P., Ponthou, L., & Seulliet, É. (2007). *Fabriquer le futur: l'imaginaire au service de l'innovation*. Village mondial.

Ospina-Delgado, J. E., Zorio-Grima, A., & García-Benau, M. A. (2016). Massive open online courses in higher education: A data analysis of the MOOC supply. *Intangible Capital*, *12*(5), 1401–1450. https://doi.org/10.3926/ic.798

Osuna-Acedo, S., Frau-Meigs, D., Camarero-Cano, L., Bossu, A., Pedrosa, R., & Jansen, D. (2017). Intercreativity and interculturality in the virtual learning environments of the ECO MOOC project. In M. Jemni, & M. K. Khribi (Eds.), *Open education: From OERs to MOOCs* (pp. 161–187). Springer. https://doi.org/10.1007/978-3-662-52925-6_9

Paillé, P., & Mucchielli, A. (2012). *L'analyse qualitative en sciences humaines et sociales*. Armand Colin.

Peltier, C., & Séguin, C. (2021). Hybridation et dispositifs hybrides de formation dans l'enseignement supérieur: revue de la littérature 2012–2020. *Distances et Médiations Des Savoirs*, *35*. https://doi.org/10.4000/dms.6414

Peraya, D. (2019). Les objets techniques dans la formation. Apport du concept de dispositif dans l'analyse des processus d'apprentissage médiatisé. In B. Albero, S. Simonian, & J. Eneau (Eds.), *Des humains et des machines. Hommage aux travaux d'une exploratrice* (pp. 206–218). Editions Raisons et Passions. https://archive-ouverte.unige.ch/unige:116760

Perrenoud, P. (2002). D'une métaphore à l'autre: transférer ou mobiliser ses connaissances? In J. Dolz & E. Ollagnier, *L'énigme de la compétence en éducation* (p. 45). De Boeck Supérieur. https://doi.org/10.3917/dbu.dolz.2002.01.0045

Picard, D., & Marc, E. (2013). *L'École de Palo Alto*. Presses Universitaires de France. https://www.cairn.info/l-ecole-de-palo-alto--9782130606628.htm

Reix, R. (2011). *Systèmes d'information et management des organisations*. Vuibert.

Rodet, J. (2016). *L'ingénierie tutorale. Définir, concevoir, diffuser et évaluer les services d'accompagnement des apprenants d'un digital learning*. JIP Éditions.

Ross, J., Sinclair, C., Knox, J., Bayne, S., & Macleod, H. (2014). Teacher experiences and academic identity: The missing components of MOOC pedagogy. *MERLOT Journal of Online Learning and Teaching*, *10*(1), 57–69.

Savoir*Devenir. (2021). MOOC disinformation step by step. https://hub5.eco-learning.eu/course/disinformation-step-by-step-oer/

Savoir*Devenir. (2022). Project Youverify! https://youverify.eu; https://savoirdevenir.net/projets

Siemens, G. (2005). Connectivism: A learning theory for the digital age. *International Journal of Instructional Technology and Distance Learning*, *2*(1), 3–10.

Simon, H. A. (1979). Rational decision making in business organizations. *The American Economic Review*, *69*(4), 493–513. https://www.jstor.org/stable/1808698

Tardif, J., & Meirieu, P. (1996). Stratégie en vue de favoriser le transfert des connaissances. *Vie Pédagogique*, *98*, 4–7.

Tremblay, D.-G. (2004). Communities of practice: What are the conditions for implementation in a virtual multi-organization community? *Organizações & Sociedade*, *11*(31), 25–39. https://doi.org/10.1590/S1984-92302004000300002

Tremblay, D.-G., Rolland, D., & Davel, E. P. B. (2003). New management forms for the knowledge economy? HRM in the context of teamwork and participation. *Research Note No 2003-14A*. Canada Research Chair on the Socio-Organizational Challenges of the Knowledge Economy.

Trestini, M. (2016). *Théorie des systèmes complexes appliquée à la modélisation d'environnements numériques d'apprentissage de nouvelle génération*. HDR, Université de Strasbourg. https://hal.archives-ouvertes.fr/tel-01432687

Vygotskij, L. S., Sève, F., & Fernandez, G. (2003). *Conscience, inconscient, émotions*. La Dispute.

Walji, S., Deacon, A., Small, J., & Czerniewicz, L. (2016). Learning through engagement: MOOCs as an emergent form of provision. *Distance Education*, *37*(2), 208–223. https://doi.org/10.1080/01587919.2016.1184400

Watson, S. L., Loizzo, J., Watson, W. R., Mueller, C., Lim, J., & Ertmer, P. A. (2016). Instructional design, facilitation, and perceived learning outcomes: An exploratory case study of a human trafficking MOOC for attitudinal change. *Educational Technology Research and Development*, *64*(6), 1273–1300. https://doi.org/10.1007/s11423-016-9457-2

Wenger, E. (1998). *Communities of practice: Learning, meaning, and identity*. Cambridge University Press.

Zacklad, M. (2013). Le travail de management en tant qu'activité de cadrage et de recadrage du contexte des transactions coopératives. *Activités*, *10*(1). https://doi.org/10.4000/activites.650

Zhu, M., Sari, A., & Lee, M. M. (2018). A systematic review of research methods and topics of the empirical MOOC literature (2014–2016). *The Internet and Higher Education*, *37*, 31–39. https://doi.org/10.1016/j.iheduc.2018.01.002

7 Fighting against disinformation

Measuring effects in Spain

Sonia Santoveña-Casal, José Javier Hueso Romero, and Javier Gil-Quintana

Introduction

Disinformation is information that is shared and partially based on reality, deliberately produced to harm, create doubt, and increase mistrust either in individuals or in groups, in institutions or in countries (Wardle & Derakhshan, 2017). It is a growing phenomenon that has become one of the main challenges of the digital society.

The exponential increase in the amount of disinformation disseminated has generated a feeling of mistrust among citizens towards the veracity of information (Magallón, 2019). This situation has led to the fight against disinformation and its new forms of dissemination becoming a priority for policymakers and many professionals affected by disinformation such as journalists (Scheibenzuber et al., 2023; Sádaba & Salaverría, 2023). In 2015, the International Fact-Checking Network (IFCN) was created by the Poynter Institute, which aims to "bring together the growing community of fact-checkers around the world and advocates of truthful information in the global fight against disinformation" (Poynter, 2015). The European Union has implemented different types of measures aimed at regulating and combating this phenomenon. In 2018, the EU *Code of Practice on Disinformation* was published, which seeks to empower individuals as consumers in the face of disinformation (European Commission, 2018). It was revised in 2022 to reinforce the accountability of the social media platforms (European Commission, 2022).

This chapter analyses the phenomenon of disinformation from the perspective of professionals from three different areas (politics, communication-journalism, and education). We considered three variables: the most problematic impacts and key players in disinformation; the main measures to be taken to combat disinformation; the role of education in the fight against disinformation. In addition, we examined the interest shown by citizens in an educational programme based on the fight against disinformation.

This research is part of a wider project, YouVerify!, which aimed to address the crucial challenges posed by fake news and to help young people develop their knowledge and skills to learn how to differentiate between real and manipulated images or videos. The project was funded by the European

DOI: 10.4324/9781003387404-10

Commission, within the "Media Literacy for All" (2020) programme. It was carried out by AFP France, National University of Distance Education (UNED) Spain, National University of Political Studies and Public Administration (SNSPA) Romania, and Savoir*Devenir France, the latter institution coordinating the project (for the full results of the policy focus groups, see Chapter 5 of this book).

7.1 Literature review

7.1.1 The most problematic impacts of disinformation

Without wishing to be exhaustive in the analysis of statistics, it seems interesting to highlight some of them, with a focus on Spain. Recent data from the European Commission show the impact of disinformation in Europe: 83% of people think disinformation threatens democracy; 63% of younger Europeans come across fake news more than once a week; and 51% of Europeans think they have been exposed to disinformation online (European Commission, 2021). According to the Eurobarometer (2022), 82% of Spanish nationals consider disinformation to be a problem in the country and 81% regularly encounter fake news or hoaxes, 54% consider that it is easy to identify fake news, and 82% consider that it distorts reality. Furthermore, very low percentages of trust in the online media are registered: only 22% of these people trust the internet and 10% trust the networks; trust in the traditional media (press 37%, radio 45%, television 32%) is relatively low as well. This has led the Spanish government to state that "hoaxes and disinformation have long represented a global threat to freedom and democracy" (Ministry of Foreign Affairs, European Union and Cooperation, s/f.).

When considering the measures for protection against disinformation in Spain, results show that among Spanish nationals, 25% consult different sources, 40% do not share the news, 37% discuss the news with a person they trust, 29% stop using the source, 28% do not pay attention to news disseminated by people whose reliability they have no reference to, 20% have greater trust in more reputable sources, and 14% do not point to any alternative or do not know (Statista, 2020). This information shows that the political and social spheres have been the areas most affected by disinformation and the dissemination of fake news.

From a political point of view, two of the most significant and probably most studied cases have been the impact of disinformation in the 2016 US elections and the Brexit referendum campaign (Grinberg et al., 2019; Shao et al., 2018). As García-Orosa (2021) argued, these cases defined the moment where concerns about the influence of the internet on democracy reached what he calls "the fourth wave", where artificial intelligence, big data, and, among others, "the validation of lies as a political strategy (among other phenomena, fake news and deep fakes)" acquired prominence (García-Orosa, 2021, p. 4).

The 2020 health emergency due to the pandemic caused by COVID-19, when disinformation had a major impact, was another defining moment. In the field of public health, networks have become, with Twitter (Kaya, 2020) standing out, a new means of communication between professionals and citizens. They have been considered a potential tool for improving health, as it favours collaboration and interaction between people with different profiles and characteristics (Moorhead et al., 2013). Social networks played a fundamental role in the dissemination of health information, whether this information was verified or not by users. However, during this pandemic period, health disinformation on networks about COVID-19 increased exponentially (Rosenberg, et al., 2020). As a consequence, disinformation has been considered another epidemic during COVID-19. False information has been on the rise and has had a serious effect on society, among which the way the control of the virus was managed. Denials, conspiracy theories, connections between political interests and healthy behaviour, links between migration and the spread of the virus, and, among others, fake news about the vaccine and its negative effects on health have been the predominant themes that have led to this phenomenon being labelled as "infodemic" by the World Health Organisation (WHO).

Disinformation activity has also been experienced exponentially with the Russia-Ukraine conflict. Since the development of this conflict in 2022, it has been one of the main targets of analysis and control by the European Union. This action is carried out, inter alia, through EUvsDiSiNFO, created in (2015), as part of the East Stratcom Task Force, a team of experts with a background mainly in communications, journalism, and social sciences, under the aegis of the European External Action Service. Their daily struggles consist of fact-checking and reporting on the spread of pro-Kremlin disinformation and the Kremlin's attempts to influence European elections through false messages.

The dissemination of disinformation or unverified information can cause serious problems in emergency situations (Kapoor et al., 2018; Laylavi et al., 2017), such as pandemics, conflicts, and elections. It calls attention to the fact that networks have a dark side that, through algorithms, manipulation, and disinformation, threaten civic life (Chapman, 2023), generating feelings of insecurity and despair (Molina, et al., 2023). As a result, the most problematic impacts of disinformation can be specified, among others, in the loss of trust, the dissemination of misinformation, the degree to which decision-making is affected, the promotion of hatred, and the undermining of truth (Wardle & Derakhshan, 2017).

7.1.2 Actors and variables responsible for disinformation

The actors responsible for disinformation include social media, algorithms, and individual actions (Chapman, 2023). Social networks, websites, and bots are among those responsible for its propagation (Lazer et al., 2017). Zannettou (2019) highlights the role of terrorist groups, political organisations, activist groups, easily manipulated individuals, and, among others, so-called conspiracy theorists. This fact is due to the influence that the ease and flexibility of the internet has had on the design, creation, and manipulation of online materials (Revuelta, 2019; Del Fresno García, 2019) and the opening of these spaces to a global citizenry. These key players vary according to the media context in which people find themselves. The media, government political campaigns, social networks, lobbies or pressure groups, or simply the users of the various networks who share information without first analysing its veracity are all part of a complex problem for which responsibility is shared.

But the phenomenon of disinformation should not be blamed exclusively on the media, social networks, or the ease or flexibility of the internet. Researchers have underlined the importance of the personal reasons and behaviour of network users in the dissemination of fake news (Vziatysheva, 2020), stressing how their cognitive processing is a decisive element in the maintenance and dissemination of false information. How we process information, personal motivations, and group rules (Wang & Fussell, 2020), personal and behavioural variables (Koohikamali & Sidorova, 2017), as well as the tendency to give advice or the emotional impact of the message (Duffy et al., 2019), have been studied as variables that influence the spread of false information.

In summary, personal variables play an important role in the influence that networks have on the spread of disinformation. Research such as that carried out by Islam et al. (2020) confirms that certain behaviours and uses of social networks have led to an increase in false information and that, for example, people with a need for self-promotion show a greater tendency to share unverified information.

7.1.3 Fighting disinformation

Governments, educational agents, and citizens are the three key actors in the fight against disinformation. Intervention by states in the development of rules and regulations, reinforcing communication processes that destroy fake news and disinformation, with clear, transparent, and detailed messages on prevention have been some of the measures implemented (Molina, et al., 2023). Research has highlighted the importance of the role of the media and the need to develop policies to combat disinformation (Larrondo-Ureta et al., 2021), as well as the decisive role of media literacy and its integration into the laws that configure education systems as a way of combating disinformation (among others, Breakstone et al., 2021; Chang et al., 2020; Roozenbeek & Van Der Linden, 2020).

Since the mid-twentieth century, it has been considered essential for education to include media and information literacy (MIL) or media education at different levels of the education system, from children education to university contexts or adult education. Teaching for and about mass and social media, social networks and digital technologies should provide students at all levels of education with an understanding of the role of media for civic participation, its benefits and challenges for society (Chapman, 2023). In fact, there has been an increase in the number of training programmes aimed specifically at this issue (Bulger & Davison, 2018; Sádaba & Salaverría, 2023), applied not only to young people but also to more adult populations, finding that older people are particularly susceptible to the phenomenon of disinformation (Moore & Hancock, 2022). Therefore, it could be argued that the fight against disinformation implies the implementation of educational strategies that allow, as Valverde-Berrocoso et al. (2022) state, the development of civic education values and critical thinking, as well as the collaborative construction of knowledge.

To sum up, the dissemination of fake news and the phenomenon of disinformation involve social, political, educational, and personal variables that require a multidisciplinary approach for their understanding and confrontation. They also require to consolidate training programmes for media literacy and education in the different stages of the educational system. A person living immersed in this society must understand not only the raw information it presents but also "its purpose, the questions that arise, the concepts that structure the information, the assumptions underlying it, the conclusions that are drawn, the implications that follow those conclusions, and the point of view that informs them" (Paul & Elder, 2005, p. 11). For this reason, "society needs to have a developed critical sense and scientific knowledge to distinguish knowledge from belief and truth from deception" (Pérez, 2018).

7.2 Methodology and corpus

7.2.1 Methodology and objectives

The methodological approach of this study was based on a mixed research that consists of analysing and integrating data collected from both qualitative and quantitative methods. Quantitative data included closed information obtained, in this specific case, from questionnaires; qualitative data resulted from open information that the research team collected through expert interviews.

The purpose of this study was to analyse the perceptions about the effects of disinformation and measure them from the perspective of Spanish professionals: the political class, journalists, and teaching teams. In addition, their point of view was contrasted with that of citizens (teachers and students) participating in a disinformation training programme, the MOOC "Disinformation Step by Step" carried within the YouVerify! project.

The specific objectives that reflected the expectations to be obtained from this study were as follows:

1 To find out what the most problematic effects of disinformation were, according to experts and ordinary citizens
2 To study who were the people who acted as key actors to implement measures against disinformation, according to the expectations of experts and ordinary citizens
3 To analyse the measures proposed for the fight against disinformation, according to experts and ordinary citizens
4 To find out the interest perceived by the students of the sMOOC "Disinformation Step by Step" in the subject matter, in relation to three dimensions: critical thinking, MIL, the production of information and disinformation

Based on these objectives, the following four research questions were raised:

RQ1. What are the most problematic effects of disinformation?
RQ2. Who are the key actors in implementing measures against disinformation?
RQ3. What are the main measures that can be taken to combat disinformation?
RQ4. What is the role of education in combatting disinformation?

7.2.2 Data collection design and analysis

This research was based on a mixed triangulation design, a quantitative part (descriptive analysis based on survey results) and a qualitative part. The quantitative study analysed the perception of students participating in a training programme, the MOOC "Disinformation Step by Step" organised on the ECO Digital Learning platform by Savoir*Devenir, with partners UNED, Agence France-Presse (AFP), and SNSPA. The Massive Online Open Course (MOOC) opened to all participants in June 2022, in particular to people interested in disinformation and MIL. The objectives of this course were: understanding what MIL is and its relationship to critical thinking; learning about the fabric of information and disinformation in the digital age; becoming familiar with and mastering information verification; understanding the nature and problems of refutation as a tool against disinformation; and developing the necessary strategies to enable participants to create their own project to combat disinformation.

To obtain the data from the participants in the training process, a satisfaction questionnaire was used (N = 187), duly revised by the project's research team and validated by the SMEMIU group (UNED), based on a Likert-type model, with five general questions (identification), four questions relating to satisfaction with the course and time management during the training; finally, a group of questions aimed at assessing the interest perceived by the students in the topics addressed. Six topics were analysed: critical thinking; MIL;

disinformation; verification and refutation; and project creation. In this study, we focused on the first three dimensions, which were the most closely related to the specific issues developed and analysed by this chapter.

The qualitative analysis was based on a discourse analysis of in-depth interviews that allowed us to delve deeper into the subject and contrast the opinions that different people, as professionals, shared in the interviews. A semi-structured interview guide was used, reviewed, and approved through a strict validation process by the research team and the SMEMIU group (UNED). This research instrument enabled the research team to conduct an in-depth exploration of a specific topic (Charmaz, 2003) and to obtain information rich in experiences, values, opinions, attitudes, feelings, thoughts, behaviours, etc., from the interviewees (Seidman, 2006). The qualitative data collection process took place during the months of October, November, and December 2021 and January 2022, with an average duration of 30 minutes per interview.

The subsequent discourse analysis on the basis of a coding processing of the content provided in these interviews was conducted according to Gibbs (2007) and Flick (2012), based on qualitative text analysis which considers coding to be "indexing or categorising text in order to establish a framework of thematic ideas about it" (Gibbs, 2007, p. 38). Six general categories of discussion topics were obtained: "Measures", "Information", "Comment", "Campaign", "Criticism", and "Reminder", as well as several specific categories within the general categories. Table 7.1 summarises this process in order to have a more precise vision of the origin and collection of the information analysed.

7.2.3 Sample

Following the guidelines of the research project, three journalists, three policy leaders, and four education experts of Spanish nationality were interviewed. Data collection was carried out by means of questionnaires and interviews. The sample consisted of 10 professionals (policy leaders, journalists, teachers) and 187 Spanish citizens (teachers, students, librarians, social workers, etc.) (see Table 7.1 for profile of interviewees).

Table 7.1 Codes and profiles of interviewees

Date	*Code*	*Profile*	*Gender*
14-10-2021	SPJP01	Policy leader	Male
10-01-2022	SPJP02	Policy leader	Female
22-12-2021	SPJP03	Policy leader	Male
23-12-2021	SPJ01	Education expert	Female
14-01-2022	SPJ02	Education expert	Female
27-12-2021	SPJ03	Education expert	Male
27-12-2021	SPJP4	Education expert	Male
03-01-2022	SPJ01	Journalist	Male
31-01-2022	SPJ02	Journalist	Female
27-12-2021	SPJ03	Journalist	Female

Table 7.2 Profile of respondents

Variable	*Descriptives*
Age	**Total: N = 187 people** (**11.2 %**) from 19 to 24 years: **N = 21** (19 women; 2 men). (**84.5%**) from 25 to 54 years: **N = 158** (135 women; 20 men; 3 dk/na). (**4.3%**) from 55 to 65 years: **N = 8** (4 women; 4 men).
Occupation/status	**Total: N = 187 people** (**61%**) Students: **N = 114** (**12.8%**) Teachers: **N = 24** (**26.2%**) Other status (Librarians, animators, social workers, etc...): **N = 49**

In relation to the questionnaire, the average age of the respondents was 37.6 years, and the majority were women 84.5% [N = 158]; 58.8% were students [N = 110], and 12.8% of those surveyed were teachers [N = 24]. Table 7.2 gives a detailed profile of the respondents, providing data on their experience of online courses, as well as their expectations of the "Disinformation Step by Step" training project and the source through which they found out about it.

According to the data obtained, the profile of the typical person surveyed was a woman between 25 and 54 years of age, a student who was familiar with the training project "Disinformation Step by Step", and was from the university itself, who sometimes took online courses and for whom this training project, to a large extent, fulfilled her objectives and expectations.

7.3 Results

The results presented in this section were in line with the objectives and research questions and were organised around categories on which the applied instruments were focused. These categories were: most problematic effects of disinformation, key actors in implementing measures against disinformation, and the role of education in combatting disinformation.

7.3.1 Most problematic effects of disinformation

7.3.1.1 Policy leaders

From the point of view of the policy leaders, disinformation entails social and health problems, etc. In terms of social problems, the subject SPSJ01 was of the following opinion:

> The contexts are distorted and how climates are generated that end up being harmful. In the end, what ends up being a hoax that is often spread with little basis and easily dismantled, ends up becoming an element of tension. In individual terms, the unease generated by a fake news story conditions people's attitudes and the way they react.

All policy experts agreed that, because of the COVID-19 health problems, many unsubstantiated news stories circulated on the internet, which led to tension and nervousness among the people. This could and may have led to instability that could have affected people's mental health. The respondents made reference to how internet hoaxes can even affect the sense of facts, such as the case of a teenager who even committed suicide because she did not know how to handle the information given on social networks. Continuing with mental health, the experts discussed the use of social networks by politicians in an attempt to explain their truth, their opinions in a way that would be accepted by the public as valid and pertinent, which also generated anxiety.

Regarding the lack of trust in the political class on the part of citizens, the subject SPJSP03 stated:

> We all have to collaborate and sometimes we collaborate negatively. When a press conference is held without questions, when certain things are done that go against disinformation and with the possibility of the journalist doing everything in his power to get our possible information, then logically we are falling down and we are collaborating in not giving all the information that is completely truthful.

The conclusion was that all media are biased in some way, which makes it impossible for politicians to be entirely transparent.

7.3.1.2 Experts in education

The qualitative sample of interviewees understood that one of the worst effects of disinformation was to create an uninformed society as it leads to major problems, especially in terms of health. Digital illiteracy helped to increase the spread of disinformation. It also led to reduced trust in the media, institutions, or politicians, as information could be manipulated for personal ends. On a psychological level, the problems were seen as linked to critical thinking: creating a tendency to absorb all the information instead of evaluating it, so that critical sense is lost, critical thinking is not developed, and, as a consequence, a critical attitude is not developed. On a psychological level, another issue was linked to decision-making, for if people are given false information, then they have a false sense of power; and, by making the wrong diagnosis, they make the wrong decisions.

One of the respondents stated that it could be very harmful to feel out of place. This expert pointed out:

> one feels out of place because one's opinion does not coincide with what one perceives. The hoaxes have that other nuance of being the only way of thinking and if you don't agree with that, with that idea, you feel alienated, as if you are out of context, and often you don't see yourself answering or replying.
>
> (SJ02)

The massive spread of these fake news stories pushed the conversation to another point and polarised people. Social media contributed to the rapid spread of this news and made people take sides one way or the other.

The experts in education also agreed that one of the most important effects of disinformation was the crisis of truth. As a consequence of this, a crisis of honesty, ethics, values, etc. was in turn fostered. In the opinion of respondent SJ04: "*people have become so accustomed to fake news that I even see it as logical*". Additionally, the justice system "*is presented as a game. As an institution, it moves from what is fair in life to what people are interested in saying. Even though we all know that this is a lie*". In the opinion of all those interviewed, this influences democracy and affects general ethics. Respondents agreed that one of the negative effects of disinformation is polarisation, which in turn could affect individual opinions and decisions.

7.3.1.3 Journalists

After analysing the journalists' answers, we can see how there are different points of view among the people working in the field of communication. For subject SPJ01:

> The main risk is the influence that people of a certain middle, low or high social class can have when facing debates of any kind. It means that fake news plays with emotions and in certain situations of confrontation or more political bias, opinions become polarised, basically, making consensus and problem solving difficult. It is practically doomed to the abyss.

Journalists also referred to the emotional instability of people with regard to mental health. They gave the example of all the hoaxes that have been created in the pandemic caused by COVID-19 and how they affected the population, creating fear and uncertainty. Subject SPJ03 believed that one of the most important harms was that disinformation manipulates and restricts people's freedom: "*Managing information is part of our freedom. We think we are very informed because we have more information and yet we are very uninformed due to an excess of information*". Disinformation is believed to be a personal threat because of the risks entailed and its effect on emotional instability. If people have access to information that is unreliable, they may make decisions that are not entirely their own, but possibly influenced by misleading information encountered in the media. This also leads to a weakening of the media system, which is called into question as an instrument not only of media manipulation but also of disinformation.

7.3.2 Key actors to implement measures against disinformation

7.3.2.1 Policy leaders

All the people interviewed who held positions of political responsibility at different levels of the Spanish state affirmed that this was a problem for everyone. Subject SPJP01 affirmed that the responsibility for implementing measures against disinformation lies mainly with public institutions. Subject SPJP02 focused above all on journalists, who finished their careers knowing well what the truth is and how to tell it, and often fail to do so.

7.3.2.2 Experts in education

As regards the fundamental aspect of education, our analysis of the data collected from the education experts showed that the main institutions that should be more actively involved in the fight against disinformation are, first and foremost, educational institutions. Schools are where all the other people in the study sample, such as journalists, politicians, etc., are trained. The elementary schools and high schools are the institutions that should be involved in addressing disinformation as it is where young people start getting in contact with deceitful content and could potentially become its victims. The school years are the age when they should learn to detect false information with structured, interdisciplinary MIL education programmes. Following this process in the education system, university institutions also have a key role to play. In this sense, journalism faculties were seen as a key institution for training people to detect false information as they have a very strong responsibility. Their role is fundamental in teaching future communicators to contextualise, interpret, and check information before it is disseminated.

Education was the response to the fight against disinformation that was repeatedly mentioned by the experts. Educational agents should contribute to the fight against disinformation, and schools in particular should play an important part in the process. Some solutions proposed were to teach students at least the basics: learn to look at a source: if it is a web page, look carefully at the URL; if you receive a message, check that it is from the person who sent it to you and that it is not false, and so on. In addition to these issues related to the field of formal and non-formal education, subject SJ04 was of the opinion that a key group in the fight against disinformation was all those who can make a financial profit from disinformation.

7.3.2.3 Journalists

In this area, we noted the statements of subject SPJ01, who believes that it is above all the family that must implement measures to combat disinformation. According to the subject:

> Parents and grandparents are the main actors in the education of children and young people. A grandparent, in the serenity of a debate, I think, is quite reliable for young people. They are the first to detect behaviours that could be dangerous in the future in a vital development under the influence of fake news.

The respondents also believed that other political and educational institutions, as well as the Church, should actively participate in the fight to avoid the radicalisation of society, thus opening up to civil co-responsibility. The government should be more involved in making laws that guarantee the truth and thus protect the rights of its citizens.

7.3.3 Key measures to combat disinformation: The role of education

7.3.3.1 Policy leaders

Subject SPJP01 stated that he was aware that the government had taken measures to fight disinformation, although he did not provide further details. In reference to social networks, the legislator has to generate a framework of security and trust: "*there is a very big responsibility of the companies that generate social networks because they are managing information and are allowing wrong ideas to circulate*". Another meaningful way to address disinformation issues were awareness campaigns in rural areas:

> The Subdelegation of the Government of Segovia has an agreement signed with the Regional Ministry of Education and the schools that are developing this type of campaign. The Town Council, together with the Guardia Civil, has also developed workshops for the elderly and senior citizens on this type of information. These workshops are aimed at the elderly so that they can be very careful with the issue of mobile phones, with the issue of scams, with the issue of learning digital literacy.
>
> (SPJP02)

In general, the policymakers believed that the measures described above were working, at least in their workplaces. They were convinced that the government must be involved in long-term measures; above all, the neutrality of the media, whether public or private, must be guaranteed. One key problem identified was that the current measures were not enough, and therefore much more work needed to be done, especially in educational centres: "*Everything that is done does not reach, does not reach the people, does not reach the street*" (SPJP02). Radio Televisión Española, to which the audience is returning, was provided as a good example (SPJP02). From the point of view of education, and in order to combat disinformation, teachers were seen as having a fundamental role to play:

> the people to work with are the future adults, adolescents and children. This involves educating them in critical judgement and free thinking, in which they develop skills that allow them to contrast information and tools that allow them to access the main, contrasted information. Critical judgement is something that has to be worked on in a transversal way, from the lowest grades onwards.
>
> (SPJP01)

Another key point was related to politicians or those in power, who should be deeply involved in addressing disinformation, as they could push legislation and take effective measures: "*they are a fundamental part, firstly because of the public media and also, as I say later, with the distribution that is made to the private media*" (SPJP03). All policymakers we interviewed believed that public awareness campaigns were one important way to address the proliferation of misleading content in the current media landscape.

7.3.3.2 Experts in education

In relation to measures to combat disinformation, respondent SJ01 was aware of the measures adopted on the UNESCO website in reference to the issue of health, especially in the wake of COVID-19 and all the disinformation that arose during the pandemic caused by this virus. Another respondent, SJ02, was aware that the Spanish Marketing Association has a code of ethics that deals with social responsibility and the truthfulness of marketing messages and actions. However, the experts expressed the feeling that the checking of disinformation was still in its infancy:

> Who is going to be interested, which government is going to be interested, which state is going to be interested in educating in criticism and freedom and the ability to protest because we are still playing the game of anything goes?
>
> (SJ03)

All respondents agreed that the Spanish government had taken some measures in education to combat disinformation, but there was a certain sense of negativism about how they worked from a media literacy perspective. Interviewees responded that education was important, not only in addressing disinformation but also in providing a more holistic view of all important social issues. Education was seen as a key means of fighting the proliferation of misleading content, even before regulating the media. Teaching critical thinking from an early age could help in the fight against disinformation. The experts made reference to past historical events where history took a turn because of deliberately misrepresented news.

7.3.3.3 Journalists

Journalists believed that special care must be provided to the most vulnerable groups, who are likely to be more susceptible to influence, such as the elderly or the immigrants. Connecting with them through awareness-raising or educational campaigns could be key to helping them cope with the dangers of disinformation. There was a strong emphasis on education, seen as the basis for the new generations.

Although considered a complicated issue, the experts believed that the use of social media could have positive outcomes. Sending messages to young people through the same social networks they use can be effective. Expert SPJ03 contributed that he believed that awareness-raising campaigns could gradually become very effective, even though they sometimes did not have immediate effects.

7.3.4 MOOCs as a tool against disinformation

The sMOOC "Disinformation Step by Step" dealt with MIL in order to implement measures against disinformation, and was developed within the YouVerify! project. This course in three languages (English, French, and Spanish) was and still is open to all participants interested in disinformation. In particular, it was aimed at educators, facilitators, teachers, librarians, journalists, and continuing education professionals. It was structured around six thematic blocks: Disinformation, Verification, Refutation, Critical thinking, MIL, and MIL project.

The MOOC was designed to address key issues of disinformation, and aimed to provide a complete training so as to allow participants to act and to implement their own projects to fight disinformation. At the end of this online training process, a feedback questionnaire was proposed, and a total of 187 Spanish people answered.

In the quantitative study, participants were asked to rate the topics presented in the training programme, based on critical thinking, MIL, and the creation of disinformation projects. The questions included in the questionnaire were measured using five-point Likert scales to determine the level of interest, appreciation, and evaluation of the respondents.

Of the respondents, 42.8% rated the proposed topics in relation to critical thinking as very interesting and 47.1% as interesting. Responses were very similar with regard to the rating of the topics: 43.9% appreciated the project as very interesting, and 48.1% as interesting. Regarding the rating of the topics in relation to MIL, 38% considered it very interesting and 50.3% as interesting. Overall, the level of interest in the topics is close to 90% when aggregating the "very interesting" and "interesting" answers. Table 7.3 shows the responses of the respondents regarding the level of satisfaction with the facilitation of the MOOC "Disinformation Step by Step" and the feedback obtained in the questions asked throughout the course (see Table 7.3).

Overall, the MOOC experience proved to be a very positive one for the people who became involved in the proposed topics, engaged in discussions, and finished most of the modules of the course.

7.4 Discussion

This study has shown that in Spain fake news was considered as disinformation or misleading information that is intentionally disseminated by power

Table 7.3 Satisfaction with the MOOC and the feedback obtained

Variable	*Descriptives*
Satisfaction in MOOC facilitation	**Total: N = 187 people** (19.8%) Very satisfied: **N = 37** (34.2%) Satisfied: **N = 64** (35.3%) Somewhat satisfied: **N = 66** (8.6%) Not very satisfied: **N = 16** (2.1%) Not satisfied at all: **N = 4**
Satisfaction with the feedback obtained in the MOOC	**Total: N = 187 people** (12.3%) Very satisfied: **N = 23** (64.7%) Somewhat satisfied: **N = 121** (23%) Not very satisfied: **N = 43**

groups (Noain Sánchez, 2021). The purpose of fake news was to manipulate and deceive the population, taking advantage of moments of crisis, such as the health crisis experienced with COVID-19 (Castillo-Esparcia et al., 2020; Fernández-Torreset al., 2021; Santoveña-Casal et al., 2021). In Spain, disinformation consisted mostly of news that did not reflect reality, but distorted it to pursue an unethical objective. All the people who took part in this study considered this type of news to be a serious problem because it did not follow a code of conduct (or ethics), but it was in fact a form of deception. Our results showed that all respondents considered that those who generate this type of news are aware that it does not conform to reality, but rather to the intention of manipulating people's opinion in the direction the sender of the news wants.

The motives for manipulating public opinion through algorithms (Esser & Pfetsch, 2020) were diverse: manipulation for political or personal interests, intention to do harm, achievement of certain objectives, economic motives, etc. Disinformation was always associated with a bad intention such as destabilising democratic societies, alternative social groups wanting to establish "correct" thinking, or certain governments (Rodríguez-Fernández, 2019b; Del-Fresno-García, 2019). The media power made use of the potential development of new media, social networks, and digital technology that have mass dissemination, to influence the thinking of citizens (Gamir-Ríos & Tarullo, 2022). Some of the people who took part in this study attributed this trend to politicians, others to the media, social networks, messaging systems such as WhatsApp, news programmes, the internet, television, mobile devices, etc. The lack of information on the use of digital technologies and the lack of real media literacy was seen as contributing to the generation of many hoaxes and their rapid spread.

All this disinformation was considered as causing damage to citizens, such as the following: social unrest, distrust in the media and in politics, and mental health problems for both the people who are victims of the fake news and its consumers; and, in stages such as adolescence, distorting content that ends up being harmful. Social unrest and a weakening of trust in the media and politics were mentioned as current problems caused by disinformation, as many media outlets were accused of showcasing their ideologies and not being faithful to the neutrality of news and misrepresenting it according to their interests. This reality affected emotions and social skills, generating the affective polarisation of people (Tucker et al., 2018).

One key takeaway of this study was that there was a real crisis of truth. When society becomes accustomed to fake news, trust in everything – institutions, politics, media, etc. – is weakened. In this sense, verification processes should be a relevant instrument to safeguard the reputation of organisations and institutions (Rodríguez-Fernández, 2019a).

The qualitative study revealed knowledge of political initiatives or regulations to curb the dissemination of lies and disinformation on social networks. Such initiatives were: *Eurobarometer*, which dealt with the perception that European citizens had about fake news; *Association of Journalists of Albacete*, where courses were set up to be taught in institutes; *Spanish Lawyers Association*, where a report was drafted to prevent contributing to the spread of this type of fake news; *Marketing Association of Spain*, with their code of ethics that mentions social responsibility and the veracity of messages, and projects such as *YouCheck!, YouVerify!* or *InVID; WeVerify*, etc. The respondents also mentioned reports developed by institutions where people who create disinformation and specifically affect that institution are noted. At the international level, websites such as "maldita.es", a project created by Clara Jiménez and Julio Montes, and "Newtral", a start-up founded by journalist Ana Pastor (Almansa-Martínez et al., 2022), were among the examples of organisations that help addressing disinformation. Other organisations were mentioned, such as the UN verification system and, in Spain, the National Police or the Civil Guard that debunk fake news through their social networks.

Several takeaways from this study could be considered in the future as starting points for policymaking to address disinformation. Firstly, there was the need for supporting MIL as "a citizen's ability to access, analyse and produce information" (Aufderheide, 1993) in schools, colleges, and universities so that young people learn how to think for themselves and develop critical thinking, thus building media competence in the face of disinformation (Pérez Tornero, 2008; Valdez López et al., 2022). In addition, the integration of MIL education in non-formal education spaces was also seen as necessary, in particular sMOOC proposals on these topics, thus opting for open and massive training based on post-digital learning in participatory virtual spaces (Hueso-Romeroet al., 2021). Following these approaches in educational contexts, steps should be taken from media literacy towards transmedia literacy, a concept of vital importance, although it was not reflected in the data obtained from this study. The integration of transmedia literacy in the classroom would enable citizens to develop "increasingly sophisticated interpretative skills to understand new narrative formats, increasingly create new content, recombine it and share it on digital networks" (Scolari, 2016, p. 9).

In the future, training actions will depend very much on the policies of the government in power, with laws that guarantee the neutrality of the media without depending on the ideology or political tendency of the group of people in government. At least in Spain, more awareness campaigns by the government or autonomous communities could reinforce what is already known and alert the population to the dangers of disinformation. Some of the key actors in this constant fight against a polluted information environment will be the journalists who have been pioneers in the fight against disinformation, since the right to truthful information is a basic need (Marinho & Sánchez-García, 2022). The university, and specifically the schools of journalism, will need to play an important part in training good journalists who are capable of always telling the truth in a neutral and balanced manner. Public institutions must play a fundamental role in all this, being transparent and generating information with as much rigour as possible. Politicians or those in power should continue to regulate the media to guarantee freedom of the press and sanction fake news. In short, from this study we conclude, coinciding with Sádaba and Salaverría (2023) and with the projection of the European Union, that citizens in general should be made co-responsible through policies to promote MIL that fight against disinformation with a set of multilevel solutions.

7.5 Conclusion

It is essential to continue researching the field of MIL and its relationship with disinformation. MIL must play a fundamental role in order to give society a new direction, a new vision of training projects and research processes with a more committed awareness of people's development (Samy-Tayie et al., 2023). We conclude this chapter with the words of Gil-Quintana:

> The exploration of the Postdigital era in which we try to develop as people, allows us to investigate the intricate relationships that occur between interacting and interacted groups of people, societies, so we will learn to feel citizenship, conscious and responsible members.
>
> (2021, p. 48)

References

Almansa-Martínez, A., Fernández-Torres, M. J., & Rodríguez-Fernández, L. (2022). Desinformación en España un año después de la COVID-19. Análisis de las verificaciones de Newtral y Maldita. *Revista Latina de Comunicación Social*, *80*, 183–200. https://doi.org/10.4185/RLCS-2022-1538

Aufderheide, P. (1993). Media literacy. *A Report of the National Leadership Conference on Media Literacy*. Aspen Institute, Communications and Society Program.

Breakstone, J., Smith, M., Wineburg, S., Rapaport, A., Carle, J., Garland, M., & Saavedra, A. (2021). Students' civic online reasoning: A national portrait. *Educational Researcher*, *50*(8). https://doi.org/10.3102/0013189X21101749

Bulger, M., & Davison, P. (2018). The promises, challenges and futures of media literacy. *Journal of Media Literacy Education*, *10*(1), 1–21. https://doi.org/10.23860/JMLE-2018-10-1-1

Castillo-Esparcia, A., Fernández-Souto, A. B., & Puentes-Rivera, I. (2020). Comunicación política y Covid-19. Estrategias del Gobierno de España. *El Profesional de la Información*, *29*(4), 1–22. https://doi.org/10.3145/epi.2020.jul.19

Chang, Y. K., Literat, I., Price, C., Eisman, J., Gardner, J., Chapman, A., & Truss, A. (2020). News literacy education in a polarized political climate: How games can teach youth to spot misinformation. *Harvard Kennedy School (HKS) Misinformation Review*. https://doi.org/10.37016/mr-2020-020

Chapman, A. L. (2023). The Good, the Bad, and the Ugly: How social media operates in the civic sphere. In *Social media for civic education: Engaging youth for democracy* (pp. 37–56). https://doi.org/10.1007/978-3-031-10865-5_3

Charmaz, K. (2003). Qualitative interviewing and grounded theory analysis. In J. A. Holstein, & J. E. Gubrium (Eds.), *Inside interviewing. New lenses, New concerns*. Sage.

Del Fresno García, M. (2019). Desórdenes informativos: sobreexpuestos e infrainformados en la era de la posverdad. *El profesional de la información*, *28*(3), e280302. https://doi.org/10.3145/epi.2019.may.02

Duffy, A., Tandoc, E., & Ling, R. (2019). Too good to be true, too good not to share: The social utility of fake news. *Information, Communication & Society*, *23*(13), 1965–1979. https://doi.org/10.1080/1369118X.2019.1623904

Esser, F., & Pfetsch, B. (2020). Comparing political communication: A 2020 update. In D. Caramani (Ed.), *Comparative politics* (5th ed., pp. 336–358). Oxford University Press. https://doi.org/10.5167/uzh-186963

Eurobarometer. (2022, April). *Standard Eurobarometer 96 - Winter 2021–2022*. https://data.europa.eu/data/datasets/s2553_96_3_std96_eng?locale=en

European Commission. (2018). Directorate-general for communications networks, content and technology. *A multi-dimensional approach to disinformation: Report of the independent High level Group on fake news and online disinformation*. EU Publications Office. https://data.europa.eu/doi/10.2759/739290

European Commission. (2021). *Disinformation: A threat to democracy—Brochure*. https://digital-strategy.ec.europa.eu/en/library/disinformation-threat-democracy-brochure

European Commission. (2022, June). *The strengthened code of practice on disinformation*. https://www.dsn.gob.es/sites/dsn/files/2022_Strengthened_Code_of_Practice_Disinformation_TeAETn7bUPXR57PU2FsTqU8rMA_87585.pdf

EUvsDiSiNFO. (2015). *Estudios e informes*. https://euvsdisinfo.eu/es/estudios-e-informes/

Fernández-Torres, M. J., Almansa-Martínez, A., & Chamizo-Sánchez, R. (2021). Infodemic and fake news in Spain during the COVID-19 Pandemic. *International Journal Environment Research Public Health*, *18*(4), 1781. https://doi.org/10.3390/ijerph18041781

Flick, O. (2012). *Introducción a la investigación cualitativa*. Ediciones Morata.

Gamir-Ríos, J., & Tarullo, R. (2022). Características de la desinformación en redes sociales. Estudio comparado de los engaños desmentidos en Argentina y España durante el 2020. *Contratexto*, 037, 203–228. https://doi.org/10.26439/contratexto2022.n037.5343

García-Orosa, B. (2021). Disinformation, social media, bots, and astroturfing: The fourth wave of digital democracy. *Profesional de la información*, *30* (6), e300603. https://doi.org/10.3145/epi.2021.nov.03

Gibbs, R. (2007). *Analyzing qualitative data*. Sage.
Gil-Quintana, J. (2021). La importancia de investigar en Comunicación y Educación. In J. Gil-Quintana, J. L. Parejo, & C. Cantillo-Valero. *Investigar en Comunicación y Educación. Teoría y práctica científica*. Tirant Humanidades.
Grinberg, N. Joseph, K., Swire-Thompson, B., & Lazer, D. (2019). Fake news on Twitter during the 2016 U.S. presidential election. *Science*, *363*(6425), 374–378. https://doi.org/10.1126/science.aau2706
Hueso-Romero, J. J., Gil-Quintana, J., Hasbun, H., & Osuna-Acedo, S. (2021). The social and transfer massive open online course: Post-digital learning. *Future Internet*, *13*(5), 119. https://doi.org/10.3390/fi13050119
Islam, A. K. M. N., Laato, S., Talukder, S. & Sutinen, E. (2020). Misinformation sharing and social media fatigue during COVID-19: An affordance and cognitive load perspective, *Technological Forecasting Social Change*, *159*. https://doi.org/10.1016/j.techfore.2020.120201
Kapoor, K. K., Tamilmani, K., Rana, N. P., Patil, P., Dwivedi, Y. K. & Nerur, S. (2018). Advances in social media research: Past, present and future. *Information Systems Frontiers*, *20*, 531–558. https://link.springer.com/article/10.1007/s10796-017-9810-y
Kaya, T. (2020). The changes in the effects of social media use of Cypriots due to COVID-19 pandemic. *Technology in Society*, *63*, 101380. https://doi.org/10.1016/j.techsoc.2020.101380
Koohikamali, M., & Sidorova, A. (2017). Information re-sharing on social network sites in the age of fake news. *Informing Science: The International Journal of an Emerging Transdiscipline*, *20*, 215–235. https://doi.org/10.28945/3871
Larrondo-Ureta, A., Fernández, S. P., & Morales-I-Gras, J. (2021). Disinformation, vaccines, and covid-19. Analysis of the infodemic and the digital conversation on twitter, *Revista Latina de Comunicación Social*, *1*(18). https://doi.org/10.4185/RLCS-2021-1504
Laylavi, F., Rajabifard, A., & Kalantari, M. (2017). Event relatedness assessment of twitter messages for emergency response, *Information Processing and Management*, *53*, 266–280. https://www.sciencedirect.com/science/article/abs/pii/S0306457316303922
Lazer, D., Baum, M., Grinberg, N., Friedland, L., Joseph, K., Hobbs, W., & Mattsson, C. (2017, May). *Combating fake news: An agenda for research and action*. Conference held February 17–18, 2017. https://shorensteincenter.org/wp-content/uploads/2017/05/Combating-Fake-News-Agenda-for-Research-1.pdf
Magallón, R. (2019). *Unfaking news. Cómo combatir la desinformación*. Síntesis.
Marinho, S., & Sánchez-García, P. (Eds.). (2022). *Trial and error in journalism and communication education: Between the classroom and industry*. Cambridge Scholars Publishing.
Molina, L., Arroba, G., Viteri-Guevara, X., Tigua-Moreira, S., Clery, A., Orrala, L., & Figueroa-Martínez, E. (2023). *Spread of fake news about Covid: The ecuadorian case. Lecture Notes Networks and Systems*, 542 LNNS (pp. 672–678). https://doi.org/10.1007/978-3-031-16072-1_48
Moore, R. C., & Hancock, J. T. (2022). A digital media literacy intervention for older adults improves resilience to fake news. *Scientific Reports*, 12, 6008. https://doi.org/10.1038/s41598-022-08437-0
Moorhead, S. A., Hazlett, D. E., Harrison, L., Carroll, J. K., Irwin, A., & Hoving, C. (2013). A New dimension of health care: Systematic review of the uses, benefits, and limitations of social media for health communication. *Journal of Medical Internet Research*, *15*(4), e85. https://doi.org/10.2196/jmir.1933

Noain Sánchez, A. (2021). Desinformación y Covid-19: Análisis cuantitativo a través de los bulos des-mentidos en Latinoamérica y España. *Estudios sobre el Mensaje Periodístico*, *27*(3), 879–892. https://doi.org/10.5209/esmp.72874

Paul, R. y Elder, L. (2005). *Estándares, principios, desempeño, indicadores y resultados con una rúbrica maestra en el pensamiento crítico*. Fundación para el Pensamiento Crítico. https://cutt.ly/0URTA1w

Pérez, L. J. C. (2018). Derecho, justicia y pensamiento crítico. *Dilemata*, *26*, 197–205. https://cutt.ly/OURTKGu

Pérez Tornero, J. M. (2008). La sociedad multipantallas: retos para la alfabetización mediática. *Comunicar: Revista Científica de Comunicación y Educación*, *16*(31), 15–25. https://doi.org/10.3916/c31-2008-01-002

Poynter. (2015). *IFCN mission statement*. Poynter Institute. https://www.poynter.org/ifcn/about-ifcn/

Revuelta, G. (2019). Comportamiento de la ciudadanía respecto a la información sobre salud: exposición, acceso y usos. *Revista Española de Comunicación en Salud*, *10*(1), 9–20. https://doi.org/10.20318/recs.2019.4448

Rodríguez-Fernández, L. (2019a). Desinformación: retos profesionales para el sector de la comunicación. *El profesional de la información*, *28*(3), e280306. https://doi.org/10.3145/epi.2019.may.06

Rodríguez-Fernández, L. (2019b). Desinformación y comunicación organizacional. *Revista Latina de Comunicación Social*, *74*(13), 1714–1728. https://doi.org/10.4185/RLCS-2019-1406

Roozenbeek, J., & Van Der Linden, S. (2020). Breaking harmony square: A game that "inoculates" against political misinformation. *Harvard Kennedy School (HKS) Misinformation Review*, *1*(8), 1. https://doi.org/10.37016/mr-2020-47

Rosenberg, H., Syed, S., & Rezaie, S. (2020). The Twitter pandemic: The critical role of Twitter in the dissemination of medical information and misinformation during the COVID-19 pandemic. *CJEM*, *22*(4), 418–421. https://doi.org/10.1017/cem.2020.361

Sádaba, C., & Salaverría, R. (2023). Tackling disinformation with media literacy: Analysis of trends in the European Union. *Revista Latina de Comunicación Social*, *81*, 17–33. https://doi.org/10.4185/RLCS-2023-1552

Samy-Tayie, S., Tejedor, S., & Pulido, C. (2023). News literacy and online news between Egyptian and Spanish youth: Fake news, hate speech and trust in the media. *Comunicar: Revista Científica de Comunicación y Educación*, *74*. https://doi.org/10.3916/C74-2023-06

Santoveña-Casal, S., Gil-Quintana, J., & Ramos, L. (2021). Digital citizens´feelings in national #Covid 19 campaigns in Spain. *Heliyon*, *7*(10), e08112. https://doi.org/10.1016/j.heliyon.2021.e08112

Scheibenzuber, C., Neagu, L. M., Ruseti, S., Artmann, B., Bartsch, C., Kubik, M., Dascalu, M., Trausan-Matu, S. & Nistor, N. (2023). Dialog in the echo chamber: Fake news framing predicts emotion, argumentation and dialogic social knowledge building in subsequent online discussions, *Computers in Human Behavior*, *140*. https://doi.org/10.1016/j.chb.2022.107587

Scolari, C. (2016). Alfabetismo transmedia: estrategias de aprendizaje informal y competencias mediáticas en la nueva ecología de la comunicación. *Telos: Revista de pensamiento sobre Comunicación, Tecnología y Sociedad*, *193*, 13–23. http://hdl.handle.net/10230/27788

Seidman, I. (2006). *Interviewing as a qualitative research. A guide for researchers in education and social sciences*. Teachers College, Columbia University.

Shao, C., Hui, P., Wang, L., Jiang, X., Flammini, A., Menczer, F., & Ciampaglia, G. L. (2018). Anatomy of an online misinformation network. *PLOS One*, *13*(4). https://doi.org/10.1371/journal.pone.0196087

Statista. (2020). *Porcentaje de población que realizó algún tipo de acción para protegerse ante la desinformación en España en 2020*. https://es.statista.com/estadisticas/1016476/principales-acciones-para-protegerse-de-la-desinformacion-espana/

Tucker, J. A., Guess, A., Barberá, P., Vaccari, C., Siegel, A., Sanovich, S., Stukal, D., & Nyhan, B. (2018). *Social media, political polarization, and political disinformation: A review of the scientific literature*. William and Flora Hewlett Foundation. https://doi.org/10.2139/ssrn.3144139

Valdez López, O. E., Romero-Rodríguez, L. M., & Hernando Gómez, Á. (2022). Competencia mediática de los/as jóvenes bolivianos/as frente a la manipulación informativa de los medios audiovisuales. *Revista Prisma Social*, *39*, 74–94. https://revistaprismasocial.es/article/view/4861

Valverde-Berrocoso, J., González-Fernández, A., & Acevedo-Borrega, J. (2022). Disinformation and multiliteracy: A systematic review of the literature. *Comunicar: Revista Científica de Comunicación y Educación*, *70*, 97–110. https://doi.org/10.3916/C70-2022-08

Vziatysheva, V. (2020). How fake news spreads online? *International Journal of Media and Information Literacy*, *5*, 217–226. https://doi.org/10.13187/IJMIL.2020.2.217

Wang, L., & Fussell, S. R. (2020). More than a click: Exploring college students' decision-making processes in online news sharing. *ACM on Human-Computer Interaction*, *4*. https://doi.org/10.1145/3375189

Wardle, C., & Derakhshan, H. (2017, September). *Information disorder: Toward an interdisciplinary framework for research and policy making*. Council of Europe. DGI. http://tverezo.info/wp-content/uploads/2017/11/PREMS-162317-GBR-2018-Report-desinformation-A4-BAT.pdf

Zannettou, S., Sirivianos, M., Blackburn, J., & Kourtellis, N. (2019). The Web of false information: Rumors, fake news, hoaxes, clickbait, and various other shenanigans. *Journal of Data and Information Quality*, *11*(3), 1–26. https://doi.org/10.1145/3309699

8 21st-century skills

Enforcing resilience and critical thinking against visual disinformation through serious games

Roberto Feltrero, Adina Ionescu, Saeta Hernando, and Cristina Sánchez

8.1 Introduction

Disinformation has emerged as one of the many risks of the digitalised and hyper-connected society. We find ourselves in a world where online disinformation threatens the veracity of information and challenges the population with great socio-educational issues. This situation calls for the necessity of creating learning opportunities for citizens to develop and train their critical thinking skills. It suggests the need for media and information literacy (MIL) interventions, with different methodological and interdisciplinary approaches at all educational levels.

False news spreads and goes instantly viral in the media and social networks, which poses a constant threat and challenge to all the actors to be active in fighting it, with multiple tools. The propagation of disinformation and the manipulation of the audience's cognitive processes are deliberately developed (Gelfert, 2018). To foil this trend, tools are required to detect and eliminate the proliferation of manipulated content, which becomes a challenge in the educational field.

To address the problem, we considered tools based on an interactive digital approach, through gamified training and the design of serious games. Multiple studies provide effective results from a gamified design to detect disinformation critically and creatively. For example, we highlighted the design in different supports such as educational websites with games for learning with the necessary steps to detect false content and verification processes (Katsaounidou et al., 2019). We noted the use of serious games to include "inoculation" against the dissemination of fake news so that, through the game experience, psychological resistance can be developed and real information can be discovered by users (Roozenbeek & van der Linden, 2019).

Disinformation is a problem that influences people's thinking and behaviour. Bastick's research (2021) shows the behavioural effects that misleading content could have. For example, he describes that "a short exposure (less than five minutes) to fake news could significantly modify people's unconscious behavior" (Bastick, 2021, p. 1). Hence, users need protection from

DOI: 10.4324/9781003387404-11

disinformation and responses that enhance cognitive and critical thinking competencies to manage their behaviour when faced with fake news. As described by Pimmer et al. (2020, p. 387), developing the cognitive skills of students is necessary for them to evaluate the credibility of information in digital spaces: "cognitive skills are part of the 21st-century skills".

Therefore, we are faced with an emerging problem that requires acquiring the necessary competences to identify, analyse, and discredit news, images, and videos that are manipulated and manipulative. The population in general, and students in particular, need to develop critical thinking and self-regulation skills to improve their digital literacy in the face of disinformation and the viralisation of fake news.

The National Literacy Trust (2018) report, in the UK, states that only 2% of children have the critical literacy skills needed to tell whether a news story is real or fake. Also, it affirms that the UK national curriculum does not equip children with the literacy skills needed to identify fake news. Though limited to the UK, such results invite us to rethink the concept of critical literacy in schools and the digital literacy training programmes that need to be implemented from an early age to foster and develop critical skills to combat disinformation.

This situation represents a serious setback for democratic societies and their educational approach, as underlined by authors such as Tascott who are rethinking the concept of education for the new generations. Tascott (2009, p. 127) stated in his work that the new generations required new skills such as critical and creative thinking and information literacy, but for this it was necessary to transform educational institutions for the use of technologies. Likewise, Pepper (2012, p. 21) indicated the need for "crucial regeneration" (a new approach meant to sustain healthy rebalancing of the education system and practices, according to the actual needs of society) to ensure students' competencies and use of technologies.

Critical thinking, as a form of information literacy, provides a means to engage critically with online content, for example by looking for evidence to support claims and assessing the plausibility of arguments, along the lines of Machete and Turpin's (2020) research. Thus, the use of gamification has been analysed for the development of critical skills by encouraging participation, creative problem-solving, and providing clear objectives, challenges, quests, feedback, competition, and cooperation (Huang & Yeh, 2017; Johnson et al., 2015).

Gamification is a pedagogical technique to enrich the student experience that has positioned itself as a solution to the challenges facing education (Kenny et al., 2017). Gamification is shown as an element of motivation and engagement in learning. In a pedagogical context, gamification becomes one of the key alternatives to traditional teaching methods (Alsawaier, 2018; Bovermann & Bastiaens, 2020). Gamification mechanics can allow users to pursue individual goals and choose between different progress paths, while the system can adapt the complexity to the user's skills (Krath et al., 2021).

Therefore, we focused on gamification as a formative and enabling model for the improvement of critical and creative thinking skills (Raisi & Huang, 2018; Saprudin et al., 2019) that go beyond entertainment and encourage participation (Caserman et al., 2020).

From a socio-educational perspective, the design of a gamified activity has to take into account patterns related to participation, interaction, and collaboration that foster both learning and entertainment. By definition, the design of a "serious game" must have a serious part for learning while also providing entertainment. Such design needs to establish a balance between meeting the learning objective of the game (Caserman et al., 2020) and considering the experience of the users who will participate in it (Silva et al., 2020). One of the biggest challenges for the success of the game is to facilitate learning and to maximise the enjoyment of the user. It is crucial to evaluate how the learning materials are implemented and how they relate to the effectiveness of the game content (Rosyid et al., 2018).

Therefore, all gamified activities that are developed in formal and non-formal contexts should be designed and planned so that the player who participates in them is proactive and develops decision-making skills and intercreativity (Sánchez-Romero and Muñoz-Jiménez, 2022). Accordingly, our gamified proposal for fighting disinformation incorporated a guided process that allowed the development of critical thinking through action research and discovery learning. The project You Verify! aimed to bring young people to acquire the aforementioned skills, through playful training based on serious games to mitigate fake news, from the development of key knowledge to understanding the difference between genuine and manipulated authentic news in an interactive digital scenario.

8.2 A game's serious responsibility: Why do we need fake news games and how do they work?

Fake news understood as counterfeit information generated to mislead its readers (Narwal, 2018) is a pressing issue in society. Harmful effects, such as polarisation and filter bubble isolation (Spohr, 2017), lack of dialogue, democratic erosion (Zhou & Zafarani, 2020), and even adopting a harmful worldview, can be silently spread to every community. Amplified by digital platforms and technological innovations (i.e., artificial intelligence, algorithms) (Bârgăoanu & Radu, 2018), disinformation is shared more by social media users and travels faster than real news (Vosoughi et al., 2018). Therefore, MIL interventions are needed in order to limit these adverse effects and offer appropriate tools to tackle disinformation.

The 21st-century skills, such as critical thinking, analytical competences, and knowledge about how to navigate the digital space (Thoman & Jolls, 2004), are necessary not only for younger generations but also for vulnerable groups (i.e., seniors) and for agents that can have an active role in combating disinformation (i.e., librarians, journalists, professors, and researchers/

experts). Changes in consumers' and learners' media consumption can be seen in an increased need for engagement, captivating narrative, immediate feedback, and digital social communication. In the fight against disinformation, it is vital to tailor the methods of teaching media literacy to the actual needs of the individuals.

Video games are an emergent instrument for tackling disinformation because they appeal to the younger generations. Many states, like Denmark, France, and Finland, include serious games and gamified interventions to promote MIL to their citizens (European Audiovisual Observatory, 2016). Games are no longer a tool for "mindless fun" (Eichenbaum et al., 2014) but are intentionally created to facilitate the comprehension of complex notions through enjoyable mechanics and dynamics embedded in the design. Multiple studies highlighted the positive effects of video games on users' attention, learning curve, engagement, and increased motivation (Peñuelas-Calvo et al., 2020; Halbrook et al., 2019; Granic et al., 2014; De Aguilera & Mendiz, 2003). As "culturally influential artifacts" (Fernandez Galeote & Hamari, 2021, p. 2), games can put forward and accentuate essential topics for society and individuals, such as climate change (Fleming et al., 2020), refugee crisis (Montag, 2020), army training (Raybourn, 2014), and disinformation created by the fake news phenomenon.

Serious games – digital educational tools oriented to transfer skills – are an innovative way to help in the fight against fake news and its attendant risks of harm. The purpose of serious games is not only the enjoyment felt by the user for simply playing the game, as in video games but also the education acquired by the user (Breuer & Bente, 2010; Bellotti et al., 2013). The latter goal, ultimately, is broken down into learning levels based on educational objectives or techniques that need to be comprehended and internalised by the learners. Serious games demonstrated positive effects on acquiring knowledge, developing analytical skills (Giessen, 2015), enhancing cognitive abilities (Susi et al., 2007; Boyle et al., 2016), and deep-thinking gains (Imlig-Iten & Petko, 2018). Game elements need to be adapted to the theoretical content in a meaningful way relevant to the learning context, the subject, learners' abilities, and desired outcomes.

A few studies indicated that serious games could increase the mental workload, decreasing learning effectiveness (Zhonggen, 2019). Therefore, researchers and game creators need to develop a balanced design to limit the negative effects, where learning levels and educational objectives are adjusted to the players' abilities.

In order to sustain the immersion of the players in the game as well as their attention and interest, creating engaging missions and obstacles is crucial but differs from commercial games design. Flow, a concept formulated by Mihaly Csikszentmihalyi (1990), is described as what emerges when the player is involved in the game or task. This immersion can lead to the "magic circle" (Zimmerman & Salen, 2004), or the particular space and time of the game that is encapsulated in the objective space and time. This profound absorption makes the games enjoyable and the reason why so many users are returning to play again. Furthermore, flow can predict positive outcomes in learning contexts and promotes knowledge retention (Alexiou et al., 2020) and self-regulation (van Schaik et al., 2011) if the levels of difficulty in the tasks increase the player's capacities. If a level is too easy, the user can become demotivated because she cannot find enough stimulants to grow on. However, if the level is too harsh, the user can feel frustrated, which impacts negatively on her perceived abilities to learn and develop. Therefore, it is paramount for serious games to balance the "tests" present in the game with the user's competencies, so as to create the desired involvement to acquire anti-disinformation techniques and tools.

To implement effective MIL interventions adapted to the new technologies and patterns of media consumption, serious games have to involve the individual in deconstructing the fabricated information at the base of every fake news.

When people encounter disinformation three scenarios are possible:

1 The individual has critical and analytical competences, she will assess that the information is fabricated, and she will move on.
2 The individual is not interested in the information, but because it is new and surprising, the "sleeper effect" (Kleinnijenhuis, 2020; Grady et al., 2021) will be activated and, after some time, the source will be forgotten, and the news will be evaluated as accurate or not.
3 The individual is unaware that the information she encountered is manipulated and will believe it immediately, possibly sharing it with others.

In the first scenario, the "mill" of disinformation will be stopped. In the other two scenarios, an intervention is needed. Because false information tends to be rapidly and widely spread, especially on social media platforms, it is a herculean task for fact-checkers to debunk the inaccurate data and promote (at least half as widely) the corrected version of the piece of news they selected for debunking.

Even with the best intentions in mind, users themselves can accelerate the spreading of disinformation. Repetition of disinformation, even if it is for debunking purposes, will create the opposite effect: the false data will be even more present and will be perceived as reality (Pennycook et al., 2018). The "continued influence effect" (Lewandowsky & van der Linden, 2021) will keep the disinformation active in the mental schemata of the citizens, and ulterior efforts of rectification will have limited effectiveness. Caulfield (2020) argued that the "backfire effect" is not absolute, and many individuals remain with the correct information after debunking, advancing a moderate viewpoint on the critique upon debunking. Lewandowsky et al. (2012) emphasised that debunking can be successful if a dose of critical scepticism is brought to the topic, paired with the corrected version. More studies need to be conducted for asserting the efficiency of debunking and for identifying the conditions to implement in order to avoid unwanted effects. So, what alternatives do we have if debunking – presenting the corrected version of the news – cannot address the entire spiral of disinformation?

Prebunking, or pre-emptive refutation (Lewandowsky & van der Linden, 2021), could attack the fake news phenomenon in a two-step intervention. Firstly, by flagging the content as unreliable and untrustworthy, an action taken by fact-checkers and some social media platforms (van Helvoort & Hermans, 2020). Facebook and Twitter, for example, provided informational warnings in their newsfeeds about the possible disinformation on COVID-19. Making users aware that malicious content could appear in their feeds and how the algorithms could amplify that the sharing of fake news is essential for the critical analysis of the mass and social media. Secondly, pre-emptive refutation is based on "inoculation" theory. Developed by McGuire (McGuire & Papageorgis, 1962; McGuire & Papageorgis, 1961; Papageorgis & McGuire, 1961), inoculation theory mirrors the vaccine prototype: a weakened argument used in propaganda or disinformation can create mental "antibodies" and make people more aware of the intentional persuasion. Recent studies demonstrated that inoculation is effective against fake news (Basol et al., 2020; Maertens et al., 2021; van der Linden et al., 2020), increasing the scepticism and slowing down cognitive biases that tend to function subconsciously and instantly (Roozenbeek & van der Linden, 2019). However, some researchers argued that prebunking could increase the reactance to persuasion (Brinson, 2022; Roozenbeek et al., 2022; Saleh et al., 2021).

Regarding exposure time, inoculation can be prophylactic or therapeutic (Compton, 2019). Prophylactic inoculation is possible when domain-specific disinformation has not even begun. One example could be the World Health Organisation's efforts and the local government's efforts to alert the citizens about the "infodemic" (WHO, 2020) and possible streams of disinformation that could appear regarding the new virus. The problem is that fake news is not just composed of new stories tailored to the current context; it tends to be already there before a particular event happens. Furthermore, fake news creates a coherent alternative worldview with the same elements that can arise in any circumstance (i.e., a secret global elite, an ill-motivated government, or a division created between different opinions). Therefore, prophylactic inoculation needs to address the potential arguments regarding a new problem and the "classic" methods and approaches that emerge.

Therapeutic inoculation, similar to the therapeutic procedure, means that the refutation will take place after disinformation (concerning a domain) has already spread (Compton, 2019). That does not mean that therapeutic inoculation is identical to debunking because the researchers will not correct the false information. However, they will make people aware that some disinformation is already present on social media platforms about the "miraculous cures" for the pandemic for example.

Regarding the user's involvement, the process of inoculation can be active or passive. Passive inoculation consists of different weakened versions of the argument created and delivered by the researchers or the MIL practitioners. Even if this approach is practical, experts in the field are becoming increasingly interested in active inoculation. The individual is directly involved in experiential learning of the concepts, techniques, and methods (Lewandowsky & van der Linden, 2021). Saleh et al. (2021) observed the positive effects of active inoculation through a serious game, "Radicalise". The game, used as a prebunking method to learn more about the methods used by extremists, improved the confidence of individuals to spot misinformation on social media platforms, increasing the ability to spot the factors that could lead to recruiting in extremist organisations, as well as detecting the techniques used by the extremists to persuade vulnerable people.

Even if inoculation is an effective method to curb the disinformation phenomena, some unintentional limitations can occur. For example, to have a relevant long-term effect "in real life", inoculation should be activated with a constant cyclicity in the form of "boosters" (Maertens et al., 2020), which makes it harder for the individual to be aware of ulterior disinformation if she is not exposed to continuous inoculation. Another issue that arises with the development of inoculation strategies to counterattack disinformation is the duality of the inoculation: it can influence both sides of an issue (Banas & Miller, 2013); therefore, it could be used with ill intentions by other entities. Lastly, inoculation can reduce the overall trust in the information encountered by the individual (Hameleers, 2023), even in official sources that share accurate information. Therefore, it remains essential to understand the conditions under which the best outcomes could be attained, especially for individuals that are part of vulnerable or marginalised groups.

Active inoculation is more and more illustrated in the form of "fake news games" or anti-disinformation serious games. Players are focused on learning about the techniques and methods used by fake news generators. They understand how disinformation is created, shared, and promoted in different groups rather than concentrating on combating specific content or theories. These "social-impact games" (Urban et al., 2018) put the user in the shoes of a fake news creator/fact-checker/troll to create a relevant context in which the player has the agency to choose what actions she wants to take. Feedback is generated instantly through likes and popularity. Real-life consequences are understood in a safe space. Serious games that involve active inoculation are perspective-taking, played in the first person, to contract the distance between the character and the player.

Active inoculation games have a multitude of benefits, such as the increased ability to spot misinformation, increased confidence that the individual is capable of detecting fake news in a real context, a more profound understanding of the persuasive techniques and methods that fake news generators are using, and, finally, a prolonged effect that lasts even after the process of prebunking is ended (Basol et al., 2020; Maertens et al., 2021; Maertens et al., 2020; van der Linden et al., 2020). A noteworthy mention is that active inoculation through serious games can become a "broad-spectrum vaccine", with games like "Bad News" having positive effects on spotting disinformation regardless of gender, age, or political orientation (Roozenbeek & van der Linden, 2019).

While the jury is still out concerning the efficiency of "inoculation", one of the long-lasting methods to tackle disinformation is through MIL interventions. Emergent MIL projects in different countries include serious games that aim at prebunking. Developing critical thinking, learning more about the fake news phenomenon, and being able to put into practice what the individual learned are among the most important effects of MIL (Frau-Meigs, 2019). Creating lasting attitudinal resistance (Saleh et al., 2021) through serious games focused on combating disinformation represents the opportunity to achieve complex learning objectives by using the multimodality of the virtual worlds.

8.3 Methodology

8.3.1 "BotBusters": General description

In the European project YouVerify!, we developed a gamified training illustrated as a scenario-based educational game – "BotBusters".[1] It was based on the InVID-WeVerify plugin, focused on analysing audiovisual media and assessing if the materials were doctored. The InVID-WeVerify was a plugin that offered several functionalities: keyframes, thumbnails, reverse image, magnifier, forensic options, reverse image search on a multitude of platforms (Google, Yandex, Bing, Tineye, Baid, etc.), contextual information and analysis of video and pictures found on social media networks (Facebook, Twitter, Instagram, and YouTube), as well, as GIFs, facilitating the effort of analysing data (video copyrights, image metadata, fact-check queries) (INVID project, 2018; Marinova et al., 2019; Teyssou et al., 2017; for more details about the InVID-WeVerify plugin, see Chapter 4 of this book). These main functionalities of the verification tool could all lend themselves to missions and tasks, which was tested in the pilot project YouCheck!, where a pilot game was created, "YouCheck! Detectives".[2]

The game was integrated into a multimodal learning approach focused on MIL, composed of a Massive Online Open Course (MOOC) platform, with diverse multimedia and text resources. To increase engagement and satisfaction levels, a gamified approach was established, where training for the usage of the InVID-WeVerify plugin also took place through the serious game, "BotBusters". The purpose of the training was to encourage young people to install the InVID-WeVerify plugin and to use it for analysing false content. The serious game "BotBusters" served two objectives: firstly, it trained the users to understand the InVID-WeVerify plugin and how to install and use it, and, secondly, it offered a virtual space in which participants could identify and verify common manipulated content found on social media platforms, specifically images and videos.

The game was a role-play, single-player type, based on therapeutic active inoculation, where the user played the role of a "Bot destroyer" that needed to verify the manipulated images and videos, with the InVID-WeVerify plugin, in order to save the world from fast-spreading lies and conspiracies. The game could be accessed online, on the official website of the project YouVerify!, and was available in four languages: English, French, Spanish, and Romanian.

In this section, we present the three components of our gamified approach: learning context (learning theories, learning objectives), game context (game type, game design, game flow), and game analysis. We opted to use the Gameplay/Purpose/Scope (G/P/S) Model for the classification of the game (Djaouti et al., 2011), the Barbosa et al. (2014) structure of game flowchart, and the Learning Mechanics-Game Mechanics Model (LM-GM) by Arnab et al. (2014) for the game play and map of the game elements.

8.3.2 Learning context

The effectiveness of a game is dependent on the context in which the game is played. The context of design (where the game designer and developer are thinking of the game) can be different from the context of use (where the participant is playing the game) (Braad et al., 2016). The "BotBusters" game was thought of as an engaging tool for young people (the main target audience) as well as other interested parties (teachers, journalists, media experts, parents, etc.). The learning context in which the game was incorporated was as a resource for using the InVID-WeVerify plugin, part of a learning section of a MOOC specially designed for acquiring the basics of disinformation verification strategies (Module 4). The serious game was aimed as a catalyst for applying the information and guidelines of MIL acquired in the other sections of the MOOC (Modules 1, 2, and 6), together with the new data on how to use a specialised tool for combatting fabricated multimedia materials (Modules 3 and 5). Integrating a serious game into the MOOC structure could accelerate the adoption/use of interactive tools (Freire et al., 2016).

Another important implication for the game's context was the time of implementation, in 2021, in the middle of the COVID-19 pandemic. Sudden changes in the schools' and faculties' way of teaching (from face-to-face to partially/entirely online), the anxiety-driven media landscape, and the acceleration of the fake news phenomenon (on and offline) made MIL interventions even more needed. With a twist specific for the new generation (but not only them), the implementation of an interactive and engaging tool capable of facilitating content retention also appeared as a natural solution.

Adopting a constructivist lens – where the meaning of the learning is construed by the learners, in the learning process (Driscoll, 2000 cited in Rooney, 2012) – "BotBusters" is based on the theoretical model of experiential learning, where the learner is actively involved in the learning process and is motivated to learn through experience (Kolb, 2015).

In the "BotBusters" game, the four stages of experiential learning were illustrated as follows: the learner/player has the concrete experience through actively choosing in the missions if the material proposed is false or true; reflection is triggered after a wrong answer and feedback from the mentors; the steps of using the InVID-WeVerify plugin and the principles behind the logic of the fake content analysis help in the generalisation of the principles and in generating new ideas about the best approach in the next mission; testing the new insight in the next mission to apply the knowledge better.

Under the umbrella of experiential learning, we also find situated-learning and problem-based learning (Rooney, 2012), both present in the serious game developed by the team of YouVerify! project (all partners provided initial and feedback to the Spanish team in charge of the game at National University of Distance Education (UNED)). Situated learning accentuates the importance of the context of use for the learner in order to assure the knowledge transfer, where the user derives the meaning of the learning process by exploring the learning space and tasks (Choi & Hannafin, 1995). The virtual space of our game was thus similar to real contexts in which the player could be involved (as a user on social networks, seeing images/videos that could be potentially manipulated).

Because learning can be a tedious process, to facilitate the assimilation of new information and problem-solving, the learning space should be able to offer guidance and support. Scaffolding is important for the user (Maybin et al., 1992), especially as beginners are supported and mentored by agents with more experience – in BotBusters' case, the mentors in the game, Sarah and Amadou. The feedback given by the mentors and the repeated information can accelerate the remembering and understanding of the tool used in the game. Problem-Based Learning (de Graaf & Kolmos, 2003; Rooney, 2012) encourages the learners to develop their understanding of the topic/concepts through a trial-and-error approach, where support from others can help in the internalisation of the concepts. It is very important to create a sense of similarity between the game situation and the real-life situation to facilitate the transfer of the skills acquired in the game world. The game designers need to replicate the real-world and/or real-life situations. The fake news phenomenon is pervasive and ubiquitous and anyone can be fooled by false claims. In our case, the game illustrated the real situation where fabricated and doctored claims and images can take place: on the internet. For this purpose, we chose images and videos that were real and shared on social networks (Facebook, YouTube, Twitter) to create a sense of authenticity between the game situation and real-life contexts.

8.3.3 Learning objectives

Because the final purpose of a serious game is educational, game mechanics and dynamics need to be connected with learning objectives, drawn from pedagogy, learning theories, and types of learners.

Learning objectives are structured after Bloom's taxonomy, revised by Anderson and Krathwohl (2001 cited in Wilson, 2016): recalling the steps for using the plugin and repeat them at every level of the game (remembering), understanding the logic behind manipulated content; applying the understanding to pragmatic choices in-game (understanding and applying), analysing the information and inspecting the context in which multimedia materials will appear (social media networks) (analysing and evaluation).

To have effective learning objectives these objectives need to be paired with game mechanics that improve the learning curve of the player.

8.3.4 Game context

The mechanics implemented in the game were: resources for learning on disinformation, resources for learning on Sustainable Development Goals (SDG)s, tasks, quests, instant feedback, player progress, badges, collecting items (numbers for a final code), and additional resources for gameplay improvement.

The "BotBusters" game took place in a world where a virus that kills critical thinking is spreading rapidly and transforms people into bots that are easy prey for false news, not only believing them but also taking an active part in sharing them everywhere. The player was part of a group of young people that wanted to fight against the bots and stop the illness, by destroying the bots through the InVID-WeVerify plugin.

The game started with a "home" screen (Figure 8.1), where the player sees three components: a video set to increase motivation and to highlight the problem of the fake news phenomenon, a button with the logo of the

Figure 8.1 The BotBusters start screen. Image by the authors.

InVID-WeVerify project that is linked to the Chrome Webstore page where the plugin could be downloaded, and a "Start" button to begin the quests. To increase attention and the intuitive user experience, both buttons had a "jiggle" effect.

After the player is primed that the disinformation is a real problem in the present world and presses the "Start" button, a presentation video about the game world appears on the second screen (Figure 8.2). In this video, the player discovers the context (a world plagued by a virus killing critical and analytical skills) and the characters (the bots, the mentors, and the teammates), and is invited to be part of the BotBusters team.

After the "Start" button is pushed again, the player is officially part of the team and is guided by two non-playable characters (NPC) that mentor her, applying the support offered by experienced characters to novices mentioned in the situated-learning approach (Figure 8.3).

The player is helped by a mentor for each component of the learning process: Sarah for navigating the game world and the principles for verifying the misleading content (MIL mentor) (Figure 8.4) and Amadou, for technical information about how to install and use the plugin (Technology mentor). Both characters offer feedback in each task: Sarah drawing attention to the correct answer and nudging the player to explore alternatives (maintaining the attention and mental schemas on combating disinformation) and Amadou explaining the results of the InVID-WeVerify plugin video/image analysis.

At the end of each story cut, in the right corner, the player has the possibility to control the cascading information, being able to go back and forth through the content, at her own pace.

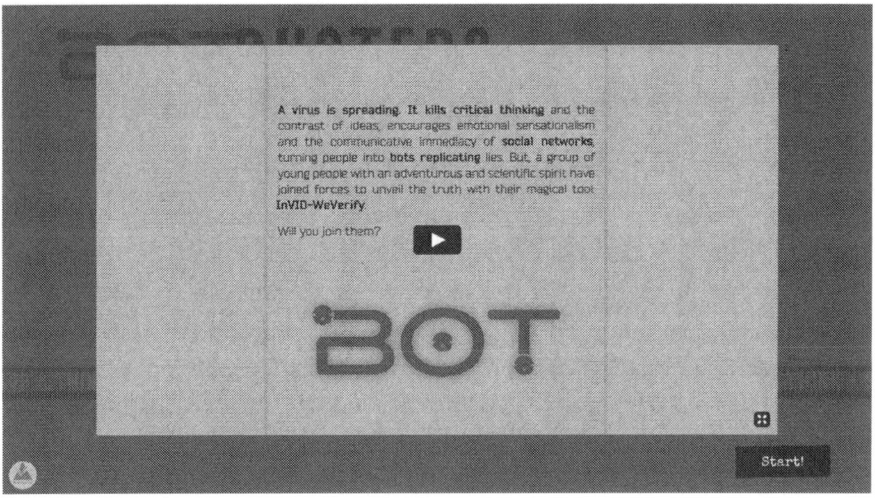

Figure 8.2 Presentation video screen. Image by the authors.

Figure 8.3 Presentation of Sarah and Amadou as mentors. Image by the authors.

Figure 8.4 Verifying principles for players in game and in real life. Image by the authors.

The information presented in the game (such as verifying principles) can help the player in the game world but it can also guide her in the out-of-the-game space, where the fabricated content can be found everywhere.

To create attitudinal resistance against visual disinformation, we chose the topic of SDGs, a topic that is present in many disinformation practices (Björk,

Figure 8.5 Screen to select one of the four missions/SDG proposed to players. Image by the authors.

2023; Chua & Khan, 2023; Sa'adAbdullahi & Pindiga, 2023). Following this subject, the game also taught about the basics of SDGs and fake news and manipulated images related to those topics (Figure 8.5). We chose four SDGs that were related to the selected fake/true news chosen for evaluation (the game main task). All the goals were represented by avatars (two male, two female) that were students in relevant fields:

SDG15: Life on Land, presented by the avatar Sanda, who studies Biology and Environment.
SDG13: Climate Action, presented by avatar Chang, who is studying Climate Science.
SDG12: Responsible Consumption and Production, presented by avatar Julia, who is an activist and studies Journalism.
SDG03: Good Health and Well-Being, presented by Ahmed, who studies Sports Medicine.

The game is a single-player type, all the other characters being NPCs, namely the four teammates and the two mentors (Sarah and Amadou).

The game had four missions, corresponding to each student of the team, and four SDGs: "Life on land", "Climate Action", "Responsible Consumption and production", and "Good health and well-being".

This approach was aligned with task-based learning (Bellotti et al., 2011), where knowledge is broken down into a sequence of small tasks that have a specific goal and instructional content. In our game, every mission had two tasks to solve, by using the In-VID-We Verify plugin. Following Barbosa and collaborators' (2014) methodology for designing the quests from a pedagogical perspective, we incorporated in each mission multiple tasks that employed the different functionalities of the plugin (video analysis, keyframes, metadata, forensics) in a different context (image/video) (see Figure 8.6 for the game flow chart). Every task needed to be solved to be able to finish the mission and to receive the motivational instruments used by the game (the code and badge pertaining to each mission).

At the beginning of each mission, an instructional video (—one to two minutes) about the particular goal (e.g., good health and well-being) was included as an educational resource that expanded the knowledge about the topic (Figure 8.7).

In each mission, the player had to solve two tasks, using the plugin, for two different types of media: image and video. Feedback was provided by the two NPC mentors (Sarah, if the answer was wrong, and Amadou, if the answer was right) after each task. Every mission had a corresponding SDG and different characters that were the user's partners. Table 8.1 summarises the structure and order of the missions and which SDG was represented along with the tasks that needed to be solved to go to the next level (see Table 8.1).

At the end of every mission, the player collected two items: a badge for completing the mission and a number. At the end of the missions, all the numbers formed a code that needed to be submitted to a secret calculator, to be able to receive the BotBuster diploma (Figures 8.8 and 8.9).

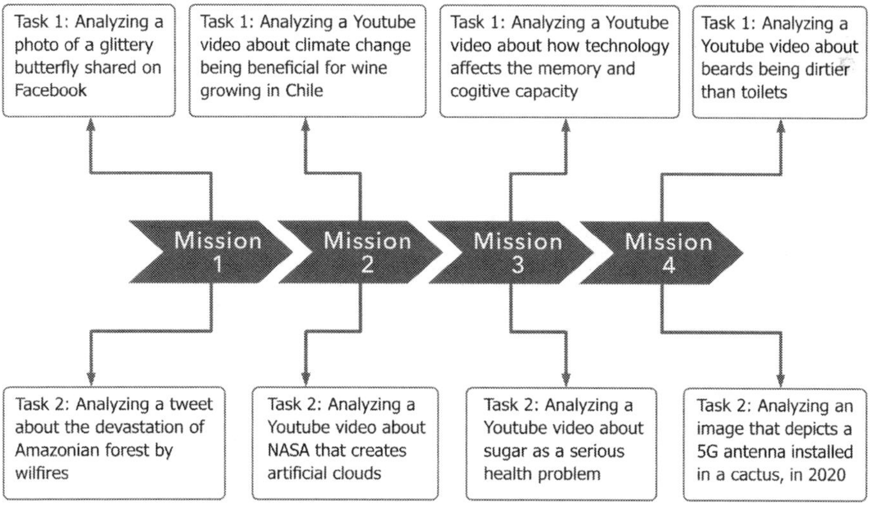

Figure 8.6 BotBusters game flow chart. Figure created by the authors.

Figure 8.7 Introductory videos at the beginning of each mission in BotBusters. Figure by the authors.

Table 8.1 Description of quests and tasks

Name	*Mission*	*Sustainable Development Goal*	*Task details*
Sanda	1	Life on Land	By using the InVID-WeVerify plugin, the player needs to assess the authenticity of a photo and a video
Chang	2	Climate Action	By using the InVID-WeVerify plugin, the player needs to assess the authenticity of two videos
Julia	3	Responsible Consumption and Production	By using the InVID-WeVerify plugin, the player needs to assess the authenticity of two videos
Ahmed	4	Good health and well-being	By using the InVID-WeVerify plugin, the player needs to assess the authenticity of a video and an image

The player collects Badge + Number after each completed mission.

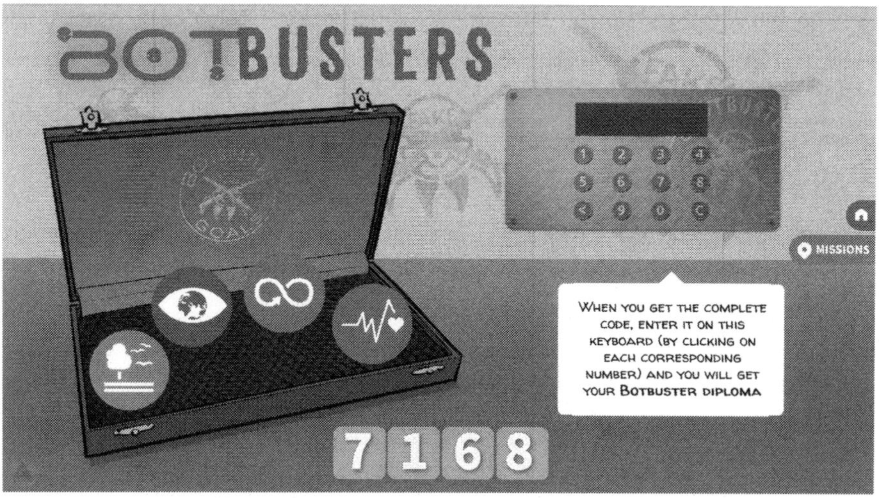

Figure 8.8 Game rewards design. Image by the authors.

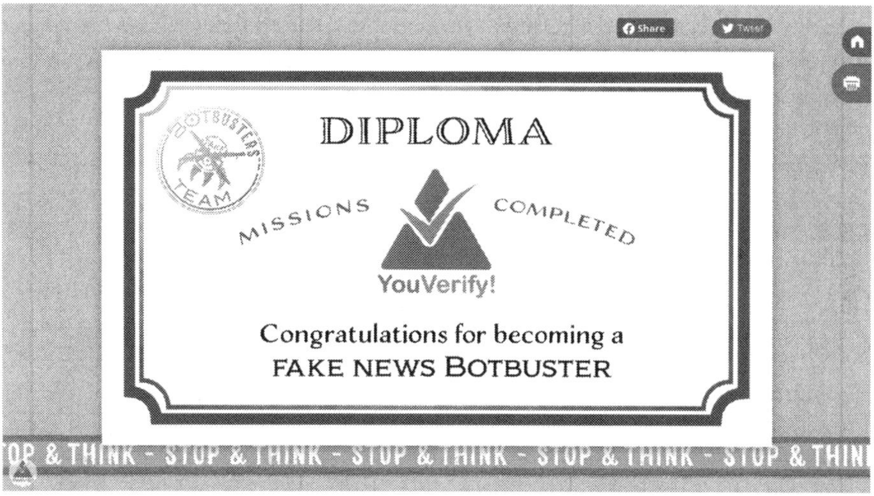

Figure 8.9 Diploma for becoming a Botbuster. Image by the authors.

The game ended with the achievement reward, the "Fake News Bot Buster" Diploma, when the player succeeded in all the missions and accumulated all the numbers needed to "crack" the code.

8.3.5 The InVID-WeVerify plugin

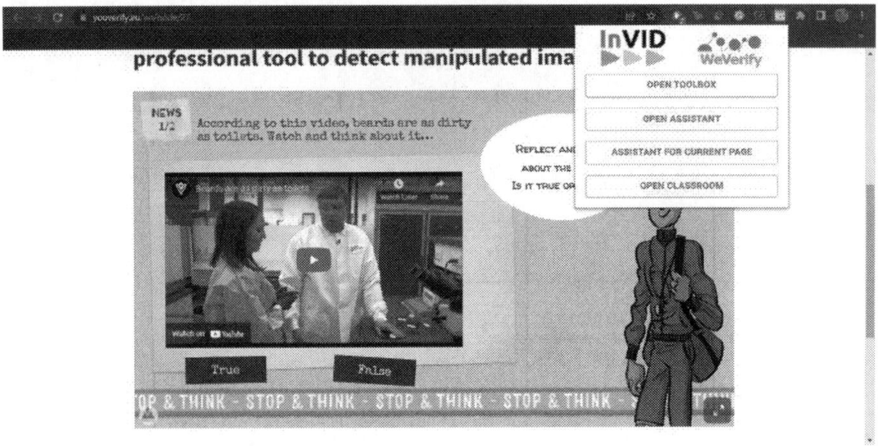

Figure 8.10 How to access the plugin. Image by the authors.

The player could expand the game universe by using the InVID-WeVerify plugin, emphasising the problem-based learning approach where an important part of the trial-and-error process of the player needs to be supported by feedback from mentors and additional resources (Rooney, 2012). The player could go to the verification landing plugin website,[3] where several options were offered to her, besides the plugin "toolbox": "tutorials", "demos", "assistant", and "classroom", with many resources (including those developed for projects Youcheck! and YouVerify! (see Figure 8.10).

The "Toolbox" section offered multiple possibilities to analyse the visual content (visual analysis, keyframes, thumbnails, video rights, and metadata) (Figure 8.11). In total, there were five videos incorporated into the tasks that the player needed to solve and she could use any of the plugin's tools. The player had the freedom to choose the order of the missions and could also explore the methods by which to identify if the video/image was part of visual disinformation.

The option "Assistant" could be activated if the player copied the URL of the video and then pasted it into the "webpage link" section, to let the assistant analyse it (Figure 8.12). The programme generated data about the video (date of uploading, likes, comments, if there were cut scenes from other videos, etc.).

Additional educational resources could be found in the "Classroom" section, where the player could read multiple documents regarding disinformation, how to tackle it, and the techniques behind it, and could also watch videos and presentations about the topic (Figure 8.13).

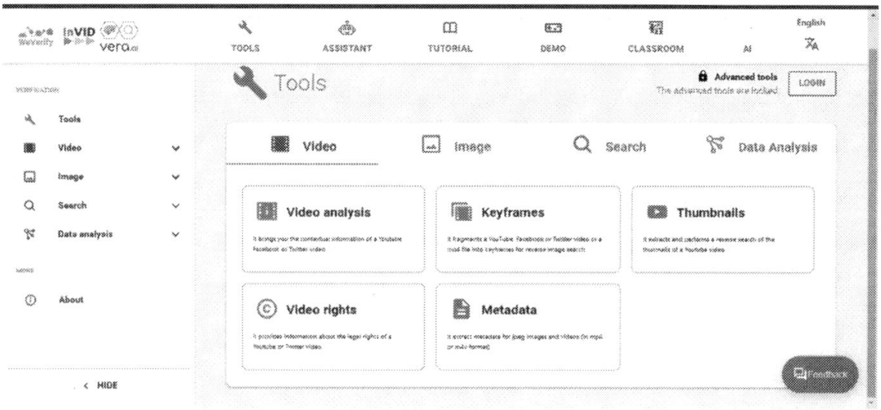

Figure 8.11 InVID-WeVerify plugin menu. Image by the authors.

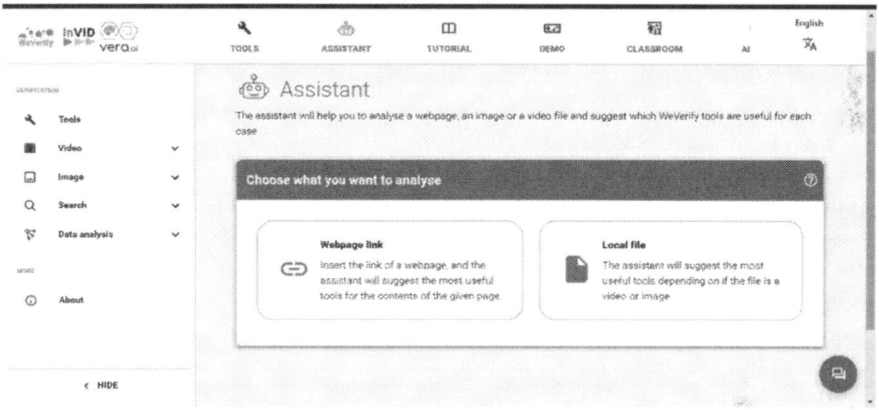

Figure 8.12 InVID-WeVerify plugin assistant. Image by the authors.

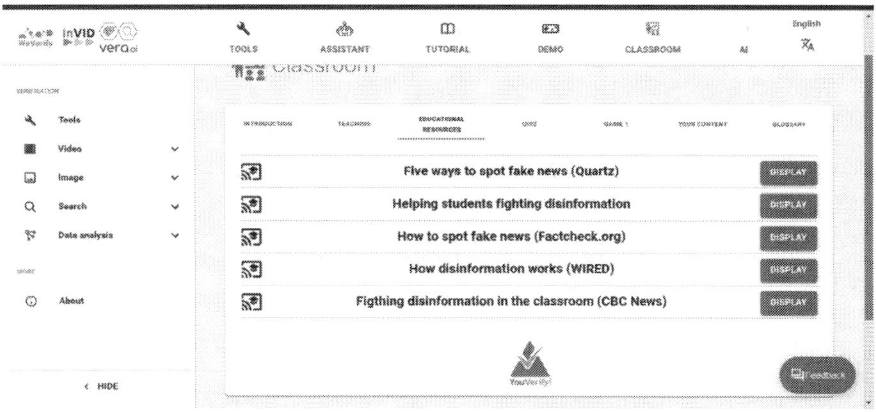

Figure 8.13 InVID-WeVerify plugin educational resources. Image by the authors.

8.3.6 Game classification

The G/P/S Model (Djaouti et al., 2011) helped in the classification of the serious game and its components. The gameplay element described how the game was played (game-based or play-based), the purpose element entailed other goals besides entertainment (message broadcasting, training, or data exchange), and the scope element referred to the audience targeted by the game (commercial or public).

The "BotBusters" fake news game had a game-based gameplay type (aligned with the Djaouti et al., 2011), where rules guided the player to choose from two options (e.g., the video you saw is false or true), instruct her to watch explicatory videos, to read the feedback and to use the InVID-WeVerify plugin. The level of exploration was low, and the player was only able to choose the order of the missions. The patterns coagulated into "GamePlay Bricks" were goals and means. The goal of the game was to match (the user needed to analyse the image and then evaluate if the image/video was true or false), and the means were select (the player needed to select the correct option) and write (because the player had to copy-paste the link of the photo into the plugin, followed by understanding what the plugin gave as a result).

The purpose of the game was twofold: broadcasting an educational message and training. Regarding the broadcasting role, the game offered information about visual disinformation, presented some principles for analysing news, and had explanatory videos at the beginning of every mission. All of these methods informed the player about the mechanisms that were behind the fabrication of misleading news. Concerning the training element of the game, the technical explanations regarding the use of the plugin were focused on cascading information that could be easily understood and then replicated individually.

In the scope part of the G/P/S Model, we needed to assess the market professional domain, the target audience, and the age. "BotBusters" was focused on the educational market, with the primary target audience being young people (15–30 years), students mainly, but it was a scalable intervention, being able to address the general public formed by parents, teachers, media specialists, journalists, etc.

In order to structure the classification of our game, we followed the editing of Djaouti and collaborators (2011).

8.3.7 BotBusters

Gameplay:

- Type: Game-based
- Goals: Match
- Means: Select, write

Purpose: Educative message broadcasting, training
Scope:

- Market: Education
- Target: Primary – 15–30 years, young people, students

Secondary: General public

In order to observe the actions and patterns of the players of BotBusters, we conducted a summative assessment, post-game, after completion based on the gameplay data (in-game analytics), as log data. The statistics were collected for each language available (English, French, Spanish, and Romanian), in the period between February 10, 2022, and April 30, 2022. The statistics came from the database provided by the gamification software Genially. The database incorporated the interactions of the players in various phases of the game, when they pressed the buttons corresponding to the different options presented to them. Based on the players' actions, the software created statistics about the number of visits to the game site, the number of players entering the game, or the number of players watching the introductory content.

The data collected referred to the number of visits, the number of players entering the game, and the number of players watching the introductory content.

The number of visits received by the game was divided based on the official languages in which the game was released (French, English, Spanish, and Romanian) (Figure 8.14).

Even if the number of visitors was high, this did not mean that all visitors played the game. Because of this, we needed to look at other log data that indicated tendencies in user behaviour.

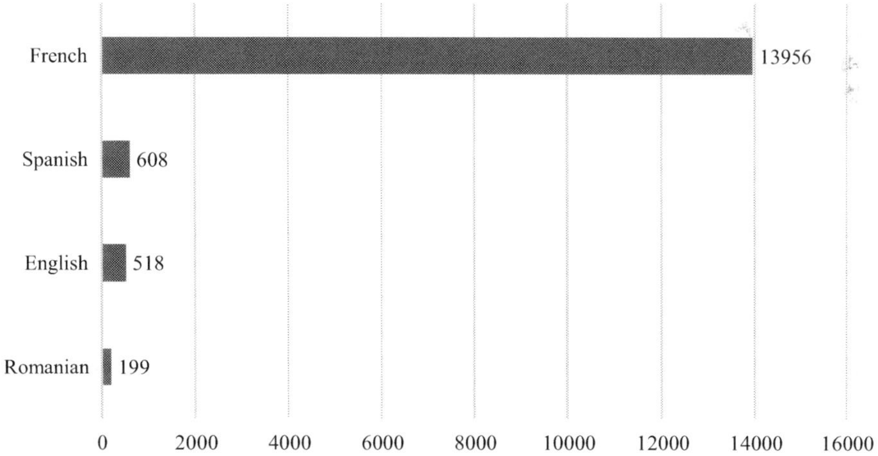

Figure 8.14 Number of visits. Graph by the authors.

8.4 Results and discussion

8.4.1 Analysis: Learning mechanics and game mechanics

For the analysis of our serious game, we used the LM-GM Model (Arnab et al., 2014), to illustrate the connection between learning objectives, mechanics, and game mechanics and the sequences in which they appeared for the user.

Based on the taxonomy of Anderson and Krathwohl (2001), Arnab and collaborators (2014) adapted Bloom's learning principles to include the Game Mechanics paired with relevant Learning Mechanics. The implementation through in-game and usage (the reason for the implementation of the game mechanics) illustrated how the learning objective was translated into in-game activities and for what purpose. We adapted the model for our game, excluding the creating section from the taxonomy of Anderson and Krathwohl (2001), which was not covered by our game and its instructions. Being a single-player game where the user was focused on identifying visual disinformation using a new tool, the focus was on the first three steps: retention, understanding, and applying (see Table 8.2).

Table 8.2 BotBusters: From learning objectives to learning mechanics

Game Mechanics	*Thinking Skills (Adapted from Bloom's Taxonomy)*	*Learning Mechanics*	*Implementation*	*Usage*
Action Points Assessment Urgent optimism	EVALUATING	Reflection	Percentage of missions completed Tasks Badges	To state the progress of the player To apply the information acquired To keep the motivation
Feedback Realism	ANALYSING	Experimentation Feedback	NPC mentors Player status Real multimedia material	To understand how to identify the fake content using InVID-WeVerify plugin End levels To have a similar context of use

(*Continued*)

Table 8.2 (Continued)

Game Mechanics	*Thinking Skills (Adapted from Bloom's Taxonomy)*	*Learning Mechanics*	*Implementation*	*Usage*
Progression Selecting/ Collecting Capture/ Elimination	APPLYING	Action/Task Demonstration Identify	Quests Numbers for the final code Warning from NPC mentors	To understand the progress To create the final code and receive the diploma Animations and feedback that could increase the attention and motivation of the players
Role-play Tutorial Cascading Information	UNDER-STANDING	Tutorial Participation	Role of the user: Botbuster Explicative video NPC mentors	To immerse the player in the game world To understand the specifics of each mission and the game world To be able to comprehend the information needed for using the tool and identifying the false content
Cut scene/ Story Goods/ Information Pavlovian Interactions Behavioural Momentum	RETENTION	Discover Generalisation Guidance Repetition Instruction	Instructional videos NPC mentors Badges Quests	To understand the context of the mission/to immerse in the game To be able to navigate with the InVID-WeVerify plugin To understand the levels and what the player needs to do To create high levels of satisfaction (dopa-mine-based) Motivation of the user and reusing the game for the next mission

Adapted from Arnab et al. (2014).

We applied the LM-GM Model to have a "more dynamic perspective" (Arnab et al., 2014) on the learning mechanics and game mechanics in the game flow. We illustrated one mission of BotBusters through the concept of game map (see Figure 8.15).

The user started with the "Start" button and was invited to choose his/her learning path (the player has the control to decide the order of the missions), exploring the tools presented in the plugin.

After a short introduction by every character, the player was invited to watch an instructional video about the SDG and why it was important to understand the basics of the field, to protect people from digital disinformation.

The player received the information step by step and in small bits (cascading information), from diverse sources: characters, videos, mentors, trial-and-error, and educational resources integrated into the plugin.

The core loop of the BotBusters game was the sequence of tasks that needed to be solved to complete the mission. Each mission counted two tasks that were focused on analysing visual materials using the InVID-WeVerify plugin. After the user finished a mission, she reactivated the loop, following the same steps in the next mission.

Motivation and engagement with the game were created by the instant feedback of the NPC mentors and the badges and numbers that the player needed to collect in order to gain her BotBuster diploma.

After visiting the game, a part of the users actually entered the game and met the characters, discovering the game universe through the ludic narrative (see Figure 8.16). The lower percentage of participants entering the game (vs. visiting) could be assigned to internal and external factors. Among the internal factors, game elements might need to be designed in order to create a hook and a desire to understand more about the game environment. Among the external factors, several could apply, such as the context of use, the mental and emotional state of the user, and the importance of the subject (acquiring skills to identify visual disinformation), as well as the familiarity of the user with this type of intervention (French version having the most entries and Romanian versions the least).

An important suggestion for analysing the statistics of low percentages of desirable actions encouraged by the game was to take into consideration the context of use and users. For example, in Romania MIL interventions were not as common as in France or Spain, with many people being reluctant to use tools that promise to facilitate the "search for the truth". With a low trust in the government and an average trust in the media institutions (Aspen Institute & Eurocomunicare, 2021), Romanians were not used to alternative educational methods (such as serious games) and that could be a potential implication of why some of the data presented low results.

Having high percentages of players that watched the introductory videos indicates that attention and interest were raised among users, influencing positively the educational purposes of disseminating disinformation educational resources offered by our game (see Figure 8.17).

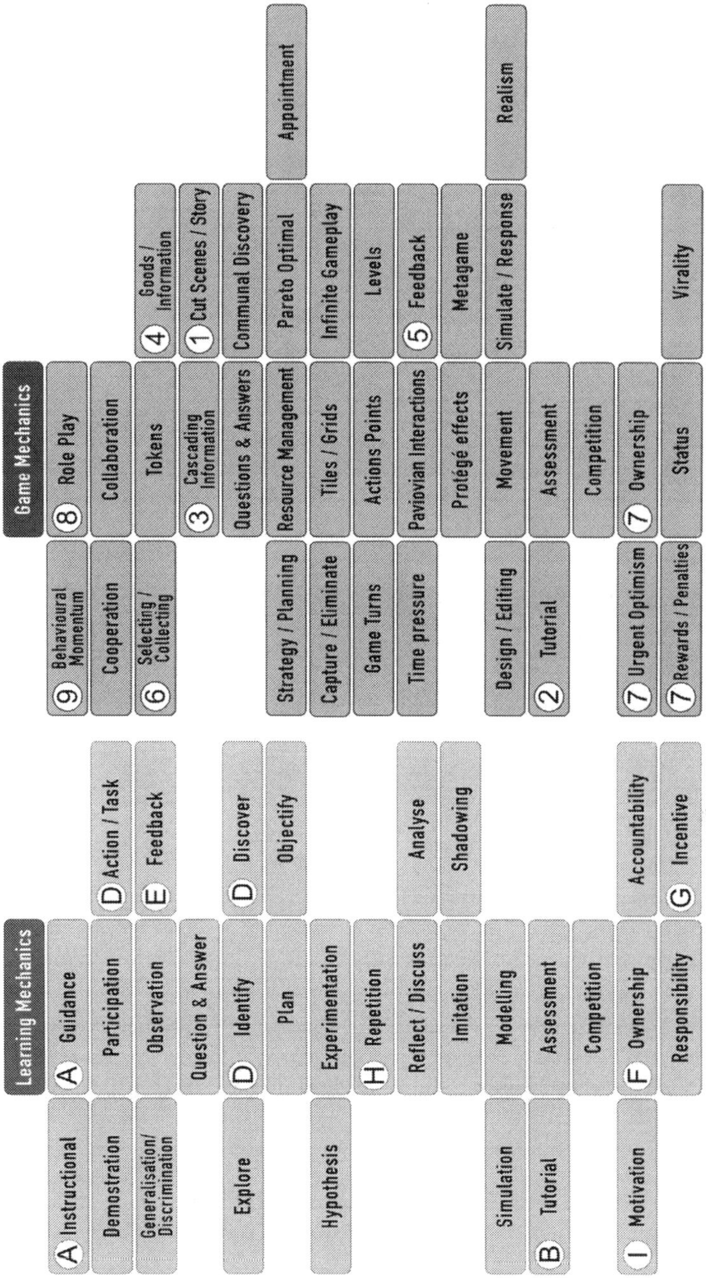

Figure 8.15 Game map of the BotBusters applying LM-GM Model (Arnab et al., 2014). Image by the authors.

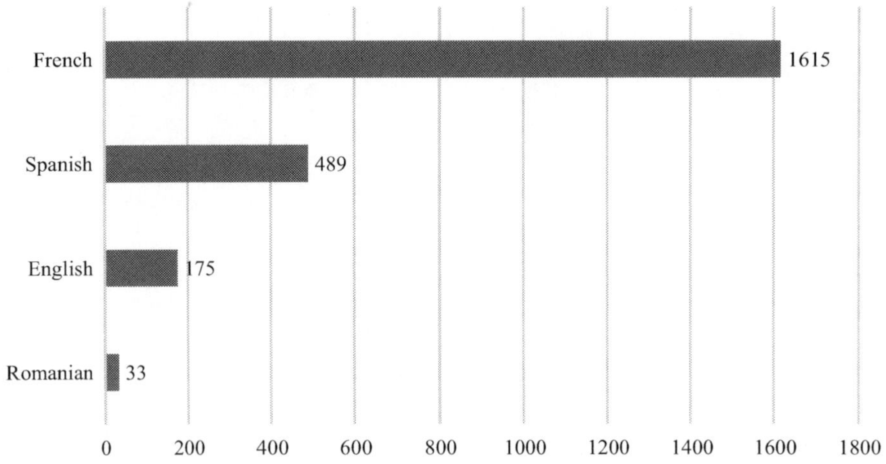

Figure 8.16 Number of players entering the game. Graph by the authors.

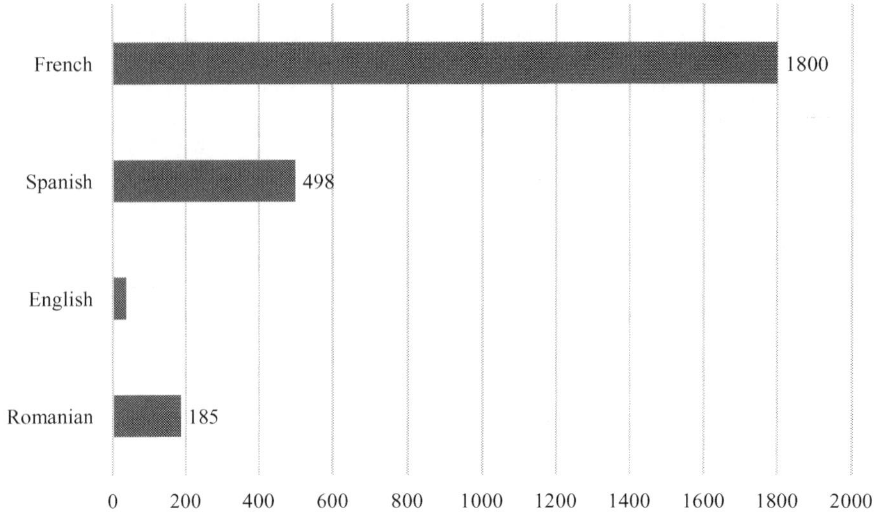

Figure 8.17 Number of players watching the introductory contents. Graph by the authors.

From the users (because they cannot be called players yet), a high percentage pressed the "Start" button after watching the introduction videos (see Figure 8.18).

We can state that the animations stimulated the users to embark on a virtual adventure and begin their journey as a player.

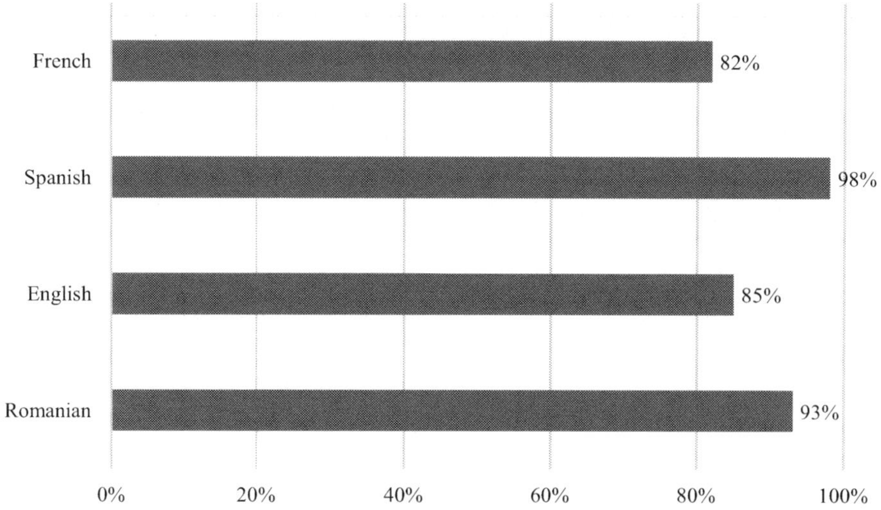

Figure 8.18 Percentages of players clicking on the "Start" Button. Graph by the authors.

Looking at the gameplay data, we can observe that many participants entered the game (2520) and more than 60% finished one mission or more, which is a good indicator for attention-grabbing, increased interest, and motivation to try playing the game. This percentage indicates that the game was sufficiently attractive for players to play the suggested "stop and think" approach when analysing possible visual disinformation present on social networks.

What is interesting in these statistics is that only 10% of participants reached the diploma, meaning that a small, yet important percentage finished all four missions embedded in the game. Even players who finished all four missions and reached the page to introduce the diploma code (248 players) seemed uninterested in printing or downloading it; just 38 of them pressed the button to obtain the document (see Figure 8.19).

An aspect that could explain the lower motivation to collect in-game items could be due to too many mechanics implemented at the same time (badge + number + diploma). The repetitive structure of the missions could impact the desire of the user to continue her exploration in the game realm. Having instant feedback and being able to retake the task, players could easily just come back to the task and push the other button (they had two choices: true/false) to finish the task, without actually trying the suggested actions.

Regarding the SDGs, the statistics provided some insights into which missions attracted players the most (see Figure 8.20).

In Figure 8.20, we observed that players first elected the "Life on Land mission" in all four languages in which the game was available. This can potentially be explained through the position of the character, because the

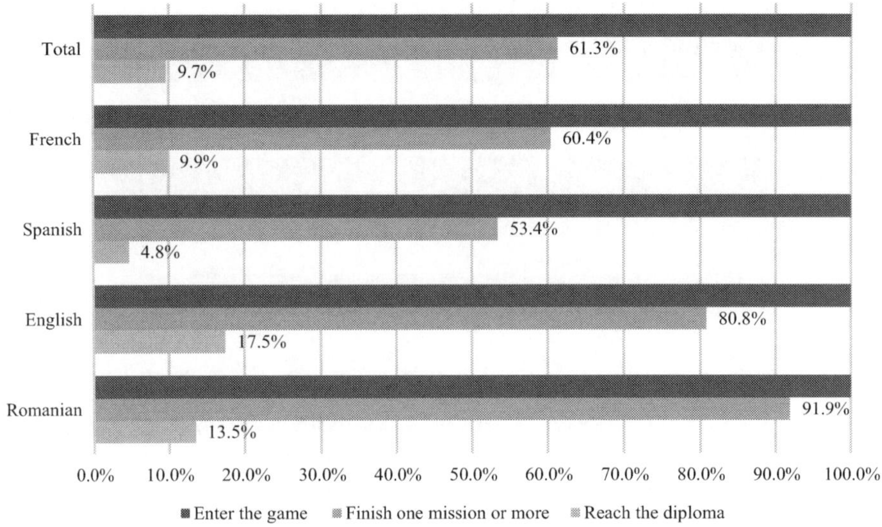

Figure 8.19 Percentage of players that reached the diploma (end of the game). Graph by the authors.

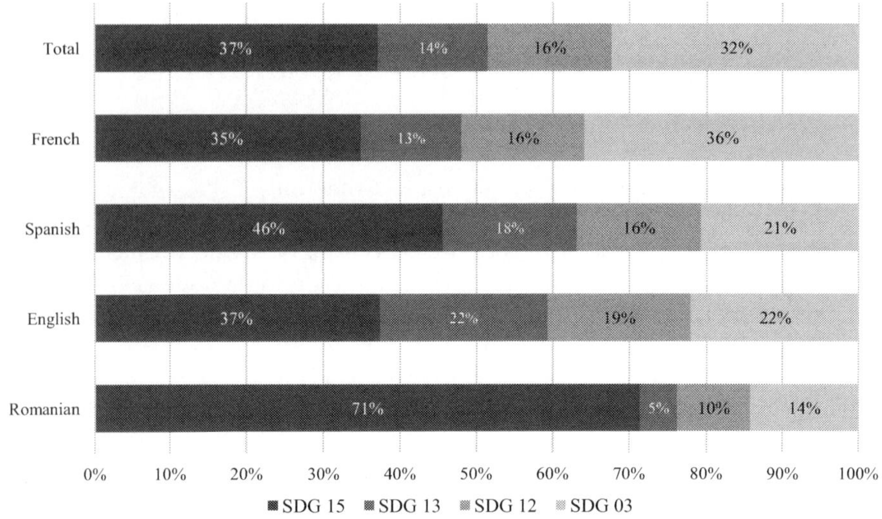

Figure 8.20 Analytics of first selection of SDG (SDG15: Life on Land, SDG13: Climate Action, SDG12: Responsible Consumption, SDG03: Good Health and Well-Being). Graph by the authors.

mission appeared first in the visual field, on the left side of the screen. However, the choices for the second, third, and fourth missions, after players became familiar with the interface of the game, were different in the countries studied. For example, the participants who spoke Spanish and English chose for their third mission SDG12 (which was the last mission, if the player respected the order). We observed that players wanted to be flexible in the game universe, after they understood the rules and how to accomplish the missions.

A potential explanation for this can be that after the user became familiar with the context of the game, she needed to explore in a non-linear manner the other components of the game, all the missions having the same pattern (start – instructional video – task 1 – feedback loop – task 2 – feedback loop – collecting badge + number – completing the mission).

Regarding the characters present in the game, another gameplay data indicated the preference for the mentors (see Figure 8.21).

In the chart, we could see that the French, Romanian, and English language players chose the MIL mentor – Sarah – as the first option. However, Spanish language players chose Amadou, the technological mentor. These differences between countries were not statistically significant, but at least showed that players had read about the two main topics of learning proposed by the game dynamics because they took this decision according to their preferences (more technological in the case of Spanish users). The players showed particular interest in the alternatives proposed by the game, hence the difference between the languages and the mentors.

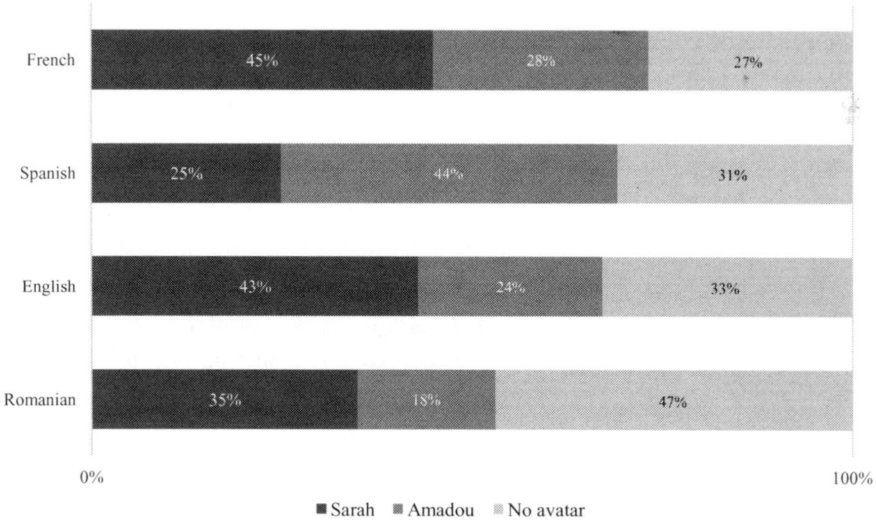

Figure 8.21 Analytics of mentor choosing. Graph by the authors.

8.5 Limitations and future studies

The objective of this game was to ensure broad dissemination of the main learning objectives of YouVerify! project. Therefore, the design was made to facilitate access to all players without any type of restriction. The users were not obliged to register or to offer personal information to be able to play the game. This design option heavily limited the data that could be extracted from the game as there were no tools to identify players (e.g., sex, age) and their exact behaviour in all the phases of the game. The in-game data available illustrated the first steps in the game environment but did not make it possible to describe the users' behaviour, to track their actions and to understand fully the players' decisions.

Future studies should concentrate more on the user behaviour, combining in-game data with analytics for different types of actions (e.g., drop-out). Another suggestion for future research could be the exploration of the players' personalities and game archetypes and their influence on game decisions and knowledge assimilation of critical thinking and analytical skills. For that purpose, the game could be useful if it was played by groups of users under supervision.

Our game analysis was limited in how deep we could dig into the player's mind and behaviour. We were mostly able to understand only general interactions with the game (entries, button clicks, etc.). More studies will need to create mixed methodology approaches in order to comprehend the motivations and perception of the game elements included in the serious game.

8.6 Conclusion

Fighting disinformation can be efficient if we shift the mindset from users as manipulated victims to users as empowered citizens that have access to interactive tools adapted to their needs. The learning process needs to be aligned with the actual context of the fake news phenomenon, facilitating skill development and real-life situations in which the player will be involved in the future, as a digital user and as a news consumer.

Serious games can become a motivational tool capable of transforming complex notions about identifying and verifying audiovisual media into small steps that all citizens can take to tackle visual disinformation by understanding how to use smart tools, such as the InVID-WeVerify plugin.

The virtual universe of the game, alongside interactive and structured information, can immerse the user and create a relevant context for learning. Anti-disinformation games are emergent, pointing to the importance of a new approach to sharing MIL notions and technical guidelines for verification tools. One of the many advantages of serious games is the flexibility in creating the learning objectives and feedback-based contexts inclusive enough to integrate a wide variety of target audiences: seniors (Elkin et al., 2023), specialists in media and journalism (Sotirakou et al., 2022), and students (Encheva et al., 2020).

The serious game "BotBusters" has been proposed to encourage young players to have a more cautious attitude against visual disinformation and provide them with the tools to identify and analyse fabricated materials through the InVID-WeVerify plugin. The high percentage of players entering the game and finishing one mission (83%) meant that most of the players were involved in the game enough for them to understand the necessity of critically approaching the news and the images or video attached to them.

The main lesson learnt from designing "BotBusters" is to create diverse game missions and tasks to increase the curiosity and retention of the users. The repetitive structure of the tasks could represent the reason why not as many participants reached the final level or received their diplomas. The game needs to be adapted to sustain an explorative repetition where even if the missions are similar, the user is met with new interactive data and opportunities to be autonomous. Many anti-disinformation games rely on providing useful information but are not necessarily encouraging the user to reflect upon what has already been learned (DeJong, 2022). Future BotBusters versions need to create a dedicated space for reflexive processes through role-play and diverse contexts for disinformation analysis. Engagement and interactivity should not be neglected but learning paths, reflection, and information sharing should be prioritised. Researchers need to focus more on understanding how to use serious games as a catalyst for prebunking and what techniques need to be implemented for the long-term positive effects to be sustained (Cernicova-Buca & Ciurel, 2022).

Disinformation poses a constant threat to the health of democracies, and serious games could become an easy, fun, interactive, and motivating space where 21st-century abilities are honed and trained through meaningful role-play, problem-solving focus, guiding, and feedback.

Acknowledgements

This chapter is the outcome of work conducted by the international team of researchers from the European project LC-01648381 – YouVerify! project.

Notes

1 https://youverify.eu/en/node/23
2 https://savoirdevenir.net/youcheck
3 https://weverify.eu/verification-plugin/

References

Alexiou, A., Schippers, M., Oshri, I., & Angelopoulos, S. (2020). Narrative and aesthetics as antecedents of perceived learning in serious games. *Information Technology & People*, *35*(8), 142–161. https://doi.org/10.1108/itp-08-2019-0435

Alsawaier, R. S. (2018). The effect of gamification on motivation and engagement. *International Journal of Information and Learning Technology*, *35*(1). https://doi.org/10.1108/IJILT-02-2017-0009

Arnab, S., Lim, T., Carvalho, M. B., Bellotti, F., de Freitas, S., Louchart, S., Suttie, N., Berta, R., & De Gloria, A. (2014). Mapping learning and game mechanics for serious games analysis. *British Journal of Educational Technology*, *46*(2), 391–411. https://doi.org/10.1111/bjet.12113

Aspen Institute & Eurocomunicare. (2021, Decembrie). *Disinformation, societal resilience and Covid-19*. (rep.) Aspen Institute. https://aspeninstitute.ro/wp-content/uploads/2022/03/DISINFORMATION-SOCIETAL-RESILIENCE-AND-COVID19_Report.pdf

Banas, J. A., & Miller, G. (2013). Inducing resistance to conspiracy theory propaganda: Testing inoculation and metainoculation strategies. *Human Communication Research*, *39*(2), 184–207. https://doi.org/10.1111/hcre.12000

Barbosa, A. F., Pereira, P. N., Dias, J. A., & Silva, F. G. (2014). A new methodology of design and development of serious games. *International Journal of Computer Games Technology*, *2014*, 1–8. https://doi.org/10.1155/2014/817167

Bârgăoanu, A., & Radu, L. (2018). Fake news or disinformation 2.0-some insights into Romanians' digital behaviour. *Romanian Journal of European Affairs*, *18*(1), 24–38.

Basol, M., Roozenbeek, J., & Van der Linden, S. (2020). Good news about bad news: Gamified inoculation boosts confidence and cognitive immunity against fake news. *Journal of Cognition*, *3*(1), 2. https://doi.org/10.5334/joc.91

Bastick, Z. (2021). Would you notice if fake news changed your behavior? An experiment on the unconscious effects of disinformation. *Computers in Human Behavior*, *116*. https://doi.org/10.1016/j.chb.2020.106633

Bellotti, F., Kapralos, B., Lee, K., Moreno-Ger, P., & Berta, R. (2013). Assessment in and of serious games: An overview. *Advances in Human-Computer Interaction*, *2013*, 1–11. https://doi.org/10.1155/2013/136864

Bellotti, F, Ott, M., Arnab, S., Berta, R., de Freitas, S., Kiili, K., & De Gloria, A. (2011). Designing serious games for education: From pedagogical principles to game mechanisms. In *Proceedings of the 5th European Conference on Games Based Learning* (pp. 26–34). Athens.

Björk, A. (2023). Facts, narratives and migration: Tackling disinformation at the European and UN level of governance. In M. Conrad, G. Hálfdanarson, A. Michailidou, C. Galpin, & N. Pyrhönen (Eds.), *Europe in the age of post-truth politics. Palgrave Studies in European Political Sociology* (pp. 177–197). Palgrave Macmillan. https://doi.org/10.1007/978-3-031-13694-8_9

Bovermann, K., & Bastiaens, T. J. (2020). Towards a motivational design? Connecting gamification user types and online learning activities. *Research and Practice in Technology Enhanced Learning*, *15*(1). https://doi.org/10.1186/s41039-019-0121-4

Boyle, E. A., Hainey, T., Connolly, T. M., Gray, G., Earp, J., Ott, M., Lim, T., Ninaus, M., Ribeiro, C., & Pereira, J. (2016). An update to the systematic literature review of empirical evidence of the impacts and outcomes of computer games and serious games. *Computers & Education*, *94*, 178–192. https://doi.org/10.1016/j.compedu.2015.11.003

Braad, E., Žavcer, G., & Sandovar, A. (2016). Processes and models for serious game design and development. In R. Dörner, S. Göbel, K. Kickmeier-Rust, M. Masuch, & K. Zweig (Eds.), *Entertainment computing and serious games. Lecture Notes in Computer Science*, vol. 9970 (pp. 92–118). Springer. https://doi.org/10.1007/978-3-319-46152-6_5

Breuer, J., & Bente, G. (2010). Why so serious? On the relation of serious games and learning. *Journal for Computer Game Culture*, *4*, 7–24.

Brinson, N. (2022). Resistance to persuasion: Examining the influence of political ideology on COVID-19 vaccine uptake hesitancy. *Frontiers in Communication*, *6*. https://doi.org/10.3389/fcomm.2021.760847

Caserman, P., Hoffmann, K., Müller, P., Schaub, M., Straßburg, K., Wiemeyer, J., Bruder, R., & Göbel, S. (2020). Quality criteria for serious games: Serious part, game part, and balance. *JMIR Serious Games*, *8*(3). https://doi.org/10.2196/19037

Caulfield, T. (2020). Does debunking work? Correcting COVID-19 misinformation on social media. *OSF Preprints*. https://doi.org/10.31219/osf.io/5uy2f

Cernicova-Buca, M., & Ciurel, D. (2022). Developing resilience to disinformation: A game-based method for future communicators. *Sustainability*, *14*(9), 5438. https://doi.org/10.3390/su14095438

Choi, J.-I., & Hannafin, M. (1995). Situated cognition and learning environments: Roles, structures, and implications for design. *Educational Technology Research and Development*, *43*(2), 53–69. https://doi.org/10.1007/bf02300472

Chua, Y.T., & Khan, R. E. (2023). Creating safe communication spaces amidst the disinformation quandary. In J. Servaes & M. J. Yusha'u (Eds.), *SDG18 communication for all*. Sustainable Development Goals Series, Vol. 1. Palgrave Macmillan. https://doi.org/10.1007/978-3-031-19142-8_8

Compton, J. (2019). Prophylactic versus therapeutic inoculation treatments for resistance to influence. *Communication Theory*, *30*(3), 330–343. https://doi.org/10.1093/ct/qtz004

Csikszentmihalyi, M. (1990). *Flow: The psychology of optimal experience*. Harper Perennial.

De Aguilera, M., & Mendiz, A. (2003). Video games and education: (Education in the Face of a "Parallel School"). *Computers in Entertainment (CIE)*, *1*(1), 1–10.

De Graaf, E., & Kolmos, A. (2003). Characteristics of problem-based learning. *International Journal of Engineering Education*, *19*(5), 657–662.

DeJong, S. (2022). Playing with fake news: State of fake news video games. *International Journal of Games and Social Impact*, *1*(1), 94–111. https://doi.org/10.24140/ijgsi.v1.n1.05

Djaouti, D., Alvarez, J., & Jessel, J. P. (2011). Classifying serious games: The G/P/S model. In F. Patrick (Ed.), *Handbook of research on improving learning and motivation through educational games: Multidisciplinary approaches* (pp. 118–136). IGI global.

Eichenbaum, A., Bavelier, D., & Green, C. S. (2014). Video games: Play that can do serious good. *American Journal of Play*, *7(*1), 50–72.

Elkin, J. A., McDowell, M., Yau, B., Machiri, S. V., Pal, S., Briand, S., Muneene, D., Nguyen, T., & Purnat, T. D. (2023). The good talk! A serious game to boost people's competence to have open conversations about COVID-19: Protocol for a randomized controlled trial. *JMIR Research Protocols*, *12*. https://doi.org/10.2196/40753

Encheva, M., Tammaro, A. M., & Kumanova, A. (2020). Games to improve students information literacy skills. *International Information & Library Review*, *52*(2), 130–138. https://doi.org/10.1080/10572317.2020.1746024

European Audiovisual Observatory. (2016). *Mapping of media literacy practices and actions in EU-28*. European Audiovisual Observatory. Council of Europe Publishing Office. https://rm.coe.int/1680783500

Fernández Galeote, D., & Hamari, J. (2021). Game-based climate change engagement. *Proceedings of the ACM on Human-Computer Interaction*, 5(CHI PLAY), 1–21. https://doi.org/10.1145/3474653

Fleming, K., Abad, J., Booth, L., Schueller, L., Baills, A., Scolobig, A., & Leone, M. F. (2020). The use of serious games in engaging stakeholders for disaster risk reduction, management and climate change adaption information elicitation. *International Journal of Disaster Risk Reduction*, *49*, 101669.

Frau-Meigs, D. (2019). *Qui a peur des "fake news"?* La Documentation Française.

Freire, M., Serrano-Laguna, Á., Iglesias, B. M., Martínez-Ortiz, I., Moreno-Ger, P., Fernández-Manjón, B. (2016). Game learning analytics: Learning analytics for serious games. In M. Spector, B. Lockee, & M. Childress (Eds.), *Learning, design, and technology*. Springer. https://doi.org/10.1007/978-3-319-17727-4_21-1

Gelfert, A. (2018). Fake news: A definition. *Informal Logic*, *38*(1), 84–117. https://doi.org/10.22329/il.v38i1.5068

Giessen, H. (2015). Serious games effects: An overview. *Procedia – Social and Behavioral Sciences*, *174*, 2240–2244. https://doi.org/10.1016/j.sbspro.2015.01.881

Grady, R., Ditto, P., & Loftus, E. (2021). Nevertheless, partisanship persisted: Fake news warnings help briefly, but bias returns with time. *Cognitive Research: Principles and Implications*, *6(*1). https://doi.org/10.1186/s41235-021-00315-z

Granic, I., Lobel, A., & Engels, R. (2014). The benefits of playing video games. *American Psychologist*, *69*(1), 66–78. https://doi.org/10.1037/a0034857

Halbrook, Y., O'Donnell, A., & Msetfi, R. (2019). When and how video games can be good: A review of the positive effects of video games on well-being. *Perspectives on Psychological Science*, *14*(6), 1096–1104. https://doi.org/10.1177/1745691619863807

Hameleers, M. (2023). The (un)intended consequences of emphasizing the threats of mis- and disinformation. *Media and Communication*, *11*(2), 5–14. https://doi.org/10.17645/mac.v11i2.6301

Huang, L.-Y., & Yeh, Y.-C. (2017). Meaningful gamification for journalism students to enhance their critical thinking skills. *International Journal of Game-Based Learning*, 7(2), 47–62. https://doi.org/10.4018/ijgbl.2017040104

Imlig-Iten, N., & Petko, D. (2018). Comparing serious games and educational simulations: Effects on enjoyment, deep thinking, interest and cognitive learning gains. *Simulation & Gaming*, *49*(4), 401–422. https://doi.org/10.1177/1046878118779088

INVID Project. (2018). *Fake news debunker by Invid & Weverify. European Union's Horizon 2020 research and innovation programme*. https://www.invid-project.eu/description/

Johnson, L., Adams Becker, S., Estrada, V., & Freeman, A. (2015). *NMC horizon report: 2015 K-12 edition*. The New Media Consortium. https://files.eric.ed.gov/fulltext/ED593612.pdf

Katsaounidou, A., Vrysis, L., Kotsakis, R., Dimoulas, C., & Veglis, A. (2019). MATHE the game: A serious game for education and training in news verification. *Education Sciences*, 9(2). https://doi.org/10.3390/educsci9020155

Kenny, G., Lyons, R., & Lynn, T. (2017). Don't make the player, make the game: Exploring the potential of gamification in education. *AMCIS 2017 – America's Conference on Information Systems: A Tradition of Innovation*, 2017 August.

Kleinnijenhuis, J. (2020). Sleeper effect. *The International Encyclopedia of Media Psychology* (pp. 1–7). https://doi.org/10.1002/9781119011071.iemp0147

Kolb, D. A. (2015). The process of experiential learning. In D. A. Kolb (Ed.), *Experiential learning: Experience as the source of learning and development* (2nd ed.). Pearson Education, Inc.

Krath, J., Schürmann, L., & von Korflesch, H. F. O. (2021). Revealing the theoretical basis of gamification: A systematic review and analysis of theory in research on gamification, serious games and game-based learning. *Computers in Human Behavior, 125*. https://doi.org/10.1016/j.chb.2021.106963

Lewandowsky, S., & van der Linden, S. (2021). Countering misinformation and fake news through inoculation and prebunking. *European Review of Social Psychology, 32*(2), 348–384. https://doi.org/10.1080/10463283.2021.1876983

Lewandowsky, S., Ecker, U., Seifert, C., Schwarz, N., & Cook, J. (2012). Misinformation and Its Correction. *Psychological Science in the Public Interest, 13*(3), 106–131. https://doi.org/10.1177/1529100612451018

Machete, P., & Turpin, M. (2020). The use of critical thinking to identify fake news: A systematic literature review. In M. Hattingh, M. Matthee, H. Smuts, I. Pappas, Y. K. Dwivedi, M. Mäntymäki (Eds.), *Responsible design, implementation and use of information and communication technology*. I3E 2020. Lecture Notes in Computer Science (Vol. 12067). Springer. https://doi.org/10.1007/978-3-030-45002-1_20

Maertens, R., Anseel, F., & van der Linden, S. (2020). Combatting climate change misinformation: Evidence for longevity of inoculation and consensus messaging effects. *Journal of Environmental Psychology, 70*, 101455. https://doi.org/10.1016/j.jenvp.2020.101455

Maertens, R., Roozenbeek, J., Basol, M., & van der Linden, S. (2021). Long-term effectiveness of inoculation against misinformation: Three longitudinal experiments. *Journal of Experimental Psychology: Applied, 27*(1), 1–16. https://doi.org/10.1037/xap0000315

Marinova, Z., Teyssou, D., Sarris, N., Spangenberg, J., Papadopoulos, S., Alaphilippe, A., & Bontcheva, K. (2019). WeVerify: Wider and enhanced verification for you – Project overview and tool demonstration. *Proceedings of the Conference for Truth and Trust Online 2019*. https://doi.org/10.36370/tto.2019.23

Maybin, J., Mercer, N., & Stierer, B. (1992). Scaffolding learning in the classroom. In K. Norman (Ed.) *Thinking voices: The work of the national oracy project* (pp. 186–195). Hodder Arnold H&S.

McGuire, W. J., & Papageorgis, D. (1961). The relative efficacy of various types of prior belief-defense in producing immunity against persuasion. *The Journal of Abnormal and Social Psychology, 62*(2), 327.

McGuire, W. J., & Papageorgis, D. (1962). Effectiveness of forewarning in developing resistance to persuasion. *Public Opinion Quarterly, 26*(1), 24–34.

Montag, V. (2020). Refugeoly: Building a serious game through refugee testimonies. *International Conference on the Foundations of Digital Games* (pp. 1–5).

Narwal, B. (2018). Fake news in digital media. *2018 International Conference on Advances in Computing, Communication Control and Networking (ICACCCN)* (pp. 977–981). IEEE.

National Literacy Trust. (2018). *Fake news and critical literacy: The final report of the commission on fake news and the teaching of critical literacy in schools.* National Literacy Trust.

Papageorgis, D., & McGuire, W. J. (1961). The generality of immunity to persuasion produced by pre-exposure to weakened counterarguments. *The Journal of Abnormal and Social Psychology, 62(3*), 475.

Pennycook, G., Cannon, T. D., & Rand, D. G. (2018). Prior exposure increases perceived accuracy of fake news. *Journal of Experimental Psychology: General, 147*(12), 1865.

Peñuelas-Calvo, I., Jiang-Lin, L., Girela-Serrano, B., Delgado-Gomez, D., Navarro-Jimenez, R., Baca-Garcia, E., & Porras-Segovia, A. (2020). Video games for the assessment and treatment of attention-deficit/hyperactivity disorder: A systematic review. *European Child & Adolescent Psychiatry, 31*(1), 5–20. https://doi.org/10.1007/s00787-020-01557-w

Pepper, D (2012). *KeyCoNet 2012 literature review: Assessment for key competences.* Key Competence Network of School Education.

Pimmer, C., Eisemann, C., & Magdalena, M. (2020). Fake news resilience through online games? Tentative findings from a randomized controlled trial in higher education. *17th International Conference on Cognition and Exploratory Learning in the Digital Age, CELDA 2020.* https://doi.org/10.33965/celda2020_202014c055

Raisi, E., & Huang, B. (2018). Weakly supervised cyberbullying detection with participant-vocabulary consistency. *Social Network Analysis and Mining, 8*(1). https://doi.org/10.1007/s13278-018-0517-y

Raybourn, E. M. (2014). A new paradigm for serious games: Transmedia learning for more effective training and education. *Journal of Computational Science, 5*(3), 471–481.

Rooney, P. (2012). A theoretical framework for serious game design. *International Journal of Game-Based Learning, 2*(4), 41–60. https://doi.org/10.4018/ijgbl.2012100103

Roozenbeek, J., & van der Linden, S. (2019). Fake news game confers psychological resistance against online misinformation. *Palgrave Communications, 5*(1). https://doi.org/10.1057/s41599-019-0279-9

Roozenbeek, J., Traberg, C. S., & van der Linden, S. (2022). Technique-based inoculation against real-world misinformation. *Royal Society Open Science, 9*(5), 211719.

Rosyid, H. A., Palmerlee, M., & Chen, K. (2018). Deploying learning materials to game content for serious education game development: A case study. *Entertainment Computing, 26*, 1–9. https://doi.org/10.1016/j.entcom.2018.01.001

Sa'ad Abdullahi, B., & Pindiga, H. I. (2023). Tracking the diffusion of disinformation on the SDGs across social media platforms. In J. Servaes & M. J. Yusha'u (Eds.), *SDG18 Communication for All.* Sustainable Development Goals Series, Vol. 2. Palgrave Macmillan. https://doi.org/10.1007/978-3-031-19459-7_6

Saleh, N., Roozenbeek, J., Makki, F., McClanahan, W., & Van Der Linden, S. (2021). Active inoculation boosts attitudinal resistance against extremist persuasion techniques: A novel approach towards the prevention of violent extremism. *Behavioural Public Policy*, 1–24. https://doi.org/10.1017/bpp.2020.60

Sánchez Romero, C., & Muñoz Jiménez, E. M. (2022). Estrategias didácticas y creatividad en contextos no formales. En J. Gil Quintana (coord.) *Didáctica de la belleza y la intercreatividad: Un reto para influencers de aprendizaje en entornos artìsticos* (p. 53–76). McGraw Hill España.

Saprudin, S., Liliasari, L., Prihatmanto, A. S., & Setiawan, A. (2019). The potential of gamification in developing pre-service physics teachers' critical and creative thinking skills. *Omega: Jurnal Fisika dan Pendidikan Fisika, 5*(1), 7–14. https://doi.org/10.31758/OmegaJPhysPhysEduc.v5i1.7

Silva, R., Rodrigues, R., & Leal, C. (2020). Gamification in management education – A literature mapping. *Education and Information Technologies, 25*(3), 1803–1835. https://doi.org/10.1007/s10639-019-10055-9

Sotirakou, C., Paraskevas, T., & Mourlas, C. (2022). Toward the design of a gamification framework for enhancing motivation among *Journalists*, experts, and the public to combat disinformation: The case of CALYPSO platform. In X. Fang (Ed.), *HCI in games. HCII 2022. Lecture Notes in Computer Science*, Vol. 13334. Springer. https://doi.org/10.1007/978-3-031-05637-6_35

Spohr, D. (2017). Fake news and ideological polarization: Filter bubbles and selective exposure on social media. *Business Information Review, 34*(3), 150–160. https://doi.org/10.1177/0266382117722446

Susi, T., Johannesson, M., & Backlund, P. (2007). *Serious games: An overview*. Technical Report HS-IKI-TR-07-001. University of Skövde.

Tascott, D. (2009). *Grown up digital. How the net generation is changing your world*. McGrawHill.

Teyssou, D., Leung, J.-M., Apostolidis, E., Apostolidis, K., Papadopoulos, S., Zampoglou, M., Papadopoulou, O., & Mezaris, V. (2017). The InVID plug-in: Web video verification on the browser. *Proceedings of the First International Workshop on Multimedia Verification* (pp. 23–30). https://doi.org/10.1145/3132384.3132387

Thoman, E., & Jolls, T. (2004). Media literacy—A national priority for a changing world. *American Behavioral Scientist, 48*(1), 18–29. https://doi.org/10.1177/0002764204267246

Urban, A., Hewitt, C., & Moore, J. (2018, November). Fake it to make it: Game-based learning and persuasive design in a disinformation simulator [Paper presentation]. *Association for Educational Communications and Technology 2018*, Kansas City.

van der Linden, S., Roozenbeek, J., & Compton, J. (2020). Inoculating against fake news about COVID-19. *Frontiers in Psychology, 11*. https://doi.org/10.3389/fpsyg.2020.566790

van Helvoort, J., & Hermans, M. (2020). Effectiveness of educational approaches to elementary school pupils (11 or 12 years old) to combat fake news. *Media Literacy and Academic Research, 3*(2), 38–47.

van Schaik, P., Martin, S., & Vallance, M. (2011). Measuring flow experience in an immersive virtual environment for collaborative learning. *Journal of Computer Assisted Learning, 28*(4), 350–365. https://doi.org/10.1111/j.1365-2729.2011.00455.x

Vosoughi, S., Roy, D., & Aral, S. (2018). The spread of true and false news online. Science, 359(6380), 1146–1151. https://doi.org/10.1126/science.aap9559

WHO. (2020). *Infodemic*. Who.int. https://www.who.int/health-topics/infodemic

Wilson, L. O. (2016). Anderson and Krathwohl Bloom's taxonomy revised understanding the new version of Bloom's taxonomy. *The Second Principle*, 1–8. https://quincycollege.edu/wp-content/uploads/Anderson-and-Krathwohl_Revised-Blooms-Taxonomy.pdf

Zhonggen, Y. (2019). A meta-analysis of use of serious games in education over a decade. *International Journal of Computer Games Technology, 2019*, 1–8. https://doi.org/10.1155/2019/4797032

Zhou, X., & Zafarani, R. (2020). A survey of fake news: Fundamental theories, detection methods, and opportunities. *ACM Computing Surveys (CSUR), 53*(5), 1–40.

Zimmerman, E., & Salen, K. (2004). The magic circle. In E. Zimmerman & K. Salen, *Rules of play: Game design fundamentals*. MIT press.

Anderson, L. W. & Krathwohl, D. (2001). *A taxonomy for learning, teaching and assessing: A revision of Bloom's Taxonomy of Educational Objectives*. Longman.

Section III

Fighting disinformation from a policy making perspective

Solutions from projects YouCheck! and YouVerify!

9 Fighting disinformation

Evidence for policy making

Nicoleta Corbu, Divina Frau-Meigs, Denis Teyssou, and Alina Bârgăoanu

9.1 Introduction

"Fake news" is a polysemic and a multilingual catch-all term built to label and classify a whole range of different concepts. Besides poor journalism, they stretch from light terms like hoaxes, satire, and clickbait to traditional terms related to propaganda, manipulation, fabricated stories, and conspiracy theories, to more recent and heavier terms such as disinformation, misinformation, post-truth, alternative facts, and cyberthreats.

Under the presidency of Donald Trump in the US, this controversial expression has also become a populist weapon to disqualify a piece of information, an opponent, and/or particular media outlets. The popularity of the term is inevitably linked to President Trump himself as the interest over time of "fake news" started to rise sharply at the end of the 2016 US presidential election (Frau-Meigs, 2019). "The president [Trump] himself adopted the term 'fake news' to describe all news that was critical or embarrassing" (p. 4), noted American scholars Benkler, Faris, and Roberts (2018) in their book *Network Propaganda*, considering the term as "a particular threat of pollution from political clickbait fabricators" (p. 9). The same book is one of the few reframing fake news in the light of the theories of propaganda, being defined as "communication designed to manipulate a target population by affecting its beliefs, attitudes, or preferences in order to obtain behaviour compliant with political goals of the propagandist" (p. 29). They thus raise the question of the definitive definition of "fake news", an important issue as it determines the kind of responses to address this phenomenon.

Despite the popularity of this simplistic all-purpose buzzword that is likely to remain in the public sphere for long, many journalists and researchers have decided to use "disinformation" instead, to detach it from the US context and its narrow focus. This is particularly the case in Europe, where a High-Level Expert Group (HLEG), mixing researchers, journalists, policy-makers, and civil society actors, was created for the purpose of defining online disinformation and the means to combat it. The HLEG described disinformation

DOI: 10.4324/9781003387404-13

> as false, inaccurate, or misleading information designed, presented and promoted to intentionally cause public harm or for profit. [...] The risk of harm includes threats to democratic political processes and values, which can specifically target a variety of sectors, such as health, science, education, finance and more. [...] It is driven by the production and promotion of disinformation for economic gains or for political or ideological goals, but can be exacerbated by how different audiences and communities receive, engage, and amplify disinformation.
>
> (High Level Expert Group on fake news and online disinformation, European Commission, 2018, pp. 3, 8, 35)

Despite its rather recent uptake, "fake news" is probably as old as humankind. For instance, writers like Vladimir Volkoff (1999) quote the Trojan Horse as the first known disinformation case in history. What has changed? Thanks to the democratisation of Information and Communication Technologies (ICTs) as well as digitalisation, it has never been easier and faster in human history to create, modify, alter, share, and spread information (as texts, images, sounds) for good and for evil purposes.

In this context, the scholarly literature on the "fake news" phenomenon has flourished since the US elections' watershed moment, along with many studies focused on possible effects (Bratich, 2020; Chen et al., 2015; Corbu et al., 2020a; Ha et al., 2019; Matthes et al., 2023), measures to address these effects (Bakir & McStay, 2017; European Commission, 2018; Frau-Meigs, 2022; Silverman et al., 2017). Various attempts to define and classify "fake news" have also emerged, from misinformation (Egelhofer & Lecheler, 2019; Lazer et al., 2018; Molina et al., 2021; Tandoc et al., 2018) to malinformation (Frau-Meigs, 2019; Wardle & Derakhshan, 2017).

However, studies questioning the audience perspective on fake news are still scarce (see, for exception, Nielsen & Graves, 2017). And yet this perspective matters as the audience is sometimes included in part of the definition, as with the HLEG, which incorporates "different audiences and communities" that can amplify disinformation and therefore play an active role in the spread and reach of the phenomenon.

In this research, we present our findings from eight focus groups, organised by the participants of the European project YouCheck! Held in four countries (France, Romania, Spain and Sweden), in 2019–2021. In each of those countries, we asked focus groups of representatives of civil society at large (teachers, civil servants, politicians, citizens) to give their own interpretation and perception about the term "fake news", and its possible effects, as well as their opinion on possible measures to combat disinformation.

Referring to Umberto Eco's (1988) concept of "*intentio lectoris*" and the role of the interpretative choice devoted to the reader, we can study here the two levels of interpretations of such an overused word: the semantic level, to gather the meaning attributed to "fake news", and the critical interpretation level, describing the formal reasons invoked by respondents to explain how "fake news" are perceived and how they should be dispelled.

9.2 Literature review

The research on disinformation has been building steadily since 2016 as "fake news" became very visible in the public sphere. It tends to consider (1) the definitions, actors, and mechanisms of the phenomenon, (2) the impact in society and the risks of harm to democracy, as well as (3) the measures taken to combat disinformation and their efficacy. We addressed all these issues in the qualitative study we conducted cross-culturally.

9.2.1 Defining "fake news"

When considering the definitions of and perceptions about "fake news", the bulk of the research focuses on forms of manipulation and the motivation of actors. Early work tried to define the scope and perimeter of disinformation. Many authors emphasised the "fuzziness" of the notion as typologies range from propaganda to plot theory but some also include satire and parody, when picked up at primary level, as some people do not recognise the content as ironically construed (Wardle & Derakhshan, 2017).

Many models for typologies and descriptions have been elaborated ad hoc, by journalists and researchers. They are very operational, as the one proposed by FirstDraft, which offers a matrix that intersects types of misinformation and types of motivations (Wardle, 2017) or the one proposed by Tandoc and colleagues (2018) that intersects intention to deceive with levels of facticity.

Other approaches are rather philosophical, focusing on making clear distinctions between genre and label (Egelhofer & Lecheler, 2019) or redefining phenomena related to misinformation, disinformation, conspiracy theory as moral panics (Bratich, 2020), etc.

Recently, many authors have argued about the lack of agreement on what "fake news" is, and proposed to avoid the use of the term as such, replacing it by other concepts, such as "information disorders" (Ali, 2022; Buehler et al., 2021; Wardle and Derakhshan, 2017). Yet the term "fake news" remains largely used by journalists and ordinary people, even if its meaning is not always clear.

Little research on audience perspectives from a sociological or cultural perspective has been written so far (Nielsen & Graves, 2017). The bulk of the literature relies on psychology and cognition to explain the mental shortcuts and illusions that create confusions in the mind and induce people to believe fake news. Terms such as cognitive dissonance, cognitive biases, and nudging have gained currency. The literature insists on what makes the audiences fall prey to fakes by pointing at cognitive biases – mostly confirmation bias and continued influence bias (Lewandowsky et al., 2012). All these biases create cognitive dissonance, when a piece of information can contradict one's beliefs, leading to the rejection of the credible information to alleviate the uncomfortable disconnect (Taddicken & Wolff, 2020).

A more recent body of literature has been looking at the effects of correction, to explain the continued influence of fake news, even after debunking (Hameleers, 2022). But even though notions such as the backfire effect (according to which correction could strengthen the belief in the myth) have been promoted to explain the persistence of fake news in public consciousness, there is no definitive agreement on the widespread effect of such notions, and robust evidence is still needed (Swire-Thompson et al., 2020).

Less research has been conducted on the new agency of users, as some of them are seen as active contributors in the spread, if not the creation, of fake news, for motives that can be ideological or financial (using social influence to monetise their creations). Such amplifiers have become influencers that can work alone or as embedded cells for other actors (especially in the case of ideological disinformation and foreign influence). They play on the vulnerabilities of algorithmic recommendation as it affects the sphere of information, peddling influence for profit, to the detriment of news quality. Publicity and propaganda can both become very porous, especially during elections when all sorts of political advertising campaigns vie for the attention of the voting citizenry (Frau-Meigs, 2018).

The rhetoric used by contributors and amplifiers has been analysed, and research shows it plays on ambiguity so that fake news can go under the radar of detection for abuse, for hate speech or defamation. Ambiguity is cultivated to wage infowars and bypass censorship on social media. It is also cultivated to enable this loose coalition of perpetrators to dissociate themselves from over-scandalising issues or figures while maintaining their overall offensive stance (Marwick & Lewis, 2017).

9.2.2 Effects of fake news

When considering the perceived prevalence and possible effects of fake news in online media, the research tends to divide its focus on political risks on the one hand and personal risks on the other hand.

At the political level, attempts to define a new risk of public harm to democratic processes (like elections) are seen in the regulatory field, at policy level (Morgan, 2018). They tend to target the platforms and the producers of disinformation described as harmful perpetrators, as well as some amplifiers amongst the users. Connecting the types of abuse with the types of perpetrators with the types of harm and the intended victims makes it possible to map the risks of harm caused by disinformation (Frau-Meigs, 2021). These risks of harm range from attacks on freedom of speech and on freedom of elections to attacks on freedom of participation as disinformation campaigns try to stifle contradictory debates, suppress voter registration, force disenfranchisement of vulnerable minorities, etc. Online content of this kind can lead to real life behaviour, like harassment, ostracism, physical threats, and censorship.

The two major impacts covered by the research in the field deal with polarisation (Hameleers & Van der Meer, 2020) and radicalisation and point at audience behaviour in terms of "selective exposure" (Guess et al., 2016, p. 11) vs "algorithmic exposure". The bulk of the research emphasises human interactions and selective exposure, with a main concern around elections, with the 2016 US elections as defining moment (Frau-Meigs, 2021). The research points to "asymmetrical polarisation", as the partisan lines show the Trump electorate more likely to visit fake news websites than the Clinton electoral base (Benkler et al., 2018). The American citizens tend to believe whatever favours their candidate, and follow social media ideologically driven (Allcott & Gentzkow, 2017). This has been described as the echo chamber effect, which is to say the selective homogeneous exposure to partisan content within a community, but with very localised circulation (Gaumon et al., 2017).

This body of research also shows that polarisation can be manipulated by foreign countries or rogue actors, weaponising fake news to destabilise the Western democracies. Such perpetrators aim at creating polemics via trolls that pretend to be part of well-established online communities. They are part of the arsenal of amplification and can objectively meet the local or national extremes that rely on that support that is described in three phases aiming at influencing audiences: "luring, taking the bait and hauling in" (Szwed, 2016, p. 7).

As for "algorithmic exposure", the research looks for guilty parties among the platform behaviour and the use of technological devices, especially bots and artificial intelligence, as they could create "filter bubbles", a kind of "information determinism" from which our current access to any new information is based on past navigation and opinions (Pariser, 2011). Algorithm-driven influence is considered as working through echo chambers and filter bubbles, in everyday life, not only during defining democratic moments such as elections (Quattrociocchi et al., 2016). It works best within a deep but restrained group of users whose political identity is identical and based on partisan affinities, thus eliminating alternative ideas and preventing deliberative conversations (Garrett & Stroud, 2014).

At the individual level, an increasing body of literature makes the distinction between individual level effects of mis- and disinformation, with societal implications. Various studies showed a range of effects, from psychological ones (Bastick, 2021; Matthes et al., 2023) to politically related ones, such as political cynicism (Lee & Jones-Jang, 2022) or political disengagement (Kim, 2022). The main concerns are related to the fact that disinformation in a poorly informed citizenry could become a real threat to democracy itself, by destabilising political institutions, delegitimising media organisations (Ognyanova et al., 2020), and influencing elections (Baptista & Gradim, 2022; Grinberg et al., 2019; Kapantai et al., 2021).

Some researchers point to the role of the internet and especially social media as paradoxical public-commercial spaces where the irrational competes with the rational (Bronner, 2019). Such paradoxical spaces give an advantage to highly motivated "believers" and influencers having an agenda built around mistrust (disguised as healthy doubt). In a generalised environment of low interest for knowledge and growing illectronism, they find a favourable ground in cognitive biases that flatter the intellectual laziness and reluctance to question their own belief systems of certain internet users. This confirms the results found by Nielsen and Graves (2017), who point out that "from an audience perspective, fake news is (...) much more about a wider discontent with the information landscape – including news media and politicians as well as platform companies" (p. 1). And they added: "When asked to provide examples of fake news, people identify poor journalism, propaganda (including both lying politicians and hyperpartisan content), and some kinds of advertising more frequently than false information designed to masquerade as news reports" (p. 1). So people seem to consider the difference between true and fake news as only a difference of degree and identify the latter as a mixture of bad journalism, polarised propaganda, and sponsored content.

In terms of policymaking, this type of research leads to finding means of self-regulation that reconstructs trusts in media at large, such as creating the Global Disinformation Index or reinforcing the fact-checking cells in all reference media. It also leads to the production of fact-checking tools funded by research such as the InVID-WeVerify verification plugin and laying the emphasis on the loyalty of social media platforms that should aim at increasing trust in quality news.

9.2.3 Fighting fake news

When considering the measures to address the fake news phenomenon and who the key actors to implement such measures are, most researchers agree that a modicum of fact-checking and media and information literacy (MIL) is key. Self-regulatory strategies and regulation are seen as a last resort, as exemplified by the EU Action plan. While promoting fact-checking and MIL, it also compelled the social media platforms to adopt a code of practice and to create a public archive of all paid political advertisements during electoral campaigns (HLEG, European Commission, 2018).

But the main actors expected to address the vulnerabilities of the audiences at large are the fact-checkers on the one hand and the media educators on the other hand. One key theme that resurfaces for both types of actors is the central issue of correction and refutation and attendant counter-discourses. Besides the bias of continuous influence that perpetuates disinformation after debiasing (Lewandowsky et al., 2012), there is the added element of vulnerability identified as "third person effect", that describes the way people tend to assume misinformation affects other people more than themselves. Corbu et al. (2020b) and Ştefăniţă et al. (2018) found that such an effect affects people's ability to spot disinformation as they tend to rate themselves as better at identifying misinformation than others. It points to the inherent risk that people will feel overconfident and will not take appropriate steps to palliate their vulnerabilities.

The difficulty of correction should lead to strategies not only of debunking but also of refutation and counter-narratives via MIL. Developing heuristics or mental routines for social media and disinformation is key as a means to build informational resilience, so as to be ready for fake news rather than to fall for them. In other words, prevention is better (and cheaper) than correction. This implies to develop critical thinking strategies because that is what seems to be suspended with disinformation: people literally suspend their critical reasoning (as we do in fiction when we suspend our disbelief) to take the lazy path of fastest and least fatiguing proposal and general mental sloth in information overload. This lazy thinking needs to be reversed and retrained, by changing mind routines and rekindling critical reasoning and critical thinking.

MIL lends itself to "prebunking" (a term preferable to "inoculation", which in media theory is not acceptable as too simplistic). It can be part of MIL techniques that build pre-emptive resilience to disinformation by describing its mechanisms, describing its perpetrators, and their motivations and promoting the use of fact-checking tools (Cook et al., 2017). Project YouCheck! illustrates this trend, as it seeks to empower the public at large by providing a smart tool that enables people to go beyond their gut feelings and double check by themselves, thus making them take charge of finding the evidence instead of being spoonfed it by toxic actors (Savoir*Devenir, 2021). The corrective mechanisms should provide an alternative cause or explanation if people are going to go through the effort of, literally, changing their mind (Nygren et al., 2021; Nygren et al., 2022).

The literature review points to some gaps and weaknesses in the research to date. If the mechanisms and perpetrators are well covered, there is not yet a critical mass of work on the diffuse and long-term effects of disinformation as well as on the efficiency of policy, fact-checking, and education measures. Other limitations of the research point to the analysis of emotions and sentiments, which remains very text based. Researchers do not yet have the ability to analyse the weight of images in disinformation and the impact of visual literacy. The quantitative approaches are the overwhelming majority, not yet accompanied by qualitative approaches, with interviews and observations of more diverse groups (in terms of age, gender, and education in particular). The identification of human factors needs to be more robust, which implies more direct interaction with users, through interviews and focus groups in particular.

In the project YouCheck! study, we investigated how citizens at large defined fake news and perceived it, as well as what they thought the solutions to prevent disinformation would or should be. We suggested using a tool designed for professional fact-checkers, the InVID-WeVerify plugin, to see if it could stimulate visual literacy, and critical thinking. We conducted this in four European countries to see also if context-based situations could explain different perspectives on fake news. The selected countries are in line with the four main models for media policy (Hallin & Mancini, 2004, revised 2011):

the "polarized pluralist model" (specific to Mediterranean countries), the "democratic corporatist model" (in North/Central European countries), the "liberal mode" (in North Atlantic countries), and "the hybrid model" (in post-communist countries).

We explored the following research questions:

RQ1. What is the audience's perspective on what fake news are?
RQ2. What is the perceived (by audience) harm of fake news at individual and social level?
RQ3. What should the measures taken to address the "fake news" phenomenon and what are the key actors responsible for implementing such measures?
RQ4. How do audience's perspectives on understanding fake news, effects, and measures to address the phenomenon vary across countries?

9.3 Methodology

Understanding the audiences' perspectives on the "fake news" phenomenon is key to addressing many social issues related to online disinformation, including media literacy practices in schools. This research has been carried out within the YouCheck! Project, whose main purpose is to raise awareness of the public at large and the education and media literacy community about disinformation and "fake news" as a threat to democracy.

In this context, we conducted eight focus groups in four European countries (France, Romania, Spain, and Sweden), to understand more in-depth how people in these countries perceive the so-called fake news phenomenon: What is "fake news", what are its consequences, and what could be realistic ways to address its negative effects? The four countries considered in this study account for the varieties of both media systems and political and social systems, and MIL practices across Europe. In recent years, the new European public policies concerning media and disinformation are very much focused on addressing the phenomenon from a variety of angles, one of which viewed as a long-term effective way of countering its negative effects is MIL (European Commission, 2018).

However, MIL practices differ to a great extent across Europe, from countries which have fully incorporated classes and topics in school curricula (such as France or Sweden), to countries which tend to consider the issue as a non-school actors' concern and for that matter do not include media literacy topics in their school curricula almost at all (such as Romania or Spain).

The focus groups were conducted in the time period of January–March 2020, and lasted on average between one hour and a half and two hours (with the shortest lasting one hour and the longest three hours). In each country, two types of people were selected. The first group was composed of high school "teachers" (with the exception of Spain, where teacher trainers at university were the respondents), teaching social sciences topics (including, in some countries, media literacy topics). The second group was composed of members of the "public at large", that is to say professionals from outside the school system, not directly involved in activities dealing with media literacy or online disinformation. They occupied a diverse range of professions (architect, IT specialist, HR specialist, engineer, fashion designer).

We used convenience samples, based on voluntary interest in participating in a discussion about fake news and online tools to address the phenomenon. The total number of teachers involved in the discussions was 34, 12 men and 22 women (France, N = 9; Romania, N = 9; Spain, N = 7; Sweden, N = 9), and the total number of people outside the education system was 30, 14 men and 16 women (France, N = 9; Romania, N = 8; Spain, N = 8; Sweden, N = 5).

The design of the study included those two categories of respondents, so as to reflect the obtrusiveness of the topic in their professional life, which could make an important difference in how they perceived certain topics and how media in general influenced their view of such topics (Weimann & Brosius, 2017). The focus group questions covered two important topics and attendant sections: the audiences' perspectives on the "fake news" phenomenon and the role of a media literacy tool, InVID-WeVerify, to fight image and video-based online disinformation. This chapter reports on the first question discussed in the focus groups. The results of the second question, using the teachers sample only, were disseminated by Nygren and colleagues (Nygren et al., 2021; Nygren et al., 2022).

We used thematic analysis, with predefined codes to explore the data from the focus groups (see Appendix 9.1). The questions pertinent for this analysis were separated into several sets. The first set was related to "news consumption patterns" (media outlets, interest in news, news exposure/avoidance). The second set dealt with "fake news" per se (definition, perceived frequency, effects, measures to fight them). The focus group closed on requests for general remarks, registering extra thoughts, insights, and suggestions.

9.4 Findings

9.4.1 Perceptions about and definitions of "fake news"

In order to understand how people perceived the fake news phenomenon, we first asked participants to discuss their context of media consumption, so as to have a general background of news consumption among the participants in the four countries.

As far as the teachers are concerned, there are important differences among countries: in Romania and Spain, they mostly prefer traditional media to alternative or social media, with TV news consumption being their media outlet of choice most of the time in Romania, and radio or online journals in Spain. Swedish teachers also prefer traditional media, generally a combination of public service radio, TV, and online press, but at the same time they are more open to new alternative sources of information, of which podcasts are explicitly mentioned. French teachers interviewed differ very much in their patterns of news consumption, with a clear preference for social media (Twitter, Facebook, Instagram, Snapchat, and YouTube) and podcasts, with TV potentially becoming entirely absent from their media diets (at least in the sample we investigated).

In the group considered as "the public at large" (or non-teachers), these differences are much attenuated, as most people in all countries use a large range of news sources, including both traditional, alternative, and social media outlets, including foreign news sources (especially in Romania). In Spain and Romania, they explicitly mention actively following news in their areas of professional expertise. In France, once again, we could trace a clear preference for social networks among respondents. Additionally, participants rarely avoid news in all countries, and they experience high levels of "incidental news exposure", which mostly they consider to be a positive thing. One notable exception is a discussion among the Romanian participants, who underline (without consensus, though) the danger of being trapped in filter bubbles and echo chambers, in a highly polarised media environment.

Against this general background, the discussion about defining "fake news" and the kind of content related to such a label provided different understandings in the different groups.

Generally speaking, the teachers in the four countries agreed that the concept is difficult to define, as "the vocabulary shifts even without us noticing it" (France). In Spain and Sweden, there seems to be a consensus about the key role played by intention, which makes the difference between disinformation, which is "strategic and deliberate" (Sweden), "information that has an *interest*" (Spain), and misinformation, which "feels more random and accidental, based on carelessness.... ignorance" (Sweden). For the Romanian respondents, "both [mis- and dis- information] are fake news. Nobody knows anymore what the intention was" (Romania).

In all countries, people agree that there are many avatars of the concept, from "partially invented news", out of context news, distorted information (Romania), to "camouflaging informational realities", "falsehood and manipulation" (Spain). Manipulation is in fact specifically mentioned and discussed in the Romanian and Spanish groups extensively, as people feel the need to make a clear connection between the two concepts (fake news and manipulation). Biased or hyper-partisan news were considered as a form of misinformation in Sweden, as

> you only see one angle... goes too fast ... or you come in without proper background information ... you may not have the correct filter to be able to read since you have an incorrect road map. In this case it doesn't have to be strategic.
>
> (Sweden)

For Romania, biased news is specifically considered as a form of fake news: "It is fake news, as it distorts information to make it advantageous for someone"

(Romania). In Romania, though, some of the respondents underline the high polarisation of the media in the country, which would ultimately not leave room for any kind of "proper news". Satire and parody are only discussed in the Romanian group, being considered as borderline genres, and only problematic if the audience does not recognise the convention behind the content.

In the "public at large" group, intention seems to play an important role for respondents in Romania and Spain:

> When we talk about news that matters, I think there is a clear purpose behind them, one that is very elaborated. I am not a supporter of conspiracy theories by any means, but I think that people who disinform know very well what they need to do, how to do it and in what direction, and they have the tools for it. It's very frustrating.
>
> (Romania)

"When there is a will to alter something to achieve a certain end" (Spain). In France, respondents talk about psychological and political motivations, which is in line with the idea of intention, while in Sweden the discussion rather focuses on "alternative facts", respondents suggesting a shift in the way people understand news, from facts to opinions: "People seem to think that their opinion weighs as heavily as facts. It's sick that there are discussions about facts versus opinions" (Sweden). Many avatars of "fake news" are mentioned in some countries, from conspiracy theories, incomplete news stories, and hyper-partisan news in Romania, to invented news, omission of content in Spain, or influencers' opinions in Sweden.

9.4.2 Perceived prevalence and possible effects of fake news in online media

The discussion about the perceived effects of fake news in the four countries was prefaced by a general outline of the perceived prevalence of fake news in the media system in each country.

In the teachers' groups, the general consensus in France and Romania is that the phenomenon is quasi-generalised, with Romanians offering estimates of 80% of all news being in some way counterfeit, showing a strong defiance in the media at large. French respondents considered the incidence of fake news "enormous". Spaniards estimate that they are "indeed exposed to false news every day", while the Swedes have a more nuanced approach: they consider (unintentional) misinformation to be more common, due to the pressure of publishing rapidly information on any given topic, while (intentional) disinformation is seen as more rare.

The "public at large" group expressed more differences about the perceived effects of disinformation. In Romania, there is consensus about a very high incidence (once again, 80% is given as an estimate), whereas in the other countries people are rather nuanced in their responses: in France, they consider the high frequency of fake news to be an overstatement (whereas teachers in France considered incidence very high) and believe that people who select their sources of information are shielded from the flow of questionable information; in Sweden, the participants deemed fake news to be very common, while Spaniards distinguished between the high prevalence of fake news on digital platforms by contrast with the traditional media.

Against this backdrop, in most of the focus groups, the effects of fake news were discussed both at societal and at personal level.

In the teachers' groups, people focused much more on the personal level. In Romania, the main concern is related to anti-vaccination and health problems ("all the stories about vaccination... I thought these stories were the most dangerous ones for the population"), while in France people talk about a general feeling of anxiety about an inescapable phenomenon ("there is an omnipresence of this anguish, no means to escape it"). Spaniards discuss effects in terms of reputation, both at individual and societal levels, as "individuals, groups, or even the media" are affected from this point of view, while Swedes fear a skewed worldview ("hard to get a fact based world view"), not shared by all.

The "public at large" group expressed views very similar to their counterparts in the educational system. Romanian respondents are very much preoccupied with health implications (the anti-vaccination campaign being considered a big part of the problem), and the possible democratic implications of "using fake news for propaganda". French interviewees talk about psychosis, social withdrawal, and generalised credulity in the population. Spanish respondents are concerned about mass influence (propaganda), viewing politics and health as the most vulnerable fields of influence, specifically mentioning implications for democracy ("Security aspects are questioned, democracy, participation, rights and legitimacy are questioned"). As in the teachers' groups, they also discussed reputation ("Fake news affects the reputation of brands, institutions and people. It affects citizens in their daily decision making").

9.4.3 Measures to address the fake news phenomenon

When discussing possible ways to fight disinformation, there are similar patterns in the two types of participants, be it teachers or the public at large. In all groups in France, Romania, Spain, and Sweden, respondents discussed education and the development of critical thinking as key.

Additionally, Romanians in both groups discussed the need for more media regulation, especially teachers "The key is the legislation and its enforcement. Because, if I know that I could do anything and not be punished for it in any way, then..." (teachers, Romania). The public at large group added the need for more technical solutions: "The fight, if you ask me, can only be fought by algorithms, as a response to the armies of bots [used in fake news viralization]" (public at large, Romania).

Spaniards also discuss the need for technical tools to address the phenomenon, to which the teachers in this country add an urge to improve the quality of news: "I see quite a few difficulties among journalists, ... they don't have tools to contrast the news" (public at large, Spain); "From the media an effort should be made to expand the agenda of collaborators, of specialists" (teachers, Spain).

In Sweden, both teachers and non-teachers also see improvement of the quality of news as the main solution to address the disinformation phenomenon: "journalists are losing their jobs and fewer journalists are paid to dig. Today media companies cannot afford to have digging journalists, making it much harder for us as readers ... to dig into a story costs money" (teachers, Sweden).

9.4.4 *Cross-country perspectives and variability*

Besides some differences between the two groups in terms of professional cultures (teachers vs others), some elements point to cultural differences and similarities across the sample and across the three subsets of questions.

In terms of similarities, the participants in the four countries shared similar views about the sense of strategic manipulation inherent in "fake news". They also shared the sense that the major negative effect of "fake news" was societal, with important democratic consequences involving propaganda. They expressed similar views on the solutions, putting education and critical thinking at the top of their priorities.

In terms of differences, the Swede respondents differed consistently from the French, Romanian, and Spanish respondents, be it in terms of understanding "fake news", perceived effects, and ways to address the phenomenon. The dominant view of the Swedes was intrinsically related to the quality of the journalism: they saw unintentional journalism errors as part of the problem; they reflected on the increased poverty of investigative journalism as an effect (and maybe cause) of disinformation; they insisted of fostering quality media as the main solution.

The other countries tended to think that policymakers are the actors that should play a central role, through measures related to both media regulation and education. France leaned towards more education to diminish gullibility in the general public. Romania focused on propaganda, manipulation, and legal enforcement. Spain showed a mix of concerns for journalism and for more regulation of the media.

9.5 Discussion

Defining "fake news" from an audience perspective is a challenging endeavour, as this study shows: not only people understand different things by the concept, but also different cultural contexts could add to the individual differences. Therefore, it is not always easy to see people's perceptions about possible effects, ways to address the phenomenon, or openness to new and inventive fact-checking tools. In this study, some insights are nonetheless worth discussing.

As far as the conceptualisation of "fake news" (RQ1) is concerned, people in the four countries analysed in this study have quite heterogeneous ways of understanding the umbrella term of "fake news". However, a common denominator is *intention*: when discussing about "fake news", people see firstly fake news as intended and secondly some other avatars of the term, such as "partially invented news", out of context news, distorted information (Romania), "camouflaging informational realities", "falsehood and manipulation" (Spain), manipulation (Romania and Spain), biased or hyper-partisan news (Romania and Sweden). In Sweden, people make a clear distinction between misinformation (unintentional mistakes under the pressure of time for journalists), which is more common, and disinformation (with intention), which is more rareSatire, and parody are mostly not considered as "fake news", provided that people recognise their intentions.

Discarding satire and parody from the definition is in line with Nielsen and Graves (2017), who showed that people usually associate satire and parody with fun content, and not with news, and different from other classifications (Derakhshan & Wardle, 2017, Tandoc et al., 2018) that include these genres under the broad umbrella of fake news. The overall results confirm the usefulness of Eco's distinction (1988) between the semantic level and the critical interpretation level: strategic intent reflected a common critical interpretation of fake news in stark contrast with many shades of semantic options for a very fuzzy term.

When discussing incidence and possible (negative) effects (RQ2), with the exception of the Swedes respondents and the French "public at large" group, all other people in the focus groups tended to agree that the incidence of fake news is very high (France, Spain), while Romanian respondents estimated that about 80% of all news being in some way counterfeit in their country. Participants referred to both individual level and societal levels for effects. Effects at the individual level were related to health (Romania), high levels of anxiety (France), reputation (Spain), and skewed worldviews (Sweden). The social implications were discussed in terms of manipulation and propaganda, negative influence of the democratic process, health, and politics being mentioned as the most vulnerable fields of influence.

Addressing the solutions to the "fake news phenomenon" (RQ3), participants thought they should be conducted through education and media literacy, development of critical thinking (France, Romania, and Spain), media regulation (Romania), technical tools, such as InVID-WeVerify (Spain), and improvement of quality news (Sweden). This is in line with three of the five measures proposed by the HLEG on Disinformation, concerning *media transparency*, *media and information literacy*, and *empowerment of users and journalists to tackle disinformation*. It resonates in particular with the need to "promote media and information literacy to counter disinformation and help users navigate the digital media environment" (European Commission, 2018, p. 5).

When looking at differences across countries (RQ4), context-based situations could explain some differences, even if the study showed that people are generally concerned with the same issues, but with nuances specific in relation to media and education practices. The Swede respondents differed consistently from the French, the Romanian, and the Spanish respondents. This would be fitting with Hallin and Mancini's models for media policy (2011).

Sweden is considered as part of the "liberal model" (North Atlantic countries), putting the responsibility on self-regulation and on media independence and quality on to the profession itself (journalists should take care of the issue), therefore also dwindling the perceived effects of "fake news" in contrast with the other countries in the sample.

The other countries put more emphasis on policymaking, regulation, and education, which is to stay the role of the state in relation to the media. France reflects the "democratic corporatist model" (Central European countries), with the notion that the state should provide for education and for the fight against disinformation. Spain reflects the "polarized pluralist model" (specific to Mediterranean countries), with its support for media regulation. Romania relates to "the hybrid model" (Post communist countries), with concern about state propaganda and support for traditional media. These results confirm that using the MIL prism enriches the media policy model by Hallin and Mancini (see Chapter 4; see also Matovic et al., 2017).

9.6 Conclusion

As with any study addressing disinformation, ours too comes with limitations. On the one hand, the convenience samples used in the four countries do not permit broad generalisations, but rather offer insights into how audiences perceive the fake news phenomenon. At the same time, following a common protocol of recruiting, conducting focus groups, and analysing data comes with many challenges, which could result in slightly different profiles of people interviewed in the focus groups or alternative ways to interpret data. Additionally, teachers recruited in this study were already interested in the topic of disinformation, which could also make generalisation of results difficult. However, we believe to have provided valuable information about one rather understudied aspect of a multifaceted phenomenon: understanding "fake news" from the audience perspective, and offering a non-normative, more pragmatic perspective on how people usually understand "fake news" and how they perceive effects and possible solutions to address the disinformation process in the European Union and in the world.

One conspicuous absence needs to be noted in all the discussions: there was little to none self-reflexive perception of the role of audiences in amplifying fake news among the participants in the focus groups. They tend to lay the source of the problem and the blame on other actors, be it the news media or the politicians, as noted by Nielsen and Graves (2017). This points to the need to develop and amplify MIL itself, in education, formal and non-formal, for young people and for adults, to ensure that audiences are aware of their role in the "fake news" phenomenon, and their role in the solutions that can be put in place, as they could acquire more critical thinking and self-reflexive competences.

Notwithstanding these limits, there are key lessons learnt, and recommendations for policymaking to fight disinformation, in line with the extant literature on the subject (for an overview, see Frau-Meigs, 2022) are as follows: (1) media literacy interventions and education in general remain the main line of addressing disinformation on long-term. Life-long learning programmes devoted to MIL and disinformation in general could change the way people think about the importance of being well informed in any healthy democracy; (2) the use of technical tools might become a way of fighting the increasingly sophisticated techniques used to alter information in a high-choice media environment; (3) a better-quality journalism should become the norm and an answer to limit the various avatars of "fake news" vehiculated not seldom through established media outlets; (4) (social) media regulation must become more strict and severe, especially in the light of the new EU Commission initiatives, such as the Strengthened Code of Practice on Disinformation and the Digital Services Act; (5) media awareness campaigns could become a standard of warning people against the various techniques and misleading narratives circulating in the media.

References

Ali, S. A. M. (2022). *How information disorder affirms authoritarianism and destabilizes democracy: Evidence, trends, and actionable mitigation strategies from Asia and the Pacific.* US Agency for International Development. https://doi.org/10.2139/ssrn.3996805

Allcott, H., & Gentzkow. M. (2017). Social media and fake news in the 2016 election. *Journal of Economic Perspectives*, *31*(2), 211–236.

Bakir, V., & McStay, A. (2017). Fake news and the economy of emotions: Problems, causes, solutions. *Digital Journalism*, 6, 154–175.

Baptista, J. P., & Gradim, A. (2022). Online disinformation on Facebook: The spread of fake news during the Portuguese 2019 election. *Journal of Contemporary European Studies*, *30*(2), 297–312.

Bastick, Z. (2021). Would you notice if fake news changed your behavior? An experiment on the unconscious effects of disinformation. *Computers in human behavior*, *116*, 106633.

Benkler, Y., Faris, R., & Roberts, H. (2018). *Network Propaganda, manipulation, disinformation, and radicalization in American Politics.* Oxford University Press.

Bratich, J. (2020). Civil society must be defended: Misinformation, moral panics, and wars of restoration. *Communication, Culture and Critique*, *13*(3), 311–332.

Bronner, G. (2019). Développement de l'esprit critique: vers une nécessaire révolution pédagogique. *Bulletin du CREAS*, *6*, 28–34.

Buehler, M., Schatz, E., Ali, S. M., Greene, C., & Sombatpoonsiri, J. (2021). How information disorder affirms authoritarianism and destabilizes democracy: Evidence, trends, and actionable mitigation strategies from Asia and the Pacific. *Asian Development Bank Economics Working Paper Series*, 1.

Chen, X., Sin, S. C. J., Theng, Y. L., & Lee, C. S. (2015). Why students share misinformation on social media: Motivation, gender, and study-level differences. *The Journal of Academic Librarianship*, *41*(5), 583–592.

Cook, J., Lewandowsky, S., & Ecker, U. K. (2017). Neutralizing misinformation through inoculation: Exposing misleading argumentation techniques reduces their influence. *PloS One*, *12*(5), e0175799.

Corbu, N., Bârgăoanu, A., Buturoiu, R., & Ștefăniță, O. (2020a). Does fake news lead to more engaging effects on social media? Evidence from Romania. *Communications*, *45*(s1), 694–717.

Corbu, N., Oprea, D. A., Negrea-Busuioc, E., & Radu, L. (2020b). 'They can't fool me, but they can fool the others!' Third person effect and fake news detection. *European Journal of Communication*, *35*(2), 165–180.

Derakhshan, H., & Wardle, C. (2017). Information disorder: Definitions. In *Understanding and Addressing the Disin-formation Ecosystem Conference* (pp. 5–12). University of Pennsylvania, Annenberg School for Communication.

Eco, U. (1988). Intentio Lectoris. The State of the Art. *Differentia: Review of Italian Thought*, *2*, 147–168. https://commons.library.stonybrook.edu/differentia/vol2/iss1/12

Egelhofer, L., & Lecheler, S. (2019). Fake news as a two dimensional phenomenon: A framework and research agenda. *Annals of the International Communication Association*, *43*(2), 97–116.

European Commission. (2018). Directorate-general for communication networks, content and technology. *A multi-dimensional approach to disinformation: Report of the independent high level group on fake news and online disinformation*. Publications Office of the European Union.

European Commission High Level Expert Group on Fake News and Online Disinformation. (2018). *A Multidimensional approach to disinformation. Report of the independent High level Group on fake news and online disinformation*. https://digital-strategy.ec.europa.eu/en/library/final-report-high-level-expert-group-fake-news-and-online-disinformation

Frau-Meigs, D. (2018). *Societal costs of "Fake news" in the digital single market*. IMCO, European Commission. http://www.europarl.europa.eu/supporting-analyses

Frau-Meigs, D. (2019) *Faut-il avoir peur des fake news?* La Documentation française.

Frau-Meigs, D. (2021). Addressing the risks of harms caused by disinformation: European vs American approaches to testing the limits of dignity and freedom of expression online. In L. Corredoira, Bel, I., & L. C. Presuel (Eds.), *Handbook of communication rights, law & ethics*. Wiley Blackwell.

Frau-Meigs, D. (2022). How disinformation reshaped the relationship between journalism and media and information literacy (MIL): Old and new perspectives revisited. *Digital Journalism*, *10*(5), 912–922.

Garrett, K. R., & Stroud, N. J. (2014). Partisan paths to exposure diversity: Differences in pro- and counterattitudinal news consumption. *Journal of Communication*, *64*(4), 680–701.

Gaumont, N., Panahi, M, & Chavalarias, D. (2017). Reconstruction of the socio-semantic dynamics of political activist Twitter networks—Method and application to the 2017 French presidential election. *PLoS One*, *13*(9), e0201879.

Grinberg, N., Joseph, K., Friedland, L., Swire-Thompson, B., & Lazer, D. (2019). Fake news on Twitter during the 2016 US presidential election. *Science*, *363*(6425), 374–378.

Guess, A., Nyhan, B., & Reifler, J. (2016). Selective exposure to misinformation: Evidence from the consumption of fake news during the 2016 U.S. presidential campaign, http://www.dartmouth.edu/~nyhan/fake-news-2016.pdf

Ha, L., Perez, L., & Ray, R. (2019). Mapping recent development in scholarship on fake news and misinformation, 2008 to 2017: Disciplinary contribution, topics, and impact. *American Behavioral Scientist*, *65*, 1–26.

Hallin, D. C., & Mancini, P. (2004). *Comparing media systems: Three models of media and politics*. Cambridge University Press.

Hallin, D. C., & Mancini, P. (Eds.). (2011). *Comparing media systems beyond the Western world*. Cambridge University Press.

Hameleers, M. (2022). Separating truth from lies: Comparing the effects of news media literacy interventions and fact-checkers in response to political misinformation in the US and Netherlands. *Information, Communication & Society*, *25*(1), 110–126.

Hameleers, M., & Van der Meer, T. G. (2020). Misinformation and polarization in a high-choice media environment: How effective are political fact-checkers? *Communication Research*, *47*(2), 227–250.

Kapantai, E., Christopoulou, A., Berberidis, C., & Peristeras, V. (2021). A systematic literature review on disinformation: Toward a unified taxonomical framework. *New Media & Society*, *23*(5), 1301–1326.

Kim, Y. (2022). How conspiracy theories can stimulate political engagement. *Journal of Elections, Public Opinion and Parties*, *32*(1), 1–21.

Lazer, D. M., Baum, M. A., Benkler, Y., Berinsky, A. J., Greenhill, K. M., Menczer, F., … & Zittrain, J. L. (2018). The science of fake news. Addressing fake news requires a multidisciplinary effort. *Science*, 359, 1094–1096.

Lee, S., & Jones-Jang, S. M. (2022). Cynical nonpartisans: The role of misinformation in political cynicism during the 2020 US presidential election. *New Media & Society*. https://doi.org/10.1177/14614448221116036

Lewandowsky, S., Ecker, U. K. H., Seifers, C. M., & Cook, J. (2012). Misinformation and its correction: Continued influence and successful debiasing. *Psychological Science in the Public Interest*, *13*(3), 106–131.

Marwick, A., & Lewis, R. (2017). *Media manipulation and disinformation online*. Data and Society Research Institute, https://datasociety.net/wp-content/uploads/2017/05/DataAndSociety_MediaManipulationAndDisinformationOnline-1.pdf

Matovic, M., Juraitė, K., & Gutiérrez, A. (2017). The role of non-governmental actors in Media and Information Literacy: A comparative media systems perspective. In D. Frau-Meigs, I. Velez & J. Flores Michel (Eds.), *Public policies in media and information literacy in Europe: Cross-country comparisons* (pp. 159–193). Routledge.

Matthes, J., Corbu, N., Jin, S., Theocharis, Y., Schemer, C., van Aelst, P., … & Zoizner, A. (2023). *Perceived prevalence of misinformation fuels worries about COVID-19: A cross-country, multi-method investigation*. Information, Communication & Society, 26(16), 3133–3156.

Molina, M. D., Sundar, S. S., Le, T., & Lee, D. (2021). "Fake news" is not simply false information: A concept explication and taxonomy of online content. *American Behavioral Scientist*, *65*(2), 180–212.

Morgan, S. (2018). Fake news, disinformation, manipulation and online tactics to undermine democracy. *Journal of Cyber Policy*, *3(1)*, 39–43.

Nielsen, R. K., & Graves, L. (2017). "News you don't believe": Audience perspectives on fake news. *Factsheet*. https://ora.ox.ac.uk/objects/uuid:6eff4d14-bc72-404d-b78a-4c2573459ab8/download_file?file_format=pdf&safe_filename=Nielsen%2B-%2BAudience%2Bperspectives%2Bon%2Bfake%2Bnews.pdf&type_of_work=Report

Nygren, T., Frau-Meigs, D., Corbu, N., & Santovena-Casal, S. (2022). Teachers' views on disinformation and media literacy supported by a tool designed for professional fact- checkers: Perspectives from France, Romania, Spain and Sweden. *Sn Social Sciences*, *2*(4). https://doi.org/10.1007/s43545-022-00340-9

Nygren, T., Guath, M., Axelsson, A., and Frau-Meigs, D. (2021). Combatting visual fake news with a professional fact-checking tool in education in France, Romania, Spain and Sweden. *Information*, *12*(5), 201.

Ognyanova, K., Lazer, D., Robertson, R. E., & Wilson, C. (2020). Misinformation in action: Fake news exposure is linked to lower trust in media, higher trust in government when your side is in power. *Harvard Kennedy School Misinformation Review*. https://misinforeview.hks.harvard.edu/article/misinformation-in-action-fake-news-exposure-is-linked-to-lower-trust-in-media-higher-trust-in-government-when-your-side-is-in-power/

Pariser, E. (2011). *The filter bubble: What the internet is hiding from you*, Penguin Books Limited.

Quattrociocchi, W., Scala, A., & Sunstein, C. (2016). Echo Chambers on Facebook, Discussion Paper 877, Harvard John M. Olin Center for Law, Economics, and Business. http://www.law.harvard.edu/programs/olin_center/papers/pdf/Sunstein_877.pdf

Savoir*Devenir. (2021). Youcheck! School interventions. *Youcheck! Project Results*. https://savoirdevenir.net/wp-content/uploads/2021/02/Youcheck-School-Intervention-EN.pdf

Silverman, C., Singer-Vine J., & Vo, L. T. (2017). In spite of the crackdown, fake news publishers are still earning money from major ad networks. *BuzzFeed News*, April 4. https://www.buzzfeed.com/craigsilverman/fake-news-real-ads

Ştefăniţă, O., Corbu, N., & Buturoiu, R. (2018). Fake News and the Third-Person Effect: They are More Influenced than Me and You. *Journal of Media research*, *11*(3), 5–23. https://doi.org/10.24193/jmr.32.1

Swire-Thompson, B., DeGutis, J., & Lazer, D. (2020). Searching for the backfire effect: Measurement and design considerations. *Journal of applied research in memory and cognition*, *9*(3), 286–299. https://doi.org/10.1016/j.jarmac.2020.06.006

Szwed, R. (2016). *Framing of the Ukraine-Russia conflict in online and social media*. NATO Strategic Communications Center of Excellence, www.stratcomcoe.org/download/file/fid/614

Taddicken, M., & Wolff, L. (2020). 'Fake news' in science communication: Emotions and strategies of coping with dissonance online. *Media and Communication*, *8*(1), 206–217. https://doi.org/10.17645/mac.v8i1.2495

Tandoc, E. C. Jr., Zheng, W. L., & Ling, R. (2018). Defining "fake news". *Digital Journalism*, *6*(2), 137–153. https://doi.org/10.1080/21670811.2017.1360143
Volkoff, W. (1999). *Petite histoire de la désinformation*. Editions Le Rocher.
Wardle, C. (2017). Fake news. It's complicated. *First Draft News*. https://medium.com/1st-draft/fake-news-its-complicated-d0f773766c79
Wardle, C., & Derakhshan, H. (2017). Information disorder: Toward an interdisciplinary framework for research and policymaking. *Council of Europe report, DGI (2017), 9*.
Weimann, G., & Brosius, H. B. (2017). Redirecting the agenda: Agenda-setting in the online Era. *The Agenda Setting Journal*, *1*(1), 63–102. https://doi.org/10.1075/asj.1.1.06wei

Appendix 9.1 Template for collecting responses across countries

General setting	Date of the focus Place where it was conducted Who conducted it Length of the focus Coding of interviewees: Focus 1 – focus with teachers Focus 2 – focus with educated people (not teachers, not journalists) Number them (do not give names): Interviewee 1, Interviewee 2, etc.
Intro	Short description of participants • Number • Gender • Age (if available) • Profession (if teachers – what they teach)
1.1 News consumption patterns	
1.1.1 Media outlets	• idea 1 • verbatim quote(s) for idea 1 (with reference to who said the words: Interviewee no, Gender, Focus no, Country): E.g.: "Fake news is nothing new. It has been around since ancient times" (Interviewee 3, female, focus 2, France) • idea 2 • verbatim quote(s) for idea 2 • idea and quotes 3,4,5…
1.1.2. Interest in political and social news	• idea 1 • verbatim quote(s) for idea 1 • idea 2 • verbatim quote(s) for idea 2 • idea and quotes 3,4,5…
1.1.3. Incidental news exposure and news avoidance	• idea 1 • verbatim quote(s) for idea 1 • idea 2 • verbatim quote(s) for idea 2 • idea and quotes 3,4,5…

(*Continued*)

1.2. Fake news	
1.2.1. Fake news definition (Refer to types, criteria; maybe add hyper-partisan news, parody and satire, other genres etc.)	• idea 1 • verbatim quote(s) for idea 1 • idea 2 • verbatim quote(s) for idea 2 • idea and quotes 3,4,5...
1.2.2. Perceived frequency	• idea 1 • verbatim quote(s) for idea 1 • idea 2 • verbatim quote(s) for idea 2 • idea and quotes 3,4,5...
1.2.3. Effects of fake news	• idea 1 • verbatim quote(s) for idea 1 • idea 2 • verbatim quote(s) for idea 2 • idea and quotes 3,4,5...
1.2.4. Measures to fight fake news	• idea 1 • verbatim quote(s) for idea 1 • idea 2 • verbatim quote(s) for idea 2 • idea and quotes 3,4,5...
1.3. Fact-checking	
1.3. Fact-checking: knowledge about, experience, prior experience with any tools (might be zero)	• idea 1 • verbatim quote(s) for idea 1 • idea 2 • verbatim quote(s) for idea 2 • idea and quotes 3,4,5...
2.1. InVID-WeVerify feedback	
2.1.1. Upper menu (Tutorials, Classroom, Interactive)	• idea 1 • verbatim quote(s) for idea 1 • idea 2 • verbatim quote(s) for idea 2 • idea and quotes 3,4,5...
2.1.2. Left menu	• idea 1 • verbatim quote(s) for idea 1 • idea 2 • verbatim quote(s) for idea 2 • idea and quotes 3,4,5...
2.1.3. Most useful, least useful	• idea 1 • verbatim quote(s) for idea 1 • idea 2 • verbatim quote(s) for idea 2 • idea and quotes 3,4,5...
2.2 Usefulness of InVID-WeVerify	
2.2 Usefulness in various professions, own personal and personal use	• idea 1 • verbatim quote(s) for idea 1 • idea 2 • verbatim quote(s) for idea 2 • idea and quotes 3,4,5...

(*Continued*)

2.3 Intention to use InVID-WeVerify in the future	
2.3. Own intention and reasons why (yes or no); recommendation to others	• idea 1 • verbatim quote(s) for idea 1 • idea 2 • verbatim quote(s) for idea 2 • idea and quotes 3,4,5…
2.4 Recommendations to make the tool better	
2.4.1 Recommendations to make the tool better: more useful, more user-friendly, more attractive, etc.	• idea 1 • verbatim quote(s) for idea 1 • idea 2 • verbatim quote(s) for idea 2 • idea and quotes 3,4,5…
2.4.2. Would they use it in a modify version?	• idea 1 • verbatim quote(s) for idea 1 • idea 2 • verbatim quote(s) for idea 2 • idea and quotes 3,4,5…
Closure	
Any floating or emerging ideas	• idea 1 • verbatim quote(s) for idea 1 • idea 2 • verbatim quote(s) for idea 2 • idea and quotes 3,4,5…
General remarks	• whatever you think it is important to add, explain, develop, etc.

10 Public policies to fight disinformation actively through media and information literacy

Flavia Durach, Loredana Vladu, Iuliana Călin, and Marina Enache

10.1 Introduction

The chapter assesses current media and information literacy (MIL) practices in three EU member states (i.e., France, Romania, and Spain), and formulates policy recommendations to strengthen current and prospective public measures in the EU for countering disinformation. The empirical data grounding the analysis were collected in the framework of the YouVerify! project (2021–2022). The project aimed to scale up and disseminate competences in image and video verification across Europe. Its goal was to address the crucial challenges brought by disinformation and help young people develop both knowledge and know-how to make the difference between genuine and manipulated images and videos. The project built on current tools and research and capitalised on the advances of a previous project (YouCheck!, 2019–2020), by focusing on critical visual literacy training so as to scale up and disseminate competences in image and video verification across Europe. Another goal of the project was to assess country readiness to develop strategies for fighting disinformation in the EU and to formulate policy recommendations in this regard.

The project was funded by the European Commission (EC), within the "Media Literacy for All" Programme (2020) of the Directorate-General for Communications Networks, Content and Technology (DG-Connect). YouVerify! was implemented by Savoir*Devenir, a French-based NGO, in partnership with press agency Agence France-Presse (AFP) in France and two universities, National Distance Education University (UNED) in Spain and the National University of Political Studies and Public Administration (SNSPA) in Romania.

Disinformation, defined as "information that is false and deliberately created to harm a person, social group, organisation or country" (Wardle & Derakhshan, 2021, p. 20), is a significant contemporary phenomenon. For the purposes of simplicity, in this chapter we use the term "disinformation" to refer to communication disorders commonly known as "fake news", although from a scholarly perspective there are important conceptual differences between fake news, disinformation, misinformation, and malinformation. These differences are explored in the literature review section of the chapter (see also Chapter 9).

DOI: 10.4324/9781003387404-14

Even if disinformation cannot be entirely eradicated, resilience against it can be developed by ensuring that new generations and their educators develop 21st-century skills, like critical thinking, understanding the present digital media ecosystem, and identifying fabricated digital content.

Jones-Jang et al. (2019) conducted a research on the importance of media, information, news, and digital literacy in identifying fake news and concluded that awareness of disinformation is highly correlated with information literacy, defined as "people's abilities to navigate and find information online that is verified and reliable" (Jones-Jang et al. 2019, p. 12). While media literacy is responsible for "critical understanding of media messages", information literacy refers to the critical assessment of information.

In a broader sense, MIL enhances the capacity of citizens to engage with information critically and meaningfully, keeping in balance the Sustainable Development Goals, as defined by the United Nations in 2015, and their fundamental human rights (UNESCO, 2021). MIL equips citizens with diverse competences: to understand information for public good, to engage critically with information, and to enjoy the full benefits of fundamental rights (Frau-Meigs, 2019).

10.2 Literature review

10.2.1 Key concepts

Communication disorders are commonly known by many names, such as fake news, disinformation, misinformation, false information, and misleading information. Since 2016, the umbrella-term "fake news" has gained significant popularity, being used by regular citizens, journalists, politicians, and some scholars. The latter recognised the need for conceptual rigour and provided several important distinctions on the typology of fake news. As Nelson and Taneja (2018) note, traditionally, fake news was narrowly used to refer to a specific television genre. In order to keep up with the emergence of new communication disorders, the term broadened its scope to refer to "false or misleading information made to look like a fact-based news story" (Nelson & Taneja, 2018, 2).

The most widely accepted differentiation between the different forms of "fake news" is the distinction between dis-, mis-, and mal-information (Wardle & Derakhshan, 2021). The two criteria used to make these distinctions are the intention to deceive and facticity (Tandoc et al., 2017). Consequently, disinformation is defined as "information that is false and deliberately created to harm a person, social group, organisation or country", misinformation as "information that is false, but not created with the intention of causing harm", and malinformation as "information that is based on reality, used to inflict harm on a person, organisation or country" (Wardle & Derakhshan, 2021, 20).

The EU institutions currently distinguish between disinformation and misinformation in the vein of the aforementioned definitions, while acknowledging that misinformation can have harmful effects even when shared in good faith. In the European Democracy Action Plan (EUC, 2020), two other concepts are considered: information influence operations (coordinated efforts to influence a target audience using deceptive means) and foreign interference in the information space ("coercive and deceptive efforts to disrupt the free formation and expression of individuals' political will by a foreign state actor or its agents") (EUC, 2020, 18). In the same document, practical implications of these conceptual differences are noted. For each type of phenomenon, different, proportional policy responses are required.

10.2.2 Effects of disinformation

The existing research on fake news effects explores a wide variety of issues. According to a systematic literature review on health-related disinformation (Melchior & Oliveira, 2022), a number of studies look at the public's reaction to fake health information: perceptions of the health issue, how the public feels about the information published, how participation in communities that debate health issues affects individual health, etc. Prompted by the context of the COVID-19 pandemic, the effects of health-related disinformation have been studied in detail. Evidence indicates that belief in conspiracy theories and spread of dis- and misinformation through social media impact COVID-19 vaccine hesitancy (Jennings et al., 2021; Loomba et al., 2021; Ruiz & Bell, 2021; Sallam, 2021). Furthermore, such belief is associated with a lesser likelihood to follow the recommendations of health officials (Romer & Jamieson, 2020).

At the political level, disinformation has been connected to election interference and influencing political attitudes and opinions. By summarising theoretical and empirical approaches in the literature, Schünemann (2022) concludes on several limited effects. Firstly, disinformation can play a significant role in elections, in terms of volume, capacity to draw attention, and clicks. Secondly, the analysis of disinformation campaigns allegedly attributed to the Russian government allows for plausible conclusions on how foreign actors successfully influenced important media mechanisms for political communication, such as agenda setting, framing, and priming. Lastly, there is "particularly little knowledge on the more substantial effects a disinformation campaign might have on public discourse and knowledge" (Schünemann, 2022, p. 41). Other political effects documented through experiment or observation by scholars include the impact on voting behaviour, reinforcement of negative evaluations of political candidates, change in attitudes, and the emergence of post-electoral regret (Iida et al., 2022). A limitation of many of these studies is that, although they find a positive correlation between belief in fake news stories and respondents' ideological orientation, they are insufficient to show that the changes in voter behaviour and perceptions of candidates were caused by the exposure to fake news (Iida et al., 2022).

Other studies focus on viralisation, contagion effect, opinion polarisation, and echo chambers (Törnberg, 2018; Vosoughi et al., 2017). Scholars note that partisan (fake) content is reshaping the whole media ecosystem, and disinformation practices are strongly ideologically biased (Benkler et al., 2017; Narayanan et al., 2018). Technology amplifies polarisation. Social media algorithms frequently distribute polarising political content by selecting what information to show in news feeds based on user preferences and behaviour (Narayanan et al., 2018), thus creating echo chambers and filter bubbles (Allcott & Gentzkow, 2017; Spohr, 2017). There is evidence that exposure to disinformation increases polarisation. One study found out that bots' capacity to flood a social network with fake news is key to driving disagreement (Azzimonti & Fernandes, 2023). Other results show an increase in the polarisation of users and URLs associated with fake news keywords and hashtags, when compared to information not labelled as such (Ribeiro et al., 2017). A study on the video sharing platform YouTube concludes that there is enhanced polarisation of views in case of fake news-oriented channels (Das et al., 2022). Furthermore, polarisation is one of the drivers of sharing political fake news on social media (Osmundsen et al., 2021).

Lastly, there is evidence that disinformation can decrease trust. Exposure to conspiracy theories has powerful negative effects on trust in government services and institutions (Einstein and Glick, 2015; Invernizzi and Mohamed, 2019). The effects of believing in conspiracy theories related to the COVID-19 pandemic have been explored in relation to prosocial behaviours such as adherence to prevention measures (Achimescu et al., 2020; Bierwiaczonek et al., 2020), and trust in the institutions involved in the management of the pandemic (Bârgăoanu, et al., 2021). Deepfakes (visual disinformation created with the help of artificial intelligence) may contribute towards distrust of news received on social media (Vaccari & Chadwick, 2020). In one study on the 2017 German Parliamentary Election, believing in disinformation alienated voters from the main governing party. Furthermore, the less they trusted in news media and politics, the more they believed in online disinformation (Zimmermann, & Kohring, 2020).

These studies on effects, which are generally survey based or experimental, provide crucial empirical evidence on the impact of disinformation. However, their conclusions can be complimented by qualitative, cross-country research data on the experts' views regarding disinformation and its societal effects. Consequently, our first research question is:

RQ1. What are the current understandings of disinformation and its effects in the three EU member states, from the perspective of relevant experts?

10.2.3 Solutions for countering disinformation

In the past decade, the EU has prioritised MIL to safeguard European values and democratic systems in the digital age (EUP, 2007). In 2010, the

Audiovisual Media Services Directive (AVMSD) defined media literacy and mandated member states to report on their citizens' levels of media literacy. In 2018, MIL, with an emphasis on critical thinking skills, became an obligation for all member states through the revised AVMSD (EUP, 2018).

The EC, the European Parliament, and UNESCO are all involved in developing and implementing media literacy policies, providing support for infrastructure, frameworks, and guidelines such as *Media Education Toolkit* (UNESCO, 2006), *Media and Information Literacy Curriculum for Teachers* (UNESCO, 2011a), and the Media and Information Literacy and Intercultural Dialogue University Network (UNESCO, 2011b). The UNESCO *Global Media and Information Literacy Assessment Framework* (2013) encourages research and reporting on MIL indicators to guide future policy development. MIL initiatives in the EU include curriculum changes, teacher training, partnerships, e-learning, and fact-checking collaborations (McDougall et al., 2018; FullFact, 2020). France and Spain are leading in media literacy policies, while Romania is at an early stage with limited official authority (Grandío et al., 2017; EAO, 2016).

The EU and online platforms have taken steps to combat disinformation (EUC, 2018a), including self-regulatory codes and policy initiatives such as *Tackling Online Disinformation: A European Approach* (EUC, 2018b) and the *Code of Practice on Disinformation* (EUC, 2018c, revised 2022). However, challenges remain in translating MIL into public policy and addressing disinformation at the national level, particularly in Romania (Nygren et al., 2022).

Against this background, we identified a gap in knowledge, in the form of insufficient comparative, in-depth analyses of current measures and future solutions for countering disinformation in France, Spain, and Romania. We addressed these issues through the following research questions:

RQ2. What are the current measures implemented in the three EU member states to fight disinformation and what is their efficiency?

RQ3. What future solutions, policy-level included, can be considered to improve resilience to disinformation in the EU member states and in the EU as a whole?

10.3 Methodology

This research aimed at developing an accurate analysis of the actual measures to fight disinformation and MIL public policies currently being put in place in France, Romania, and Spain as well as providing key recommendations, insights, and indicators for country readiness in establishing MIL policies for disinformation in the EU. It proposed a reliable assessment, at member state level, of the impact of anti-disinformation strategies through MIL practices, while, at the same time, identifying personalised approaches to media literacy implementation and public policies. Specifically, the research objective was to explore current and prospective public measures in the EU to counter disinformation through MIL, by focusing on the experiences of three member states: France, Romania, and Spain.

The research method used to attain the mentioned objectives and thus to answer the research questions is the in-depth semi-structured interview, as it is an appropriate tool to explore possible solutions to tackle the complex phenomenon of disinformation. The main instrument is the interview guide, created in a standardised form in order to offer consistency and comparability among interviewers and countries (Patton, 2015, p. 440). It consisted of 11 questions clustered in 3 groups dedicated to each of the 3 research questions (see Appendix 10.1).

The interview guide was pretested with two Romanian experts, and, afterwards, it was shared with all partners in the project, in order to be used in all three countries. The interviews were conducted in the national language of each project partner; each produced a national report, which was translated to English, with verbatim quotes. The first thematic cluster included four questions on the distinction between different types of "fake news" based on intentionality, scope, and perceived prevalence, the reasons for spreading false information and their main source and the most dangerous effects both at personal and at social levels. The second group of questions referred to the interviewees' knowledge about the studies conducted in their institution or by other entities in their country to combat disinformation, as well as about other measures implemented so far to fight actively this phenomenon. The third set of questions focused on the effectiveness of the measures taken so far and the changes foreseen on them, the category of population prioritised in this regard, other solutions to fight the disinformation in the future, the way the key actors should address this phenomenon, and the types of policies that could prove effective.

A series of in-depth, semi-structured interviews were conducted between January and March 2022 in the three mentioned countries, with the participation of 30 relevant stakeholders. There were 10 policymakers (members of the parliament, members of the government, advisers on educational policies, and members of regulatory bodies in the field of media), 12 experts in MIL, media studies, or disinformation research (members of the research community, academia, librarians, the NGO sector, and cultural institutions), and 8 journalists (covering the spectrum of media organisations in all three countries included in this project). The interviews were conducted in the national language of each partner, and they were held online, on the Zoom platform, or by phone. The participants were coded for anonymity purposes as follows: country abbreviation (FR for France, RO for Romania, SP for Spain) + P (for policymaker)/E (for expert)/J (for journalist) + number. For instance, a policymaker from France appears as FRP01, whereas a journalist from Romania appears as ROJ01 (see Appendix 10.2).

Talking to experts, especially when the interviewers and the interviewees have a common scientific background, can lead to gathering data more efficiently and in a shorter time, as it increases the level of motivation and eliminates the need for further justification (Bogner et al., 2009). On the other hand, the selection process of experts and their personal biases can restrict the advantages of semi-structured interviews (Von Soest, 2022). In order to limit the disadvantages of this research method, this project targeted experts from different relevant fields, yet with a common agreement on salient issues, as other studies confirmed (Dorussen et al., 2005).

10.4 Findings

The comparative analysis of the results, based on the main topics tackled in the interview, revealed a wide spectrum of effects of disinformation, the current types of countermeasures taken so far in all three countries and possible solutions which need to be implemented in the future.

10.4.1 Effects of disinformation

10.4.1.1 Policymakers

Policymakers in France insisted on the threat to democracy, be it at a political or an individual level. They pointed to the paradox of a very highly educated population and the rise of disinformation (FRP03). Disinformation is being weaponised by rogue countries to destabilise democratic societies, based on the fact that in a democracy the freedom of expression cannot be controlled (FRP04). Elections are particularly risky periods in this regard, especially presidential elections (FRP01, FRP04). According to Romanian respondents, numerous dangerous effects of disinformation are "destabilisation of democracy, erosion of public trust, attack on democratic institutions" (ROP01), "affecting our narrative about the state, the democracy" (ROP02).

Disinformation weakens trust in media, institutions, and elites. The example of the COVID pandemic illustrates the role of false experts, of loss of hierarchy of knowledge and expertise (FRP01, FRP03). There is a fake equivalency between the voice of experts and other opinion-makers, posing a real threat to democracy and "esprit de raison" (FRP03). The weakened trust in the political class was mentioned as well by a Spanish respondent, referring to the negative collaboration: "when a press conference is held without questions" or "not all the information is given in a completely truthful way" (SPP03).

At the individual level, the negative effects of disinformation could run deeply into people's belief system, social relationships, and affiliation to a community, leading to division and polarisation (FRP01). Romanian respondents emphasised the lack of critical thinking and the automatic process of believing everything, as the "Facebook generation do not filter anything and don't have complex technological skills" (ROP01).

Disinformation has a real-life impact on decisions, resulting in real life death in some cases (FRP03). False information not only harms the accuracy of the data but can also generate "inappropriate attitudes and reactions towards things or situations" (ROP03). In Spain, during the COVID crisis, a lot of unsubstantiated news was circulating on the internet, with distorted contexts, which led to tension and nervousness among the people, affecting their mental health (SPSJ01). Fake news can be particularly toxic on young people's minds and can have lasting effects as for example the belief in chemtrails, antivax, or hate speech (FRP04).

Cognitive biases are augmented when people are caught in a false information loop. Fake news can negatively influence the entire cognitive and experiential process of creating worldviews, by "confirming the individual's theory, increasing or lowering the trust in authorities or even legitimating the action against a public authority" (ROP03).

The challenge is to make people understand that not all news is equal. Giving labels (from public institutions or platforms) can be double-edged because it increases distrust that affects all media in the end. This can be the worst effect of all because it induces undesirable long-term effects of distrust (FRP01, FRP02, FRP03).

At a cultural level, a degradation of public conversation, turning very aggressive on social media, has been noticed. This is where disinformation meets "cancel culture" (FRP02), and the public and cultural debate is sterilised and impoverished.

10.4.1.2 Experts in MIL/media studies/disinformation research

All *experts* agreed that the impact of disinformation could be dangerous, potentially fatal in some situations, "affecting the individual and public health" (ROE02, FRE02, FRE01). The uninformed status of our societies and their digital illiteracy increase misinformation. We are now facing a crisis of truth which leads to a crisis of democracy, honesty, ethics, values, and justice. Disinformation is a threat to democracy due both to the dissemination of anti-democratic ideas and values, polarisation of the debates, and distrust in institutions and to propaganda and cyberwar (FRE03, FRE04).

According to the experts, at the macro level, misinformation can alter the ability of citizens to trust their leaders, government, and media, affecting the institutional reputation and image and, therefore, their credibility as a reliable source of information, which is considered "a problem in relation to the democratic functioning of our societies" (FRE02). Civic education could be affected because people do not believe that their governmental institutions will deliver social well-being. However, the important impact television still has (FRE03) could mitigate some of the threats of the online fake news.

A real insidious and important problem at the individual level is that exposure to fake news provokes a lot of anxiety and negative thinking, that develops and grows in online communities, polarising (FRE03) and contributing to online harassment, which can have very serious consequences: reinforcement of isolation, disintegration of close social relations (FRE02), lack of dialogue and hate speech, and loss of freedom of choice and opinion (FRE04). All these will make it "very complicated to ensure equal opportunities in the public space for those who are different from us" (ROE02).

Disinformation creates mistrust, suspicion in others and in oneself, and hinders the decision-making process: "Without a minimum of trust in both personal and social interactions, you are blocked" (ROE01). Being blocked means that the individual doesn't have the necessary tools to analyse and find alternative methods to understand the world and therefore a diminished desire to understand other perspectives. The most dangerous effects are not only "intolerance, radicalization, extremism" (ROE02, FRE01, FRE04) but also polarisation of opinions (as mentioned by the Spanish respondents).

10.4.1.3 Journalists

According to the interviewed *journalists*, individuals are affected by the quality of information received, which impacts both the quality of one's decisions, regarding public agenda, voting behaviour, social measures, fiscal measures, etc., and the individual's health and emotional stability.

Fake news plays with emotions and in certain situations of confrontation or more political bias, opinions become polarised, basically, making consensus and problem-solving impossible. It is practically doomed to the abyss (SPJ01).

Thinking of the particular case of the COVID-19 pandemic, one Romanian interviewee noted that people who are most vulnerable to fake news end up making poor choices not only for their personal but also for their collective health (ROJ02). In Spain, people were directly affected by different hoaxes during the pandemic, which created a climate of fear and uncertainty (SPJ03). The sanitary crisis has revealed a fracture of people outside the system who live in alternative reality and with whom no rational argumentation works (FRJ01).

Disinformation offers false explanations for significant social and political events, and provides a fake context for these events, which, in itself, is toxic for citizens. It induces distorted perceptions, influences attitudes and behaviours, and sows confusion. Fake news manipulates and restricts people's freedom, making them "very uninformed due to an excess of information" (SPJ03). At a political level, disinformation is a threat to democracy and to our own countries, especially during massive political campaigns aimed at influencing a situation in another country (FRJ02).

At the systemic level, one of the most severe consequences is the "total annihilation" (ROJ02) of trust. Vulnerability to disinformation increases in societies (such as Romania) where trust in the public institutions is already low, caused by real-life experiences, like unfortunate experiences with public authorities, the chaotic crisis management, and slow reactions of the authorities.

Trust in the media is also affected. For those who have access to multiple sources of information and can apply some critical filters, to discover that certain media sources "indulge in fake news" can have "an effect of distrust on the media in general" (ROJ03). For those who do not engage in critical thinking and do not have a diverse media diet, fake news can create a false sense of trust in the actors who spread fake news. These actors are more concerned with validating their audience's beliefs and prior behaviours than with accuracy of information, thus creating a false sense of agreement, trust, and loyalty for these audiences. Social media influencers who make a habit of sharing fake news also cultivate distrust in the traditional media.

Another social impact is on authoritative sources, such as scientists, experts, and professional media. Disinformation takes advantage of the speed of information transmission and the popularity of social networks and non-mainstream platforms, to viralise false information very quickly. Fake news is then very difficult to dismantle later by authoritative sources and social media.

10.4.2 Measures to fight disinformation

10.4.2.1 Policymakers

Policymakers in Romania stressed that domestic measures to fight against disinformation are at the beginning, with many initiatives in media literacy education and isolated measures such as awareness campaigns, fact-checking platforms, and media regulation projects on their way. According to one Romanian expert, all the endeavours of media literacy and fighting against disinformation initiated by the EC and Parliament should be promoted to the public and localised to the national background, digital infrastructure, and educational system: "There is a directive from European Union that is now in the Senate, specifically in the Culture Commission, based on which we will be able to monitor the online space and intervene where it is needed" (ROP01). Another respondent pointed out that the focus should be not only on the legislative level but also on new generations in the long term: "Maybe the National Audio-Visual Council can regulate social media, but it will be hard. The accent should be put on the youth and its competencies" (ROP03).

Fact-checking platforms are not a common tool used by the citizens of Romania, yet more and more investigative journalists tend to integrate this tool into their writing process. In France, fact-checking needs to be properly funded, to help traditional media in the process (FRP01). For journalism and the press, considered as the best or second best "rampart against disinformation" (FRP02), the Ministry of Culture has competence, but the levers are not the same because the press is mostly made of private companies (FRP02). The Ministry of Culture has supported the creation of the Press Ethics Committee/Comité d'éthique de la presse, after consultation with the French public authority for the regulation of audiovisual and digital communication/l'Autorité de régulation de la communication audiovisuelle et numérique (ARCOM), with initial aid. "Anything helping the self-regulation of the profession is good because it allows the state to keep its distance, and to keep self-regulation away from the platforms" (FRP02).

Critical thinking is a paramount ability for navigating the present times, and media literacy interventions can be implemented in schools' educational programmes or optional courses: "In high schools, we have <Media Education> classes, where they develop fact-checking abilities and understand how to spot fake news" (ROP02). Other types of educational interventions against false information are projects supported by the Centre of Independent Journalism and workshops and training on legal education (ROP02). Another way to tackle disinformation is by making awareness campaigns and contacting opinion leaders, with access to a large audience (ROP01).

All French respondents have either initiated, participated, or contributed to measures in their institution. Their support for measures in media regulation comes after a feeling of "a deficit of analysis and interpretation as to the platforms and their economic model" (FRP01). In France, there are two legislative levels to be taken into consideration, the European and the national one. It is important to articulate both to induce change (FRP01). It is at the European level that policy texts and rules are taken and then are transposed in national legislation. This is the case with platform regulation, e-commerce directive, and copyright law directive. The European level is important for some issues like taxation and "dismantling" of platforms, as well as for the negotiations with the US government "to make lines change" (FRP01).

The advent of the law on "the manipulation of information" is considered "an important step" (FRP03), based on which "full transparency of algorithms, with independent and regular audits" (FRP01, FRP04) can be required. France also created an agency at the Ministry of Defence for the fight against foreign interference and manipulation of information (FRP03). And another set of measures touched French Authority for audiovisual oversight, ARCOM (ex-CSA), for the circulation and amplification of disinformation via the platforms.

MIL measures are "imperious necessity" in France because of its amplification and virality (FRP01) and partly because of the lack of human resources among the regulators (FRP04). It should be taught as a discipline all through the curriculum, with dedicated full-time teachers, not just "at random", as is done now. ARCOM publishes a yearly report on what they do for MIL, and they have a dedicated taskforce of experts that works with them (FRP04). This discipline goes hand in hand with digital education (coding), to raise the competences for the digital economy for all (FRP01) and also with journalism and teachers and librarians training (FRP02, FRP03).

The key actors of the perimeter of culture are libraries and media libraries, according to "Plan Bibliothèques" (FRP02), because "they are present all over the territory, they are free and their public is very diversified". Librarians are trained to do "mediation"; they have "very rich and complete collections, including of the press" (FRP02).

In Spain, in reference to social networks, there is a legislator who has to generate a framework of security and trust, as "there is a very big responsibility of the companies that generate social networks because they are managing information and are allowing wrong ideas to circulate" (SPP01). The only solution for social media is to make memes or upload real news on social media to combat misinformation (SPP03). There are also some awareness-raising campaigns in rural areas (SPP02).

10.4.2.2 Experts in MIL/media studies/disinformation research

The Spanish *experts* mentioned that their government has put in place some measures in education to combat misinformation, without going into details, but there is a certain sense of negativism about how they work from a media literacy perspective. There are, however, measures taken at UNESCO in reference to the health issue, especially in the wake of COVID-19 and all the misinformation that arose during the pandemic caused by this virus (SPE01). Also, the Spanish Marketing Association has a code of ethics that talks about social responsibility and the truthfulness of marketing messages and actions (SPE02).

In Romania, working with experts, especially on fact-checking, is a growing initiative with examples, such as Misreport – a project supported by journalists from Press One and True Story Project, both monitoring and writing about online disinformation, with "some sort of debunking in this area" (ROE03). NGOs and other independent associations are focused on training and workshops targeting youth and teachers, like the Independent Journalism Center, which has a pilot programme that covers 100 schools, meant "to train the teachers who will incorporate media literacy concepts in their subjects" (ROE04).

In Romania, media regulation needs to be cautiously implemented, to avoid the limitation of the content by law and preserve freedom of speech: It is the journalists' responsibility to be aware of the importance of their professionalism and their role in democracy (ROE02).

The best advice for journalists is to rely on self-regulation and ethical systems that are already part of academia and civil society, and, if not, other actors, such as NGOs should point out the consequences of disinformation (ROE02).

Media literacy measures are mentioned by Romanian respondents as part of academic efforts, such as fake news courses and a new master's degree (ROE02). Media literacy interventions have proven benefits in the learning path of the students, and, according to one Romanian expert, member of the International Fact-checkers Network, "education and media literacy is the only thing we know that does not hurt" (ROE04).

In France, publishing and spreading fake news has been illegal since the law on the press of 1881. New European and national laws punish people or companies for the same reasons. Also, a specific law against fake news has been designed in France and passed in 2019.

The Ministry of Education from France has a specific structure to deal with MIL as a whole, including disinformation – the CLEMI, an operator that proposes teacher training, educational resources, tools, and communication campaigns such as the "Semaine des médias et de la Presse à l'école". A specific effort is made towards the youngsters (FRE01).

The French Ministry of Culture supports associations working on MIL. The calls for proposals have become very much focused on the creation of tools, training of trainers, and evaluation, but there are very few projects which are submitted (FRE02).

The Ministry of Culture has also developed an MIL training programme (EMILE) for its agents and high-ranking decision-makers in all sections and missions of culture, conducted by NGO Savoir*Devenir (FRE04). It also created a plan for libraries, quite active in developing actions to fight disinformation, often with schools, but also with their own publics including adults and seniors, with workshops, events, and publications (FRE02, FRE03).

The Ministry of the Interior also supports MIL initiatives via its Marianne Fund (FRE02). Lots of civil society associations, MIL associations, popular education mediators, and journalists develop advocacy, actions, and tools to fight against disinformation (FRE04).

A number of tools are being developed in France to help fight disinformation by the Ministry of education and many actors in the non-formal educational or associative fields. Most are targeting the youth, even if adults should also be a key target. One part of the issue is that young people are easier to reach (at school), adults less so, even in libraries (FRE03, FRE01).

These tools are rather numerous and propose a variety of formats (text, videos, serious games, comics, etc.), but they are scattered, with no standards, being developed by actors without coordination or collaboration. This is the reason why the Ministry of Culture has supported the creation of the mediae ducation website,[1] that references all MIL resources (FRE02).

10.4.2.3 Journalists

Journalists in Romania are aware of media literacy initiatives, awareness campaigns, as well as regulations and state-driven initiatives. Although media literacy is not part of permanent courses in the formal education framework, a number of initiatives led by civil society exist, sometimes in partnership with secondary schools and high schools. "There are various non-governmental organisations, but no initiatives are coming from the state" (ROJ01). In this regard, ROJ03 mentioned Şcoala de Valori (School of Values) and the Centre for Independent Journalism.

There is growing public discussion, prompted by some media outlets, about what fake news means. Sometimes, controversial topics are analysed by journalists "with applicability to the topics of the day when appropriate" (ROJ03). Media outlets which are dedicated to informing their audiences correctly have one thing in common: access to experts "to clarify certain things", to specialists "to verify contradictory information", even to authorities when necessary (ROJ03).

In one opinion, state-owned media are the least biased and the most transparent out of the whole media ecosystem in Romania and should be put at the forefront of the fight against fake news: "The Ethics Commission only exists on public television" (ROJ02).

In Romania, there is no permanent regulatory framework with respect to online disinformation. Audiovisual media are regulated by the National Audiovisual Council. But, as one expert emphasises, "the deficiencies in The Council's activity are extremely pronounced, as certain false information goes unnoticed, and the complaints take a long time to be analysed" (ROJ03).

Additionally, there are some free and publicly accessible online platforms dedicated to fact-checking, among which are factual.ro and veridica.ro. Some of these are embedded in media organisations (Verificat Europa FM, Verificat AFP). ROJ03 mentioned LARICS, a laboratory of research and analysis, which is involved in research projects related to defence, foreign affairs, national security, and information warfare.

In Spain, the secretary of state approved a commission to study fake news led by the Department of Homeland Security (SPJ01). There are awareness-raising campaigns carried out by the Bar Association and international consultancy firms to rank reputation and make companies aware of the importance of a good name (SPJ02).

In terms of regulation of platforms, in France there is a need to have "the editorial responsibility of platforms clearly identified" (FRJ01), as they should be considered producers of information. Another fight in France focuses on copyright, which is connected with the issues of disinformation because it is about funding and financial health of media, "that is a guarantee of independence in relation to political power" (FRJ01).

In France, there is an enormous "chantier" (*work in progress*), conducted by FRJ01 for years at the Ministry of Culture, with "A mantra: educate to doubt" (FRJ01). Also, there was ARPEJ (association for youth) that was engaged in media education, as well as APEM, recently. These associations have many punctual actions that explain the mechanisms of information and show its added value in the fight against disinformation.

In Spain, there are many awareness-raising campaigns and policies, for example on the topic of climate change (SPJ01). Also, the Association of Journalists of Albacete organises many courses that are repeated every year in high schools. It is believed that awareness campaigns aimed at a very wide audience could be vital to avoid misinformation or to learn how to detect it.

In terms of challenges, media organisations should step up their collaborative efforts, from aggregating resources, such as recordings of evidence obtained by a particular newsroom, to warning each other about cases of fake news (ROJ03). The media in France has shown their utility and mobilised against disinformation (FRJ01). The local and regional press should get close to audiences, to meet professionals and discuss with them (FRJ02). The

Europorters project has been developed to encourage young people to produce informational content about Europe. The best productions are published in local papers, to create a "*showcasing effect*" and "*effet d'entrainement*" (*ripple effect*) (FRJ02). The challenge is to give young people the right reflexes to verify information, take a distanced perspective, and avoid falling prey to the "traps of manipulation" (FRJ02).

10.4.3 *Future solutions*

10.4.3.1 Policymakers

French *policymakers* proposed to create future platforms in "new conditions that are not the Chinese model of social credit with state surveillance nor the American model of surveillance capitalism" but are based on a more human and virtuous model, with sharing of progress and wealth (FRP01). In their opinion, journalists should do fact-checking "as part of their job", while being guaranteed their independence (FRP03), and influencers need to be also involved in this activity, by commenting news on their social media channels (FRP03).

In Romania, policymakers' opinion is that little to no importance was given to academic research as the main tool for tackling disinformation and the base for public policies. ROP03 expressed his expectation towards researchers who should present quantitative results confirming that disinformation is a serious problem, like other state priorities, not a topic for communication sessions. All the Romanian respondents believe that the fake news phenomenon needs to be monitored, documented, and evaluated to assess its magnitude and to implement policies that are following the reality. One solution for accelerating the research on fake news is the association of "schools and universities" (ROP02) and the "cooperation between academics and members of the Parliament" (ROP03). Social media and new apps can be prolific mediums for sharing information about how to not be swayed by subtle fake news, "such as vlogs or even influencers and, in the formal education, through peer learning and international Erasmus+ mobilities" (ROP02).

In Spain, the majority agreed that the alternative is education, especially of the young people "to have criteria and critical thinking" (SPP02). Awareness-raising campaigns are also considered very positive, but they cannot reach everything and everyone. The media should be willing to stand by the truth and suspicious news items should be quarantined before their veracity is checked.

10.4.3.2 Experts in MIL/media studies/disinformation research

French *experts* consider that there is the political will to fight disinformation, and the trend is positive. There should be MIL training of the decision-makers at the highest levels (FRE04), but also a discipline in school, dealing with disinformation, media literacy, and digital culture at large (FRE01, FRE02) as well as part of the life-long training of all citizens. While MIL is perceived as a key, fact-checking is seen as not being so efficient at the societal level (FRE02). Pedagogy at schools and universities should be rethought to develop competencies necessary to develop critical thinking and fight disinformation (collaboration, peer to peer learning, mutual support, creativity) (FRE03). According to French experts, the problem is mainly with Google, Apple, Facebook, Amazon, Microsoft (the GAFAM), and measures should be directed to these companies, as disinformation has to do with their economic model. More regulation to address moderation is needed, starting from the European level, by imposing economic sanctions. Some actions have been taken in terms of moderation (FRE01), but lots remain to be done, even if there are big financial interests at stake (FRE02). Heavier and more effective prosecution should target people spreading disinformation (FRE02).

The experts in Romania illustrated three perspectives: assuring citizens' basic needs, solving systemic issues, and adapting international MIL projects to the Romanian socio-economic background. Fake news has a strong impact not only because it is heavily manipulated or just because people lack critical thinking skills, but also due to the degradation of the state's role and the democratic processes, unfortunately heavily overlooked, having various consequences in people's dissatisfaction (ROE03).

As the digital landscape is continuously changing, the battle against disinformation should be adapted and updated, targeting all types of individuals: "the best measure is to remain open to test as many things as possible in this area" (ROE04).

In Spain, the alternative way to reach out, especially to young people, is to send messages on social networks, because fake news and warnings should be in the same place. There is not a feeling of much positivity right now until critical thinking is taught in schools or good legislation and enforcement provided. Spanish experts believe that a lot of people make a living out of this fake news because it generates a lot of money, which leads to the idea of regulation because punishing lies will be more effective than carrying out campaigns to stop hoaxes. According to expert, "there has to be legislation that forces or convinces the originators of false information of the need for truthful information" (SPE04).

10.4.3.3 Journalists

The French *journalists* emphasised that the Ministry of Culture's aids for journalists, projects, and initiatives (like "Assises du journalisme") are not enough, as the press should be supported very concretely (FRJ01). Also, a new relationship of trust between journalists and audiences should be created (FRJ01, FRJ02), along with an extensive dialogue on information, on its contribution to the common good, to the individual good, to better knowledge, beyond MIL in the classroom (FRJ02). Moreover, there must be economic and military intelligence measures meant to prevent foreign intervention in public debate, but it has not reached journalism so far (FRJ02).

In Romania, journalists stressed the decisive role of education and MIL, especially in synergy with other types of measures, such as regulation (ROJ01). In partial disagreement, another opinion is that education should be the main driver of resilience to disinformation, and that regulation can open the doors to censorship (ROJ02). Compulsory media literacy courses would help secondary education students understand how to assess and fact-check news and information. As technological advancements move the focus from written text to visual communication, educational interventions should be centred around visual literacy (ROJ02). Greater transparency of the media ownership and sponsorship of content would also bring good results. In Romania, it is difficult to say who is behind a particular piece of disinformation, but this lack of accountability can be overcome with the help of "extant tools that can be refined to find those responsible and bring them to justice" (ROJ03). The respondents expressed their support for additional efforts, with the expectation of measures that would limit the freedom of expression.

In Spain, it is believed that special care must be taken with the most vulnerable groups, such as older people or immigrant groups, who are likely to be manipulated. Connecting with them through awareness-raising or educational campaigns can be the key to avoiding this. There is also a strong emphasis on education, which is the basis for the new generations in detecting hoaxes.

10.5 Discussion

10.5.1 Current understandings of disinformation and its effects

The salience of disinformation as a contemporary phenomenon led to shared understandings of the concept in all the three countries. Even when respondents could not provide an exact definition, they described disinformation as information known to be partially true or completely false, disseminated intentionally to mislead and manipulate. This particular understanding of the phenomenon corresponds to current definitions used by scholars and policymakers (EUC, 2020; Tandoc et al., 2017; Wardle & Derakhshan, 2021). Responses stressed the fact that the phenomenon is not new. However, the technical means at disposal today greatly amplify its impact and capacity to influence, radically alter its configuration, and transform it into a new phenomenon in terms of its scope, and the scale of its impact on society. In this context, the dialogue and cooperation among stakeholders becomes essential, a fact highlighted by policymakers, experts, and journalists alike.

Transformations in the modern information environment do not lead to the same results in all countries and political systems, though our analysis reveals a high consensus across countries on the generally pervasive effects of online disinformation. In the interviews, distinctions have been made between systemic and individual effects. Systemic effects include destabilisation of democracy, erosion of public trust (especially trust in the state institutions, but also in media and experts), election interference, polarisation of opinions, and engineering of social movements. These expert views on systemic effects of disinformation are confirmed by the empirical evidence in the literature on political effects (Iida et al., 2022; Schünemann, 2022), disinformation and polarisation of opinion (Azzimonti & Fernandes, 2023; Das et al., 2022; Törnberg, 2018; Vosoughi et al., 2017), and impact of disinformation on trust in the media and institutions (Bârgăoanu, et al., 2021; Einstein and Glick, 2015; Invernizzi and Mohamed, 2019; Vaccari & Chadwick, 2020). Disinformation can become a tool for propaganda and hybrid warfare.

Individual effects mentioned by experts include exposure to low-quality information, poor decision-making, captivity in echo chambers, distorted perceptions of social and political events, a loss of freedom of choice and opinion, and amplification of negative feelings, especially anxiety. This list of potential individual effects is supported by studies on disinformation and poor health choices, such as vaccine hesitancy (Melchior & Oliveira, 2022; Sallam, 2021) or lack of compliance to health guidelines during the COVID-19 pandemic (Romer & Jamieson, 2020), as well as by studies exploring the interplay between disinformation and emotions (Corbu et al., 2021, Horner et al., 2021).

The influence of disinformation differs, however, according to the level of social contentment, the level of education of the population, the way education cultivates critical thinking, and the degree of people's confidence in their own governance system and in the leadership of their country. So, when we talk about the impact of transformations in the information ecosystem, we also need to consider the realities of the social ecosystem, an idea expressed, in particular, by journalists and by respondents in Romania.

10.5.2 Assessment of current measures

In France, Romania, and Spain, there are several measures put in place to fight disinformation. These measures include media literacy projects, educational policies, regulations, NGO/university-led projects and analyses, academic research, and fact-checking tools. Despite a shared preoccupation with countering disinformation in all three countries, the levels of sophistication, diversity, and efficiency of measures vary, including in the field of MIL – a finding that supports and complements prior studies (Frau-Meigs et al. 2017; Grandío et al., 2017).

France has a very advanced framework for countering disinformation. Furthermore, all French respondents have had direct experiences with the design or implementation of measures, some at a national level, others both at national and European levels. Experts mentioned the existence of dedicated structures (i.e., an agency at the Ministry of Defence for the fight against foreign interference and manipulation of information), and the role of ARCOM in limiting the circulation and amplification of disinformation via the online platforms. In France, regulation against fake news passed in 2019, but some shortcomings were noted to persist. For instance, in France there is a need to have the editorial responsibility of platforms clearly identified. Furthermore, authorities can put in place requests for transparency of algorithms and moderation, but they cannot sanction the US-based online platforms.

Media literacy as a tool for countering disinformation is a strong preoccupation in France; the field is supported through institutional mechanisms. Experts mentioned the existence of a dedicated structure in the Ministry of Education to deal with MIL as a whole, including disinformation-related topics. Additionally, the French Ministry of Culture supports associations working on MIL. The same ministry is also responsible for training its agents and high-ranking decision-makers in all sections and missions of culture in MIL. The Ministry of the Interior supports MIL by providing funding. Numerous civil society actors, such as non-profit associations, popular education mediators, and journalists develop advocacy, actions, and tools to fight against disinformation. In the field of journalism, the French Ministry of Culture has supported the creation of the Press Ethics Committee after consultation with the French public authority for the regulation ARCOM.

In Romania, domestic measures to fight against disinformation are at the beginning. The most numerous initiatives at the moment of conducting the research can be found in the field of media literacy education. Although media literacy is not part of permanent courses in the formal education framework (primary and secondary education), NGOs and other independent associations are focused on measures such as training and workshops for youth and teachers. Romanian experts mentioned other isolated measures as well, such as awareness campaigns and the availability of fact-checking platforms. The possibility to draft regulations in the field is mentioned as an emerging topic for debate in the national institutions. In Romania, there is no permanent regulatory framework with respect to online disinformation, and some Romanian experts expressed a clear concern that media regulation could hinder journalistic freedom. Self-regulation and ethical guidelines that are already part of academia and civil society were presented as better alternatives.

In Spain, the government has taken some measures for fighting disinformation, including awareness campaigns in vulnerable areas, education measures, and research led by the Department of Homeland Security. Professional associations rely on codes of ethics to limit the manipulation of information (e.g., the Spanish Marketing Association has a code of ethics that talks about social responsibility and the truthfulness of marketing messages and actions). The Association of Journalists of Albacete organises annual courses for high school students. However, Spanish respondents expressed a certain degree of scepticism on the efficiency of media literacy interventions undertaken until now in the country.

Overall, the expert opinions on the MIL framework in each country confirm prior analyses that highlighted differences between countries in their implementation of MIL policies, with France and Spain being the most advanced, and Romania, in an earlier stage of the process (YouthWiki, 2021a, 2021b; Grandío et al., 2017; EAO, 2016). As a novelty of the present study, we were able to gather updated information and evaluations on the key components for a reliable MIL policy framework (Frau-Meigs et al. 2017): conceptual framework, public policies, allocation of resources, and mapping of stakeholders. Furthermore, by interviewing different categories of stakeholders, we could explore the importance each category of stakeholders gives to the elements of the MIL framework. Policymakers stressed the importance of formalising MIL in the education system. Experts from academia and other relevant professional areas were able to give numerous concrete examples of MIL initiatives, and assessed the contribution of stakeholders in this regard; they also inked MIL with fact-checking initiatives. Lastly, journalists had the least in-depth knowledge of MIL policies, although they touched on the subject at a more superficial level.

The approach of the present study differs from other analyses focusing on MIL in a number of ways. Firstly, the study goes beyond the theoretic and conceptual approach of MIL (UNESCO, 2013) by gathering consistent empirical data of a qualitative nature. Secondly, we focus on the collection and analysis of the expert opinions of different types of practitioners, whereas other studies looked at national reports (Frau-Meigs et al. 2017) or existing studies on MIL frameworks (Becerra & Lau, 2020). Thirdly, we follow up on the new directions for research established by scholars (Frau-Meigs et al. 2017), more specifically issues related to the governance of MIL. Lastly, while other studies focused exclusively on MIL, we consider education the MIL framework in conjunction with other measures for countering disinformation.

10.5.3 Future solutions: A whole-of-society approach in countering disinformation

Another added value of our study is the strong focus on recommendations for strengthening the current framework for countering disinformation in France, Romania, and Spain. Furthermore, these recommendations highlight the importance and impact of MIL when considered in conjunction with other measures (including regulation). In this section, we discuss the respondents' propositions for future solutions; these target all the components of the MIL framework and take into consideration national differences, as well as similarities. We draw recommendations based on the insights received from the experts participating in the research.

In the field of countering disinformation, there are two issues that coexist and influence each other. The first concerns the radical transformations in the information ecosystem, which are fostering the potential for fake news to go viral. In addition, the rapid pace of communication and digital transformations generates a certain level of confusion in terms of defining terms, conceptualising, establishing taxonomies in the sphere of disinformation, reporting risks and dangers, and identifying appropriate courses of action/measures. The second issue concerns the social immunity and permeability of citizens and democratic institutions to the negative effects of disinformation.

Both issues emerged during the interviews and were addressed in-depth by respondents, leading to two strategically significant lines of action: the first concerns the manipulation of information in the digital space; the second is aimed at strengthening social immunity and re-establishing trust in the media, in experts, and in state institutions. The two sides of the problem – the creation of disinformation on one hand, and resilience and trust on the other – need to be linked in order to foreshadow a response. Thus, a twofold policy response is envisaged, which considers both the very nature of the digital ecosystem and the societal resilience, including public trust, MIL interventions, and relevant regulations.

In France, respondents believe the emphasis should be put on media regulation, independent and frequent audits, legal and economic sanctions for not limiting fabricated content, more funding, and educational policies that give MIL greater importance within the education system. Respondents in Romania see a significant need for better educational policies in the field of MIL, with a more decisive involvement of the Ministry of Education, media regulation that targets disinformation, and extensive research on the phenomenon. Similarly, Spain highlighted the importance of media education, public awareness campaigns, and regulation to prevent fake news.

As there is diversity in the MIL approaches of the three investigated countries, as well as diversity in the types of entities involved, the first recommendation is that MIL stakeholders and policymakers should create additional opportunities for joint initiatives for research and practice in the field of MIL, under the umbrella of public–private civic partnerships and programmes. The experience of project YouVerify! and its outcomes suggest that cross-country cooperation, under the umbrella of public–private civic partnerships and programmes, is one of the most fruitful approaches for advancing MIL in Europe, and for reducing discrepancies between sectors or countries.

The data suggest that France, Romania, and Spain each go through particular challenges in the implementation of an MIL framework, with France being most advanced in this area, and Romania and Spain still in more early stages. This diversity of the domestic background, of the influence of particular success factors and barriers call for a careful tailoring of measures and approaches. Initiatives should be promoted to the public and localised to the national background, digital infrastructure, and educational system. Amidst significant differences in terms of an emerging framework for MIL interventions in many countries, it is useful to adapt the disinformation response measures to the MIL development in each country (i.e., early/advanced/very advanced stages), and capitalise from a cross-country exchange of experiences and lessons learned.

No matter the envisaged implementation option, MIL needs to be formalised in the education system, and be provided with adequate resources, in order to have a decisive, and systemic contribution to countering disinformation. Otherwise, single or isolated MIL initiatives could only have very limited impact, with poor follow-up, and sustainability potential. To this view, it is recommended to increase the role of compulsory media education in the school curriculum and allocate financial and specialised human resources adequately. MIL should be a form of mandatory discipline with dedicated hours and dedicated teachers, and the curriculum should be developed with the help of experts who have proven effective in countering disinformation. Pedagogy at schools and universities should be re-thought to develop competencies necessary to develop critical thinking and fight disinformation (collaboration, peer to peer learning, mutual support, creativity). Educational policies should focus on making media literacy a full-fledged subject, adapted to age and school cycle, in tune with current disinformation trends (i.e., an emphasis on visual literacy). Where possible, MIL should be included in the relevant legislation, to ensure a uniform implementation in all regions.

For longer term efficiency, MIL could go beyond formal education. More non-formal types of MIL interventions can be implemented by the civil society, such as MIL through the media (e.g., information verification handbooks, dedicated TV programmes, and podcasts). This involves a close collaboration with the non-profit sector and other civic groups.

Access to education is an important aspect to be considered when calibrating MIL. According to the respondents, MIL measures are effective, but they fail to reach important segments of society. Thus, less visible, vulnerable target groups, such as seniors, migrants, and socially disadvantaged communities, might require special actions aimed at closing the learning gap. Systemic problems, such as functional illiteracy and early leavers from education and training can decisively hinder MIL efforts. Efforts need to be made to improve the overall quality and access to education as a precondition for the success of MIL. MIL policies should go beyond targeting students in primary, secondary or higher education, to make MIL part of the life-long training of all citizens. Other target groups to consider are public servants and decision-makers who need to overcome their own deficit in media literacy; social networks users; vulnerable groups, such as seniors or immigrant groups.

Many experts mentioned that there is a persistent lack of coordination among stakeholders in the field of MIL, and between public, private, and civic initiatives. To tackle this aspect, it is necessary to establish clear intersectoral mechanisms at ministerial level, as well as an MIL collaboration framework with permanent connections between public, private, and civic actors. As a corollary, there is a need to increase the public visibility of the

MIL collaboration framework through dedicated networking opportunities, and awareness campaigns. The collaborative mechanisms should lead to better coordination between government institutions, academia, the non-profit sector, journalists, and online platforms. The quality of collaboration is more important than the form of collaborative structures. As such, MIL needs to be institutionalised as a national priority through a private–public partnership.

Nevertheless, an evaluation methodology featuring relevant MIL Key Performance Indicators should be developed to measure the impact of MIL interventions. The existence of comprehensive standards for evaluating the impact of MIL interventions can foster delay of evidence-based policies in this area. Once designed and validated, such an evaluation methodology should be implemented in a coherent and uniform manner, to inform further actions and strategies on the topic.

There is compelling evidence on the efficiency of MIL interventions for countering disinformation. In a broader sense, MIL enhances the capacity of citizens to engage with information critically, to make better decisions, and navigate information online in reliable ways. Nevertheless, what emerges clearly from our study is that MIL should not act as a stand-alone solution. Current and future measures for countering disinformation identified by the French, Spanish, and Romanian experts consider MIL as an important pillar in a larger framework.

The data suggest that the public conversation about countering disinformation in France, Romania, and Spain takes quite different shapes. While the three countries share a common understanding of the different forms of manifestation of fake news (i.e., disinformation, misinformation, propaganda, etc.) and the severity of its effects at individual and societal level, each country is in a different stage with respective corrective measures. Given this context, measures undertaken at the EU level should meet national needs, and that each member state should be equally considered in the process. EU measures for countering disinformation need to be responsive to domestic needs, and the outcomes of EU efforts should benefit all countries.

Respondents stressed that the national and EU levels should partner in countering disinformation. They have stressed repeatedly how policies and international guidelines from the EU and the EC should be supplemented by localised interventions, at local level. Consequently, the conclusions of this study can inform policymakers at the EU level on how to support this need for a more country-centred and localised approach (e.g., by facilitating the exchange of best practices among member states, by providing funding for cross country cooperation, by training domestic stakeholders working in relevant fields, and by supporting the academic community).

Significantly, all recommendations formulated by respondents imply the idea of transdisciplinarity, and comprehensive approach. Disinformation is undoubtedly a process associated with the sphere of social and public communication. In the context of contemporary technological developments, however, in order to devise measures to counter disinformation, it is necessary to address this phenomenon in a transdisciplinary manner, in its multiple dimensions – social, administrative, political, and technological, with the involvement of a vast array of actors.

The challenge posed by disinformation, its multiple dimensions, and its impact on various spheres of activity call for a broad and coherent response, coordinated and meaningful actions between the various stakeholders, all designed against a backdrop of respect for fundamental human rights, freedom of expression, and fundamental democratic values. The centre of gravity of disinformation therefore remains in the field of communication, but its analytical perspectives need to be diversified in order to capture the complexity of the phenomenon. The idea of concerted actions involving stakeholders from various sectors, institutions, and domains is very close to the concept of "whole-of-society approach" in tackling disinformation, where the focus is on empowering all relevant actors and building social consensus on the need for action to combat disinformation (Maddox et al., 2021). In this view, the following categories of actors are targeted: state authorities, regulators, media, digital platforms, actors involved in online advertising, website owners, academia, civil society representatives, etc. A whole-of-society framework for responding to misinformation involves communication activities, resilience-building activities, disruptive activities (interrupting the cycle of misinformation), and, nevertheless, regulatory activities.

Despite the relatively small sample of 30 participants in the research, the results allow for an in-depth understanding, from an expert perspective, of the current issues and challenges for countering online disinformation in France, Romania, and Spain. The insights gathered from multiple perspectives (policymakers, journalists, and experts in relevant professional and academic fields) provide a nuanced, diverse mapping of current and prospective measures for countering disinformation. The relatively small sample is compensated by the quality and depth of the analytical conversation – measured by the high level of detail and the complexity of information provided by participants, and thus could be hardly considered as an insuperable limitation of the research. Findings are based on the expert type of opinions and create the grounds for exploring specialists' perspectives on the specificities of the MIL frameworks in each country. Moreover, findings reveal the extent to which different categories of experts approach MIL as a viable line of action in building individual and societal resilience to online disinformation. Overall, the similarity in topics and concerns across countries and categories of respondents allowed the clustering of key issues in the data and the formulation of adequate policy recommendations, in line with the objectives of the YouVerify! project.

10.6 Conclusion

The digital media – and social networks in particular – have created a new reality of news consumption, one that presents not only new opportunities but also new vulnerabilities for democratic societies. Online disinformation has pervasive effects at both the individual and the social level, and the efforts to identify the best policy responses need to consider the diversity of forms in which misinformation circulates, and the challenges the public experiences in identifying disinformation and exercising critical thinking.

The challenges discussed in this chapter lead to two strategically significant lines of action: the need to design new policies to formalise and standardise MIL intervention across the EU, and the need to consider MIL as part of a broader set of measures to counter disinformation, following a whole-of-society approach. In all three countries, additional measures in all key areas are also necessary (research and fact-checking, MIL, regulation, and quality journalism). Measures against disinformation are not very impactful in isolation. Policymakers should consider a holistic societal approach, covering six fronts: (1) research and understanding, (2) fact-checking; (3) national strategy for countering disinformation; (4) co-regulation; (5) quality journalism; (6) MIL.

Furthermore, there is a need for strengthening the role of both national and EU-level experts in the design and assessment of public policies for countering disinformation. Although disinformation narratives are transnational, the phenomenon itself is highly contextual, depending on numerous national and regional factors that impact individual resilience. Conversations across experts from multiple fields (policy, journalism, academia, MIL, fact-checking, etc.) would contribute to a better understanding of the sometimes-unanticipated weaknesses and biases that are exploited by the perpetrators of disinformation actions. Moreover, by enhancing the dialogue between the national and the European levels, the vulnerabilities, challenges, as well as the prospective solutions to disinformation could be mapped more accurately. Also, responses could be formulated in a concerted yet relevant manner.

Disinformation is bound to be a problem of the public sphere, a communication-related phenomenon with anchors in numerous sectors. Its roots are social, administrative, political and technological, thus requiring a transversal, multidisciplinary, and interinstitutional approach.

In a nutshell, systemic coherence and consistency are needed to obtain comfortable levels of resilience, and to secure societies against the negative effects of disinformation. Well-tailored MIL strategies are one key tool in the countries that are determined to implement a whole of society approach to fighting disinformation. Horizontal and vertical collaboration among stakeholders in different sectors and at all administrative levels (i.e., local, regional, national, EU) help mitigate conflicts, avoid polarisation, and build cohesion. Within this systemic view, MIL can be an essential and ambitious enabler of a whole-of-society approach to fighting disinformation.

Appendix 10.1 Templates for the interviews

Interview guide for policymakers

Introduction

a *Start with introducing the project and thanking the participant for agreeing to participate to the interview.*
b *Introduce yourself.*
c *If he/she did not complete a written consent form, ask them to agree to record an oral consent form; then stop and save the recording.*
d *Ask them to briefly introduce themselves.*
e *Ask permission to start recording the entire interview.*

Effects of disinformation

The "fake news" phenomenon, online disinformation, computational propaganda, etc. have been given a lot of attention lately. We would like to invite you to discuss together these phenomena.

Q1. First of all, what does "fake news" mean to you?

Explore distinctions mis-/disinformation; intentionality, scope (types of fake news), perceived prevalence, etc.

Q2. What do you think are the reasons for spreading false information?
Q3. What are the main sources of false information?
Q4. People often talk about the danger of fake news exposure, disinformation, misinformation, etc. What would be, in your view, the most dangerous effects both at personal and at social levels?

Explore:

- Weakening trust in media; trust in politicians; trust in institutions
- Human's psychological conditions (high anxiety levels, uncertainty)
- Threat related to individual decisions and choices
- Online reputation (personal and institutional, including public figures' reputation)
- Threats to democracy
- Personal threats (such as health threats)

Measures to fight disinformation

We would like now to discuss what has been done to combat the negative effects of disinformation so far. First of all, based on your experience:

Q5. Are there any studies, reports, etc. that have been conducted to combat disinformation in your institution? Are you aware of other such studies conducting by other institutions in [COUNTRY]?

Q6. To your knowledge, has your institution so far implemented any measures to actively fight disinformation? Could you provide details? How about other institutions that you know of?

Explore:

- Media literacy measures (i.e., curricula changes, optional courses, workshops, teaching resources, etc.)
- Technical tools (such as tineye; reversed image search; InVID-WeVerify)
- Awareness campaigns
- Media regulation measures
- Fact-checkers
- Large-scale projects

(As much as possible, refer to the effects discussed in the first part of the interview.)

Future solutions against disinformation

We have so far discussed what has been done so far to actively fight against disinformation. We would like now to open the dialogue about what could be done in the future.

Q7. You have already mentioned some measures that have been taken so far. To your knowledge, were they effective in some way? If yes, could you give some examples? Were there any particular populations prioritised in this regard?

Q8. How about the future? Do you see any changes in any of the measures taken so far in the future? *Explore each of the measures already mentioned by the interviewee in Q6.*

Q9. Do you see any other solutions (that has not been implemented yet) to fight the disinformation phenomenon in the future?

Q10. Who do you think should be the key actors (including institutions) to address the disinformation phenomenon and how?

Explore: politicians, ministries, parties, media, institutions

Q11. If you think of policymaking to fight disinformation, what would be one of the first types of policies (education, media regulation, etc.) you believe could prove effective? Do you have anything more concrete, detailed, in mind about what these policies could be all about?

Q12. What would you do if you had the position and the resources to decide on immediate and mid-term measures to fight disinformation?

CLOSURE

We have covered issues related to disinformation, its effects, and ways to fight this phenomenon. Do you think there is anything else that you consider important, and we should talk about before closing the interview?

Interview guides for experts

Introduction

a *Start with introducing the project and thanking the participant for agreeing to participate to the interview.*
b *Introduce yourself.*
c *If he/she did not complete a written consent form, ask them to agree to record an oral consent form; then stop and save the recording.*
d *Ask them to briefly introduce themselves.*
e *Ask permission to start recording the entire interview.*

The "fake news" phenomenon, online disinformation, computational propaganda, etc. have been given a lot of attention lately. We would like to invite you to discuss together these phenomena.

Q1. First of all, what does "fake news" mean to you?

Explore distinctions mis-/disinformation; intentionality, scope (types of fake news), perceived prevalence, etc.

Q2. What do you think are the reasons for spreading false information?
Q3. What are the main sources of false information?
Q4. People often talk about the danger of fake news exposure, disinformation, misinformation, etc. What would be, in your view, the most dangerous effects both at personal and at social levels?

Explore:

- Weakening trust in media; trust in politicians; trust in institutions
- Human's psychological conditions (high anxiety levels, uncertainty)
- Threat related to individual decisions and choices
- Online reputation (personal and institutional, including public figures' reputation)
- Threats to democracy
- Personal threats (such as health threats)

Measures to fight disinformation

We would like now to discuss what has been done to combat the negative effects of disinformation so far. First of all, based on your experience:

Q5a. Are there any studies, reports, etc. that you know of, which have been conducted as a baseline for measures to combat disinformation in [COUNTRY]?
Q5b. Which would be the key institutions or groups of people that you believe should be most actively involved in fighting disinformation?
Q6. To your knowledge, has any of these institutions or groups of people so far implemented any measures to actively fight disinformation? Could you provide details?

Explore:

- Media literacy measures (i.e., curricula changes, optional courses, workshops, teaching resources, etc.)
- Technical tools (such as tineye; reversed image search; InVID-WeVerify)
- Awareness campaigns
- Media regulation measures
- Fact-checkers
- Large-scale projects

(As much as possible, refer to the effects discussed in the first part of the interview.)

Future solutions against disinformation

We have so far discussed what has been done so far to actively fight against disinformation. We would like now to open the dialogue about what could be done in the future.

Q7. You have already mentioned some measures that have been taken so far. To your knowledge, were they effective in some way? If yes, could you give some examples? Were there any particular populations prioritised in this regard?
Q8. How about the future? Do you see any changes in any of the measures taken so far in the future?

Explore each of the measures already mentioned by the interviewee in Q6.

Q9. Do you see any other solutions (that has not been implemented yet) to fight the disinformation phenomenon in the future?
Q10. Who do you think should be the key actors (including institutions) to address the disinformation phenomenon and how? Do you think the kind of organisation that you are part of should play an active role in this? In what ways?

Explore: politicians, ministries, parties, media, institutions, own organisation

Q11. If you think of policymaking to fight disinformation, what would be one of the first types of policies (education, media regulation, etc.) you believe could prove effective? Do you have anything more concrete, detailed, in mind about what these policies could be all about?

Q12. What would you do if you had the position and the resources to decide on immediate and mid-term measures to fight disinformation?

CLOSURE

We have covered issues related to disinformation, its effects, and ways to fight this phenomenon. Do you think there is anything else that you consider important, and we should talk about before closing the interview?

Interview guides for journalists

Introduction

a *Start with introducing the project and thanking the participant for agreeing to participate to the interview.*
b *Introduce yourself.*
c *If he/she did not complete a written consent form, ask them to agree to record an oral consent form; then stop and save the recording.*
d *Ask them to briefly introduce themselves.*
e *Ask permission to start recording the entire interview.*

The "fake news" phenomenon, online disinformation, computational propaganda, etc. have been given a lot of attention lately. We would like to invite you to discuss together these phenomena.

Q1. First of all, what does "fake news" mean to you?

Explore distinctions mis-/disinformation; intentionality, scope (types of fake news), perceived prevalence, etc.

Q2. What do you think are the reasons for spreading false information?
Q3. What are the main sources of false information?
Q4. People often talk about the danger of fake news exposure, disinformation, misinformation, etc. What would be, in your view, the most dangerous effects both at personal and at social levels?

Explore:

- Weakening trust in media; trust in politicians; trust in institutions
- Human's psychological conditions (high anxiety levels, uncertainty)
- Threat related to individual decisions and choices
- Online reputation (personal and institutional, including public figures' reputation)
- Threats to democracy
- Personal threats (such as health threats)

Measures to fight disinformation

We would like now to discuss what has been done to combat the negative effects of disinformation so far. First of all, based on your experience:

Q5a. Are there any studies, reports, etc. that you know of, which have been conducted as a baseline for measures to combat disinformation in [COUNTRY]?
Q5b. Which would be the key institutions or groups of people that you believe should be most actively involved in fighting disinformation?
Q6. To your knowledge, has any of these institutions or group of people so far implemented any measures to actively fight disinformation? Could you provide details?

Explore:

- Media literacy measures (i.e., curricula changes, optional courses, workshops, teaching resources, etc.)
- Technical tools (such as tineye; reversed image search; InVID-WeVerify)
- Awareness campaigns
- Media regulation measures
- Fact-checkers
- Large-scale projects

(as much as possible, refer to the effects discussed in the first part of the interview.)

Q6b. What part do you think that the media have played so far in the fight against disinformation? And what were the challenges of the media in this regard?

Future solutions against disinformation

We have so far discussed what has been done so far to actively fight against disinformation. We would like now to open the dialogue about what could be done in the future.

We have so far discussed what has been done so far to actively fight against disinformation. We would like now to open the dialogue about what could be done in the future.

Q7. You have already mentioned some measures that have been taken so far. To your knowledge, were they effective in some way? If yes, could you give some examples? Were there any particular populations prioritised in this regard?
Q8. How about the future? Do you see any changes in any of the measures taken so far in the future?

Explore each of the measures already mentioned by the interviewee in Q6.

Q9. Do you see any other solutions (that has not been implemented yet) to fight the disinformation phenomenon in the future?

Explore: politicians, ministries, parties, media, institutions, media

Q10. If you think of policymaking to fight disinformation, what would be one of the first types of policies (education, media regulation, etc.) you believe could prove effective? Do you have anything more concrete, detailed, in mind about what these policies could be all about?
Q11. If you think of policymaking to fight disinformation, what would be one of the first types of policies (education, media regulation, etc.) you believe could prove effective? Do you have anything more concrete, detailed, in mind about what these policies could be all about?
Q12. What would you do if you had the position and the resources to decide on immediate and mid-term measures to fight disinformation?

CLOSURE

We have covered issues related to disinformation, its effects, and ways to fight this phenomenon. Do you think there is anything else that you consider important, and we should talk about before closing the interview?

Appendix 10.2 Description of the interviewees (codes, gender, institution)

No.	*Code*	*Gender*	*Institution*	*Platform*
1	FRP01	F	French National Senate	Zoom
2	FRP02	M	Ministry of Culture, France	Zoom
3	FRP03	M	French National Assembly	Zoom
4	FRP04	F	French audiovisual authority	Zoom
5	ROP01	F	Romanian National Council of Audio-Visual	Zoom
6	ROP02	M	Institute of Education Sciences, Romania	Zoom
7	ROP03	M	Romanian Parliament	Zoom
8	SPP01	M	Direction of Educational Programs of the Community of Madrid	Teams
9	SPP02	F	Cortes of Castile and León (Senate of the autonomous community)	Teams
10	SPP03	M	Cortes of Castile and León (Senate of the autonomous community)	Teams
11	FRD01	F	Ministry of Education, France	Zoom

(*Continued*)

No.	*Code*	*Gender*	*Institution*	*Platform*
12	FRD02	F	Ministry of Culture, France	Zoom
13	FRD03	F	Public Library of Information, France	Zoom
14	FRD04	F	Ministry of Culture, France	Zoom
15	ROD01	F	National University of Political Studies and Public Administration (SNSPA)	Telephone
16	ROD02	M	University of Bucharest	Zoom
17	ROD03	F	Media Research Center	Zoom
18	ROD04	F	Funky Citizens (fact-checker)	Zoom
19	SPD01	F	Association for the Defense of the Public Image of Women	Teams
20	SPD02	F	Market Real Consultores S.L.	Teams
21	SPD03	M	Valladolid University	Teams
22	SPD04	M	WordPress	Teams
23	FRJ01	M	Radio France Internationale, Assises du journalisme	Zoom
24	FRJ02	M	Association for Media literacy, APEM	Zoom
25	ROJ01	F	Antena 3 TV	Zoom
26	ROJ02	M	TVR1 (public broadcaster)	Zoom
27	ROJ03	M	B1TV and Radio Europa FM	Zoom
28	SPJ01	M	COPE Radio	Teams
29	SPJ02	F	Communication Office of the UNED	Teams
30	SPJ03	F	"El Objectivo" and "El Español"	Teams

Note

1 https://mediaeducation.fr/

References

Achimescu, V., Sultanescu, D. and Sultănescu, D. (2020). The pathway from distrusting Western actors to non-compliance with public health guidance during the COVID-19 crisis in Romania. *SocArXiv*. https://doi.org/10.31235/osf.io/bu45a

Allcott, H., & Gentzkow, M. (2017). Social media and fake news in the 2016 election. *Journal of Economic Perspectives*, *31*(2), 211–236. https://doi.org/10.1257/jep.31.2.211

Azzimonti, M., & Fernandes, M. H. (2023). Social media networks, fake news, and polarization. *European Journal of Political Economy*, *76*, 102256. https://doi.org/10.1016/j.ejpoleco.2022.102256

Bârgăoanu, A., Corbu, N., Buturoiu, R., & Durach, F. (2021). Managing the COVID-19 pandemic: Predictors of trust in institutions in Romania. *Kybernetes*, *51*(7), 2398–2415. https://doi.org/10.1108/k-12-2020-0913

Becerra, T. D., & Lau, J. (2020). MIL competency framework: Mapping media and information competencies. *Anagramas Rumbos Y Sentidos De La Comunicación*, *19*(37), 49–67. https://doi.org/10.22395/angr.v19n37a3

Benkler, Y., Faris R., Roberts H., & Zuckerman E. (2017). Study: Breitbart-led right-wing media ecosystem altered broader media agenda. *Columbia Journalism Review*. https://www.cjr.org/analysis/breitbart-media-trump-harvard-study.php

Bierwiaczonek, K., Kunst, J. R., & Pich, O. (2020). Belief in COVID-19 conspiracy theories reduces social distancing over time. *Applied Psychology: Health and Well-Being*, *12*(4), 1270–1285. https://doi.org/10.1111/aphw.12223

Bogner, A., Littig, B., & Menz, W. (2009). Introduction: Expert interviews—An introduction to a new methodological debate. In *Palgrave Macmillan UK eBooks* (pp. 1–13). https://doi.org/10.1057/9780230244276_1

Corbu, N., Bârgăoanu, A., Durach, F., & Udrea, G. (2021). Fake news going viral: The mediating effect of negative emotions. *Media Literacy and Academic Research*, *4*(2), 58–87.

Das, M., Singh, P., & Majumdar, A. (2022). *Investigating dynamics of polarization of YouTube true and fake news channels*. Springer (pp. 73–112). https://doi.org/10.1007/978-981-16-5268-4_4

Dorussen, H., Lenz, H., & Blavoukos, S. (2005). Assessing the reliability and validity of expert interviews. *European Union Politics*, *6*(3), 315–337. https://doi.org/10.1177/1465116505054835

Einstein, K. L., & Glick, D. (2015). Do I think BLS data are BS? The consequences of conspiracy theories. *Political Behavior*, *37*(3), 679–701. https://doi.org/10.1007/s11109-014-9287-z

European Audiovisual Observatory (EAO). (2016). *Mapping of media literacy practice and actions in EU-28*. Strasbourg Publishing.

European Commission (EUC). (2020). *The European democracy action plan*. Communication from the Commission to the European Parliament, the Council, the European Economic and Social Committee and the Committee of the Regions. Brussels. COM (2020) 790. https://eur-lex.europa.eu/legal-content/EN/TXT/PDF/?uri=CELEX:52020DC0790

European Commission (EUC). (2018a). *A multi-dimensional approach to disinformation: Report of the independent High level Group on fake news and online disinformation*. European Commission, Directorate-General for Communications Networks, Content and Technology. Publications Office. https://data.europa.eu/doi/10.2759/0156

European Commission (EUC). (2018b). *Tackling online disinformation: A European approach* |Shaping Europe's digital future. European Commission. https://digital-strategy.ec.europa.eu/en/library/communication-tackling-online-disinformation-european-approach

European Commission (EUC). (2018c). *Code of Practice on Disinformation*. European Commission, Directorate-General for Communications Networks, Content and Technology. Publications Office. https://digital-strategy.ec.europa.eu/en/policies/code-practice-disinformation

European Parliament (EUP). (2018). Directive *(EU) 2018/1808* of the European Parliament and of the Council of 14 November 2018 amending Directive 2010/13/EU on the coordination of certain provisions laid down by law, regulation or administrative action in Member States concerning the provision of audiovisual media services (Audiovisual Media Services Directive) in view of changing market realities. https://eur-lex.europa.eu/legal-content/EN/TXT/PDF/?uri=CELEX:32018L1808&from=EN

European Parliament (EUP). (2007). *A European approach to media literacy in the digital environment - Communication from the Commission to the European Parliament, the Council, the European Economic and Social Committee and the*

Committee of the Regions. Commission of the European Communities. https://eur-lex.europa.eu/legal-content/EN/TXT/?uri=celex%3A52007DC0833

Frau-Meigs, D. (2019). Information disorders: Risks and opportunities for digital media and information literacy? *Medijskestudije/mediastudies*, *10*(19), 10–28. https://doi.org/10.20901/ms.10.19.1

Frau-Meigs, D., Velez, I., & Michel, J. F. (2017). Mapping media and information literacy policies: New perspectives for the governance of MIL. In D. Frau-Meigs, I. Velez, & J. F. Michel (Eds.), *Public policies in media and information literacy in Europe: Cross-country comparisons* (p. 22–88). Taylor and Francis.

FullFact. (2020). *Media and Information Literacy – lessons and interventions from around the world*. Fullfact Information Literacy Group. https://infolit.org.uk/media-and-information-literacy-lessons-and-interventions-from-around-the-world/

Grandío, Maria del Mar, Dilli, Sirin, & O'Neill, Brian. (2017). 3 Legal frameworks for Media and Information Literacy. In Divina Frau-Meigs, Irma Velez, & Julieta Flores Miche (Eds.), *Public policies in media and information literacy in Europe: Cross-country comparisons* (pp. 116–129). Taylor and Francis. https://doi.org/10.4324/9781315628851

Horner, C. G., Galletta, D. F., Crawford, J. J., & Shirsat, A. R. (2021). Emotions: The unexplored fuel of fake news on social media. *Journal of Management Information Systems*, *38*(4), 1039–1066. https://doi.org/10.1080/07421222.2021.1990610

Iida, T., Song, J., Estrada, J. A. C., & Takahashi, Y. (2022). Fake news and its electoral consequences: A survey experiment on Mexico. *AI & Society*, 1–14. https://doi.org/10.1007/s00146-022-01541-9

Invernizzi, G. M., & Mohamed, A. E. (2019). Trust nobody: How voters react to conspiracy theories. *Journal of Experimental Political Science*. http://doi.org/10.2139/ssrn.3507190

Jennings, W., Stoker, G., Bunting, H., Valgarðsson, V. O., Gaskell, J., Devine, D., McKay, L., & Mills, M. (2021). Lack of trust and social media echo chambers predict COVID-19 vaccine hesitancy. *medRxiv (Cold Spring Harbor Laboratory)*. https://doi.org/10.1101/2021.01.26.21250246

Jones-Jang, S. M., Mortensen, T., & Liu, J. (2019). Does media literacy help identification of fake news? Information literacy helps, but other literacies don't. *American Behavioral Scientist*. *65*(2), 372–388. https://doi.org/10.1177/0002764219869406

Loomba, S., De Figueiredo, A. M., Piatek, S. J., De Graaf, K., & Larson, H. J. (2021). Measuring the impact of COVID-19 vaccine misinformation on vaccination intent in the UK and USA. *Nature Human Behaviour*, 5(3), 337–348. https://doi.org/10.1038/s41562-021-01056-1

Maddox, J. D., Gentzel, C., & Levis, A. (2021). Toward a whole-of-society framework for countering disinformation. *Modern War Institute*. https://mwi.usma.edu/toward-a-whole-of-society-framework-for-countering-disinformation/

McDougall, J., Zezulkova, M., van Driel, B., & Sternadel, D. (2018). Teaching media literacy in Europe: Evidence of effective school practices in primary and secondary education: Analytical report. (NESET II; p. 90). *Publications Office of the European Union*. https://data.europa.eu/doi/10.2766/613204

Melchior, C., & Oliveira, M. (2022). Health-related fake news on social media platforms: A systematic literature review. *New Media & Society*, *24*(6), 1500–1522. https://doi.org/10.1177/14614448211038762

Narayanan, V., Barash, V., Kelly, J., Kollanyi, B., Neudert, L. M., & Howard, P. N. (2018). *Polarization, partisanship and junk news consumption over social media in the US*. Cornell University Library.

Nelson, J. A., & Taneja, H. (2018). The small, disloyal fake news audience: The role of audience availability in fake news consumption. *New Media & Society*, *20*(10), 3720–3737. https://doi.org/10.1177/1461444818758715

Nygren, T., Frau-Meigs, D., Corbu, N., & Casal, S. M. S. (2022). Teachers' views on disinformation and media literacy supported by a tool designed for professional fact-checkers: Perspectives from France, Romania, Spain and Sweden. *SN Social Sciences*, *2*(4). https://doi.org/10.1007/s43545-022-00340-9

Osmundsen, M., Bor, A., Vahlstrup, P. B., Bechmann, A., & Petersen, M. B. (2021). Partisan polarization is the primary psychological motivation behind political fake news sharing on Twitter. *American Political Science Review*, *115*(3), 999–1015. https://doi.org/10.1017/s0003055421000290

Patton, M. Q. (2015). *Qualitative research & evaluation methods: Integrating theory and practice*. SAGE. https://worldcat.org/title/890080219

Ribeiro, M. H., Calais, P. H., Almeida, V. A., & Meira Jr, W. (2017). "Everything I disagree with is #FakeNews": Correlating political polarization and spread of misinformation. *arXiv preprint arXiv*. https://doi.org/10.48550/arXiv.1706.05924

Romer, D., & Jamieson, K. H. (2020). Conspiracy theories as barriers to controlling the spread of COVID-19 in the U.S. *Social Science & Medicine*, *263*, 113356. https://doi.org/10.1016/j.socscimed.2020.113356

Ruiz, J. B., & Bell, R. S. (2021). Predictors of intention to vaccinate against COVID-19: Results of a nationwide survey. *Vaccine*, *39*(7), 1080–1086. https://doi.org/10.1016/j.vaccine.2021.01.010

Sallam, M. (2021). COVID-19 vaccine hesitancy worldwide: A concise systematic review of vaccine acceptance rates. *Vaccines*, *9*(2), 160. https://doi.org/10.3390/vaccines9020160

Schünemann, W. J. (2022). A threat to democracies? An overview of theoretical approaches and empirical measurements for studying the effects of disinformation. In *Cyber security politics*. Routledge (pp. 32–47).

Spohr, D. (2017). Fake news and ideological polarization. *Business Information Review*, *34*(3), 150–160. https://doi.org/10.1177/0266382117722446

Tandoc, E. C., Lim, Z. J., & Ling, R. (2017). Defining "fake news." *Digital Journalism*, *6*(2), 137–153. https://doi.org/10.1080/21670811.2017.1360143

Törnberg, P. (2018). Echo chambers and viral misinformation: Modeling fake news as complex contagion. *PLOS ONE*, *13*(9), e0203958. https://doi.org/10.1371/journal.pone.0203958

UNESCO. (2021). *Media and information literate citizens: Think critically, click wisely! UNESCO Publishing*. https://unesdoc.unesco.org/ark:/48223/pf0000377068?posInSet=1&queryId=N-12a50add-cf8c-4846-b283-04280d8128c2

UNESCO. (2013). *Global media and information literacy assessment framework: Country readiness and competencies*. UNESCO. https://unesdoc.unesco.org/ark:/48223/pf0000224655

UNESCO. (2011a). *Media and information literacy curriculum for teachers*. UNESCO. https://unesdoc.unesco.org/ark:/48223/pf0000192971

UNESCO. (2011b). *Media and information literacy and intercultural dialogue university network*. MILID. https://www.unesco.org/en/communication-information/media-information-literacy/milid-network

UNESCO. (2006). *Media education: A kit for teachers, students, parents and professionals*. UNESCO. https://unesdoc.unesco.org/ark:/48223/pf0000149278

Vaccari, C., & Chadwick, A. (2020). Deepfakes and disinformation: Exploring the impact of synthetic political video on deception, uncertainty, and trust in news. *Social Media and Society*, *6*(1). https://doi.org/10.1177/2056305120903408

Von Soest, C. (2022). Why do we speak to experts? Reviving the strength of the expert interview method. *Perspectives on Politics*, *21*(1), 277–287. https://doi.org/10.1017/s1537592722001116

Vosoughi, S., Mohsenvand, M., & Roy, D. (2017). Rumor gauge. *ACM Transactions on Knowledge Discovery from Data*, *11*(4), 1–36. https://doi.org/10.1145/3070644

Wardle, C., & Derakhshan, H. (2021). *Information Disorder: Toward an Interdisciplinary Framework for Research and Policymaking. Council of Europe Report*, DGI (2017)09. http://tverezo.info/wp-content/uploads/2017/11/PREMS-162317-GBR-2018-Report-desinformation-A4-BAT.pdf

YouthWiki. (2021a). *Media literacy and safe use of new media*. European Commission. https://national-policies.eacea.ec.europa.eu/youthwiki/chapters/spain/68-media-literacy-and-safe-use-of-new-media#ftn3

YouthWiki. (2021b). *Media literacy and safe use of new media*. European Commission. https://national-policies.eacea.ec.europa.eu/youthwiki/chapters/romania/68-media-literacy-and-safe-use-of-new-media

Zimmermann, F., & Kohring, M. (2020). Mistrust, disinforming news, and vote choice: A panel survey on the origins and consequences of believing disinformation in the 2017 German parliamentary election. *Political Communication*, *37*(2), 215–237. https://doi.org/10.1080/10584609.2019.1686095

Conclusions: Research on MIL, fact-checking, and disinformation debunked

MIL checkmates fake news

Nicoleta Corbu and Divina Frau-Meigs

11.1 Introduction

After three years of constant work on disinformation, during the additional and unexpected COVID-19 pandemic, the task of debunking remains a herculean labour for fact-checkers as they must choose among the daily fare of fakes to spend time and energy on the few they have selected. For media and information literacy (MIL) practitioners, the labour is different as they provide people with the strategies and tools for dealing with the bulk of fakes on their own, aiming at user agency and autonomy. This labour is not "inoculation" (Compton, 2019), a misnomer that may give the sense that only a "booster" from time to time is enough to stave of the infodemic (Frau-Meigs, 2022), thereby minimising the work to build resilience. This labour is a sustained and scaffolded process, whose performance and efficacy lays on the critical thinking competences more even than the outcome of debunking.

The nature of disinformation, as we get to understand it better and better, lies in the fact that by now the terrain in which fakes develop is already prepared, so that when a new falsehood or conspiracy theory appears, for instance, it meets with a context that fits into a coherent alternative worldview, as "alternative fact" as famously said by Trump's campaign manager, Kellyanne Conway. Consequently, any new fake, be it on climate change or health, or any other topic, feeds a narrative where causality and blame can be cast on, inter alia, the global elite, reptilians, us *vs.* them – a polarised system where the first casualty is truth. Calling on the anti-vax movement for instance, brings together the other traits of this alternative worldview, be it anti-abortion, anti-wokeism, etc. To this alternative worldview, MIL opposes a holistic approach that is not based on a single fake news but on the sense-making mechanisms that foster adherence to disinformation per se, by contrast with fact-checking.

Projects YouCheck! and YouVerify! altogether spanned three crucial years in Europe, with major crisis around disinformation: coronavirus pandemic confinements and concerns, sanitary crisis and plot theories on health, war in Ukraine, and cyberthreats on democratic societies. The combined results confirmed the need to frame MIL as a pilar of democracy as it fosters values of citizenship, cross-cultural collaboration, sharing, and scaling. They also

DOI: 10.4324/9781003387404-15

demonstrated the need to promote MIL as a full-fledged digital transliteracy, with a special focus on digital visual literacy and data literacy, empowered by smart tools such as the plug-in InVID-WeVerify. These projects, their rationale, and their theory of change support the need to move MIL to a scientific field of its own that embraces the convergence produced by mediatisation, documentarisation, and datafication. This is one of the privileged and sustainable ways to foster transformative education, across mental, intellectual, and power borders.

Drawing from these projects as sense-making practices, it is apparent that the lack of alignment with core competences and outcomes can be a hindrance to scaling-up MIL in an inclusive way. In a context of polarised and radicalised issues, deploying MIL pedagogies and practices that draw on people's experiences and foster their competences can engage citizens to discuss these matters openly without putting themselves excessively at risk while enjoying other digital opportunities for creativity and participation.

11.2 Confirming theory of change and research design

Methodologically, these various tenets and angles confirmed the theory of change pertaining to transliteracy, as developed by the UNESCO chair "Savoir*Devenir in durable digital development at Sorbonne Nouvelle University, with the acronym AIR (Analyse, Interpret, React). Transliteracy brings together the two strands of MIL revealed by research about MIL effectiveness: the strand that increases knowledge and critical thinking, and the strand that aims at creative thinking and attitude change (Jeong, 2012). Transliteracy also confirms that media literacy interventions tend to be more impactful if they are embedded in programmes reinforced through multiple iterations (Nygren et al., 2021; Tully et al., 2020), as occurred with the MOOC Disinformation Step by Step (see Figure 11.1).

Following Brest (2010) and Clark and Taplin (2012), the joint YouCheck! and YouVerify! projects confirmed some tenets that can structure MIL interventions and foster their sharing, in particular to fight disinformation:

Assumptions: the fight against disinformation would be better understood if embedded in a series of activities and tools that also foster quality information and freedom of expression. This was consistently asked by teachers and educators at large.

Inputs: besides identifying the need to train teachers, educators and journalists as multipliers and amplifiers, the resources created as input offered content to create not only a solid knowledge base but also remediation strategies and activities. This was particularly developed in the "Disinformation Step by Step" MOOC that proposed modules on verification tools, refutation strategies, and project-building, via several workshops and collective activities on Padlet.

Outputs: the results expected from the inputs led to appropriation of knowledge, especially on visual literacy, and increased relationships between the developers of InVID-WeWerify and participants in the project. This was visible in the additions made to the website of the plug-in, that reflected some of the teachers and users at large requests, such as a database of verified fakes, tutorials, and a chatbot.

Outcomes: the levels of engagement of the partners and the participants in both projects were sustained. Some resulted from the planned activities (MIL roadmaps, class interventions, etc.), some from the constant negotiation across partners to produce specific outputs (quizzes, tests, templates, reports, etc.) and the necessary feedback between phases and iterations.

Impacts: the quantitative and qualitative evidence induced by the outcomes showed some tangible benefits among the partners and participants. The interest in the open badges offered to the participants in the MOOC (more than 300), which were requested mainly by Romania and Spain, point to the economic options opened by an MIL certification. Beyond building personal resilience, the other tangible impact was collective, as societal resistance emerged from interviews and focus groups, calling for institutional support of teachers (in YouCheck!) and regulation, in favour of public policies for MIL (in YouVerify!).

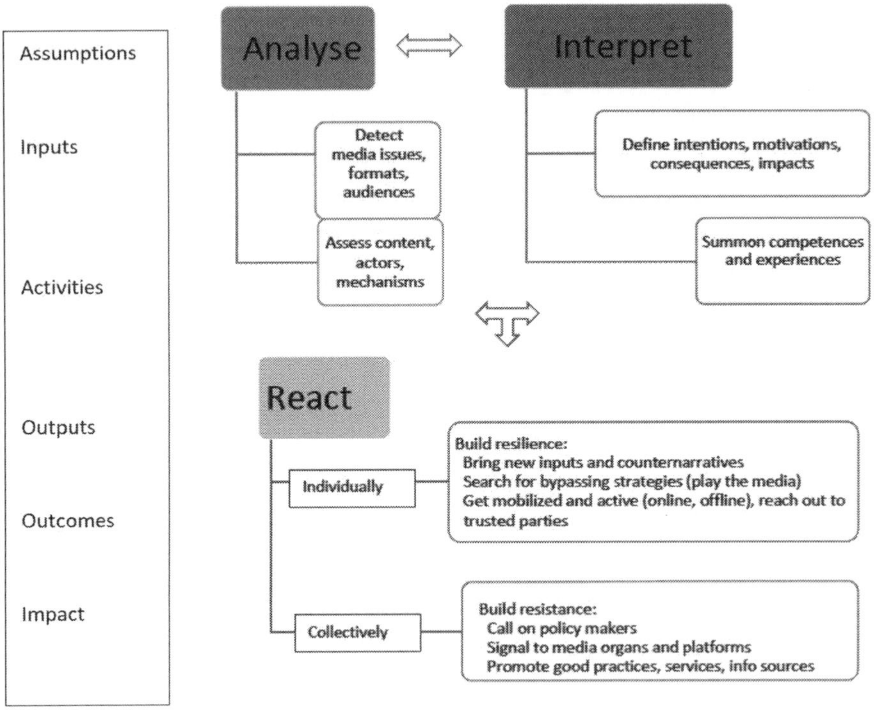

Figure 11.1 AIR theory of change, confirmed.

Source: Frau-Meigs et al., 2018.

11.3 Aiming at transferable sense-making practices

The other tangible impact of both projects resulted in the number of activities and workshops spawned by the projects, in several countries and regions of the world. This impact is directly related to the sustainability of the projects, as it shows that the intention for producing transferable resources and strategies met with success.

Since it ended in 2022, project YouVerify! has been extended in various directions. Impact overall has been validated by the transfer of competences to other countries and other regions. In that sense it fits the term of "sensible practice" and answers some elements of the "tool for analysis of sense-making practices" in the Digital Citizenship Education framework by the Council of Europe (Frau-Meigs et al., 2017a). The tool proposes various criteria for analysis, besides the usual elements of actors, target, and funding, such as "sense-making rationale and vision", "evaluation and performance", "governance levels", and "impact".

In the case of YouCheck!/YouVerify!, the rationale and vision of the project was about solving the problem of disinformation, using MIL as a lever for change and showcasing IT tools and fostering practices with several communities of practice. The evaluation was both formative and transformative for target groups that benefited from certificates and open badges; it was also iterative as several seasons of the MOOC were offered, and the MOOC itself was modified after the first evaluation. The governance levels were multiple: the European region was first, with trickling down to countries such as France Romania, Spain, and Sweden. But then the project went beyond, to two other regions, Latin America and French-speaking Africa. This expansion directly relates to impact, besides the proven efficacy of the original project. It showed that the processes put in place in both YouCheck! and YouVerify! were reproductible, transferable, sustainable, and inclusive.

In France, the Savoir*Devenir team was able to transfer the MOOC and its design to French-speaking countries (OIF) such as Cameroun, Ivory Coast, the Republic of the Congo, and Haiti. In these countries, the outputs and outcomes confirmed the importance of training trainers as multipliers. Most of the participants were youth leaders, NGO representatives, university students, and online influencers (see Table 11.1).

Table 11.1 Transfer in French-speaking countries

Workshops held	13 (N = 2,540)	6 in Cameroun (N = 1,400), 5 in Ivory Coast (N = 1,060), 2 in Haiti (N = 80)
Badges delivered	50 +	28 in Cameroun, 15 in Ivory Coast, 7 in Haiti
Identification of "remarkable" projects	19	12 in Cameroun, 4 in Ivory Coast, 3 in Haiti

Among the "remarkable" projects (a terminology used by OIF), some are worth noting for their capacity-building and their localisation, adjusted to local situations and ways of learning and teaching: the "MIL caravan" with a bus to go to rural areas; the "fresco of disinformation" to play with examples and strategies; "the little secrets of Alex" campaign on Facebook to reach online users, replicating some of the main contents of the MOOC; the "Bénévoles de l'EMI" to entice university students to train people in MIL; the "MIL cartoon" made from the MOOC to explain MIL in visual and accessible ways (see Figure 11.2).

These results were prolonged in Madagascar and Republic of the Congo, with the production by Savoir*Devenir of a paper version with four booklets. In France, Savoir*Devenir also transformed the MOOC in four NOOC (nano-MOOCs), to make the contents accessible in a shorter version, for the agents and decision-makers of the Ministry of Culture. The French-speaking partners decided to create a network called "MIL without Borders" to keep sharing experiences, and Cameroun created a regional centre for MIL, called Centre Regional d'Education aux Médias (CREM), active as of 2023.

In Spain, the UNED team, besides expanding activities in Spain, reached out to Latin America. The MOOC "Disinformation Step by Step" was followed by participants in Cuba. It spawned another MOOC "Otras formas de educar para el siglo XXI", with the support of UNESCO Cuba and the Ministry of Higher Education, Science, and Technology (MESCYT) of the Dominican Republic. It was a highly successful MOOC that trained more than 2,000 people and received very good feedback from the participants. Gamification was the guiding thread, and UNED created MIL "spirits" that accompanied and guided the participants throughout the course, sending them challenges at each learning stage (see Figure 11.3).

UNED also developed interesting projects in Colombia, with project CRECER (**C**apacitación en est**R**ategias para mejorar la **E**ducación a distancia y la **C**alidad **E**ducativa para la **tR**ansición digital). The objective is for UNED to carry out actions to promote teacher training at the University of Cartagena in Colombia through the transfer of its own open and virtual education technologies, involving training developments adapted to the local needs of this Colombian university.

UNED, through its research group "Social Media and Inclusive and Ubiquitous Media Education" (SMEMIU) and the spin-off ECO-LEARNING, has the necessary experience in distance education strategies and production of digital content for lifelong virtual training. All this, thanks to its specialisation in disruptive technologies for the creation of inclusive, adaptive, and accessible to all educational courses and resources. The international cooperation with the University of Cartagena is expected to lead to the creation of open virtual courses and content adapted to the social needs of the region to promote MIL development.

In Romania, the National University of Political Studies and Public Administration (SNSPA) team was able to expand its activities in Romania.

Figure 11.2 The MIL cartoon developed by EdukMedia Cameroun.

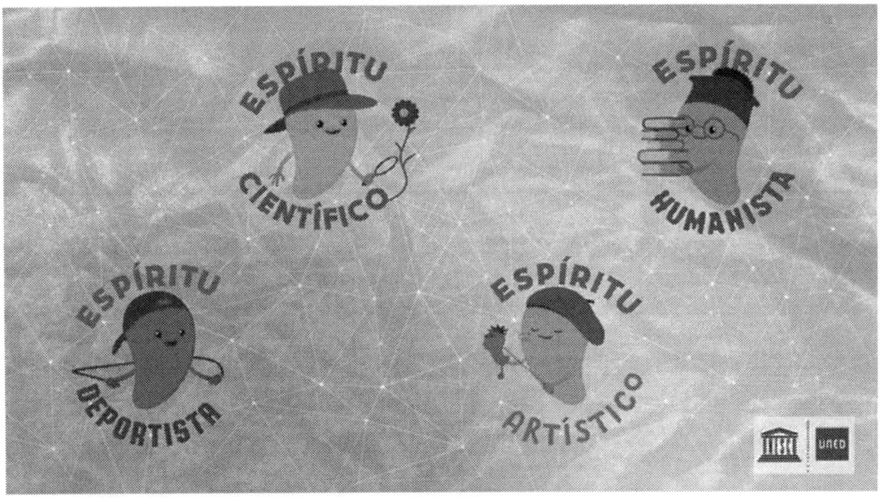

Figure 11.3 The gamification in MOOC "Otras formas de educar para el siglo XXI".

The transfer and spillover of the two projects led to SNSPA being part of the consortium that obtained the Horizon project for Bulgarian-Romanian Observatory for Digital Media (BROD), one of the 14 European Digital Media Observatory (EDMO) hubs. The lead partner also became an expert in the EDMO Expert Group on Structural Indicators for the Code of Practice on Disinformation (European Commission).

SNSPA was able to reach out to key media literacy actors in Romania, as a result of the two projects, via the French Institute in Romania. Parts of the MOOC documents were integrated in SNSPA media effects and disinformation classes at the university. And an EMIF-funded project was won by the Romanian team, Factboost[1] with civil society organisation, Eurocomunicare, that was part of the original projects (see Figure 11.4).

11.4 Validating MIL strategies and solutions

11.4.1 Lifelong and long-distance learning

As shown by the examples of Savoir*Devenir and UNED, long-distance options and lifelong training options are important strategies to foster MIL, as long as it remains clear that MIL is about teaching about media, not using media for learning about other topics – even though this limit is more and more porous due to the enveloping environment created by interconnected media systems. Nonetheless, it remains crucial to have a reflexive and critical view on media, and a place where their role, even in teaching, can be viewed from a meta-position.

These different strategies show the potential for more intervention and participation in culture and media. They point to a need for professionals and users at large to adjust to different media and modify their uses and

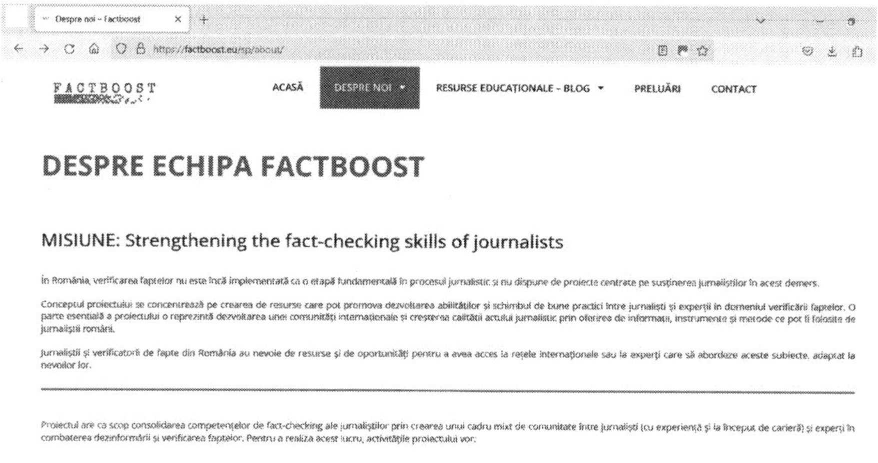

Figure 11.4 Website of EMIF funded project, Factboost.

interactions with different situations and tools. In each case, there are mass, social, and, increasingly, synthetic media that will help them stay attuned to their communities and fans, whatever the activity. This points to the need for multi-competences, among which online presence and online creativity, changing the production and working conditions, in a context of ecological and digital transitions and crises.

This also calls for collective intelligence in the face of artificial intelligence, the recent challenge since starting YouCheck! and YouVerify! projects. Diversity in teams and collaboratives helps augment distributed competences and transfer of know-how and ideas, as well as enhance the agility needed to adjust to transformational situations (as a health crisis for instance or an AI panic). This also harks at the need for specific cultures and institutions brought in for MIL, beyond media organisations: libraries, museums, and other places of culture (cinemas, theatres, etc.) that can become new territories for MIL be it for information or creation. Their functions can change or be augmented (with MOOCs, Metaverse installations, etc.) to address the largest possible public.

11.4.2 MIL design

Designing MIL projects requires pedagogical strategies and practices that are agile and iterative. The two projects YouCheck! and YouVerify! built on each other and involved each two iterations of the intervention, for improvement and localisation. This iterative process needs to be built in the early stages of the design, to ensure reflexivity and transfer. This helps build trust across very heterogeneous MIL stakeholders, the "You!" that appears at the end of both project acronyms.

The iterative process made it possible to validate some basic MIL methodological principles:

1 Modular approach (stand-alone quizzes and games)
2 Authentic documents and examples (not produced in lab, which is crucial for disinformation cases)
3 Multi-stakeholder involvement (not just teachers and journalists but also developers, policymakers, librarians, etc.)
4 Competence based (with a clearly defined framework)
5 Critical thinking (reflexive learning)
6 Creative thinking (creating innovative tools, hands-on approach, publishing productions, etc.)
7 Attention to information quality (crucial in the fight against disinformation)
8 Focus on uses and practices (for instance, stop amplification, not stop algorithms)

In conjunction with the AIR theory of change, this kind of approach leads to a conceptual framework for the design of MIL projects and interventions, always with the user at the centre of the process:

1 The level of user awareness and competence required to master the impacts of MIL
2 The level of user agency and empowerment in relation to MIL policymaking and governance (Frau-Meigs, 2023)

The level of awareness and mastery is well covered by competences and activities to ensure that they are well appropriated by MIL learners. The level of agency and empowerment deals with engagement and advocacy as MIL learners put their recently acquired awareness to use, in whatever place of power or control they can be. They can act as voters, militants, advocates, volunteers, etc. Many roles open up to them where they can contribute to policy shaping and to monitoring of governance tools. In some cases, they can go as far as being stakeholders in governance institutions. This is the case of the MILID network of universities created by UNESCO in 2011, which unites many UNESCO MIL chairs around the world in coordinated activities that culminate in the UN-labelled Global MIL week (always the last week in October).

11.4.3 Policy takeovers

Both projects had a policy dimension, especially YouVerify!, to be coherent with the two-level conceptual framework. Making policy recommendations is not expected in pure research projects but can be a welcome outcome of research intervention projects. The development of indicators for evaluating MIL interventions is crucial to touch policymakers and convince them about the impact of MIL. This can also result in more funding as often evidence-based evaluation triggers more resources.

In this sense, MIL policymaking is still in full swing, with many decisions enacted at various levels of governance: the EU level (for Directives and for funding in particular), the national level (adjusting the Directive on Audiovisual Media Services to national law), the more local levels of civil society, universities, and other institutions. Some aspects of policy are recurring in the research projects:

1 The protection of audiences, as in the case of the fight against disinformation where the challenges to social cohesion are also challenges to democratic institutions. Moderation and regulation of platforms as well as algorithmic biases become key in the face of persisting stereotypes and discrimination;
2 The regulation of mass media and social network platforms, with their attendant systemic risks: manipulation of information, dissemination of false information and hate speech; systemic risks with regard to data use, including privacy and digital citizenship matters;
3 The economics of media and their production: piracy and illicit content issues, influence marketing and alternative business models; geopolitics of internet governance, etc.

At the end of the two projects analysed in this book, there are some important takeovers for policymaking in MIL, across Europe: (1) a better delineated MIL definition, which is cohesive and sense-making as well as age-specific (young children, teenagers, adults); (2) a baseline to measure performance; (3) design considerations for learning about MIL and its role in an increasingly mediated society; (4) a coordination process to assemble all MIL projects and actors so as to share know-how.

11.4.4 Future research on disinformation is inextricably related to MIL

When discussing the future of research related to information disorders, there is a need to understand the rapid developments of technology, which fosters better and better tools of disinformation to mimic successfully the real word. The next wave of disinformation will most probably be AI-driven, with viral fakes as generative adversarial networks (GANs), algorithmic data mining and advanced image manipulation technologies. Of particular concern are "deepfakes" that can be fabricated using advanced neural network approaches to manipulate video content (swapping faces and bodies in a quasi-undetectable manner). The lessons learnt in the two MIL projects point towards a necessary rapid adaptation of disinformation detection tools to the AI-driven avatars of fabricated content. At the same time, keeping pace with the changes brought about by the new technologies becomes more and more challenging, which gives MIL an even more prominent role in educating the new generations in the spirit of critical thinking, constant questioning of available information and informed decision-making.

The future research in MIL projects should aim towards including more and more automated methods of data analysis, capable of making sense of the unprecedently huge amount of (dis)information available on social networks. To this end, there are important European initiatives to regulate to some extent the very large online platforms (VLOPs) and very large search engines (VLOSEs) through the Code of Practice on Disinformation, and, even more importantly, to obtain free and secure access to platforms data for researchers, via the Digital Services Act (Article 40 in particular).

Additionally, there is a need for valid ways to measure AI-literacy and resilience, with a scalable framework as recommended in the Directorate General for Education and Culture “Guidelines for teachers and educators on fighting disinformation and promoting digital literacy through education and training” (European Commission, 2022).

The increasing inclusion of AI-generated content into all sectors of social life leads to a need to address the issue of constant training and rapid replication of training with face-to-face interactions and conversations to ensure the human is back in the process, to strike a balance between machine results and human discoveries, compatible with daily life uses of information search.

To conclude, the future of research in MIL points towards a few key directions: (1) building AI-literacy and resilience within an MIL framework (instead of creating a different line of literacy), as a response to the increasing technological sophistication of fabricated disinformation content; (2) using automated data analysis combined with manual validation of the new computational social science methods to ensure a thorough identification of misleading narratives in the current high choice media environment; (3) fighting for free and secure access to big data generated by VLOPs and VLOSEs being made available for research; (4) building and including new technological tools capable of AI-generated fake content identification; (5) keeping the human presence in MIL trainings and interventions; (6) scaling up MIL-related training and research.

11.5 Recommendations for policymaking in fighting disinformation

The research conducted in YouCheck! and YouVerify! points towards recommendations for policymaking, with the aim of strengthening MIL practices in Europe and beyond, and actively fight mis- and disinformation.

11.5.1 MIL education

First, there are currently very big differences across countries in terms of the level of MIL practices being integrated in the formal curricula in school. Therefore, media education should have an increased presence in the European curricula (especially in countries such as Romania, where elements of MIL are only sporadically thought and integrated into other classes curricula). This goes hand in hand with finding the financial and human resources to support such endeavours.

Second, even though there is solid evidence that MIL measures are effective, they often fail to reach certain segments of society. Oftentimes, these segments, such as the elderly, people coming from economically disadvantaged backgrounds, people with low education and limited literacy and numeracy skills, etc., are the most vulnerable to mis- and disinformation (Buturoiu et al., 2021). Therefore, the efforts of scaling up MIL trainings and practices should target such groups in the future.

Moreover, the field of MIL shows a persistent lack of collaboration and coordination among key stakeholders. For instance, there is still a serious gap between researchers and practitioners in the field, between policymakers and the public, between the regulating institutions and their beneficiaries, etc. Creating clear intersectoral mechanisms for permanent collaboration has been pointed out by previous research (Frau-Meigs et al., 2017b). Important steps have been made in this direction, through the European initiatives, such as the EDMO hubs or the dedicated Horizon grants, that bring together, to an unprecedented degree, practitioners, researchers, stakeholders, and the public at large. However, these are but small steps towards creating the much-needed mechanisms of collaboration and coordination.

Finally, there are no common, clear standards of evaluating the impact of MIL interventions, not only across countries but also between similar initiatives in a single country. Creating a baseline, with a unified methodology for measuring the impact of various types of MIL interventions, is much needed, providing golden standards of evaluation, for constant improvement of methods, tools, and teaching methods.

11.5.2 Fact-checking

Fact-checking remains one important tool of actively and constantly fighting mis- and disinformation thought the world (Chan et al., 2017; Walter et al., 2020). The number of fact-checkers has increased constantly in the last years, and important steps have been made in an attempt to regulate the standards these organisations need to obey in order to ensure a transparent, balanced, and neutral identification and debunking of misleading information (for an overview, see Chapters 1 and 2 in this book). However, these efforts are still far from making fact-checkers visible to large audiences and convincing them to check dubious information when they come across it. In this context, the integration of fact-checking initiatives into MIL interventions, both in schools and in life-long learning settings, could foster the habit among the larger public to check to most prominent/viral questionable information via fact-checking websites.

Moreover, constant efforts are being made to create repositories of fact-checks, which could help integrate the efforts of fact-checkers and making them available to larger and larger audiences. Such an initiative is currently conducted within the EDMO hubs, via the Truly Media platform (https://app.truly.media/fact-checking). The aim is to create repositories with fact-checks produced by all fact-checkers active in the EDMO hubs, searchable by source, publication date, hub, and language. Nonetheless, such efforts are still designed to help researchers and journalists, and it might take a long while until they become tools to be used by large audiences. Still, such repositories could become important source of data analysis for researchers who try to investigate the dominant disinformation narratives in online and social media and important sources of data checking for journalists.

Notwithstanding the limits of fact-checking as a tool to fight disinformation actively, it remains one of the important means to search for misleading information. Integrating the efforts of fact-checkers with research, especially via automated methods designed to identify prominent (viral) disinformation narratives, may make their endeavours more visible not only to researchers and journalists but also to large audiences.

11.5.3 Quality journalism and media awareness campaigns

In the last years, there have been ample debates and compelling evidence about the ever-decreasing quality of journalism, due to dramatically reduced time of news production and pressure of audience metrics (Fürst, 2020), economic pressure and commercialisation (Picard, 2014), reduced newsroom resources and automated journalism (Danzon-Chambaud, 2021), etc.

In this context, the data gathered in the two MIL projects show that there is a general concern among both experts and the public in general about the declining quality of journalism and decline in trust in the media in general. The initial and continuous training of journalists in MIL could contribute to the re-evaluation of standards of journalism and data quality checking before publishing, to foster news quality in general.

Journalists are part of the problem of misinformation in general, but also a key part of the solutions to disinformation. Embedding fact-checking routines into journalist practices and constant MIL training could lead to better news quality, even under the pressure of time and immediacy in reporting the next scoop.

Additionally, mass media need to play a more important role in reaching large audiences to make them aware of the dangers of disinformation. Mass media awareness campaigns, in which the national broadcasters could have an important say, may be a means to sensitise the segments of the audience identified as difficult to reach, such as the elderly or people with low literacy levels.

11.5.4 Social media regulation

Last, but not least, in the last few years, the discussions about the need for social media regulation have reached an unprecedented pick. At least at the level of the European Union, the Code of Practice on Disinformation (2018, revised 2022) has proposed new ways of social media self-regulation, with the help of its signatories, among which all important players designated as VLOPs and VLOSEs, except for X (former Twitter).

Several initiatives are emerging to propose new means of evaluating the indicators of the Code of Practice, which is presently a very difficult, inefficient, and problematic endeavour. Among them, there is the EDMO Expert Group on Structural Indicators for the Code of Practice on Disinformation, coordinated by the Centre for Media Pluralism and Media Freedom at the European University Institute and the DG CNECT project on Monitoring Framework for the Code of Practice on Disinformation. Additionally, the Digital Services Act and the Digital Market Act are EU-level regulation instruments, whose aims are "to create a safer digital space in which the fundamental rights of all users of digital services are protected and to establish a level playing field to foster innovation, growth, and competitiveness, both in the European Single Market and globally" (EU Commission, 2023).

All these initiatives are important steps towards involving the VLOPs and VLOSEs in the collective effort of reducing the amount of disinformation on social media platforms. Such initiatives should be continued with the constant input coming from researchers, practitioners, and stakeholders in the field.

Note

1 https://factboost.eu/sp/

References

Brest, P. (2010). The power of theories of change. *Stanford Social Innovation Review*, *8*(2), 47–51. https://doi.org/10.48558/NPZS-C374

Buturoiu, R., Udrea, G., Oprea, D. A., & Corbu, N. (2021). Who believes in conspiracy theories about the COVID-19 pandemic in Romania? An analysis of conspiracy theories believers' profiles. *Societies*, *11*(4), 138. https://doi.org/10.3390/soc11040138

Chan, M. P. S., Jones, C. R., Hall Jamieson, K., & Albarracín, D. (2017). Debunking: A meta-analysis of the psychological efficacy of messages countering misinformation. *Psychological Science*, *28*(11), 1531–1546. https://doi.org/10.1177/0956797617714579

Clark, H. & Taplin, D. (2012). *Theory of change basics: A primer on theory of change*. Actknowledge.

Compton, J. (2019). Inoculation theory and metaliterate learning. In T. P. Makey & T. E. Jacobson (Eds). *Metaliterate learning for the post-truth world* (pp. 63–79). Neal-Schuman.

Danzon-Chambaud, S. (2021). A systematic review of automated journalism scholarship: Guidelines and suggestions for future research. Open Research Europe, *1*. https://open-research-europe.ec.europa.eu/articles/1-4

European Commission. (2022). Directorate-general for education, youth, sport and culture. In *Guidelines for teachers and educators on tackling disinformation and promoting digital literacy through education and training*. Publications Office of the European Union. https://data.europa.eu/doi/10.2766/28248

European Commission. (2023). The Digital Services Act Package. https://digital-strategy.ec.europa.eu/en/policies/digital-services-act-package

Frau-Meigs, D. (2022). How disinformation reshaped the relationship between journalism and media and information literacy (MIL): Old and new perspectives revisited. *Digital Journalism*, *10*(5), 912–922. https://doi.org/10.1080/21670811.2022.2081863

Frau-Meigs, D. (2023). *Policy brief on AI and MIL*. UNESCO.

Frau-Meigs, D., O'Neill, B., Tome, V., & Soriano, A. (2017a). *Competences in digital citizenship education*. Council of Europe Publishing.

Frau-Meigs, D., Velez, I., and Flores Michel, J. (Eds.). (2017b). *Public policies in media and information literacy in Europe. Cross-country comparisons*. Routledge.

Frau-Meigs, D., Velez, I., & Garreau, P. (2018). *Fresh AIR, the INEDU handbook: Lessons plans and resources on key MIL themes*. IREX/Savoir*Devenir. https://Savoirdevenir.net/ressources

Fürst, S. (2020). In the service of good journalism and audience interests? How audience metrics affect news quality. *Media and Communication*, *8*(3), 270–280. https://doi.org/10.17645/mac.v8i3.3228

Jeong, S-H. (2012). Media literacy interventions: A meta-analytic review. *Journal of Communication*, *62* (3), 454–472.

Nygren, T., Guath, M., Axelsson, C.-A., & Frau-Meigs, D. (2021). Combatting visual fake news with a professional fact-checking tool in education in France, Romania, Spain and Sweden. *Information*, *12* (5), 201. https://doi.org/10.3390/info12050201

Picard, R. G. (2014). The economics of journalism and news provision. In T. Vos (Ed.), *Journalism* (pp. 281–296). De Gruyter.

Tully, M., Vraga, E. K., & Bode, L. (2020). Designing and testing news literacy messages for social media. *Mass Communication & Society*, *22*(1), 22–46. https://doi.org/10.1080/15205436.2019.1604970

Walter, N., Cohen, J., Holbert, R. L., & Morag, Y. (2020). Fact-checking: A meta-analysis of what works and for whom. *Political Communication*, *37*(3), 350–375. https://doi.org/10.1080/10584609.2019.1668894

Index

Pages in *italics* refer to figures, pages in **bold** refer to tables, and pages followed by "n" refer to notes.